THEORY AND INTERPRETATION OF NARRATIVE
James Phelan, Peter J. Rabinowitz, and Robyn Warhol, Series Editors

NARRATIVE THEORY

NBOUND

Queer and Feminist Interventions

EDITED BY

Robyn Warhol AND Susan S. Lanser

THE OHIO STATE UNIVERSITY PRESS • COLUMBUS

Library of Congress Cataloging-in-Publication Data

Narrative theory unbound : queer and feminist interventions / edited by Robyn Warhol and Susan S. Lanser.

    pages cm

 Includes bibliographical references and index.

  ISBN 978-0-8142-1280-6 (cloth : alk. paper) — ISBN 978-0-8142-9385-0 (cd-rom)

  1. Discourse analysis, Narrative. 2. Queer theory. 3. Feminist theory. I. Warhol, Robyn R., editor. II. Lanser, Susan Sniader, 1944– editor. III. Series: Theory and interpretation of narrative series.

  P302.7.N3824 2015

  809'.923—dc23

2014046216

Cover design by Janna Thompson-Chordas
Text design by Juliet Williams
Type set in Adobe Minion Pro
Printed by Thomson-Shore, Inc.

♾ The paper used in this publication meets the minimum requirements of the American National Standard for Information Sciences—Permanence of Paper for Printed Library Materials. ANSI Z39.48-1992.

9   8   7   6   5   4   3   2   1

CONTENTS

$\mathcal{I}$LLUSTRATIONS

ACKNOWLEDGMENTS

This book began as a conversation among the presenters and participants who gathered in Columbus, Ohio, from May 12 to May 14, 2011, to explore new directions in queer and feminist narrative theory. We are grateful to all who organized and participated in this Project Narrative Symposium sponsored by The Ohio State University for their vital contributions to the intellectual substance of this project. In addition to those whose essays appear this volume, we want to thank everyone else who was actively involved in the symposium, including presenters Frederick Luis Aldama, Ann Cvetkovich, Helena Michie, James Phelan, Sangeeta Ray, and Rebecca Wanzo; respondents Chad Allen, David Herman, Brian McHale, Guisela Latorre, James Braxton Peterson, Hilary Schor, Maurice Stevens, and Marlene Tromp; and discussion leaders Adéléké Adééko, Katra Byram, Helen Davis, Tommy Davis, Molly Farrell, Lynn Itagaki, Sandra Macpherson, Linda Mijezewski, Sean O'Sullivan, Delores Phillips, and Karen Steigman. We can hear echoes of all their voices throughout this book.

Co-workers at The Ohio State University, including Kelli Fickle, Lauren Parkins, Nicole Cochran, and Lizzie Nixon, helped with the administrative details that made the symposium possible. Equally crucial was the moral support we received from English Department chairs Valerie Lee and Richard Dutton, as well as the financial support from Arts and Humanities Dean Mark

Shanda for the symposium and from former dean John Roberts for Project Narrative.

Working with The Ohio State University Press, we feel lucky to have collaborated with series co-editors Jim Phelan and Peter Rabinowitz, acquisitions editors Sandy Crooms and Lindsay Martin, and the extraordinary Malcolm Litchfield, former director of the press. We also received a brilliant response from an anonymous external reader, to whom we are indebted for improvements in the book's conception and execution.

As always we are grateful to our families for their good-natured support in all our efforts. Robyn thanks her boys Seth Warhol-Streeter and Max Kriff, and especially her astonishingly understanding partner, Peter Kriff. Sue thanks her spouse Jo Radner, oral historian and storyteller, for her fresh and challenging perspectives on a genre that we share as a field of study and that she practices so brilliantly. Sue is also grateful to Robyn for creating the 2011 symposium that gave birth to the book and for inviting her to co-edit this volume. And finally, we thank each other for patience, flexibility, and diligence in getting this work done in the face of pressing personal, medical, professional, and familial obligations. We took turns being the one who needed to apologize to the other for slowness in responding to an email or a call, ultimately reaching the balance that made this book a profoundly collaborative and satisfying effort.

INTRODUCTION

ROBYN WARHOL and SUSAN S. LANSER

nbound: a term of Promethean audacity for a field that is no stranger to derivations from the Greek. We choose this name, with admitted *hubris,* to loose some chains of narrative thinking, to transgress some theoretical boundaries, to unbind some narratological constraints. Our subtitle makes a second bold move by claiming for queer and feminist approaches the power to intervene in narrative theory *tout court.* If both of these bold moves are intentional, they are also provisional. Our subtitle recognizes that "queer and feminist" are not the only sites for intervention in narrative study. But we do aim to place gender and sexuality at the center of an inquiry about the production and reception, forms and functions of narrative texts. And we believe that the range, depth, and innovation that characterize this collection show why gender and sexuality belong at the heart of all narrative inquiry and how unbinding these concepts can unbind narrative theory as well.

Under the rubric of *Narrative Theory Unbound,* then, we gather a diverse and sometimes dissonant spectrum of theoretical challenges. Although the two of us have long preferred the term "feminist narratology" to describe our own practice, the more capacious and less contentious rubric of "narrative theory" better reflects the diversity of approaches gathered here. In this introduction as in the essays that follow, the terms "narratology" and "narrative theory" will both appear. Within the field, the two terms are sometimes used interchangeably to refer to the systematic study of how narrative forms make meaning. But the phrase "feminist narratology" remains under pressure from two directions: from *echt* narratologists who assert that culturally invested and category-resistant approaches cannot properly be called narratological, and from scholars of gender and sexuality who remain suspicious of narratology's formalist priorities and binary frames. Indeed, narratology's roots in an ahistorical structuralism seemed at first to preclude a feminist or queer approach. When analysis depends on "either-or" categorizations, as it did in the narratology of the 1970s and 1980s, the rich multiplicity not just of genders and sexualities but also of narrative practices could indeed get reduced into essentialist and universalizing generalizations. Feminist narratology has been aware of this potential problem from the beginning, but *Narrative Theory Unbound* embeds itself in a consciousness of intersectional challenges, a commitment to pluralist *bricolage,* and a comfort with messy complexities that we believe foster an enabling flexibility without sacrificing theoretical rigor. In this sense, too, we hope to have loosened the field to embrace multiple pathways by recognizing a diversity—even a clash—among queer and feminist investments in narrative and indeed among understandings of narrative itself. We also embrace capacious understandings of both "feminist" and "queer." We recognize feminism as a set of move(ment)s designed to address—that is, to understand, analyze, and intervene to rectify—oppressive and repressive systems and practices that perpetuate limitations and inequalities rooted in assumptions about biological sex or social gender. Likewise, we recognize "queer" as the sign for move(ment)s that challenge—and again, aim to understand, analyze, and rectify—heteronormative systems and practices and their attendant binary assumptions about sex, gender, and sexuality. We recognize, however, that "feminist" and "queer" may foster divergent and even conflicting projects, whether on the stage of politics or on the page of scholarship; *Narrative Theory Unbound* reflects this multiplicity.

Feminism and narratology joined forces in the 1980s when literary and cultural critics, perhaps especially in the United States, were becoming highly self-conscious about articulating the theoretical principles governing their critical practice. In recent years, the theoretical imperative has become less distinct. Much of what was spelled out by structuralists, poststructuralists, new historicists, neo-marxists, queer theorists, postcolonialists, and feminists during the heyday of the "theory wars" has now become naturalized within critical practice; epistemological and methodological assumptions are now more often enacted than explained. Narratology still requires the articulation of method, however, particularly since the many developments in narrative theory—for instance, cognitive and mind-centered approaches, "unnatural" or antimimetic narratologies, and rhetorical and ethical narrative theories—differ in significant and sometimes irreconcilable ways. Mapping out those differences is essential to the project of narrative theory, as competition and collaboration among the various branches continue to build new ways of thinking about narrative. Today as in the 1980s, criticism inspired by theories of gender and sexuality continues to bring to light aspects of narrative that other narratologies, however different their investments, tend to overlook or underemphasize. For all the differences within and between queer and feminist approaches, what unites them is precisely this primacy of commitment to regard narrative and gender/sexuality as coequal terms.

This volume brings together scholars of literature, performance studies, biography, and popular culture who are exploring the many ways in which narrative represents, structures, and constitutes gender and sexuality, as well as the ways these concepts inflect narrative itself. With its origins in a three-day Project Narrative Symposium organized at The Ohio State University by Robyn Warhol in May 2011, the book collects current work by three generations of narrative critics who are affiliated with gender and/or sexuality studies. Though only a few would call themselves feminist or queer narrative theorists, all the scholars in this collection draw on feminist or queer theory in making their critical arguments, and all are concerned with the specific workings of narrative. Each of the essays in this book speaks to the question "What are the theoretical principles driving my current work on gender, sexuality and narrative?" The authors pause to consider what it is about their work on narrative that is feminist or queer, and what it is about their work in feminist or queer studies that is guided by theories of narrative. While "feminism" may still connote an exclusive focus on women in some circles, queer and feminist narrative theories are united in viewing sex, gender, and sexuality as constructions pertaining to women, men, bi-, trans- and gender-queer people across other diversities of culture, race, ethnicity, class, age, (dis)ability, religion, and nationality.

In this introductory chapter, we will sketch out a brief history of feminist and queer narrative theory, then make some generalizations about the present and some predictions for the future of the field before turning to the specific contributions that comprise *Narrative Theory Unbound*. To avoid reifying a hierarchy between "feminist" and "queer," we have chosen a self-consciously random fluctuation between "queer and feminist" and "feminist and queer." We begin from the premise that although feminist inquiry emerged earlier, neither queer nor feminist narrative theory could exist in its current form without the other. Indeed, the two approaches overlap in respects that make them difficult to tease apart even though they also live in fruitful tension.

Some projects lean more heavily on sexuality and some on gender, but much of the work in this volume is inflected by both.

Feminist narrative theory emerged as both an engagement with and a challenge to the body of theory that students of narrative were building primarily upon the principles of structuralism and semiotics. This enterprise—so much equated with the term "narratology" that structuralist narratology is now widely called "classical"—sought to elaborate a narrative grammar (as A. J. Greimas called it), a poetics of prose (in Tzvetan Todorov's formulation) that could account for all narrative texts. Like structural anthropology and structural linguistics, narratology was to apply equally to all narratives, regardless of when they were produced or where they came from, and while prose fiction was the overwhelming generic focus, the new narrative grammars soon sought to account as well for film, drama, narrative poetry, and "non-fictional" narrative genres. Fostered especially by the translation into English in 1980 of Gérard Genette's *Discours du récit* (1972), the new narratology also instantiated an array of terms, categories, and distinctions that, while remaining contested, provided a dazzling critical vocabulary on which students of narrative began quickly to rely.

During the same period that classical narratology was gaining its academic foothold, however, feminist literary criticism was also burgeoning, especially in the United States and western Europe, not only as a method of interpretation but as an inquiry into method itself. Feminist literary theorists began to ask whether "androcentric" epistemologies, models, and approaches were even applicable to female-written texts or could elucidate the historically contingent gender dynamics now understood to structure all textual and social arrangements. These scholars insisted upon grounding their theories in the lived experience of "women," conceived at first naïvely as a unified category simply designating the opposite of "men." Structuralism, with its differently totalizing goals and its formalist abstractions, seemed among the theoretical approaches least likely to be influenced by the historicizing turn that feminist criticism was pioneering. Elaine Showalter's *A Literature of Their Own* (1977), for example, took all formalisms to task for "evad[ing] the issue of sexual identity entirely, or dismiss[ing] it as irrelevant and subjective" and thus in effect "desexing" both women and the field (8).

Such challenges, however, ended up expanding rather than foreclosing the intellectual space for a feminist understanding of narrative. Mieke Bal's 1977 book translated into English in 1985 as *Narratology: Introduction to the Study of Narrative* had already loosened the canon, if not the context, by focusing on works by Duras and Colette as well as the canonical Flaubert. In a direct critique of new narratological tenets, Nancy K. Miller's 1981 "Emphasis Added: Plots and Plausibilities in Women's Fiction" identified Genette's notions of plot and plausibility as male-centered constructs masquerading as universals and argued that "the implausible twists of plot" common to many women's novels constituted "comment on the stakes of difference within the theoretical indifference of literature itself" (44). Pointing to the "complete disregard of gender in the formalist study of narrative voice" (46), Lanser's *The Narrative Act* (1981) aimed explicitly to forge a poetics of point of view that would recognize the imbrications of ideology, context, and form to accommodate women's writings and feminist concerns. From a psychoanalytic perspective, Teresa DeLauretis's "Desire in Narrative" (reprinted in *Alice Doesn't,* 1984) exposed the gendered Oedipal structure both of narrative desire and of the language in which narrative had been characterized. Margaret Homans (1983), Mária Minich Brewer (1984), and Rachel Blau DuPlessis (1985) likewise challenged conventional thinking about plot by exploring what they saw as the different dynamics of women's narratives.

In this same period each of us--committed to the larger project of narrative poetics and deeply interested in women's writings though not yet acquainted with one another's work—likewise asked what happens to narratology's models when they are tested against gendered representations. We came separately to conclude that androcentric narratology had overlooked the structures we found in women's writing. The tipping point arguably occurred in 1986 through the simultaneous publication of Warhol's "Toward a Theory of the Engaging Narrator" and Lanser's "Toward a Feminist Narratology," both of which spoke from within the sphere of classical narratology to call for a gender-conscious poetics. Positing a distinction between "distancing" and "engaging" narrators, Warhol argued that the engaging narrator had been undertheorized and devalued because of its association with women writers and "sentimental" novels. Lanser proposed that "feminist criticism, and particularly the study of narratives by women, might benefit from the methods and insights of narratology" and that "narratology, in turn, might be altered by the understandings of feminist criticism and the experience of women's texts" (342). Warhol's *Gendered Interventions* (1989) further demonstrated the ways in which nineteenth-century women novelists, barred from addressing the public in person, used novels as a form of direct address, while Lanser's *Fictions of Authority* (1992) explored the limits and possibilities of different instantiations of narrative voice in novels by European and American women. Significantly, the essays we published separately in 1986 received far more, and more vituperative, criticism than the books we published a few years later; by end of the decade, the tide had turned for feminist narratology. The publication in *PMLA* of Susan Winnett's "Coming Unstrung: Women, Men, Narrative, and Principles of Pleasure" (1990) sits at that turning point by advancing a bold critique of the masculinist assumptions founding major theories of narrative, especially Peter Brooks's *Reading for the Plot* (1992). In *Ambiguous Discourse: Feminist Narratology and British Women Writers* (1996), Kathy Mezei collected a dozen essays by scholars explicitly aligning themselves with the new approach. *Narrative Theory Unbound* is the first collection of feminist narrative theory to appear since 1996 and the only collection of queer narrative theory published to date.

Since the 1990s, feminist narrative theorists have focused richly, productively, and diversely on women (and sometimes men) writers, narrators, plots, and sometimes characters, as well as on the gendered and gendering impact of particular narrative strategies upon flesh-and-blood readers. Theorists have emphasized that gender is a process created in and through culture, "mapping" as Susan Stanford Friedman put it in her pathbreaking work, the complex intersections of culture, identity, and transnational geography that forge narrative practices.[1] Conversely, in an equally important development, narrative theorists began to recognize in feminist approaches a model for other culturally conscious explorations of narrative. Indeed, feminist narratology has been widely credited with the "postclassical turn" from a universalizing structuralism to a contingent understanding of "narrative grammar" as inseparable "from questions about the contexts in which narratives are designed and interpreted" (Herman 11).

Like feminist theory itself, feminist narrative theory has grown over its three decades in both the scope of its interests and the depth of its insights. What began as a focus on the impact of culturally constructed gender upon the form and reception of narrative texts has broadened to feminist narratolo*gies* that recognize race, sexuality, nationality, class, and ethnicity as well as gender in formulating their theoretical and analytical projects. One of the most important developments of recent decades has been an acknowledgment of what legal scholar Kimberlé Crenshaw has called "intersectionality." An intersectional approach foregrounds the conviction that sexuality, race, class, nationality, age, and ability—to name just the most frequently cited categories of difference—intersect with one another to form intricate

---

1. In addition to the specifically literary work we have been discussing, feminist narratology has significantly inflected such fields as discourse analysis, folklore, and linguistic anthropology. In *Literary and Linguistic Approaches to Feminist Narratology* (2006), Ruth Page pioneered a methodology that synthesizes literary and discourse analyses.

variations upon oppression and privilege. Generalizing about the oppression of "nineteenth-century women in the United States," for example, makes no sense if race, region, and class are not part of the analysis, since middle-class white women lived so differently from their counterparts who worked in factories, and both lived so differently from women who were enslaved or relocated from their ancestral homes to reservations. For that matter, when sexuality, age, disability, religion, and ethnicity come into the analysis, middle-class white American women even lived differently from one another. An intersectional approach tries to track the influence of as many identity categories as possible and to scrutinize the imbrications of those tracks when working out an argument, while remembering that the identity categories themselves are fluid within groups and even within individual persons.[2] This intersectional approach further implicates gender and sexuality as mutually constitutive systems and expands the potential for alignments between feminist and queer approaches, especially where those approaches share understandings about identity.

In this regard, Judith Butler's model of performativity has been profoundly transformative in aligning queer and feminist approaches and in understanding what it means to "act." Although a perceived opposition between theory and activism has plagued academic feminism as well as queer studies, we understand theory as itself a form of academic activism, in that it continually overturns assumptions which have served to keep gender inequalities and heteronormative epistemologies in place. For feminist and queer narrative theory, gender matters, in the sense that gender makes a difference in the production and reception of texts, and also in the sense that the gendering of writing and reading has its basis in—and an impact upon—lived experience in the material world. Today feminists generally join queer theorists in understanding gender difference to be a cultural construction, not a biological given, and in recognizing that both gender and sexuality exist along a variegated spectrum that individual subjects experience in shifting ways across a lifetime. Within this framework, gender and sexuality are not *who you are,* but rather *what you do,* and they never settle into a solid or coherent identity. While gender and sexuality are therefore not an essence but a performance, these and other identity categories, however constructed and fluid, nonetheless have real implications and effects. And as many essays in this volume underscore, narratives are critical to constructing, maintaining, interpreting, exposing and dismantling the social systems, cultural practices,

---

2. For a useful outline of intersectional feminist methodology from a scholar based outside the United States, see Lykke.

and individual lives that shape and are shaped by performative acts. Feminist and queer narrative theorists identify and demystify the workings of those norms in and through narrative, and expose the dominant stories keeping the binaries in place.

Indeed, this recognition of the power of narrative pervades queer theory and underwrites its longstanding investments in thinking about narrative. Although work explicitly calling itself "queer narratology" is presently modest—a circumstance this volume might ameliorate—theorizing about narrative has been intimately intertwined with queer theory from the inauguration of sexuality studies. The centrality of narrative in shaping heteronormativity and with it queer subjectivity has been acknowledged by virtually every major queer theorist from Roland Barthes to Eve Sedgwick and Judith Butler to Lee Edelman. A key aspect of this queer engagement has been the question of whether and how narrative might be turned to queer ends; if Marilyn Farwell's *Heterosexual Plots and Lesbian Narratives* (1996) would have it in the affirmative, D. A. Miller's *Bringing Out Roland Barthes* (1992) and Judith Roof's *Come As You Are* (1996) insist on the heteronormativity of narrative itself. Bringing psychoanalysis and deconstruction to bear on questions of reading and desire, queer/feminist theorists have deconstructed notions of narrative teleology as both masculinist and heterosexist. The idea that narrative itself is heterocentric in its future-oriented drive has also become powerfully influential in the work of Judith Halberstam, Paul Morrison, Jane Gallop, and especially Edelman, who has argued that futurity is inextricable from the reproductive imperative. Edelman's insistence on positing a queer temporality that does not focus on the future has profoundly influenced queer studies of narrative. Attention to temporality also raises questions about queer history and the ways that gay, lesbian, bisexual, and transgendered experience have been effaced by mainstream accounts of the past. The project of reconstructing a queer archive that would ground a new kind of history, as practiced by Ann Cvetkovich and others, asks how the materials of that archive would be arranged into a new narrative of the queer past and present. The field of queer performance studies has also intersected with narrative theory in books such as Joseph Litvak's study of theatricality and sexuality in the nineteenth-century novel, *Caught in the Act,* and Claudia Breger's *An Aesthetics of Narrative Performance,* which brings together narrative studies and performance studies to analyze contemporary German novels and films.

From their diverse vantage points, all the essays gathered in *Narrative Theory Unbound* are working with narrative-theoretical terms and concepts, some more explicitly than others. While feminist and especially queer narrative critics often distance themselves from the scientistic posture of structuralist narratology with its seemingly relentless binaries, structuralism and its descendants among postclassical narratologies still provide much of the vocabulary enabling the theorists in this volume to make their arguments. Peggy Phelan offers the boldest dramatization of this fact by taking "hypothetical focalization"—David Herman's refinement of Gérard Genette's term for describing "who sees" in a given narrative text—as the starting point for an essay that speedily departs from the disciplined application of narratology to enact a queer textual performance of personal grief. "Spatiality" (invoked here by Hillary Chute) and especially "temporality" (explicitly central to the essays by Chute and by Jesse Matz, and likewise crucial to the arguments made here by Valerie Rohy, Paul Morrison, and Wendy Moffat) hold the same prominence in these essays as they do in other kinds of contemporary narrative theory. Claudia Breger writes here of narrative "worldmaking" and Warhol uses the word "storyworld," terms developed within mind-centered or cognitive narrative theory. Several of the authors draw on narratological terms for describing the organization of materials in a story, from the "narrative teleology" (the selection and ordering of story elements that lead up to the narrative's ending) invoked by Moffat and the "narrative etiology" (assumptions about the source and origins of particular narratives) explored by Rohy and taken up by Ellen Peel, to the "emplotment" discussed by Judith Roof and Shalyn Claggett, to Rohy's discussion of "closure." Narratology's attempts to catalog narrative forms are mentioned by Roof as "taxonomies of story structure." Sue J. Kim and Suzanne Keen both build upon Keen's earlier research on "narrative empathy," and Abby Coykendall draws on Genette's formulation of the "paratext." Both Lanser and Warhol use concepts that have been central to feminist narratology from its inception, including in Lanser's case "free indirect discourse" and in Warhol's, the "structure of address." Warhol talks about "metanarration" (self-reflexive narrative practices referring to the constructedness of a text), which is not to be confused with Roof's "metanarratives" (narratives about other narratives). This last distinction points to the disciplinary need for precision in facing a plethora of terms, one reason why narratology has developed so many of its notoriously clunky, Greek-based neologisms. But on the whole, the contributors to *Narrative Theory Unbound* strive to avoid "jargon" in our commitment to speak to a broad audience; the specialized terms we do evoke in this volume have specific denotations that allow narrative theorists to point directly to correspondences between textual features and narrative effects.

This volume also hopes to make a modest contribution to addressing the narrowness of the canon on which feminist and queer narratological models are built. As Lanser notes in her essay for this book, just as the structuralists' canon was too male and too European to yield insight into the forms of women's writing, feminist narratology's canon has generally been too white, too heterosexual, too female, and too centered in nineteenth- and early twentieth-century fiction, while queer narratology has been centered mostly in twentieth- and twenty-first-century man-made films and novels, with Henry James as leading man. Feminist and queer narrative theories need both to test our models against a broader range of world narrative forms and to learn from that process the limits of our current understandings of narrative form and function. Queer and feminist narrative theories also would benefit from elaborating a literary history that takes into account the forms and structures our research has observed. So far the field has tended to operate in a piecemeal fashion, elucidating the narrative structure of a single text or of a carefully delimited set of texts. Insofar as a universalizing model of narrative is out of the question and a homogeneous chronology of developments impossible for a contextualist narrative theory, we might conceive of a history of gendered and sexed narrative forms built on something like the example of Franco Moretti's maps, graphs, and trees. If our methodologies are ever to break free from the static and binary traces of structuralism that still lurk behind our practice, queer and feminist narrative theories might try out theoretical models that have recently proved fruitful in transmedial studies, such as Bruno Latour's actor-network theory, and in queer/postcolonial/intersectional studies, such as Gilles Deleuze and Félix Guattari's concept of assemblages.[3] And, too, after thirty years of dwelling on the politics of form, feminist and queer narrative theories may be ready to turn from poetics and hermeneutics to take on a politicized aesthetics, conceived perhaps as an erotics of narrative that would be focused on the reader's body, and working, perhaps, in concert with the gendered neuronarrative approach (combining empirical research and psychoanalysis) that Kay Young and Suzanne Keen have both been pioneering.

At the 2011 Project Narrative Symposium on Feminist and Queer Narrative Theories, we took stock of what our field has failed so far to do so that we could consider what it can do in the future. The impetus for the conference itself was our recognition that feminist and queer narrative studies, though grounded in similar theories and methodologies, have not been as closely in dialogue as they might be. The present book, an outcome of that symposium, is one means of bringing that conversation into being.

---

3. See the recent work of Frank Kelleter for explorations of serial narratives as actor-networks, and see Puar for groundbreaking work that brings assemblages into the discussion of intersectionality.

We have structured this volume into four sections of full-length essays, a fifth section comprised of challenging commentaries, and a compelling afterword. While we could have organized the essays in many different ways, we have clustered them into groups that seem to us to be in implicit conversation with one another around a burning issue in the field. "Narrative Discourse Unbound" presents four essays that exemplify a range of queer/feminist engagements with—and departures from—principles of narratology. "Intersectional Narrative Theories" brings together the three essays that rely most explicitly on intersectionality theory to advance queer/feminist understandings of narrative. "Lifewriting, Gender, Sex" reflects the challenges wrought by diverse biographical and autobiographical forms from the written and oral to the graphic and digitized. "Emplotment, or the Shapes of Stories" gathers essays that explore the impact of queerness, gender, and embodiment upon narrative practices; the overlap between this topic and lifewriting is profound. The commentaries that comprise our fifth section, "Challenges: Un/doing Narrative Theory," cut across these topics to suggest points of solidarity and resistance among theorists with divergent commitments to our three anchoring concepts—narrative, feminist, queer. We include these challenges to the collection's longer essays to open out the topics under discussion and thus to underscore the provisional nature of any project of theoretical inquiry. Taken together, the twenty contributions to this book map the present state of feminist and queer narrative theory, while each individual essay works to expand the boundaries of what a particular approach has enabled thus far. The afterword by Irene Kacandes takes the next step beyond the genealogy articulated in this introduction to glance back at the past so as to gesture towards areas that are open for exploration by new generations of narrative theorists who are also committed activists.

Revisiting the kinds of questions she raised in "Toward a Feminist Narratology" (1986), Susan S. Lanser opens the section we've called "Narrative Discourse Unbound" by calling for an approach that is not only queerer and more feminist but more narratological. Lanser makes the case for the power of narratology to elucidate the dynamics that story aims to conceal. She argues for recognizing narrative form as cultural content in order to forge a deeper understanding of the ways in which such social vectors as gender and sexuality, class, race and nationality shape historically and geographically diverse narrative practices. She proposes, however, that extending the still limited scope, reach, and relevance of narratology might require further reform of narratological terms and concepts and even of narratological priorities.

Judith Roof takes a very different and arguably queerer approach in "Out of the Bind: From Structure to System in Popular Narratives," shifting the analytical model from "structure" to "system" and revealing the limits of conventional narratological taxonomies. Focusing on variant versions of "Red Riding Hood," Roof demonstrates the "potential for morphing" intrinsic to the definition of character and exposes the insecure logic of story that enables elements within a system to "shift and recombine" into "non-binary multiples." Roof's systems perspective thus offers a complex account of narrative as a persistent, recombinant process as she shows how a systems model can militate against the hegemonic conventions of heteronormative closure that structuralist approaches can reify.

From different angles, Robyn Warhol and Peggy Phelan also turn the tables on conventional narratological concepts. Drawing on Judith Butler's *Giving an Account of Oneself,* Warhol focuses on televisual form, showing how camera angles and editing practices efface the subjectivity of "real" women. The misogyny of Bravo TV's *Real Housewives* series, she argues, inheres less in its content than in its narrative form. She offers as a contrasting example the mockumentary *The Office,* in which characters address the camera directly while talking about their experiences and feelings in narratives that represent the ambivalence and confusion omitted in the autobiographical sequences on *Real Housewives.* Ironically, Warhol concludes, the hyperrealist representations of fictional people on *The Office* come closer to signifying subjectivity than the depictions of "real" people in reality TV. In making this argument, Warhol also demonstrates the critical place of formal analysis in understanding gendered representations of subjectivity.

The expanded understanding of focalization proposed by David Herman becomes the starting point for Peggy Phelan's "Hypothetical Focalization and Queer Grief," at once a moving autobiographical meditation and a queer/narratological intervention. Drawing on concepts of performance, Phelan sees in hypothetical focalization a haunting *"might have been"* that evokes the doubt, uncertainty, and blurred vision attendant upon the articulation of queer lives and a caveat against taking "clarity and precision" as methodological goals potentially inadequate to "messier and blurrier" (queer) textual performances. Phelan weaves theory and—and as—narrative while evoking the "twin experiences" of queer "love and grief" by way of Eve Sedgwick's life and work, particularly as Sedgwick's presence touched upon the death of Phelan's lover and collaborator, Lynda Hart.

Our introduction and Lanser's essay both argue for an intersectional approach to narrative subjects, plots, and practices. The three essays constituting our second section approach intersectionality from distinct though compatible vantage points. Susan Stanford Friedman elucidates an aspect of identity and culture—religious affinity—that she deems an "overwhelming absence" from feminist theory, parsing out the ways in which religion itself constitutes a multiplicity of force fields—theological, cultural, and institutional—that converge in narrative. Friedman maintains that religion is an axis not of power but of difference, and she sees the *Bildungsroman* as "a specific testing ground for an intersectional queer/feminist narrative theory in which religion generates narrative structures well outside the agonistic patterns of oppression and resistance." Focusing on coming-of-age novels by Ahdaf Soueif, Leila Aboulela, and Randa Jarrar that grapple with generational tensions in Muslim diasporic communities, Friedman calls for a "fundamental shift" not only in conceiving narrative but in conceiving intersectionality.

Narrative empathy is the focal point of essays by Suzanne Keen and Sue J. Kim that likewise provide new intersectional perspectives. Keen's "Intersectional Narratology in the Study of Narrative Empathy" expands her well-known work on this topic by exploring the "complex overlays" of form, content, and context that account for diverse responses to narrative. Using the framework delineated by psychologist C. Daniel Batson and focusing on popular fiction as an understudied (and gendered) genre, Keen asks how readers' identities shape responses to characters, particularly "when narrative empathy reaches across boundaries of difference." In turn, Keen shows how intersectional identities also shape the contexts of production and reception in the literary marketplace.

Sue J. Kim provides a particularly positive instance of intersectional empathy in "Empathy and 1970s Novels by Third World Women." Building on Keen's theories to recognize empathy as a "complex, historically and institutionally embedded concept," Kim shows how social change can emerge from "crossing and changing existing borders between different groups of women," in this case Third World women and U.S. women of color. In demonstrating how "specific narrative strategies" helped women to "map out the kinds of oppressions, repressions, and erasures that women of color shared" in the 1970s "across ethnic and national boundaries," Kim is also able to shed light on the more limited potential of a present-day "fetishizing global capitalism." Kim's powerful conclusion that readerly empathy has social force is thus also conditioned by historical contingencies.

The section called "Lifewriting, Gender, Sex" begins with Alison Booth's "Screenshots in the *Longue Durée*: Feminist Narratology, Digital Humanities, and Collective Biographies of Women," a report on the Collective Biographies of Women (CWB) project, which gathers and sorts nineteenth- and twentieth-century collections of short biographies of famous women. Having developed an analytic schema, Booth and her research team have identified patterns of structure and content in the forgotten genre of collective biography. Booth places her project within the history of feminist narrative theory, emphasizing the collaborative nature of her work and collective nature of her subject matter. Her immersion in digital humanities leads Booth to think in terms of systems and social networks, new moves for feminist narrative theory. Booth's essay adds dimensions to our concept of lifewriting, our understanding of "evidence" in feminist-narrative literary analysis, and our access to the history of mainstream representations of the female subject.

In "The Space of Graphic Narrative: Mapping Bodies, Feminism, and Form," Hillary Chute sketches out a history of women comics artists' autobiographical works, and then explores the ways in which comics are an especially fruitful field for feminist narrative studies. Emphasizing the interdisciplinary approach required for analysis of comics' verbal-and-visual texts, Chute embraces the "enabling formalism" required for study of the medium. While comics' unabashed constructedness invites analysis of its formal codes and conventions, the medium also foregrounds issues like embodiment that are central to feminist and queer narrative theory's concerns. Acknowledging the importance of temporality to comics studies, Chute emphasizes that comics also raise equally pressing questions about spatial positioning. The essay illustrates Chute's method with brief readings of images from Alison Bechdel's *Are You My Mother?* and Phoebe Gloeckner's *A Child's Life and Other Stories,* which collapse time, space, and multiple selves to explore ambivalent desire for (as well as disavowal of) the past.

Wendy Moffat's essay makes "The Narrative Case for Queer Biography." Having written a life of E. M. Forster, Moffat argues that a biography of a queer person is not necessarily a queer biography, and reflects on the disconnection between gay social history and queer theory. Like other essayists in our collection, including Morrison, Rohy, and Matz, Moffat considers the part that temporality plays in queer conceptions of narrative. Narrative, Moffat argues, is not a dead issue for queer theory. She lingers with Eve Sedgwick's later work to point out that while Sedgwick repudiated teleological narrative, she did not advocate putting some kind of antinarrative in its place. Moffat discusses the new historicist and poststructuralist penchant for narrating "a case," weighing the appropriate scale on which to write a queer life.

Like Moffat, Jesse Matz takes up queer theory's critique of teleological narrative in "'No Future' vs. 'It Gets Better': Queer Prospects for Narrative Temporality." Here Matz juxtaposes Lee Edelman's trenchant critique of the reproductive imperative implicit in narrative's emphasis on futurity to Dan Savage's "It Gets Better" YouTube campaign aimed at potentially suicidal queer teenagers. Matz points out that although Edelman's and Savage's projects would seem to oppose each other directly enough to cancel each other out, they share a form of queer dissent that opens up new ways to think about "what narrative temporality means for queer possibility." Matz outlines an understanding of temporality as pedagogy, calling for queer narrative theorists to shift attention "from time-schemes that shape our lives to those that are shaped by our practices and rhetorics."

The first two essays in "Emplotment, or the Shapes of Stories," are closely related to the work on queer lifewriting in the previous section. Paul Morrison's "*Maurice,* or Coming Out Straight" reads Forster's most explicitly homosexual novel to show the ways in which heterosexuality turns out to reproduce sameness among normative persons and plotlines, while homosexuality opens up the possibility for divergence and difference, even though "hetero" denotes difference and "homo" means sameness. Morrison's essay has as much to say about Freud as it does about Forster, contending that "Freud makes possible the situation in which homosexuality can mean either nothing or everything, as homophobic convenience dictates." As long as the story of homosexuality seems to fit the heteronormative plot, as in the gay marriage movement, it doesn't signify, but when "the hetero reproduction of the same is threatened with difference, or . . . exposed for what it is," homosexuality suddenly explains everything.

Valerie Rohy's "Strange Influence: Queer Etiology in *The Picture of Dorian Gray*" begins with prevailing accounts of what explains homosexuality, or rather, with stories of where homosexuality comes from. She approaches the etiology of homosexuality as a narrative form that could enable us to "think causality differently," looking to Oscar Wilde's novel as a model for how that might come about. Homosexuality is, in this novel, both an absent cause and an absent effect. The essay considers the undecidability of Wilde's own sexual transgressions in the context of his trial, and ends on the contention that homosexuality "exerts its own . . . strange influence, pitting the closure of etiological narratives against the queerness of sexuality as such."

Susan Fraiman's "Gendered Narratives in Animal Studies" shifts this section's focus to a field that has not yet received much attention from queer and feminist narrative theorists. Fraiman identifies four widely circulated anecdotes about encounters between humans and animals (from Jacques Derrida, Barbara Smuts, Carol Adams, and Donna Haraway), examining each of these very short stories for signs of gender. Fraiman suggests that the brevity of these stories already marks them as "feminine," but her essay's purpose is to analyze the gendering of the narratives themselves. For her, this entails looking at the gendering of the narrators, actors, affective tenor, and narrative arc in each of the four stories; emplotment is only one of the narrative concepts guiding her analysis, but it is crucial to her argument. While a modification to theories of narrative is not among Fraiman's immediate goals, narrative theory provides a framework for grounding her feminist intervention into animal studies.

Bringing narrative theory together with neuroscience, Kay Young's "Sex—Text—Cortex" examines the sexed and gendered emplotment of "the brain's story." Young tackles the controversial question of whether or not sexuality and gender differences are hard-wired into the physiology of the brain, and points to ways in which queer and feminist narrative theories can help explain the stories presented as answers to that question. Her essay examines researchers' stories about where gender and sexual orientation originate, showing breakdowns in cause-and-effect plots that resonate with Rohy's and Morrison's observations. Young ends her essay by directly addressing the question that framed the 2011 symposium session in which she participated: "Feminist/Queer and Cognitive/Neurological Narrative Theories: Can We Talk?" According to Young, a conversation between these subfields of narrative theory must happen in order to complicate and diversify the developing story of the human brain.

The commentaries that we gather into the final section, "Challenges: Un/doing Narrative Theory" offer both provocative perceptions and a stark reminder of the limiting linearity of print. Robyn Warhol built into the 2011 symposium an exciting innovation: to begin the second and third mornings with a set of reflections on "the conference thus far." These reflections were of course stimulated by, and in turn stimulated, the wide-ranging and intense discussions that followed each paper, creating, over three days and some thirty-five speaking voices, a cumulative intellectual heft that exceeds representation. Only a full transcript could begin to give the flavor of those days, and only hypertext could begin to map the myriad of linkages from thought to thought. The five short papers that comprise the volume's final section are transformations of selected "conference thus far" commentaries into trenchant theoretical interventions that offer new, often provocative points of view. Abby Coykendall pushes back on two major assumptions that ground this volume: the compatibility of "queer" and "feminist" and the centrality of "narrative." She cautions that "combining feminist and queer" risks construing feminism as unqueer and queer as unfeminist, and she challenges the "tacit primacy" we grant to narrative theory. Reversing the paradigm, Coykendall presents narrative studies as a "specialized application of feminist and queer studies" since "the sole center of gravity around which queer subjects can circulate is their collective resistance" to regulatory cultural narratives. Thus,

for Coykendall, queer theory is effectively narrative theory, and indeed a critical corrective to a narratology that treats gender and sexuality as "peripheral
to its core interests and practices." In contrast to Warhol and Lanser's call to
recuperate narratology, Coykendall would "unburden" narrative theory from
narratology's institutional legacy.

Martin Joseph Ponce advances a queer-of-color critique from an angle
even more skeptical of any project that aims "to break down the current
conundrums and competing interests operating in queer studies and ethnic
studies and their encounters with narrative theory." Ponce doubts the possibility of "reciprocal engagements across queer, feminist, and narrative theory"
because of the "incongruous intellectual histories and political commitments"
of these fields. Ultimately, Ponce sees as the most viable option an approach
that recognizes "feminist, queer, black, and other ethnic studies" as necessarily
grounded in "highly contingent and variable" relationships both to narrative
and to narrative theory. He likewise points to tensions within queer theory in
its failure to attend sufficiently to racial and ethnic diversity.

For Claudia Breger, the merger of feminist/queer/narrative has a different valence, one that pushes against both old theories and new universalisms to forge what she calls a "critically affirmative theoretical bricolage." It
is precisely by moving away from a lines-in-the-sand drawing of boundaries
that queer/feminist narratologies are able to forge new interventions. Taking "'polyamorous relations' between affect and sexuality" as one instance,
Breger calls upon scholars to map "the multifaceted, plural, and contextually changing ways in which feelings are sexualized and desires imbricated in
affective orientations."[4] But where Coykendall might prefer revolt against the
traffic cop of narratology, Breger asks theorists to "calm" their well-trained
"inner hermeneutist of suspicion" in order to create fruitful provisional alliances with fields and positions that might be less congenial for permanent
relationships.

Each of these five commentaries draws attention to specific contributions
to *Narrative Theory Unbound,* and none more than Ellen Peel's. In "Narrative Causes: Inside and Out," Peel shows the ways in which several of our
contributors have collectively "brought the notion of causality back to life"
by offering a new understanding of two different aspects of causality: the first
intratextual and focused on the relationship of one event to another; the second extratextual and focused on the relationship between text and reader.
Exploring especially the contributions to this volume of Sue J. Kim, Valerie
Rohy, Paul Morrison, and Jessie Matz, and coming to terms through them

---

4. See also Ann Cvetkovich, "Public Feelings" 462.

with Lee Edelman's provocative *No Future: Queer Theory and the Death Drive* (2004), Peel argues that queer investigations of causality set the stage for a new concept of reproduction.

In a final commentary, Shalyn Claggett takes on what she sees as an "overlooked and undertheorized" problem at the heart of queer and feminist narrative theory: how to "take stock of extratextual significance while at the same time distinguishing between real-world context and its representation." She calls on queer/feminist theorists to consider "how the arsenal of techniques narrative theory has accumulated since its structuralist beginnings can be used to examine character understood as human personality, rather than exclusively focusing on character as literary device." Evoking Jonathan Adler's research on the ability of narrative to forge rather than simply reflect agency, Claggett underscores the value of narrative as a "tool" for the self-actualization of marginalized groups. Claggett reverses the paradigm that gives primacy to fiction and treats the referential world as its analogue, asking narrative theorists to make a new "bid for relevance" by bringing the tools of narrative theory to bear on the nonfictional genres that are so influential in today's fraught world.

Irene Kacandes takes up those ethical and activist imperatives in the afterword to the volume as she reminds us that it's the "afterward that will count." Evoking her transformative encounter with the writer Toni Cade Bambara, Kacandes places herself historically as a scholar who grew up with second-wave feminism, profoundly influenced not just by Bambara's field-defining ideas, but also by her refusal to participate in the academic star system. Kacandes offers a meditation on three messages inspired by Bambara: the need to break down hierarchies within academia and within our own ranks, the importance of developing strategies for managing our envy of colleagues' presumed access to authority on issues of identity and privilege, and the insight that projects of feminism and queer theory can only work if we enact alliances among ourselves. Kacandes relates her impressions of how three generations of feminist and queer narrative theorists interacted at the 2011 Project Narrative Symposium, and frames our debates with the contemporary realities of oppression, discrimination, and human-rights violations that prove we still have work to do in the world. Kacandes expresses a faith that not just storytelling but also feminist and queer accounts of narrative can support that work.

We hope this introduction gives an indication of why we took the bold step of naming this volume *Narrative Theory Unbound* and why *Queer and Feminist Interventions* might become a vanguard for all narrative inquiry. We also hope we have underscored the importance of narrative to queer and feminist theorizing and to the reconstructive activism of feminist/queer praxis in the interests of social change. We look forward to a neo-Promethean future of positions and perceptions about narrative that no one has yet conceived. Among all the movements in U.S. literature departments that emerged during the theory revolution of the 1980s, narrative theory in general, and narratology in particular, was probably the most uncool, the approach considered least likely to have a future. As it turns out, and as this volume testifies, contextual narratologies had a future then and have one now: our story is not likely to come to closure any time soon.

Works Cited

Bal, Mieke. *Narratology: Introduction to the Theory of Narrative*. Toronto: U of Toronto P, 1985.

Breger, Claudia. *An Aesthetics of Narrative Performance: Transnational Theater, Literature, and Film in Contemporary Germany*. Columbus: The Ohio State UP, 2012.

Brewer, Mária Minich. "A Loosening of Tongues: From Narrative Economy to Women Writing." *Modern Language Notes* 99.5 (1984): 1141–61.

Brooks, Peter. *Reading for the Plot: Design and Intention in Narrative*. New York: Knopf, 1984.

Crenshaw, Kimberlé. "Mapping the Margins: Intersectionality, Identity Politics, and Violence Against Women of Color." *Stanford Law Review* 43.6 (1991): 1241–99.

Cvetkovich, Ann. *An Archive of Feelings: Trauma, Sexuality, and Lesbian Public Cultures*. Durham: Duke UP, 2003.

———. "Public Feelings." *South Atlantic Quarterly* 106.3 (2007): 459–68.

DeLauretis, Teresa. *Alice Doesn't: Feminism, Semiotics, Cinema*. Bloomington: Indiana UP, 1984.

Deleuze, Gilles, and Félix Guattari. *A Thousand Plateaus*. Trans. Brian Massumi. Minneapolis: U of Minnesota P, 1987.

DuPlessis, Rachel Blau. *Writing Beyond the Ending: Narrative Strategies of Twentieth-Century Women Writers*. Bloomington: Indiana UP, 1985.

Edelman, Lee. *No Future: Queer Theory and the Death Drive*. Durham: Duke UP, 2004.

Farwell, Marilyn. *Heterosexual Plots and Lesbian Narratives*. New York: NYU P, 1996.

Friedman, Susan Stanford. *Mappings: Feminisms and the Cultural Geographies of Encounter*. Princeton: Princeton UP, 1998.

Gallop, Jane. *The Deaths of the Author: Reading and Writing in Time*. Durham: Duke UP, 2011.

Genette, Gérard. *Narrative Discourse: An Essay in Method*. Trans. Jane E. Lewin. Ithaca: Cornell UP, 1980.

Greimas, A. J. *Structural Semantics: An Attempt at a Method*. Trans. Ronald Schleifer, Alan Velie, and Danielle McDowell. Lincoln: U of Nebraska P, 1983.

Halberstam, Judith. *In a Queer Time and Place: Transgender Bodies, Subcultural Lives*. New York: NYU P, 2005.

Herman, David. *Narratologies: New Perspectives on Narrative Analysis*. Columbus: The Ohio State UP, 1999.

Homans, Margaret. "Her Very Own Howl: The Ambiguities of Representation in Recent Women's Fiction." *Signs* 9.2 (1983): 186–205.

Kelleter, Frank, ed. *Populäre Serialität: Narration–Evolution–Distinktion.* Bielefeld: Transcript, 2012.

Lanser, Susan S. *Fictions of Authority: Women Writers and Narrative Voice.* Ithaca: Cornell UP, 1992.

———. *The Narrative Act: Point of View in Prose Fiction.* Princeton: Princeton UP, 1981.

———. "Towards a Feminist Narratology." *Style* (20) 1986: 341–63.

Latour, Bruno. *Reassembling the Social: An Introduction to Actor-Network Theory.* Oxford: Oxford UP, 2005.

Litvak, Joseph. *Caught in the Act: Theatricality in the Nineteenth-Century English Novel.* Berkeley: U of California P, 1992.

Lykke, Nina. *Feminist Studies: A Guide to Intersectional Theory, Methodology, and Writing.* New York: Routledge, 2012.

Mezei, Kathy, ed. *Ambiguous Discourse: Feminist Narratology and British Women Writers.* Chapel Hill: U of North Carolina P, 1996.

Miller, D. A. *Bringing Out Roland Barthes.* Berkeley: U of California P, 1992.

Miller, Nancy K. "Emphasis Added: Plots and Plausibilities in Women's Fiction." *PMLA* 96.1 (1981): 36–48.

Moretti, Franco. *Graphs, Maps, Trees: Abstract Models for a Literary History.* New York and London: Verso, 2005.

Morrison, Paul. *The Explanation for Everything: Essays on Sexual Subjectivity.* New York: NYU P, 2001.

Page, Ruth. *Literary and Linguistic Approaches to Feminist Narratology.* New York: Palgrave, 2006.

Puar, Jasbir. "'I would rather be a cyborg than a goddess': Becoming-Intersectional in Assemblage Theory." *philoSOPHIA* 2.1 (2012): 49–66.

———. *Terrorist Assemblages: Homonationalism in Queer Times.* Durham: Duke UP, 2007.

Roof, Judith. *Come As You Are: Sexuality and Narrative.* New York: Columbia UP, 1996.

Showalter, Elaine. *A Literature of Their Own: British Women Novelists from Brontë to Lessing.* Princeton: Princeton UP, 1977.

Todorov, Tzvetan. *The Poetics of Prose.* Trans. Richard Howard. Ithaca: Cornell UP, 1977.

Warhol, Robyn. *Gendered Interventions: Narrative Discourse in the Victorian Novel.* New Brunswick: Rutgers UP, 1989.

———. "Toward a Theory of the Engaging Narrator: Earnest Interventions in Gaskell, Stowe, and Eliot." *PMLA* 101.5 (1986): 811–18.

Winnett, Susan. "Coming Unstrung: Women, Men, Narrative, and Principles of Pleasure." *PMLA* 105.3 (1990): 505–18.

PART I

*N*arrative Discourse Unbound

SUSAN S. LANSER

Toward (a Queerer and)
More (Feminist) Narratology

"The story had held us, round the fire": With this classic lure, Henry James inaugurates both *The Turn of the Screw* and the large conundrum that his small novel poses for the project of narrative. For James's homage to the power of story is complicated almost immediately when the text disclaims its ostensible purpose: we're about to get a story, but "the story *won't* tell," or at least "not in any literal, vulgar way" (8). In a more than trivial sense, this gesture reminds us that, as my graduate professor David Hayman was fond of saying, narrative is the art of not telling a story. And if "the story won't tell," then that art of narrative is also decidedly queer.

I begin with this passage to suggest that it is precisely to the extent that "the story *won't* tell . . . in any literal, vulgar way" that narrative needs narratology. To the extent that narrative succeeds by covering the tracks of its own strategies, narratology provides a critical pathway to understanding how stories work and thus also to how they "hold" us. To the extent that those narrative strategies function as narrative content, stories cannot even be apprehended unless we can read them as form. And to the extent that the gender arrangements on which narrative depends—and the narratives on which gender arrangements depend—are complex, subtle, and sometimes elusive, feminist and queer studies might be among narratology's particular beneficiaries. In advancing these opening claims, I am reversing the emphasis of my earlier work: if in the 1980s and 1990s I was urging narrative studies to be queerer and more feminist, I'm now urging feminist and queer studies— and even narrative studies—to be more narratological. While feminism and narratology have made a fruitful marriage that produced contextual narratology as its sturdiest offspring, the benefits of narratology remain undertapped. Tapping those benefits, however, may require some reform in narratological theories and practices, not least a shift to inductive and intersectional approaches and a hard interrogation of terms and priorities.

In the quarter century since the publication of Robyn Warhol's *Gendered Interventions* and my own "Toward a Feminist Narratology," feminism and narratology have certainly formed a visible intersection on the literary map, with an impressive dossier of achievements. The extensive bibliography to Ruth Page's *Literary and Linguistic Approaches to Feminist Narratology* provides a case in point, as does any web search on the two terms. And as "the earliest and most established strand of contextual narratology," feminism has rightly been credited for helping to move narratology from structuralist to postclassical paradigms (Sommer 61). But can narratology take credit for influencing feminist or queer studies with parallel force? To what extent does narratology matter to scholars who do not practice it as its own end? Has the widely touted "narrative turn" across the human sciences been a narratological turn as well? Where does narratology reside today beyond the small world of specialist journals and conferences? Why, conversely, has narratology refused to die—rather like the ghosts that James's governess sees or imagines—when its death has been proclaimed so frequently? Why, in short, was David Lodge ultimately wrong when he wrote, three decades ago in his novel *Small World*, "Hasn't [the narratologist's] moment passed? I mean, ten years ago everybody was into that stuff, actants and functions and mythemes and all that jazz. But now . . ." (134).

In this essay, I would like to make several interventions as a way of staking the terms for a narratological future that also furthers feminist and queer intellectual aims. I will argue that feminist and queer narratologies have worked with canons that are too narrow, and I will suggest the importance of extending their historical and geographic maps. I will propose that an intersectional narratology may assist that cartographic project while also moving beyond the confines of literary scholarship to reveal the narrative formations in feminist and queer studies broadly conceived. I will argue that questions of representation, and especially of queer representation, are as much questions of form as of content and that narratological concerns thus lie at the heart of debates about the queer capacities and limits of narrative. In the end, I will hope to persuade you that "the story *won't* tell" unless we study narrative form as narrative content, a strategy that might also help to mend the continuing—and in my view false—division between cultural and formal approaches evident, for example, in the tacit breach between theory of the novel and theory of narrative. And I will speculate that feminist and queer literary scholarship, along with other ideologically charged or identity-focused inquiries, might benefit in particular from narratology insofar as the mimeticist tendencies of those critical practices overlook the transgressions, subversions, and contingencies embedded in form. Finally, I will argue that narratology is well worth retaining as both word and practice, but that narratology may be too important to leave to narratologists: we might need new approaches to address the terminological and topical terrors—and, I dare say, missteps—that the field inspires. And because all of this is too much to cover in one essay, I will also have to take the risk that this essay *won't* tell, or—worse—will tell only in literal and vulgar ways.

We might start with a report card. If we take feminist and queer narratologies as a test case for addressing the questions I've outlined, there is cause for both celebration and concern. On one hand, the work of queer and feminist scholars, including those represented in this volume, has advanced narrative theory in ways as rich and varied as their many books, essays, and conference papers indicate. Indeed, so much has been accomplished that we can now chart achievements on multiple axes to see precisely where feminist and queer narratologies have made major inroads and which terrains are barely traversed. On the other hand, the rough data I found in, say, the *MLA Bibliography* charts a narrower path not only of feminist and (especially) queer narrative theory but of narrative theory *tout court*. My subject searches on women and feminism yielded a whopping 69,000 entries. Gender added a sizeable 14,000, sexuality another 8,000, and the combined indices "lesbian," "gay," "queer," "bisexual," and "transgender" about 2,000 more—for 93,000 subject entries in all. Searches combining any of these subjects with "narrative"—itself over 52,000 entries strong—were much more modest: respectively, 2,077 entries for women, 445 for gender, 219 for sexuality, and just 50 for lesbian, queer, gay, bisexual, and (the nonexistent) transgender combined. Equally surprising, "narrative theory" and "narratology" together yielded only about 2,000 subject entries, with narratology comprising but 15 percent of these, and subject searches combining narrative theory or narratology with *all* of the terms denoting women, feminism, gender, or sexuality were minuscule at 125.[1] To be sure, MLA searches can be faulty and MLA classifications

---

1. I undertook these particular searches in mid-2013; needless to say, the *MLA Bibliography* is an ever-shifting entity. But data from 2011 and 2013 were not appreciably different.

complex, and narrative theorists might want to inquire about current parameters.[2] But we also know that search terms perpetuate critical practices.

It's also sobering, therefore, to acknowledge the narrow literary canon that
these MLA entries draw upon, for they support the probability that feminist
and queer narrative studies has been forging a field on a very small portion
of the world's texts, indeed primarily from a small body of novels by white,
nineteenth- and twentieth-century English and American women and queer
men, with a few films offering modest generic diversity. In my tally of MLA
citations, fully three-quarters of the essays engaging feminist and queer narrative theory were drawn from these sources. Postcolonial and pre-1800 texts
were striking for their paucity, and a bare handful of entries considered works
by male novelists not known as queer. A search of the twenty-odd entries on
"women writers" and "narrative voice" suggests a potentially wider canon of
narratological *practice,* which may indicate not only the *MLA Bibliography's*
limited ability to discern what counts as narrative theory but a deeper need
to integrate that broader canon into the theoretical formulations that guide
the field. Like many feminist projects of the 1980s, feminist narratology was
effectively born essentialist despite finer intentions, its universalizing gender oppositions ironically replicating the either/or tendencies of structuralist
narratology itself. As Ruth Page rightly noted of my own work, feminist narratology at the outset was "embedded in . . . a binary model of gender that
emphasized difference" between men and women and tended "to construct
the category 'women' as if it were a universal group" (46–47). While theorists such as Margaret Homans and Susan Friedman challenged this initial
model early on, it's telling that the only edited collection that uses "feminist"
and "narratology" in its title, Kathy Mezei's wonderful *Ambiguous Discourse,*
is explicitly focused on British women writers from Jane Austen to Jeanette
Winterson. My own *Fictions of Authority* is barely broader in its attention to
the United States and Europe, while queer narrative theory reveals a disproportionate penchant for British modernists. It's not implausible that the narrow contours of this dominant corpus unwittingly imply an equally narrow
role for narratology itself.

As the work of several contributors to this volume should demonstrate,
feminist and queer narrative theorists might thus find a useful concept in the
intersectional approach now pervasive in feminist scholarship yet still undertapped for the study of narrative.[3] Named by the legal scholar Kimberlé Cren-

---

2. For example, Robyn Warhol's *Gendered Interventions* turned up only under "narrative
discourse" and "sex roles" and my *Fictions of Authority* only under "women writers" and "narrative voice." Susan Friedman's *Mappings* was nowhere in the MLA database at all.

3. The summer 2013 special issue of *Signs* provides some of the most recent thinking—and

shaw, intersectionality argues that multiple aspects of identity—gender, race, ethnicity, class, nationality, global position, age, sexuality, ability, religion, language, historical moment—converge and interact to create actual or perceived social positions, meanings, experiences, and representations in a world patterned by structural inequalities. Identity categories are thus never simply additive; each vector produces and is produced within a set of social locations where "traffic" differentially affects the movements of individuals and groups and indeed where what even counts as traffic and movement is socially contingent. As Chun, Lipsitz, and Shin observe, "no individual lives every aspect of his or her existence within a single identity category. Every person is a crowd, characterized by multiple identities, identifications, and allegiances" (923). Thus, as Cho, Crenshaw, and McCall remind us, intersectionality challenges "single-axis thinking" to examine more complex "dynamics of difference and sameness" across multiple academic and more-than-academic inquiries (787).

While recognizing pervasive inequalities wrought by global structures of power, then, intersectional thinking would question not only gender binaries but all notions of fixed categories read outside their specific configurations in time and space. To take a common example: motherhood can hardly be considered simply a "universal" female experience when, just for starters, we contrast the one-child policy of China to the pronatalism of some cultures in the Middle East or consider the economics of in-vitro fertilization. In the United States, staying home full-time to care for an infant has positive valence for the well-to-do mother but negative valence for the poor one who, it is assumed, should not be having babies in the first place; more provocatively, it has been legally accepted for the state to remove to protective custody the infants of black cocaine addicts but not babies born to white well-to-do alcoholics, even though "the injury to a fetus from excessive alcohol far exceeds the harm from crack exposure" (Roberts 177).[4] In European countries where women rearing infants receive state support, yet another set of values and distinctions applies to the notion of "stay-at-home" parenting, and a different one still in countries like Sweden where a portion of parental leave is allocated exclusively to fathers. Thus even across a specific slice of time, motherhood as "female experience" effectively does not exist; it is always constituted within, and in turn constitutes, multifaceted social locations.

debate—about intersectionality, its meanings, and its value for both scholarship and social action.

4. In one study where "the rate of positive results for [substance abuse by] white [pregnant] women (15.4 percent) was slightly higher than that for Black women (14.1 percent)," black women were nonetheless "ten times more likely than whites to be reported to government authorities" (Roberts 175).

To be sure, given women's lower status in virtually every portion of the globe, particularly in relation to structures of public power, some aspects of maternity, along with other social and cultural phenomena, may well offer gendered patterns that cross time and place. But intersectional thinking demands that feminism no longer assume that such patterns exist or that we can predetermine them.

Whether we are studying historical or fictional narratives, then, intersectional theory calls on us to observe the structural and circumstantial effects of particular convergences of persons in particular locations rather than to presume commonalities that may once have passed as "common sense." Intersectional thinking would reject an approach to narrative that assumes identities to be predictable or predictive, yet would understand that narrative genealogies, along with our ways of thinking about them, are doubtless shaped by intersectional configurations. To take another quick example, the election of a black president in a country riven by race and riddled by racism is reminder enough that intersectional maps do not determine the behaviors of individuals or groups. Yet surely we cannot tell even the shortest story of this presidency without recognizing the implications of Barack Obama's biracial parentage, African paternity, Hawaiian birth, and Arabic middle name, along with his athletic masculinity, his heterosexuality, and his elite education, to name only a few significant vectors.

While intersectionality theory, like any theory, carries its own problems and challenges, it seems to me a particularly fruitful ground for a narratology that is pliable enough to address feminist and queer interests and comprehensive enough to advance historical and cross-cultural inquiry.[5] As an extended metaphor the intersection is strikingly close to Bakhtin's notion of the chronotope, the temporal–spatial nexus that "assimilate[s] real historical time and space" to literary expression in recognition of "the intrinsic connectedness of temporal and spatial relationships that are artistically expressed in literature." Both the intersection and the chronotope assume that certain kinds of social persons converge in ways that enable, complicate, or prevent certain actions. Bakhtin indeed conceives the chronotope as an "intersection of axes" that "defines genre and generic distinctions . . . [and] determines to a significant degree the image of man in literature [which] is always intrinsically chronotopic" (84–85). Hence Bakhtin's primary emphasis on the road, with all its social and temporal capaciousness, in contrast to what he implies to be the static and socially restricted drawing room.

---

5. It is important to acknowledge that the wide application of intersectionality theory has been contested as appropriative and dematerializing of its origins in black feminist thought. See, for example, Nash.

But Bakhtin's is hardly a gender-neutral comparison, and these two locations—road and drawing room—might therefore suggest another example
of a fruitful intersectional project. It has long been said—and has sometimes
been true—that historically men and boys have taken to the road, while
women and girls, to recall Virginia Woolf, sit and feel in a drawing room. It
would be illuminating to map roaming plots on intersectional premises to
see how gender, class, race, and ethnic values have shaped representations
of mobility. In the European novel alone we might compare the sixteenth-
century pícara Justina or the eighteenth-century Moll Flanders to a confined
Princesse de Clèves or Clarissa Harlowe and consider the price for adventure
paid by a Maggie Tulliver. We might interrogate the racial and class contours of the outlaw worlds created by such contemporary novels as Sue Monk
Kidd's *The Secret Life of Bees* (wildly popular and in my view disturbingly
appropriative) or Toni Morrison's grimmer and less popular *Paradise,* both
of which create spaces controlled by poor black women who operate more or
less outside the social order; we might want to ask why the young protagonist of Kidd's novel has to leave her proper white world, in effect, to *have* a
plot, and whether similar outlaw communities could function in realist fiction if the characters were black men. And we might return to Nancy Miller's
provocative claims in "Emphasis Added: Plots and Plausibilities in Women's
Fiction" to ask whether the "poetics of women's fiction" Miller posits through
the resistant alternative verisimilitude of *La Princesse de Clèves* and *The Mill
on the Floss* attaches only to women writers, as Miller surmised and as Miller's moment needed, or is more expansively a function of the dynamics of
power and desire that attach to female characters under certain restrictive
conditions.

In calling for an intersectional practice, I am not proposing to reduce
literary texts to social programs, to impose crude categories onto complex
characters, or to forge simplistic explanations for narrative events. I do think,
however, that we might venture the kind of large-scale inquiry that Franco
Moretti models in *Graphs, Maps, Trees,* bringing an intersectional understanding of time and place to an analysis of how individual narratives and
groups of narratives work out the dynamics of identity (i.e., character) and
movement (i.e., plot), and then map those dynamics across the vast field of
the world's narratives in a new kind of historicist project that would offer a
"distant reading" of narrative form. We might trace a single narrative practice—say, autodiegetic narration (i.e., by a protagonist), charting its rise in
early seventeenth-century Spain and eighteenth-century France and England,
its diminution in the nineteenth-century West and early emergences in nineteenth-century Japan and China, its imbrications with anticolonial struggles

in turn-of-the-century Latin America and postcolonial South Asia, and its massive worldwide popularity today. We might then correlate the identities and strategies of different kinds of narrators with what we know about their time, place, and authorship in order to see how these different patterns of narration map onto literary history. Such projects might help us to test the validity of studying texts according to the social identities of their writers and thus either reinvigorate, reshape, or put to rest the assumptions of authorial difference on which some feminist narratologists, myself included, have staked claims.

Queer narratology demands equally intersectional attention, along with a calibration between queer and feminist approaches that might explore, if not resolve, the thorny tensions between them that several contributors to this volume identify. For example, my own work on narrative voice has argued that the gender of an otherwise unmarked heterodiegetic (i.e., "third person") narrator will derive from the gender of the textually inscribed author. So compelled was I to attribute gender to narrators that in some quarters that linkage came to be dubbed "Lanser's rule." I speculated, however, that the authority conventionally given to male voices might override that link in the case of a woman writer, in effect already queering my own proposition. A still queerer lens might suggest that when a heterodiegetic narrator's gender is unmarked, heterodiegesis becomes the very emblem of gender indeterminacy. We're all doubtless familiar as teachers with the students who say, "in this novel *it* says . . ."; perhaps that is not simply a sign of ignorance, as I certainly have lamented on more than one occasion, but a sign of the queerness, and historical instability, of heterodiegesis itself. What sex do today's readers confer on the narrator of *Adam Bede*: the sex of George Eliot or that of Marian Evans? Might it be more accurate and more useful to say that the narrator of *Adam Bede* is queer? Robyn Warhol implies as much, *avant la lettre,* when she writes in *Gendered Interventions* that "assigning a gender" to this narrator "is no straightforward task" (115). Might heterodiegesis itself be sex-and-gender-queer in essence, enabling an indeterminacy open to the breadth and instability of human voice? And does feminist narratology lose something if, instead of insisting that the narrator of *Mansfield Park* who wants to let others dwell on "odious subjects" is female, we say that "it" is queer?

An intersectional queer narratology might likewise consider mapping free indirect discourse and its etiology. If Frances Ferguson is right that free indirect discourse is the novel's "one and only formal contribution to literature" (159), then it would be all the more illuminating to ask whether novels attempting queer representation might make particular uses of FID as a complex strategy of intimacy, authorization, and distance, or whether the genealogy of FID is dominated by outsiders from Lafayette and Austen to Hurston and Toomer. It might be worth putting to the narratological test D. A. Miller's proposal that formal innovation may be the displaced project of queer fiction. Is it accidental, for example, that Henry James, Virginia Woolf, Dorothy Richardson, Marcel Proust, Colette, Nella Larsen, Djuna Barnes, Katharine Mansfield, and Gertrude Stein—and maybe James Joyce— were queer(ish) folk as well as modernists who pioneered the practice of FID? That is, would an intersectional narratology along either authorial or representational axes—in this case, queer writers or queer texts—help us to understand how and why particular narrative strategies are deployed in particular contexts?

Most importantly, I suggest, for both feminist and queer studies an intersectional narratology will demand much more attention to Asian, African, and Latin American narratives—and much more work in the archives—if it is to achieve a global and historical narrative knowledge. Indeed, the dual tracking of narrative elements with configurations of gender and sexuality over time and place could lay the narrative groundwork for astonishingly new insights into both the history and the possibilities of narrative. This "excavation of forgotten literary forms," extended in space as well as time, might also assist the move from poetics to aesthetics that Margaret Cohen advocates in her "Narratology in the Archive of Literature," which lays out a map for working with narrative historically in ways that could also be extended spatially.

Such projects of narrative mapping would be inductive and thus effectively empirical, working upwards to narratological theory from the careful study of many and diverse textual instances. They implicitly challenge a conviction, or at least a practice, dear not only to classical but to feminist and even queer narratologies: deriving general principles—whether about narrative, about gender, or about sexuality—from a reasoned understanding of social or textual behaviors without an extensive scrutiny of narrative works. Consider D. A. Miller's argument, for example, that gay narrative is simply not feasible. Miller uses for his touchstone Roland Barthes's painful recognition of exclusion when he comes upon a wedding at the church of Saint-Sulpice. Miller is right, of course, that this marrying couple "is in full and open possession of a story, a story, moreover, that one hardly exaggerates in our culture to call *the* story." Miller goes on to opine that "the dismal more recent efforts to 'homosexualize' our culture's omnipresent marriage plot with stories of boy meeting boy, or girl getting girl, suggest that its heterosexist bias is at all corrigible through a policy of equal opportunity. The very notion of a 'gay version' here only tends to analogize gay experience to the structure of its own thereby all the more deeply denied oppression," that "the gay version never ceases to convey its own factitiousness in the comparison, not unlike one of the wedding ceremonies where the couple writes their own service, as though to conceal from themselves the compulsory character of the ritual whose established phrasing—'man and wife!'—peals none the less through their clunking but forgettable modifications" (D. A. Miller 45–46). Miller's judgments may be reasonable enough, and yet they tell us nothing, in the end, about actual "gay" marriage narratives and what they look like: how they are structured, how they resemble or depart from heterosexually hegemonic ones, what effects they might have on readers.[6]

The tension between deductive and inductive methodologies plagues the history of narratology as much as it plagues the history of sexuality and gender. In a provocative essay exposing this methodological faultline between classical and contextual narratologies, Roy Sommer argues that while a top-down imposition of narrative categories of the kind practiced by classical narratologists may be valid for projects attempting to describe all narrative possibilities, this approach falters for fields such as "postcolonial or intercultural narratologies" that are concerned with "specific features of specific texts embedded in specific cultural and historical contexts" (70). These contextual projects, Sommer claims, must therefore build an inclusive but specific corpus of texts from which to theorize.[7] Such a project puts texts and their intellectual frameworks ahead of narratological analysis for its own sake. Thus, even as Gerald Prince seeks a description of narrative that is "systematic and universal," his "On Postcolonial Narratology" also recognizes the particular need for such a narratology to address "matters commonly, if not uncontroversially, associated with the postcolonial" such as "hybridity, migrancy, otherness, fragmentation, diversity, [and] power relations" (373). Rather than starting with categories and rubrics, Prince starts with the needs of a field, confident that a postcolonial narratology will already "likely take into account" many "(well-established) narratological concepts and achievements" (379). Allowing postcolonial topics precedence over standard narratological priorities—priorities often articulated in a daunting terminology—points the way toward a practice of narratology that can make its own case for relevance.

---

6. For one such inquiry, see Julia Wexler's dissertation in progress (Brandeis University), "Queering Happily-Ever-After: The Evolution of Closure in Contemporary Gay & Lesbian Novels." Miller is of course not alone in questioning the possibility of a "queer story"; see as well Judith Roof, *Come As You Are: Sexuality and Narrative* (New York: Columbia UP, 1996) and Lee Edelman, *Homographesis* and *No Future: Queer Theory and the Death Drive* (Durham: Duke UP, 2004).

7. Given the universalizing tendencies of cognitive narratology, Sommer's equation of "postclassical" with "contextual" could now be misleading.

While of course no narrative poetics is either entirely separable from or entirely dependent on individual instances, the more central difference beneath inductive and deductive thinking concerns the extent to which it is desirable, or even possible, to develop a meaningful narrative poetics that can account for all texts. In my view we need both the delineation of general rubrics built on an explicitly diverse textual canon, and an interrogation into specific intersectional formations; Prince too said as much when he agreed with Robyn Warhol in 1995 that expanding his excessive male-heavy canon would benefit narratology in general ("On Narratology" 74). We still don't really know whether particular bodies of texts, whether delimited by authorship, genealogy, or representational emphasis, can be empirically differentiated. Large, digitally enabled studies suggest one path for addressing and perhaps provisionally settling some of the thornier issues, for example, about the relationship between authorial identities or intersectional context and textual properties, and we can surmise that the broader the corpus, the more precise and encompassing the narratological system. It may be useful to consider a provisional halt to deductive methods until our narratological findings are far more inclusive and diverse, and our understanding of them far more intersectional, than any narratologies, feminist and queer narratologies included, can currently boast.

Acknowledging not only that narrative is effectively intersectional but that intersectionality is effectively narrative may increase the value of narratological tools and methods across genres and disciplines by integrating formal patterns with social ones. Certainly we can see the limits of narratology's purview when we venture beyond the disciplinary confines of the *MLA Bibliography*. Sandra Heinen, writing in the volume *Narratology in the Age of Cross-Disciplinary Research*, has already recognized that "the attempts to apply narratological theory to non-literary narratives" are "few and far between" (196). The interdisciplinary database Academic Search Premier confirms with impressive numbers the "narrative turn" in the humanities and social sciences, with over 25,000 subject entries on "narrative," a good proportion of which are drawn from journals outside literary studies. And despite a similarly strong number of subject entries on the aggregate of feminism/gender/women/sexuality/lgbtq, the conjunction of these terms with narrative is but a modest 1,000. Moreover, if Academic Search Premier is a test case, the "narrative turn" in scholarship is not a turn to narrative theory as such; Academic Search Premier does not even recognize "narrative theory" as a rubric. Ironically, though, it does recognize "narratology" and codes as narratological some 300 items, though only 17 of these are subject entries, and the vast majority of the 300 are works by literary scholars about literary texts.

Still, that search does bring up a score of articles conjoining narrative with feminism, gender, or sexuality in journals as diverse as *Affilia: Journal of Women and Social Work, International Feminist Journal of Politics, Journal of the American Academy of Religion, Journal of Sociology and Social Welfare, Qualitative Inquiry, Journal of LGBT Issues in Counseling, Boston College Journal of Law and Social Justice,* and *Nursing Philosophy* that reveal a broad range of narratological influences or use the term "narratology," if in ways that literary narratologists might not recognize.[8] The journal *Nursing Philosophy* alone, for example, offers a good dozen essays that collectively use theoretical works ranging from Paul Ricoeur's *Time and Narrative* to Susan Friedman's *Mappings* in order to explore, for example, how "informed consent" might be understood in narrative terms when working with persons with dementia (McCormick), how dialogues on a hospital floor might reflect the split subjectivity of narrative voices (Cash), how a clinical picture might integrate the possibly fictional narratives through which patients tell their medical stories (Lorem), and how distinctions between narrative and story argue against the romanticization of narratives in health care (Paley and Eva). Indeed, probing below the surface of Academic Search Premier has also suggested that the relationship between narrative theory and the "other" disciplines need not be a one-way street; it seems clear that research projects like those described in *Nursing Philosophy* could help literary scholars to delineate approaches to narrative that might be most useful for studying both "natural" and "unnatural" narratives in ways that have fascinating "real-world" implications.

It might therefore also be useful for literary scholars to try our hand at "non-literary" explorations. In recent presentations, I have suggested that the concept of negative or reverse plotting might be one avenue for exploring the intersectional strategies not only of literary works but also of sociological formations, case histories, and feminist thought. I refer here to narrative situations in which specific event sequences or full stories take their meaning from textually triggered, though not necessarily textually inscribed, antitheses. In effect, one plot shadows the other, and the second plot derives its meaning from its relationship with its antecedent plot. A classic example would be the anti-fairy tale: Anne Hussey's poem "Cinderella Liberated," for instance, presents a speaker who "sleep[s] with / my feet in the fire / destroying the evidence / one glass shoe / melting like butter / both feet black as briquettes / while the prince / in a world of questions / searches for an answer." While literature is rich with negative plotting and women writers may deploy it with particular frequency, I have also characterized the narrative dimensions of

---

8. See, for example, Buser et al. and Zeiner.

feminist theory according to a set of "masterplots" that deploy the dynamics of negative plotting as a way to demonstrate the value of narratological thinking for feminist thought. In a similar vein, Ruth Page's *Literary and Linguistic Approaches to Feminist Narratology* provides a fruitful model for studying the press by exploring "media narratives of success and failure" concerning Hillary Clinton and Cherie Booth in their capacity as 1990s "first ladies" of the United States and the United Kingdom, respectively.

Infusion from the disciplinary "outside" of literary studies constitutes yet another way in which the implications of narratology for literary study—feminist, queer, and otherwise—remain to be mined. But this mining ultimately rests not simply on Morettian mappings or on interdisciplinary sleuthwork; it rests first and foremost on how we read. It is worth noting as well that while such practices would seem to fall within the realm of "distant reading," which Moretti identifies with "an ambition [that] is now directly proportional *to the distance from the text*" ("Conjectures" 57) a narratological version of large-scale study actually entails the *close* reading of specific aspects of narrative form that, I argue, must rightly be understood as textual content. And though what I'm going to suggest is far from novel, it remains undervalued in what are still, in the profession at large, mimeticist hermeneutics. Which brings me back to Henry James and the story that won't literally tell. In her famous essay "Turning the Screw of Interpretation," Shoshana Felman makes the case for narratology when she looks at the dilemma posed by James's novel and indeed by story in general: "Our reading of *The Turn of the Screw* would . . . attempt not so much to *capture* the mystery's solution, but to follow, rather, the significant path of its flight; not so much to solve or *answer* the enigmatic question of the text, but to investigate its structure; . . . The question underlying such a reading is thus not '*what* does the story mean?' but rather '*how* does the story mean?'" (119). Felman's position here is strikingly close to that of Susan Sontag's pathbreaking "Against Interpretation": "Interpretation, based on the highly dubious theory that a work of art is composed of items of content, violates art . . . . What is needed, first, is more attention to form in art. . . . What is needed is a vocabulary—a descriptive, rather than prescriptive, vocabulary—for forms. . . . The function of criticism should be to show how [a text] is what it is, even that it is what it is, rather than to show what it means" (sections 8–9).

Is this not precisely what narratology offers, even in its low-level definition by the OED: "the study of the structure and function of narrative, esp. (in structuralist and post-structuralist theory) as analogous to linguistic structure; the examination and classification of the traditional themes, conventions, and symbols of the narrated story"? And what is perhaps especially memorable about Sontag's understanding of criticism is that her very next sentence, the one that crowns "Against Interpretation," links that *how*—the study of form—with "an erotics of art.": When she connects the pleasure of the text with the function of the form, effectively uniting the narratological and the postmodern Roland Barthes, Sontag also marries poetics and aesthetics.

But whether or not one wishes to eschew interpretation, feminist and queer narrative studies are particularly diminished, I think, when we forget that form functions *as* textual, historical, and social content. The narratological study of narrative offers us the opportunity to learn precisely what the story doesn't tell "in any literal, vulgar way." Literary theorists from Aristotle to Jameson have long acknowledged that form is a kind of content and, as such, socially meaningful. Yet the relationship between narrative theory and novel theory—to take one important example—still remains something of a standoff, and nowhere more vividly than on the turf of history. In 2010, the journal *Eighteenth-Century Fiction* issued a call for papers that reads as follows:

> Is there a place for "formalist" criticism in the study of the eighteenth-century novel? Given the current dominance of historical, thematic, and cultural studies approaches to the eighteenth-century novel, can we usefully speak of novelistic form? Does the novel as a capacious and almost anti-formal "form" leave any space for formalist approaches? Does the sheer variety of narrative types that constitute the novel in the eighteenth century render the notion of "novelistic form" meaningless? Or is there in the period an emerging and dominant formal pattern, a consensus about the properly novelistic form of narrative fiction, that is worth extracting and articulating? (as posted on C18-L)

While narratologists might groan at the possibility that one could study the novel *without* considering its formal qualities, literary historians might equally groan at how "little interest" narratologists have shown, as Monika Fludernik has noted, "in the history of narrative forms and functions" (331). John Brenkman makes a similar claim when, concerning "voice," he speaks of "narrative theory and novel theory as antagonistic genres" (281)—and this almost a half century after Lucien Goldmann argued that "the novel form seems to me, in effect, to be the transposition on the literary plane of everyday life in the individualistic society created by market production. There is a rigorous homology between the literary form of the novel . . . and the everyday relation between man and commodities in general, and by extension between men and other men, in a market society" (7). Of course both novel historians and narrative theorists acknowledge that some of the most important contributions to narrative studies are rich amalgams of theory and history; think for example of Erich Auerbach's *Mimesis,* Ian Watt's *Rise of the Novel,* the work of Bakhtin, Gyorgy Lukács, and Goldmann himself, and we might recall that Fredric Jameson's *Political Unconscious* relies almost as much on Greimas as on Marx. Such examples easily support Ansgar Nünning's conviction that "the more narratological literary and cultural history becomes and the more historically and culturally oriented narratology becomes, the better for both" (345).

An essay I published in Jan Alber and Monika Fludernik's *Postclassical Narratology* offers a modest contribution to that aim by studying narrative form as sexual content in the context of lesbian literary history. In tracing one structure—first-person narration by female narrators to their female narratees—across the long eighteenth century, I hope to have shown that we have something to learn about both the history of sexuality and the history of the novel from studying narrative form. By attending to *narrative relations* rather than to textual events, I can argue that female same-sex desire underwrites the eighteenth-century novel in ways that disrupt the conventional totalizing argument that the "rise" of the novel entailed only the formation of heterosexual subjects under the sign of sexual difference. By looking at the structures of *confidence* in domestic novels, I suggest that erotic intimacy between women is preserved at the level of narrative interaction and that the interaction sometimes also bleeds into the plot. In ways too little noticed, this imbrication characterizes—and queers—the mid-eighteenth-century's two most famous novels, Samuel Richardson's *Clarissa* (1747–48) and Jean-Jacques Rousseau's *Julie, ou la Nouvelle Héloise* (1762), in which movement beyond the plot's ostensible closure turns a death sentence into a fleeting fantasy of same-sex marriage. Here form is effectively the outing of content, which makes the novel's history of gender and sexuality incomplete unless it encompasses a history of formal practices. And this is but one aspect of what I hope could become a history and geography of narrative form *as* narrative content, all the more in arenas such as sexuality where content may have been closeted by circumstance—as is arguably true of *Turn of the Screw*—and where the story thus can't tell in any literal let alone vulgar way.

A rapprochement between novel theory and narrative theory could also help to advance what I believe is still narratology's thinnest arena: the study of character, a particularly challenging topic because it raises so many mimeticist traps. I've been surprised at the rather slim attention by narrative theorists to a book that I consider among the most promising recent contributions to the formal study of character, Alex Woloch's *The One vs. the Many: Minor*

Characters and the Space of the Protagonist in the Novel. Although the book made a splash in Victorian studies and does get mentioned in Robert Scholes's revised *Nature of Narrative,* it remains underknown to narratologists because it falls on the other side of the narrative theory / novel history divide despite Woloch's own characterization of his work as narratological, just as Hilary Dannenberg's award-winning *Coincidence and Counterfactuality* suffers from falling on the other side of this dividing line and thus being understudied by novel theorists despite its historical span and historicist investments. Woloch's project, as he describes it, is "to redefine literary characterization in terms of [a] distributional matrix: how the discrete representation of any specific individual is intertwined with the narrative's continual apportioning of attention to different characters who jostle for limited space within the same fictive universe." Woloch's method rests on the creation of what he calls "two new narratological categories," the temporality of "character-space" and the spatial distribution that he calls "the character-system" (13–14). I would love to see a broader narratological project that takes us beyond "flat" and "round" characters and shows form as the "outing" of character by looking at complex character spaces and systems of the kind Woloch describes—in conjunction with Suzanne Keen's theories of empathy, Jim Phelan's rhetorical rubics (mimetic, synthetic, thematic), and the familiar Greimasian and Proppian notions of actants and functions—to provide a holistic theory of character that also grapples with the intricate relationships between mimesis and semiosis that lie at the heart of fictional representation but that avoids mimeticist traps. And I would argue that nowhere is the narratology of character more sorely needed as an intervention against such entrapment than vis-à-vis the cathexis with characters as if they were "real" people. Notwithstanding the signal importance of "caring about" literary characters as a project of empathy and "poetic justice," to borrow terms from Blakey Vermeule and Martha Nussbaum respectively, it may take a narratological deconstruction of the sign systems that produce character to inhibit the more imitative and uncritical investments in literary character that we see, for example, in the current fandom around Jane Austen's heroines.

Throughout this essay, I have insisted on the word "narratology" despite pressures from within feminist and queer narrative theory to eschew it. Indeed, as my title means to emphasize, I want to argue strongly for the retention of narratology as word, concept, and critical practice for the structural rigor and illuminative capacities of its approach. I have tried to suggest through the examples I've chosen that the most classical narratological inquiry can help us to map not only texts but their social contexts because, as Gerald Prince has persuasively argued, those contexts are already embedded in the formal practices of texts, not least in the construction of narratees that Prince's work has enabled. But in making the case for narratology "proper," I must also confront the problems laid out in Ansgar Nünning's witty insider history of the field:

> Narratologists turned out to be ingenious model-builders, manic systematizers, and unbeatable coiners of fanciful terms. They soon became renowned for their mind-boggling taxonomies . . . and highly scientific language, consisting almost entirely of unintelligible neologisms, which sounded awe-inspiring and arcane to anyone who did not happen to belong to the elect few. Structuralist narratologists developed a special predilection for unusual compounds beginning with prefixes like extra- and intra-, or meta- and hypo-, especially those ending with the word 'diegetic.' To the utter bewilderment and dismay of generations of undergraduates, even narratological terms beginning with the prefixes hetero- and homo- did not have anything to do with sex. (347)

In my view, the worst effect of this terminological mania is not that it turns off would-be practitioners—though that is certainly a large problem—but that it flattens the field, implicitly giving equal importance to every distinction. Surely some distinctions matter more than others, at least in specific contexts and perhaps *tout court*. I worry that narratology is still doing a good deal of business the significance of which is not readily apparent, which is why I have quipped that narratology may be too important to be left to narratologists. Like the spot the size of a shilling at the back of one's head that Virginia Woolf describes in *A Room of One's Own*, narratology's blind spots need to be exposed by theorists and scholars whose primary commitments lie outside narratology.

I would thus call on feminist and queer scholars of narrative to engage in two simultaneous projects: to scrutinize narrative concepts so as to promote those with broad applicability and resonance, and then to scrutinize and re-evaluate the terms we associate with those concepts. Let us use the lens of the outsider—the radical queer theorist or the reader of, say, *Nursing Philosophy*—to learn which concepts they find particular fruitful. Let us interrogate the terms associated with those concepts to ask whether they need to remain literally or figuratively "Greek"—whether Greek in origin, or "greek to me." This may also mean—to evoke yet another coded meaning of Greek—that our terms and concepts might be *queerer*; from my *Narrative Act* onward, I have argued that binaries are less useful than spectra, and in an age of both gender-queer and digital morphing we might also ask where blurring the boundaries is useful, as I've suggested might be the case with heterodiegesis. Certainly the thin line between ghost story and psychodrama continues to haunt James's *Turn of the Screw* and to dupe its readers into seeking an impossible reduction; knowing that the *very same* formal strategies enable this literal duplicity might also encourage us to dislodge narratology from equating precision with exclusion and singularity. As Laura Buchholz's work on free indirect discourse as "morphing" also reminds us, and as digital photography makes even more evident in such images as the series of "George W. Obama / Barack O'Bush" transformations that are ubiquitous on the internet, both/and may be more accurate than either/or, rending word as well as image as queer as *The Turn of the Screw* renders story.

Although I have been emphasizing exhortation over celebration in this essay to emphasize the necessity of forward movement that keeps any field vital and to chart some of the directions in which that forward movement might take us, I want to close by honoring the indisputable: feminist and queer narratologies have changed the literary landscape and, if more modestly, the feminist/queer landscape as well, and in ways unthinkable when Wayne Booth published his *Rhetoric of Fiction* or Genette his *Figures III*. (Indeed, one wonders whether any *double-entendre* was even envisioned when Genette acknowledges that in exploring narrative poetics he "went regularly to the most *deviant* aspects of Proustian narrative" [265; emphasis in original].) David Lodge may have speculated in 1984 that narratology was dying, but in fact the field has continued to grow fruitful and multiply. With so many new directions to follow, and with our own ingenuities female, male, and queer, it's probable that the project of a queer/feminist narratology—indeed the project of *narratology*—has just begun.

Works Cited

Bakhtin, M. M. "Forms of Time and of the Chronotope." *The Dialogic Imagination.* Ed. Michael Holquist. Trans. Caryl Emerson and Michael Holquist. Austin: U of Texas P, 1981. 84–258.

Brenkman, John. "On Voice." *Novel: A Forum on Fiction* 33 (2000): 281–306.

Buchholz, Laura. "The Morphing Metaphor and the Question of Narrative Voice." *Narrative* 17 (2009): 200–219.

Buser, Juleen K., Kristopher M. Goodrich, Melissa Luke, and Trevor J. Buser. "A Narratology of Lesbian, Gay, Bisexual, and Transgender Clients' Experiences Addressing Religious and Spiritual Issues in Counseling." *Journal of LGBT Issues in Counseling* 5 (2011): 282–303.

Cash, Penelope. "'I await your apology': A Polyphonic Narrative Interpretation." *Nursing Philosophy* 8 (2007): 264–77.

Cho, Sumi, Kimberlé Williams Crenshaw, and Leslie McCall. "Toward a Field of Intersectionality Studies: Theory, Applications, and Praxis." *Signs* 38.4 (2013): 785–810.

Chun, Jennifer Jihye, George Lipsitz, and Young Shin. "Intersectionality as a Social Movement Strategy: Asian Immigrant Women Advocates." *Signs* 38.4 (2013): 917–40.

Cohen, Margaret. "Narratology in the Archive of Literature." *Representations* 108 (2009): 51–75.

Crenshaw, Kimberlé. "Mapping the Margins: Intersectionality, Identity Politics, and Violence Against Women of Color." *Stanford Law Review* 43 (1991): 1241–99.

Dannenberg, Hilary P. *Coincidence and Counterfactuality: Plotting Time and Space in Narrative Fiction.* Lincoln: U of Nebraska P, 2008.

Felman, Shoshana. "Turning the Screw of Interpretation." *Yale French Studies* 55–56 (1977): 94–207.

Ferguson, Frances. "Jane Austen, *Emma,* and the Impact of Form." *Modern Language Quarterly* 61.1 (2000): 157–80.

Fludernik, Monika. "The Diachronization of Narratology." *Narrative* 11 (2003): 331–48.

Friedman, Susan. "Lyric Subversion of Narrative in Women's Writing: Virginia Woolf and the Tyranny of Plot." *Reading Narrative: Form, Ethics, Ideology.* Ed. James Phelan. Columbus: The Ohio State UP, 1989, 162–85.

Genette, Gérard. *Narrative Discourse: An Essay in Method (Discours du récit).* Trans. Jane E. Lewin. 1972. Ithaca: Cornell UP, 1980.

Goldmann, Lucien. *Toward a Sociology of the Novel (Pour une sociologie du roman).* 1964. Trans. Alan Sheridan. London: Tavistock, 1975.

Heinen, Sandra. "The Role of Narratology in Narrative Research Across the Disciplines." *Narratology in the Age of Cross-Disciplinary Research.* Ed. Sandra Heinen and Roy Sommer. Berlin: De Gruyter, 2009. 193–211.

Homans, Margaret. "Feminist Fictions and Feminist Theories of Narrative." *Narrative* 2 (1994): 3–16.

Hussey, Anne. "Cinderella Liberated." *The New Yorker.* 19 Aug. 1974. 77.

James, Henry. "The Turn of the Screw." *The Two Magics.* London: Macmillan, 1898.

Lanser, Susan S. *Fictions of Authority: Women Writers and Narrative Voice.* Ithaca: Cornell UP, 1992.

———. "Sapphic Dialogics: Historical Narratology and the Sexuality of Form." *Postclassical Narratology: Approaches and Analyses.* Ed. Jan Alber and Monika Fludernik. Columbus: The Ohio State UP, 2010, pp. 186–205.

———. "Toward a Feminist Narratology." *Style* 20 (1986): 341–63.

Lodge, David. *Small World.* New York: Macmillan, 1984.

Lorem, Geir. "Making Sense of Stories: The Use of Patient Narratives within Mental Health Care Research." *Nursing Philosophy* 9 (2008): 62–71.

McCormick, Brendan. "The Person of the Voice: Narrative Identities in Informed Consent." *Nursing Philosophy* 3 (2002): 114–19.

Mezei, Kathy, ed. *Ambiguous Discourse: Feminist Narratology and British Women Writers.* Chapel Hill: U of North Carolina P, 1996.

Miller, D. A. *Bringing Out Roland Barthes.* Berkeley: U of California P, 1992.

Miller, Nancy. "Emphasis Added: Plots and Plausibilities in Women's Fiction." *PMLA* 96 (1981): 36–48.

Moretti, Franco. "Conjectures on World Literature." *New Left Review* 1 (2000): 54–68.

———. *Graphs, Maps, Trees: Abstract Models for Literary History.* London: Verso, 2005.

Nash, Jennifer C. "'Home Truths' on Intersectionality." *Yale Journal of Law and Feminism* 23 (2011): 445–70.

Nünning, Ansgar. "Towards a Cultural and Historical Narratology. A Survey of Diachronic Approaches, Concepts, and Research Projects." *Anglistentag 1999 Mainz. Proceedings.* Trier, 1999. 345–73.

Nussbaum, Martha. *Poetic Justice: The Literary Imagination and Public Life.* Boston: Beacon, 1997.

Page, Ruth. *Literary and Linguistic Approaches to Feminist Narratology.* New York and Basingstoke: Palgrave Macmillan, 2006.

Paley, John, and Gail Eva. "Narrative Vigilance: The Analysis of Stories in Health Care." *Nursing Philosophy* 6 (2005): 83–97.

Phelan, James. "Character, Progression, and the Mimetic-Didactic Distinction." *Modern Philology* 84 (1987): 282–99.

Prince, Gerald. "On a Postcolonial Narratology." *A Companion to Narrative Theory.* Ed. James Phelan and Peter J. Rabinowitz. Malden, MA, and Oxford: Blackwell, 2005. 372–81.

———. "On Narratology: Criteria, Corpus, Context." *Narrative* 3 (1995): 73–84.

Roberts, Dorothy. *Killing the Black Body: Race, Reproduction, and the Meaning of Liberty.* New York: Random House, 1997.

Sommer, Roy. "Contextualism Revisited." *Journal of Literary Theory* 1 (2007): 61–79.

Sontag, Susan. *Against Interpretation, and Other Essays.* New York: Farrar, Straus and Giroux, 1961.

Vermeule, Blakey. *Why Do We Care About Literary Characters?* Baltimore: Johns Hopkins UP, 2011.

Warhol, Robyn. *Gendered Interventions: Narrative Discourse in the Victorian Novel.* New Brunswick: Rutgers UP, 1989.

Woloch, Alex. *The One vs. the Many: Minor Characters and the Space of the Protagonist in the Novel.* Princeton: Princeton UP, 2003.

Zeiner, Carol L. "Marching Across the Putative Black/White Race Line: A Convergence of Narratology, History, and Theory." *Boston College Journal of Law and Social Justice* 33 (2013). <http://lawdigitalcommons.bc.edu/jlsj/vol33/iss2/2>.

JUDITH ROOF

Out of the Bind

From Structure to System in Popular Narratives[1]

*T*his is about a story of hegemony and resistance, or put another way, a story of narrative and its discontents. Or a story of the ideological state apparatus and the uninterpellated citizen. Or the structuralist/capitalist aegis of modern Western culture and the noncompliant socialist. Or the heteronormative, heteroreproductive, Mosaic, determinist, natural, and pre-ordained order of things and the perverse. Or structure and system. Or interspecies desire. Or how binary notions of complementary gender turn into non-binary multiples. Or *Little Red Riding Hood*.

This story never goes away. A little girl dons her favorite red velvet hood to visit her ailing grandmother who lives in the woods. On the way, the little girl meets a wolf who suggests that she pick some flowers to take to her grandmother. The girl dallies while the wolf rushes to Grandma's house, and finding Grandma in bed, swallows her. Disguising himself as the grandmother, the Wolf takes her place. Little Red Riding Hood finally makes it to Grandma's abode, where the wolf swallows her as well. Sated, the wolf falls asleep and snores loudly, the noise rousing the interest of a passing hunter who investigates, finds the wolf, cuts him open (in the Grimm tale with scissors), and

---

1. With thanks to Hannah Biggs.

releases the two victims who both live happily ever after while the hunter takes the grim remainder—the wolf's skin—home with him.[2]

Like all fairy tales, "Little Red Riding Hood" is a cautionary story. The obvious lesson of the Grimm version is to avoid wandering from the straight-and-narrow, or, in its more modern guise, "don't talk to strangers." In its doublings (two female victims, two male assailants), repetitions (two ingestions), reversals (assailant becomes victim, victims are unswallowed, or perhaps reborn via a crude Caesarean), the tale is easy fodder for Proppian analysis.[3] Critics read the tale as a political allegory, a sex/gender/predation allegory, as fodder for psychoanalytic interpretation, and have interpreted it as an interrogation of the relation between narrative injunction and behavior and as a specimen text illustrating the problem of the construction of the body and the book, "bound and unbound" in texts.[4] The tale could also easily be read in relation to one or several of the following: pedophilia, rape, voyeurism, seduction, exhibitionism, cougar-phobia, oral sex, anal sex, and bestiality, or as a coming-of-age narrative. There have been at least five scholarly books or edited collections on the tale since 1989, and, of course, innumerable popular cultural versions in children's books, puppet shows, children's theatre, and films.[5]

Little Red Riding Hood has also repeatedly been made into animations. Many of the cartoon versions, particularly from the 1930s and 40s, torque the narrative towards the more overtly sexual, bestial, and curiously anal, producing such variations as the married wolf actually going for bigamy with the grandmother in the 1931 Van Beuren Studio's Little Red Riding Hood, with a Riding Hood that looks like Minnie Mouse.[6] In the 1931 Betty Boop Dizzy

---

2. This is a summary of the Grimm Brothers' version of the tale, available at http://www.pitt.edu/~dash/type0333.html#grimm.

3. Vladimir Propp's analyses of folktale elements in Morphology of the Folktale would characterize the various elements of this tale as fitting into functional categories, such as, for example, "The Hero Leaves Home" (Red Riding Hood) or "The Villain Is Defeated" (The Hunter kills the wolf) that recur in many tales as structural elements. These are "structural" not only because they play among series of opposites but also because the practice of breaking story processes down into smaller parts derives from the practices of structural linguistics.

4. As political allegory, see Raufman and Ben-Canaan, "Red Riding Hood"; as sex/gender/predation, see Attwood, "Who's Afraid of Little Red Riding Hood?"; as a psychoanalytical inquiry, see Joosen, "To Be or Not To Be Tamed?"; Dundes, "Interpreting Little Red Riding Hood Psychoanalytically"; Laruccia, "Little Red Riding Hood's Metacommentary"; and Pettit, "Books and Bodies, Bound and Unbound."

5. For example, Sandra Beckett, Recycling Red Riding Hood (2002), and Red Riding Hood for All Ages: A Fairy-Tale Icon in Cross-Cultural Contexts (2008); Alan Dundes, Little Red Riding Hood: A Casebook (1989); Ann Martin, Red Riding Hood and the Wolf in Bed: Modernism's Fairy Tales (2006); Jack Zipes, The Trials and Tribulations of Little Red Riding Hood (1993).

6. Although there are various claims that Disney sued Van Beuren for its characters' similarities to Disney's Mickey and Minnie Mouse, I can find no record of such a suit.

Red Riding Hood, Betty consummates something with her dog, Bimbo, who is dressed in wolf's clothing. Tex Avery resets his 1943 *Red Hot Riding Hood* in Hollywood with a predatory Grandma and a burlesque Riding Hood. In the Bugs Bunny remake, *Little Red Riding Rabbit* (1944), a gawky, unattractive Riding Hood begs for the attentions of a wolf who is far more preoccupied with Bugs. The Bugs Bunny version ends with the hapless wolf, balanced spread-legged over a fire and weighted down with every piece of iron Fritz Freleng's crew can conjure, trading places with the dorky Riding Hood, who is left to grill in the Wolf's weighted and enflamed "split" position. Monty Python's version transforms Red Riding Hood into a John Cleese amazon, Grandma's house into NASA, and the wolf into Buzz Aldrin, while the contemporary "Bedtime Story" version transforms Red Riding Hood into a savvy Y-Gen youth who speaks psycho-babble and has the wolf castrated.[7] And preceding all of these, the medieval Renard the Fox tales feature a trickster—the clever red fox Renard (like a vulpine Riding Hood) and his archenemy, the institutional wolf, Ysengrin.[8] Many of the cartoon versions refigure Red Riding Hood as a trickster, merging these foxy types.

This range of versions is not simply testimony to the tale's longevity or media creativity. Something in the basic terms of this narrative itself produces multiple versions not as merely variations on the same pattern, but also as continually generated from its open set of possibilities. Whether we see these as "variations" (simple substitutions within the same paradigm) or as "versions" (broad recombinations of widely analogized story elements instigated by an openness to multiples and added according to a rule) depends upon how we conceive of narrative itself. If we envision narrative as a structure that proceeds according to a conventional paradigm—journey, danger, disaster, salvation—by which tensions are resolved, then the arrangement of events in relation to one another and to the character types possible offers only a few possibilities for alteration. We can always find the same pattern.

Reading *Little Red Riding Hood* as a paradigm assumes that narrative is a structural pattern defined by binary elements in the tradition of Propp, Lévi-

---

7. There are innumerable animated versions of the tale that also tell the story "straight." The context of these torqued cartoons is that with the exception of the online versions, they were the studio cartoon accompaniments packaged as a part of an evening's film fare and were therefore aimed at adults.

8. *Le Roman de Renart* is a French folklore character whose tales were first written in the twelfth century by Pierre de Saint-Cloud. The satirical fabliaux play on the cleverness of the underdog red fox against the stiff bêtises of the institutional Wolf. Although the Grimm version of "Little Red Riding Hood" is not satirical, many of the animated versions are. See for example, Paulin Paris, *Le Roman de Renart*. Red Riding Hood's trickster qualities, evident in the torqued retellings, suggest some collapse of the *Renart* figure with the Red Riding Hood narrative.

Strauss, Brooks, and Barthes—in fact in the tradition of most theories of narrative.[9] In the long tradition of structuralist analyses of narrative, narrative theorists and narratologists have conceived of narrative in the binary terms that have informed structural linguistics and narratology. We cannot talk about narrative except through narrative, and all of the elements we might identify arrive already as binaries distributed into passive/active, boundary/passage, inside/outside positions in the story. This, for example, is the argument Teresa de Lauretis astutely corrals in her chapter on "Desire in Narrative" in the 1984 *Alice Doesn't*. Showing that concepts of male and female are aligned with active and passive roles in the distribution of positions in plot, de Lauretis demonstrates how structural notions of narrative delimit the female role to "plot-space, a topos, a resistance, matrix and matter," while the male (or masculine—there is some slippage here) hero is an active human subject, "the establisher of distinction, the creator of differences" (119). De Lauretis's argument also demonstrates the self-generating circle between narrative structure and gender as necessarily binary.

The concept of narrative is not only dependent upon the tenets of structuralism, its underlying pattern is the looming and inescapable story of Oedipus, from which there seems to be no alternative or outside insofar as trying be outside of Oedipus might be an Oedipal move. Roland Barthes famously reads this "Oedipal pleasure" as the desire "to denude, to know, to learn the origin and the end" and continues, characterizing narrative pleasure not as suspense, but as "intellectual . . . if it is true that every narrative (every unveiling of the truth) is a staging of the (absent, hidden, or hypostatized) father—which would explain the solidarity of narrative forms, of family structures, and of prohibitions of nudity" (*Pleasure* 10). In his *The Pleasure of the Text* (1975) as well as arguably in his semiotic decoding of Balzac's "Sarrasine" in the earlier *S/Z* (1974), Barthes is already looking for ways around the apparent hegemony of this Oedipal narrative of narrative by focusing on "neither culture nor its destruction"—the apparent joy of oedipal narrative—but instead on the erotics of "the seam between them, the fault, the flaw, which becomes so" (7).

Thinking of narrative as primarily structural in this way envisions structure as defining the possibilities and arrangement of cause–effect relations

---

9. Following the insights of structural linguistic and structural anthropology, both Peter Brooks and Roland Barthes offer accounts of narrative as a structural process. In "Introduction to the Structural Analysis of Narrative," Barthes undertakes an extended analysis of narrative in structural terms. In "Freud's Masterplot" as well as in *Body Work*, Peter Brooks develops an account of narrative in relation to desire, which ultimately reaffirms the curiously binary character of some psychoanalytic accounts of desire (i.e., Freud's *Beyond the Pleasure Principle*) as well as conceptions of the body itself.

within a certain pattern that matches our imaginary of sexuality and capitalism.[10] If we hypothesize that events in a narrative are constrained by their necessary alignment with the conventional taxonomies of story structure and tension, then only certain kinds of variations are possible for any story—and these only appear as *variations* of the same structure—as substitutions slotted in archetypal roles deployed in archetypal patterns.

If we apprehend narrative as a system instead of a repeated paradigmatic activity, we understand narratives as persistently generated by their own systems' rules instead of being the product of a grander paradigmatic substitution. A system is a set of elements that interrelate according to a system "rule" or generating principle. Each version of a story recombines a range of possibilities according to this rule. This "rule" distinguishes the elements of one story system from other story systems as well as from the environment in which these systems function. A systems perspective on *Little Red Riding Hood* would mean that the elements—the characters, relationships, and objects—comprised by the designation "Red Riding" ("Little" and "Hood" being the constantly changing titular terms) can manifest in any permutation and combination conceivable within the rule of the "Red Riding" system. The rule of the "Red Riding" system consists of three elements: (1) Host and guest characters whose relation is interrupted by a third, (2) the serial ingestion of characters, and (3) the transformability of characters. In relation to this system rule, changes in elements, cause–effect relationships, and actors can occur at any point in the process instead of conforming to a paradigmatic exigency that requires oppositions (protagonist/antagonist, good/bad, beginning/end, or even the finer binary distinctions developed by narratologists). Within the system many elements can shift and recombine as long as these processes cohere with the system's rule. Characters' personalities and relative positions of empowerment and roles in the system can change. Actions such as ingestion, which can be imagined as anything within the conceivable range of alternatives, substitutes, analogies, or ironic contradictions (i.e., sexual predation, marriage, victimization), can occur in any of a number of possible settings with characters and character traits that draw from a broad range of permutations.

As a story generated by this "rule" "Red Riding" also has a relation to the larger environment of all narrative. The "Red Riding" system belongs to and is a set of story versions in an environment of narrative practice that consists of multiple contexts, different media, audiences, and literary traditions. The system "Red Riding" incorporates its relation to this larger narrative envi-

---

10. See Robert Scholes, *Fabulation and Metafiction* 26; and Judith Roof, *Come As You Are.*

ronment as an aspect of its system so that the system "Red Riding" not only generates stories according to its own rule, it also manages that operation in its relation to the larger environment of narrative it has included as a part of its own system. This means that understood within a systems logic, "Red Riding" is a system composed of a rule, sets of elements, and the relation between that rule and the environmental conventions of narrative in relation to which its rule might operate. All of this functions within a larger environment of narratives, narrative conventions, media, and contexts. Different narratives may be generated from different systems, but these systems can interact with one another and with the larger environment of narrative convention, media, and context.[11]

The rules of the "Red Riding" system generate points (or nodes) where the operation of the system produces the convergence of elements (character and character, character and setting, character and action, etc.). These points elicit alternatives; like *The Wizard of Oz* scarecrow, these nodes offer multiple directions as long as the choices comply with the systems' rules. Not only can the characters veer at the literal junctures on the path to Grandma's (i.e., end up in Hollywood instead of the woods), the characters themselves may also morph into any number of different versions of a triad of the guest, host, predator, and rescuer, who then triangulate with and morph into one another in a variety of possible ways. Each choice shifts the possibilities for the next in a feedback effect that shapes the version. Choosing Hollywood, for example, as a setting might define the characters as performers and vice versa. As long as the "Red Riding" rule governs the choices, almost any track within the logic of the system might be used to get from beginning to end. The same dynamic may be reconstituted in multiple versions that work that same dynamic in any number of different ways.

A systems perspective, thus, offers a more complex account of narrative as a persistent choosing within a broad range of elements that always coexist as the material of a generating system. Versions of *Little Red Riding Hood* are, thus, not merely variations of the same paradigm, but multiple versions generated from possibilities produced by the "Red Riding" rule itself. This helps account for its perverse shifts in context, in character personality, in what counts as ingestion and its reverse generated by the system's rule. We recog-

---

11. Although systems thinking is a large field, the simplest understanding of system comes from Humberto Maturana and Francisco Varela's *Tree of Knowledge,* Cary Wolfe's *What Is Posthumanism?* and Bruce Clarke's *Posthuman Metamorphosis.* There is a systems version of Little Red Riding Hood in which every element is laid out in relation to its own register and system. See Tomas Nilsson's *Slagsmålsklubben,* <http://www.youtube.com/watch?v=Y54ABqSOScQ>. Accessed 30 Jan. 2012.

nize the tale because we already know what the range of permutations can be, not because the tale is a pattern to be reiterated as variations, but because we know its rule and can imagine the permutations it might generate.

The transformational aspect of "Red Riding"'s rule means that while the system appears to provide definitive agents—Red Riding Hood, Grandma, Wolf, Hunter—the tale forms around characters who openly morph or betray a potential for morphing as an intrinsic part of their definition as character. Characters within the "Red Riding" system contain in themselves potential perversity in the etymological sense of the word as "a turning away from." The possibilities of this transformational capacity are subject only to the rule's other tenets—host/guest/predator, ingestion and its reversal, transformabil-ity—that organize the system. The Wolf turns into Grandma or a playboy or an automobile or sexual prey (and in the past few years has turned into a Were-wolf, a sort of meta-metamorpher), who can fall in love with, eat, pursue, or ogle Red Riding Hood or Grandma or Bugs, who can end up dead, at the altar with Grandma, beside a rabbit, or as Buzz Aldrin. Grandma can become a victim or a rejuvenated cougar who turns into fodder and/or sexual prey and ends up reborn, happy, pricked, or jilted at the altar. Red Riding Hood morphs into fodder/prey/vixen/sadist/enlightened child. The hunter takes off with the skin to do what, we don't know—except that the skin is the thing that emblemizes the trope of metamorphosis itself.

The transformational rule of "Red Riding" not only accounts for the char-acters' ranges of forms, but also shifts the narrative from a moral-producing lesson to a variety of increasingly perverse scenarios (perverse in the Freud-ian sense that the aims and objects do not mesh with any reproductive impe-tus). So, for example, at the point where the Wolf first encounters Little Red Riding Hood played by Boop, her dog Bimbo may already have taken over the Wolf's skin, transforming himself from pet to predator. Or at the point where the Wolf is about to eat Grandma, she transforms into a lascivious vixen (predictably wearing red) and pursues him. Because these possibilities are generated by the operations of the system's "rule" instead of slotting into a pre-existent paradigm, *Little Red Riding Hood*'s versions do not necessarily replay the heteroreproductive, capitalist narrative structure of joinder and completion to which we are accustomed as the premise of narrative satisfac-tion. Using a generating rule, story systems easily produce nonbinary, non-oppositional, nonhierarchical, and even potentially nonideologically driven dynamics of telling, including the possibility that desire might torque away not just from the heteronormative and heteroreproductive, but also from urges towards completion, satisfaction, and quiescence—in other words, from ends themselves as well as from any impetus we might identify as sadistic, masochistic, or even curious. Although the Grimm version of *Little Red Riding Hood* ends with a lesson—knowledge as the gain of conflict—many other renditions simply leave off with perpetuated lust, predation, and/or oscillating morphings.

A good example of all of these alternatives is Tex Avery's 1943 cartoon, *Red Hot Riding Hood*. Beginning with a traditionally prosaic exposition of what appears to be the conventional tale, the characters rebel in a self-reflexive moment, transforming from *Little Red Riding Hood* stereotypes into the jaded personae of typecast Hollywood performers playing parts. The cartoon recommences as *Red Hot Riding Hood* set in Hollywood, and featuring a Wolf who has become a sexual predator, a Riding Hood who has become a nightclub performer who sings like Betty Grable and talks like Katharine Hepburn, and a cougar Granny who pursues the Wolf. The positions of host, guest, and third-party predator are completely interchangeable. As the Wolf goes after Red Hot Riding Hood, she turns him down and escapes to Grandma's penthouse, where the Wolf encounters the energetically horny Grandma. Her pursuit apparently teaches the Wolf the evil of his ways, and although he pricks Granny with a pin, sending her sky high, he swears off his oglings, returns to the nightclub, and, promising himself if he stares he'll kill himself, he stares and kills himself. As a ghostly remainder, he continues his ogling.

This text lends itself to two obvious readings. One, Red Riding Hood and the Wolf, neither of whom is what she or he seems to be (a fact that is revealed in that early meta-cartoon moment), proceed nonetheless to play out their roles as host/victim and guest/predator, although it becomes less clear which is which. In the Grimm version, the grandmother is a host/mediator, a middle figure who, upon having been eaten, becomes a liminal being neither human nor animal, female nor male, alive nor dead, but all and none. There is, however, no end to desire in the Tex Avery version. Grandma, too, is a predator and the chase continues. Even death does not wither the wolf's constant res-erection, and the moral might be that no matter how far and in what guise we wander, the "rule" lives on.

In a second reading, the Avery version's reversal of the traditional tale seems to realign the relative powers of male and female through a Chinese-box series of enframements. The version consists of a self-reflective outer frame, a second frame of the traditional story of the wolf pursuing Red Riding Hood, and a third enframed narrative in which the male/female, guest/host roles appear to be reversed, Grandma chasing the Wolf, where the Wolf, the apparent victim, becomes the victor, though arguably Grandma also gets the pricking she wants. Ingestion has become lust. Red Riding Hood's apparent control over the scenario also reverses the relative empowerment of male/female, but leaves in place the relation between human/tamer and untamed/beast. At the same time, the enframed narrative of younger beast/older woman appears to offer a misogynistic and ageist response to what is presented as the absurdity of the lusty older woman. This enframed Grandma/Wolf narrative is literally surrounded by the male/predator, female/prey narrative of the Wolf and Red Riding Hood in which neither is the victor and nothing is decided. Red Riding Hood continues to perform (which we could argue is a position both of power and of objectification), and the Wolf continues as an enthusiastic yet unsatisfied voyeur without either side having any resolution—that is, getting to stop or getting to "eat." We could read this as a vaguely feminist tale, as Red Riding Hood—the tricky Renard (red is the clue) of Avery's version—always fools the Wolf, even though she ends up in a perpetual burlesque loop on stage. The cartoon's self-referential frame, however, poses the traditional tale as a hovering alternative version and point of perpetual comparison, making *Red Hot Riding Hood* simultaneously a version of a traditional tale and something else, a version born of intrinsic morphing that never ends at all, as Avery produces a sequel, *Little Rural Riding Hood* (1949), in which Red Hot Riding Hood appears again, singing the same song on the same stage, but this time doubled by a truly goofy country cousin.

From its metanarrative frame, Avery's *Red Hot Riding Hood* elicits a comparison to the Grimm version, morphs that tale into two different narratives about what appear to be cautionary tales of sex and power, then offers two endings, both ambivalent. In its multiply enframed versions of predation, *Red Hot Riding Hood* does not offer a definitive cautionary tale about sex, gender, rebellion against the Man, sex with older women, or anything else. We might conclude, in a fairly reductive way, that the text is woman-friendly if ageist, insofar as the male figure is depicted as an animal who never gets the eponymous heroine but is left with Grandma. Or, as a current critical fashion might suggest, *Red Hot Riding Hood* is really the tale of interspecies desire and of how a civilized humanocentric cleverness overcomes the predator/guest/beast, who nonetheless never goes away—who is, like Derrida's cat, always looking.[12]

If the Avery version were simply a variant of a dominant narrative, it might be a cautionary tale based on distinct binaries premised on sex/gender. Its ingestions are sexual; its reversal and remainder are also sexual. But what if the tale consists of the metanarrative of circulating and perpetuated desire

---

12. Jacques Derrida's *The Animal That Therefore I Am* commences with a question raised by the author's experience of being seen naked by a cat.

itself? There would not be two sexes in the tale, but many gender regimes that spread among species, ages, roles, and circumstances.[13] Everyone is predator, prey, seducer, onlooker; everyone is trickster, tricked, unsatisfied, clever, and thwarted. Everyone can transform into something else, as long as the dynamic works via the system's rule. But is concluding this just a matter of thinking differently? Does working in an "other" way change the story and our story of the story, or is that "otherness" already a part of the story to be recontained by the story itself?

Non-Paradigmatic Others; or How Systems Envision Multiples, Delivering Gender from Binary Conceptions

"Red Riding" is also a system that depends on the perpetual interruption of the guest and host figures by a third interloper. This interruptive pattern inaugurates something other than a binary structure, a concept taken up by both Ross Chambers and Michel Serres. Chambers fleshes out the ways narrative may not align with what Barthes defined as narrative's Oedipal impetus. Chambers's 1991 *Room for Maneuver,* for example, specifically addresses the way narrative itself might provide some sort of opposition to structures of dominant power transposed from the narrative to the political. The tome commences with an epigram from Michel Serres's *The Parasite* (2007) that evokes the tale of the fox and the wolf in an uncanny reverberation of Red Riding Hood's incorporation of elements from both classical and the Renard traditions. Serres's book plays with the idea that any relation between two beings defined by a rule of hospitality will always be interrupted by a third party whose advent both repeats the host–guest relation and alters the relative roles of the participants, offering a third function and perspective. All binaries ultimately consist of a series of triadic relationships. This scenario, governed by a rule by which the parasite/guest always turns into a host in an unending process of serial addition, produces the sense of this third party or "tranche" as the element whose advent transforms the roles of the first two, much in the same way as the advent of the wolf transforms both Riding Hood and Grandma from one function to another. At the same time, this interloping third is also the perspective from which the positions of the first two can be perceived. Three is always a necessary appurtenance of binaries

---

13. Deleuze and Guattari's notion of a "regime" in *A Thousand Plateaus* is that it is a "specific formalization of expression" (111). This formalization, they declare, "constitutes a semiotic system" which, as they warn, "is always a form of content that is simultaneously inseparable from and independent of the form of expression, and the two forms pertain to assemblages that are not principally linguistic" (111).

insofar as three is always implied by two (according to Lacan's interpretation of Fregeian numbers).[14]

In evoking Serres's "third tranche," *Room for Maneuver* opens up an entirely different realm of narrative possibility in Serres's systemic rule of a serial opening out into a perpetuated shifting premised on the relations among three functions. As illustration of how this principle of transformed position functions, Chambers cites Serres's passage from *The Parasite* about the fox and the wolf of La Fontaine's fable, which Serres offers as illustration of a narrative machine of undecidability around a desire produced by a third-term illusion—the illusion that something exists—the interloper, the unattainable object—that would satisfy a desire. In La Fontaine's fable, the fox, looking in a well, sees a reflection of the full moon which he mistakes as a wheel of cheese. The hungry fox jumps into the well's pail, which descends into the bottom of the well, where the fox is trapped, his illusion of cheese having disappeared in the waves produced by his own catastrophe. The fox waits until the wolf comes along and invites him to share the cheese/moon which is now no longer a wheel, but a partial crescent. The wolf jumps into the opposing pail and descends, lifting the fox out of the well and trapping himself. Serres's question, cited in part by Chambers, is:

> Of the fox and the wolf, which one is better, the stronger or the smarter? I think by playing the game of competition, playing this game of slyer, stronger, crueler, these species have disappeared, leaving man alone to play this game of destruction. But before there were no more foxes or wolves, a question about intelligence could be asked. In fact, it was this question that killed the foxes and the wolves. Aesop chose the fox and La Fontaine the wolf; teachers like to classify things. I think that they are equivalent, and I think that it all depends. Sometimes it's Achilles, sometimes Ulysses; sometimes the pendulum swings one way, sometimes the other. This game is a machine that comes and goes like the balance beam of an assay scale. Our justice or our scourge? (74)

Serres's reading of the fabulists appears to reconfirm the binary character of the narrative project, especially insofar as the question of intelligence seems to have eliminated a multiplicity of species from the scene in favor of the one and same—in favor of what he deems "equivalent." Competition would seem to consist of opposing parties who embody a binary distinction, except

---

14. Jacques Lacan's use of Frege's numbers suggests that any number is a set that can only be perceived from the position of the next number. For example, 3 is 4, 4 is 5, and so on. See Jacques-Alain Miller's "Suture: On the Logic of the Elements of the Signifier."

as a list of thinkers from Derrida to Irigaray would suggest, these opposites are always versions of the same.[15] And the essential equivalence of binaries may be precisely the point insofar as the assay scale is not a machine of the binary at all, but always turns on a third term. This third term—the balancing point of the assay scale, the interloping third party—enables infinite change-ability that may free narrative from its overdetermined oedipality along with the binaries any structural analysis both produces and requires. The question exemplified by Red Riding Hood's persistent morphings and Serres's assay scale is how systems thinking might assay the assay: how breaking up binaries generates change. An effect of this is the dissolution of all binaries into non-oppositional, interconstitutive multiples. And insofar as binary gender is a product of narrative just as narrative might be a product of binary gender (in a rehearsal of systemic interconstitutionality), the introduction of perpetuat-ing multiples breaks even gender up into genders whose relation is no longer oppositional or complementary, but simply differential, sliding, varietal, much like Deleuze and Guattari's concept of the "assemblage."[16]

A systems concept of narrative, thus, might alter the ways we conceive of the binary sex/gender pretexts such theorists as Barthes, de Lauretis, and others have suggested subtend narrative. Does *Little Red Riding Hood's* trans-formational economy provide an opportunity and even perhaps the assump-tions through which we might envision sex/gender/sexuality as more broadly multiple, changing, unpredictable, and unloosed from the oedipal heterore-productive aegis that narrative reproduces as its own etiology? What, in other words, if Serres is wrong? What if the never-quite-oppositional fox and the wolf both survive, eclipsed perhaps by the anxious human, but never quite the same, and never quite equivalent? What if their transformative capacities continue to play, which, as we have seen, appears to be the case in "Red Rid-ing" versions? Answers to this question may not, as Barthes, Chambers, et al. might wish, escape ideological complicity, but they might make that complic-ity less clear, more chaotic and multiply invested.

---

15. In their differing ways and contexts, both Jacques Derrida and Luce Irigaray under-stand oppositions as versions of a single phenomenon. See, for example, Derrida's "Before the Law" in *Acts of Literature* and Irigaray's "This Sex Which Is Not One" in *This Sex Which Is Not One*.

16. According to Deleuze and Guattari in *A Thousand Plateaus*, an "assemblage" exists on two axes. The "horizontal" axis "comprises two segments, one of content, the other of expres-sion" (88). This axis is both a "machinic assemblage of bodies, or actions and passions, an intermingling of bodies reacting to one another," and "a collective assemblage of enunciation, of acts and statements, of incorporeal transformations attributed to bodies" (88). Deleuze and Guattari's "vertical axis" consists of "*territorial sides,* or reterritorialized sides, which stabilize it, and *cutting edges of deterritorialization,* which carry it away" (88).

If conceptions of gender are loosed from attachment to binary paradigms and if conceiving of stories as systems enables that loosing, then what might define genders? If each "story" is a system generating versions, then narrative as a practice is less a paradigmatic practice than sets of assemblages in Deleuze and Guattari's sense of the term as amalgamations of desires, significations, interactions, and transient meanings and functionings. Given the rules of story systems and the range of material available, stories may well play against paradigmatic and ideological imperatives, ranging into all kinds of possibilities. Narrative is an assemblage of regime/first-order systems whose evocation, marked by morphing nodal points (which are often not quite so self-referentially visible as they are in "Red Riding"), instates multiple possibilities and imports different systemic imperatives without necessary regard to any overriding metanarrative or ideology. Insofar as our making sense of narrative tends to reduce it to sets of binaries organized within a specific hetero-ideological impetus, this unbinding might seem to be unlikely. However, the vagaries of interpretation suggest that metanarratives are themselves up for grabs, often depending on the assumptions that govern the interpretive process itself. Do we seek, for example, closure or infinite play? Singularity or multivalency? The old critical questions.

What we have to account for is how, at any given point in what we regard as a story, every possibility coexists as a knowable set of selections. The intersections of these multiple systems constitute points where choices have and can be made. The nodes appear as morphings that might veer or sidetrack the valences and actions of characters and offer infinite and irreducible variety at points where conventional binaries might have held sway. The characters' morphing does not reliably occur at any traditional narrative plot point associated with transformation, but instead travels with and as an effect of a certain understanding of character as that which turns. The characters of *Little Red Riding Hood* are the equivalent of Barthes's provocative "seams," except they open outwardly instead of providing a peep. The nodes' systemic intersections do not make all of the competing systemic imperatives visible as such, but instead represent a choice already made that turns the logic of the story itself into something else. Whatever impetus seems to have governed the anticipated direction of the story to closure shifts to a different set of operations—from a morality lesson, say, to an exhibition of desire for its own sake. And the character agents of this are no longer bound to oppositional roles, including genders themselves as necessary binary.

At the beginning of *Red Hot Riding Hood*, for example, the Wolf suddenly reveals that he is an actor playing a role with which he is not too happy. This self-conscious shift evokes the discourses of animation, metacinema, self-referentiality, class, the traditional tale, the imperatives of censorship, and Tex Avery as an auteur, at a minimum. The text alters from the anticipated "Grimm" *Little Red Riding Hood* to a dynamic of self-consciousness and rebellion that morphs and restarts the story according to a different set of presumptions about setting and character. Even within this shift the Wolf's morphing from suave man-about-town to rowdy horndog enacts another intersection of systemic logics and imperatives—this time about class, Hollywood cinema, celebrity culture, and slapstick. What these nodal morphings demonstrate is that what we might regard as the story of the story constantly changes in the middle, moving in different directions, not randomly, but in relation to which systems (and their adherent imperatives) might take over at any given point. And that which takes over engages as much perverse variety as the choices already made permit, which means that given a necessarily perverse trajectory, characters display idiosyncratic attributes that remove them from conventional gender taxonomies.

As the versions of Red Riding Hood show, not only are we well aware of the range of possibilities and keep them in mind, but one choice or another can change the story vastly, much as we may try to recuperate it either via comparison to the origin (and hence it becomes a variation) or via interpretation itself—another narrative that reinstalls structure or susses out what structure might be operating to the exclusion of other kinds of dynamics. Red Riding Hood anatomizes the nature of the story itself as never a secure logic, but as always up for grabs. Another way to envision this evisceration of narrative logics is to regard narrative itself as a system that can observe how all of the story systems in its environment work. Narrative hosts the perpetual intersecting of systems that make desire itself visible, not as the necessary engine or effect of narrative nor even as the dominant mode of the story of the story with which we have long been familiar, but as a selective impetus bound to no single dynamic. Narrative is a desire machine that returns to something in the subject, but which is nonetheless detached from it. This machinic Desire operates in a way analogous to Francisco Varela's notion of the "micro-identity": as the "readiness-for-action proper to every . . . situation" (10).

In all of this, the determining attributes of any paradigmatic conception of narrative fade into the environment. To the extent to which narrative is understood as a rehearsal of cultural ideologies that defines the positions proper to agency while reiterating the conventional contexts within which they operate, narrative both produces and reconfirms a very binary notion of gender as complementary and asymmetrical opposites. But to the extent to which narrative might equally be regarded as a system of systems, it may host as well an emancipation from the kind of thinking that assumes structure at the cost of non-oppositional multiplicity, variety, and possibility. When it comes to gender, this shift offers conceptual tools for revising the impasses of gender inequality and the inevitable binaries of "queer" thinking by offering a mechanism for recounting stories, agencies, and genders outside of any paradigmatic necessity.

Works Cited

Attwood, Feona. "Who's Afraid of Little Red Riding Hood? Male Desire, Phantasy and Impersonation in the Telling of a Fairytale." *Thamyris: Mythmaking from Past to Present* 6.1 (1999): 95–105.

Barthes, Roland. "Introduction to the Structural Study of Narratives." *Image, Music, Text.* Trans. Stephen Heath. New York: Hill and Wang, 1977. 79–124.

———. *The Pleasure of the Text.* Trans. Richard Miller. New York: Hill and Wang, 1975.

———. *S/Z: An Essay.* Trans. Richard Miller. New York: Hill and Wang, 1974.

Beckett, Sandra. *Recycling Red Riding Hood.* New York: Routledge, 2002.

———. *Red Riding Hood for All Ages: A Fairy-Tale Icon in Cross-Cultural Contexts.* Detroit: Wayne State UP, 2008.

Brooks, Peter. *Body Work: Objects of Desire in Modern Narrative.* Cambridge: Harvard UP, 1993.

———. "Freud's Masterplot." *Literature and Psychoanalysis: The Question of Reading Otherwise.* Ed. Shoshana Felman. Baltimore: Johns Hopkins UP, 1982. 280–300.

Chambers, Ross. *Room for Maneuver: Reading (the) Oppositional (in) Narrative.* Chicago: U of Chicago P, 1991.

Clarke, Bruce. *Posthuman Metamorphosis: Narrative and Systems.* New York: Fordham UP, 2008.

de Lauretis, Teresa. *Alice Doesn't: Feminism, Semiotics, Cinema.* Bloomington: Indiana UP, 1984.

Deleuze, Gilles, and Félix Guattari. *A Thousand Plateaus: Capitalism and Schizophrenia.* Trans. Brian Massumi. Minneapolis: U of Minnesota P, 1987.

Derrida, Jacques. *The Animal That Therefore I am.* Trans. David Wills. New York: Fordham UP, 2008.

———. "Before the Law." *Acts of Literature.* Trans. Derrick Attridge. New York: Routledge, 1991. 181–220.

Dizzy Red Riding Hood. Dir. Dave Fleischer. Fleischer Studios, 1931.

Dundes, Alan. "Interpreting Little Red Riding Hood Psychoanalytically." *The Brothers Grimm and Folktale.* Ed. James M. McGlathery, with Larry W. Danielson, Ruth E. Lorbe, and Selma K. Richardson. Champaign: U of Illinois P, 1988. 16–51.

———, ed. *Little Red Riding Hood: A Casebook.* Madison: U of Wisconsin P, 1989.

Grimm Brothers. *Little Red Cap.* <http://www.pitt.edu/~dash/type0333.html#grimm>. Accessed 30 Jan. 2012.

Irigaray, Luce. "This Sex Which Is Not One." *This Sex Which Is Not One.* Trans. Catherine Porter. Ithaca: Cornell UP, 1985. 23–33.

Joosen, Vanessa. "To Be or Not To Be Tamed? Bruno Bettelheim, Jacqueline Rose and Gillian

Cross on the Unconscious in 'Little Red Riding Hood.'" *Phrasis: Studies in Language and Literature* 48.1 (2007): 7–27.

Lacan, Jacques. *The Seminar of Jacques Lacan, Book II: The Ego in Freud's Theory and in the Technique of Psychoanalysis, 1954–1955*. Trans. Sylvana Tomaselli. New York: Norton, 1991.

Laruccia, Victor. "Little Red Riding Hood's Metacommentary: Paradoxical Injunction, Semiotics and Behavior." *Modern Language Notes* 90.4 (1975): 517–34.

Little Red Riding Hood. Dir. Harry Bailey, John Foster. Van Beuren Studios, 1931.

"Little Red Riding Hood." Dir. Terry Hughes, Ian McNaughton. *Monty Python Live at the Hollywood Bowl*. Columbia Pictures, 1982.

Little Red Riding Hood. Bedtime Stories, uploaded by MyDamnChannel at <http://www.youtube.com/watch?v=fZVBZTS2ntk>. Accessed 30 Jan. 2012.

Little Red Riding Rabbit. Dir. Fritz Freleng. Warner Brothers, 1944.

Little Rural Riding Hood. Dir. Tex Avery. MGM, 1949.

Martin, Ann. *Red Riding Hood and the Wolf in Bed: Modernism's Fairy Tales*. Toronto: U of Toronto P, 2006.

Maturana, Humberto, and Francisco Varela. *Tree of Knowledge*. Trans. Robert Paolucci. Boston: Shambhala, 1987.

Miller, Jacques-Alain. "Suture: On the Logic of the Elements of the Signifier." *Symptom: Online Journal for Lacan.com*. <http://www.lacan.com/symptom8_articles/miller8.html>. Accessed 30 Jan. 2012.

Nilsson, Tomas. *Slagsmålsklubben* <http://www.youtube.com/watch?v=Y54ABqSOScQ>. Accessed 30 Jan. 2012.

Paris, Paulin. *Le Roman de Renart*. Paris: Editions Pierre Belfond, 1966.

Pettit, Thomas. "Books and Bodies, Bound and Unbound." *Orbis Litterarum* 64.2 (2009): 104–26.

Propp, Vladimir. *Morphology of the Folktale*. Trans. Lawrence Scott. 2nd ed. Austin: U of Texas P, 1968.

Raufman, Ravit, and Rachel Ben-Canaan. "Red Riding Hood: Text, Hypertext, and Context in an Israeli Nationalistic Internet Forum." *Journal of Folklore Research* 46.1 (2009): 43–66.

Red Hot Riding Hood. Dir. Tex Avery. Loew's, MGM, 1943.

Roof, Judith. *Come As You Are: Narrative and Sexuality*. New York: Columbia UP, 1996.

Serres, Michel. *The Parasite*. Trans. Lawrence Schehr. Minneapolis: U of Minnesota P, 2007.

Scholes, Robert. *Fabulation and Metafiction*. Urbana: U of Illinois P, 1979.

Varela, Francisco. *Ethical Know-How: Action, Wisdom, and Cognition*. Palo Alto: Stanford UP, 1999.

Wolfe, Cary. *What Is Posthumanism?* Minneapolis: U of Minnesota P, 2009.

Zipes, Jack. *The Trials and Tribulations of Little Red Riding Hood*. New York: Routledge, 1993.

ROBYN WARHOL

Giving an Account of Themselves

Metanarration and the Structure of Address in
The Office and *The Real Housewives*

*A*mong reality TV shows, the *Real Housewives* franchise is an obvious target for feminist criticism. Focusing on nouveau-riche women attempting to live up to their husbands' incomes in prosperous urban America, *The Real Housewives* is one of the most overtly misogynist U.S. television programs circulating today. If the series' title seemed to promise a glimpse into the actual lives of women in American cities whose work entails raising their children and maintaining their homes, the "reality" is a carefully crafted representation of women who (with a few exceptions) don't need to work either inside or outside the home, because someone else is lavishly supporting them. Evidently the show's project is to represent women who are or have been married to wealthy men as not quite human. Their faces and bodies disfigured by the manifest signs of multiple plastic surgeries, the people identified as "housewives" in these series are monsters, uniformly grasping, rapacious, hostile, volatile, and utterly self-centered. In their two-dimensionality, they do not seem much like real housewives—or like real people of any kind. Indeed they seem to me much less like real people than do characters on many fictitious programs, not just on the long-form serials of "quality TV"[1] but even on some popular network situation comedies. It would be easy

---

1. Jason Mittell prefers to call long-form television serials with high production values "complex TV"; for defenses of the term "quality TV," see the essays in McCabe and Akass.

to attribute this effect to the cartoonish behavior of the women represented on *The Real Housewives* shows, but a feminist-narratological approach to the series' formal structures will show that the dehumanization of the "housewives" occurs at a level deeper than the overt content of the episodes. I will argue here that the televisual narrative conventions of *The Real Housewives* militate against the women's being represented as full-blown subjects. By contrast, I will examine the narrative conventions of *The Office*, a mockumentary TV sitcom whose fictional characters ironically come off more like real people than the women represented on such supposedly reality-based shows as *The Real Housewives.*[2] Contrasting *The Office* with *The Real Housewives* can highlight a difference between the formal conventions of reality TV and the conventions of what I will call "hyper-realism" in mockumentaries like *The Office*, while at the same time revealing one way mainstream media continues working to present women (in this case the so-called real housewives) as not really human.

My assertion about the seeming reality of this particular mockumentary sitcom's characters is corroborated by any of the online fan sites for both the British and American versions of *The Office*, as well as some of the Wikipedia entries for characters on the series. All these sources provide evidence that devotees of *The Office* frequently slip into what Wikipedia's editorial community criticizes as "in-universe" discourse.[3] That is, fans of *The Office* tend to speak of the characters' actions and experiences in the past tense rather than the continuous present, implying that they think of these events as having happened in the extradiegetic world. The ontological status of reality-TV characters, however, presents a problem Wikipedia has not acknowledged in its editorial policies. Contributors are writing from an "in-universe" perspective about figures on *The Real Housewives* in accordance with the shows' claim to be recording the actions of real people; however, as I will explain in more detail below, the staging and editing of reality shows renders the characters'

---

2. I am referring here to the characters on both the British version of *The Office*, starring Ricky Gervais, and the U.S. adaptation of that series, originally starring Steve Carrell, which ran for nine seasons on NBC, but particularly to the male leads in both series: Jim, who is the U.S. version of the British Tim; and Michael and his British original, David.

3. For the Wikipedia Style Manual's description of the problem with in-universe writing, see <http://en.wikipedia.org/wiki/Wikipedia:Manual_of_Style_(writing_about_fiction)>. Evidence of confusion between the ontological status of characters on *The Office* and real people surfaces, for example, under the "Talk" tab on the pages for "Creed Bratton." The *Office* entry on Bratton has been flagged by editors (as of 19 Mar. 2013) as being "in-universe," treating the character as a real person, which no doubt reflects confusion partly because the actor, whose name is also Creed Bratton, has a separate Wikipedia entry full of undocumented biographical information. See <http://en.wikipedia.org/wiki/Creed_Bratton_(character)> and <http://en.wikipedia.org/wiki/Talk:Creed_Bratton>.

represented actions largely fictitious. Stars of reality TV are supposed to be simply themselves, but their actions are directed and edited in such a way as to simplify and distort the characteristics that go into making those "selves." Even what they say to one another—invariably presented as spontaneous natural speech—is laid out on storyboards, filmed in multiple takes, and edited into a final form that presents nothing more than an illusion of conversation.[4] Given that the "real housewives" are supposed to be real and the characters on the mockumentary are not, I ask: What makes it possible for The Office's fictional representations of people to come across on television as more authentic than characters on reality TV who are supposed to be actual people?

To be sure, like the characters on The Office, the stars of reality shows are *not* persons but representations of persons—their presentation in the televisual text is the result of an elaborate production process. Just as in a heavily scripted sitcom like The Office, plots and characterization in reality TV are created through storyboards, producers' decisions, and directors' guidance. Creating "frankenbites" by splicing together pieces of conversations that took place in different contexts or even on different days, the editors of reality TV exert a kind of authorship after-the-fact, shaping characters' speech and behavior to better fit their assigned roles as villains or protagonists. The formal difference, then, between a mockumentary sitcom like The Office and a *real* reality TV show like The Real Housewives does not inhere in the truth-status of the shows' content. I attribute the reality effect achieved by The Office to the contrast between that series' structure of address and the structure of address in reality TV.[5] By "structure of address" I mean the answers to some of the basic questions about voice that narratology asks: Who is speaking? To whom? In what circumstances?[6]

While potential answers to these questions have been very thoroughly theorized for prose fiction, television's narrative structures have only recently come under serious scrutiny by scholars such as Gaby Allrath and Marion Gymnich, Jason Mittell, and Sean O'Sullivan who are sketching out a poetics for TV narrative. Like them, I am interested in identifying the conventions and practices that television shows use for telling stories, and like them, I use the language of narrative theory to account for how those stories achieve

---

4. See TV Tropes on "Manipulative Editing" for a list of ways reality-TV editors remodel characters' utterances into "frankenbites" made up of fragments from different speeches: <http://tvtropes.org/pmwiki/pmwiki.php/Main/ManipulativeEditing>.

5. My use of the term "reality effect" is inspired by, but more literal than, the term Roland Barthes coined in 1968.

6. These are among the motivating questions for the foundational narrative theories of Booth, Genette, and Chatman, to mention foundational examples.

their effects. My project is a little different from theirs, though, in the same way that my approach—feminist narratology—is different from structuralist narratology or from the other postclassical narrative theories that have grown out of it and that are being developed today. Thus, while my questions about the structure of address could be found in a narrative analysis coming from almost any approach, my ways of answering them take into account the texts' staging of gender, sexuality, class, and race in order to tackle the larger question besetting all literary and cultural criticism: What difference does it make?

As I scrutinize the degree to which characters on reality TV and mockumentary come across as "real," I will break down the narrative conventions that go into creating what I will call the reality effect. My purpose is to contrast the mechanics of mockumentary's reality effect with its opposite: an implication that the characters on *The Real Housewives* are somehow other than human. All of the televisual narrative techniques I will be discussing are present across the genre of reality-TV shows that purport to depict people's everyday lives. Different reality shows have varying agendas for setting up dramatic conflict by placing people in close contact with personalities likely to clash with their own, a practice originally developed over the decades-long run of MTV's *The Real World,* the common ancestor of all reality shows that fabricate micro-communities, tape hundreds of hours of fly-on-the-wall footage of people's interactions, and then edit all that material down into episodes. I could make similar arguments about other reality shows, but I am focusing here on *The Real Housewives* franchise because its deep misogyny is as troubling as is its proliferation.[7] Using a feminist narrative approach, I can locate that misogyny not just in the series' content but, more profoundly, in its structure. The "real" in *The Real World* has always carried layers of irony, referring both to the show's young characters' first attempts to live outside their parents' homes and to the show's pretense of depicting people's actual behavior. The "real" in *The Real Housewives* is doing another kind of work: it has to beg the question of the characters' reality, because the show's form does so much to drain the women of any semblance of human subjectivity. The ways that this happens only became visible to me by contrast to the strategies of formal hyper-realism in *The Office.* These strategies include presentation of the characters' individual relationships to the virtual persons holding

---

7. For a detailed analysis of the ways *The Real Housewives* contrives to present each of its characters as the archetypal "rich bitch," see Lee and Moscowitz. They discuss the double-bind of class and gender as it plays out in the New York cast. At the time of this essay's composition there had been seven U.S. "Real Housewives" shows, set in Orange County, New York City, Atlanta, New Jersey, Beverly Hills, Miami, and Washington, D.C., all following the same formal structure. There have also been at least four international versions, in Brazil, Canada, France, and Australia.

the cameras; the degree of the characters' evident awareness of the camera crew on the scene; and the amount of ambivalence evident in each character's delivery of lines. In the next two sections of my essay I will illustrate the contrasting management of the cameras' presence in *The Office* and *The Real Housewives,* and in the final section, I will take some cues from Judith Butler to show how characters in these two series give the impression of having a greater or lesser degree of subjectivity, depending on how much ambivalence the narrative form allows them to express when they are "giving an account of themselves."

Reality Effect 1: Visual Metanarration[8]

In reality TV and mockumentary, as in classic Hollywood film and most fictional television programming, cameras, lights, microphones, and crew are never seen. As in film, this is achieved in reality shows through the use of the single-camera style, where scenes are enacted and shot multiple times from various angles and distances, then edited and spliced together to produce the familiar visual vocabulary of reaction shots, shot-reverse-shots, and point-of-view shots, as well as the conventional movement between long shots, medium shots, and close-ups.[9] Imitating news reporting and other factual TV genres, the camera angle in reality television and mockumentary generally remains at eye level, minimizing manipulations of viewpoint which could remind a viewer that the images presented are being mediated. The premise of reality TV implies that cameras of course have to be present in the diegetic space to be recording the characters' speeches, movements, and reactions, but in reality-TV programs the cameras are, by convention, invisible, their mediation of events occluded. *The Real Housewives* series follow the reality-TV convention not just by keeping the camera operators and their equip-

---

8. I use the term "metanarration" as defined by Neumann and Nünning. The device draws attention to the fact of its own status as narrative, much as "metafiction" draws attention to fictionality. It is more specific than "reflexivity," used by Hight, or "metacinematic," used by Royal, to refer both to metanarration and metafiction in their excellent formal analyses of mockumentaries.

9. "Single-camera" does not necessarily mean there is only one camera on the scene at any given time; it is used in opposition to "multi-camera," the style where four cameras are fixed in place around a set or stage. Jeremy Butler points out that *The Office* was one of four single-camera sitcoms in NBC's Thursday-night lineup for the 2006–7 season. The adoption of single-camera style (which was not new, but had been common on the sitcoms of TV's golden age) contrasted with the fixed multi-camera style that had dominated the popular sitcoms of the previous two decades, signifying NBC's attempt to recapture the prestige of what used to be its "must-see TV" Thursdays (174).

ment off-camera, but also by consistently ensuring that if the characters in the process of filming ever glanced at or commented about the cameras, those glances and comments get edited out. As in classic Hollywood cinema, the unacknowledged and undetectable cameras are part of the machinery of formal realism, treating the screen as if it were a window on a reality unshaped by art or craft. Until its eighth and final season, *The Office* also followed this reality-TV convention to the extent of keeping the cameras and their operators outside the visual frame, but, like other mockumentaries, *The Office* has, throughout its run, acknowledged the presence of invisible camera operators and cameras frequently. If the fiction that there are no cameras is part of classic cinematic and televisual realism, I am claiming that these direct and indirect allusions to the presence of cameras is one of mockumentary's hyperrealist gestures.

The Office is full of the kind of metanarratorial references to its own status as TV show that reality series like *The Real Housewives* are consistently careful to avoid. While we are accustomed to thinking of metanarration (or the self-reflexive activity of narrators who draw attention to the text's status as an act of narration) as a convention for interrupting the reality effect of narrative, or for disrupting mimesis with reminders of the diegesis that makes it possible, I am arguing that metanarration in mockumentary has the opposite effect.[10] I propose to show in this section of my essay that the more the mockumentary text manipulates structures of address to heighten the audience's experience of metanarration's effects, the more real its constructed people can appear to be.

Paradoxically enough, one of the trademarks of hyperrealist style in both the British and American versions of *The Office* is also one of its biggest differences from "real" reality-TV shows, that is, the way each of the characters acknowledges the cameras' presence in the storyworld. Until the very end of the series, no one ever explains why this documentary about office life is being made, where the financing for it might be coming from, or who the intended audience is to be. The cameras are just *there,* and the characters are individually more or less reconciled to this intrusion on their daily lives. Unlike characters on reality-TV shows, these mockumentary characters did not sign up to be the subject of a camera's constant surveillance, and each of them repeatedly registers awareness of the fact that they are being filmed. A wonderful remix from an *Office* fan site collects representative moments

---

10. For exemplary criticism assuming metanarration and metafiction necessarily have this disruptive effect, see Malina as well as recent work on impossible narrative situations and "unnatural narrative" by Brian Richardson (in Herman et al.), Jan Alber and Rüdiger Heinze, and others.

of characters' acknowledging the camera by glancing at it and registering in their facial expressions their attitudes about having the cameras in their space.[11] These attitudes are nearly always unspoken, registered in the characters' look back at the camera that is perpetually looking at them. Series protagonists Jim and Pam appear to become friends with the camera operators (a development that is confirmed by the final season's storyline), directing their gazes outside the visual frame and straight into the camera when they ask the camera people to share information about other characters' secret activities or include the unseen operators in their private jokes. Though their side of the conversation is silent and invisible for seven seasons of the show, the camera operators sometimes even initiate conversations with Jim and Pam, as in the scene where the couple is confronted with video footage of their sneaking away from the office on a secret date. Angela, the accountant who hates everybody, shoots hateful glances at the camera operators, too; Jan the boss, who turns out to be clinically insane, demonstrates her paranoia in her evident uneasiness about and hostility towards the cameras' following her. Dwight, who wants so much to be Assistant Manager and not Assistant to the Manager, as Michael repeatedly reminds Dwight that he is, bosses the camera operators around as much as he does his co-workers, beckoning them to follow him or waving them away from a closed door. Although they do not until the very end reach the embodied and visualized status of cameramen in that ultimate filmic genre of metanarration, *cinéma vérité*, the unseen people holding the cameras emerge in these interactions as the equivalent of minimally realized characters, a palpable presence on the scene. The unseen camera people inhabit a double status, simultaneously acting the part of a fictitious and invisible documentary camera crew and serving as the actual camera crew for the TV series itself. Of course, the cameras' functions in these two roles are markedly different, in that the fictional operators never ask their subjects to reenact a scene to enable the cameras to shoot reactions and alternating points of view, whereas the frequent cuts among viewpoints are evidence that the actual film crew has recorded numerous takes of every scene.[12]

---

11. See YouTube, "The Office: The Cameras See Everything": <http://www.youtube.com/watch?v=ZTmE7zaAJ_M>.

12. Jeremy Butler has identified a TV instance of mock *cinema vérité* in "Ambush," the one live-broadcast episode of the single-camera hospital drama *ER*. An actor playing a production assistant peers into the camera lens in a fish-eye extreme close-up, wipes something off the surface of the lens, and moves out of the camera's line of sight. Butler says this move connotes "a particular sense of realism" in the way that handheld cameras do, but his identifying the "production assistant" as an actor nicely illustrates the distinction I am making between the fictitious camera crew and the actual one (145–46).

The character Jim has a special relationship with the cameras during action scenes (as opposed to the interpolated "interviews" with selected characters in each episode, about which I will say more below), indicated by his frequent looks at the camera. This repeated action has the dual effect of emphasizing the character's self-conscious discomfort with finding himself in this degrading work situation while at the same time constructing the character as a subject who can connect intellectually and emotionally with the actual viewer. His glances at the camera usually imply that no matter how absurd the people around him may be, he wants to make sure that the camera operators (and the implied audience for whom the camera operators stand in as observers) know that *he* knows better.[13] There are at least three YouTube videos on fan sites collecting Jim Halpert's "camera faces," which eventually became so predictable a part of the show's substance as no longer to have the surprise they had in the earlier seasons.[14] Sharing a joke, squirming in embarrassment, flinching at the unavoidable revelation of his own hurt feelings, Jim consistently returns the camera's gaze, much more often in the earlier seasons than the other characters do. If, as the receiver of Jim's glances, the camera operators are the visual equivalent of the TV text's narratee, representing the implied fictional audience who will eventually see the documentary, they are also standing in for the actual viewers, engaging them structurally in the intersubjective experience of Jim's emotions.

In *The Office* the implied presence of the camera people in the storyworld is a constant reminder to the actual audience of what it might be like to have a real documentary crew following your every move. They move through televisual space without ever visibly inhabiting it, constructing a liminal place in the storyworld that is unseen and yet diegetic.[15] The action often marks the camera operators' presence as when, for instance, the camera's gaze aggressively chases Michael under his desk where he is trying to hide in order to make a private phone call, or when Karen spots an embarrassed Jim sitting in a parked car wearing a disguise. In this latter scene, Karen is not expecting to see Jim, and so might have walked past without noticing him, but her attention is drawn to the parked car by the presence of the camera crew filming Jim through the passenger window, obvious to her but invisible to the

---

13. This pattern is hilariously satirized on another office-based single-camera sitcom where characters glance at the camera, *Parks and Recreation,* in which the foolish but well-meaning Andy frequently directs knowing looks at the camera as if seeking the viewer's reassurance when he has said something silly that he hopes isn't wrong.

14. See, for example, YouTube, "70 Jim Halpert Camera Faces in 70 Seconds": <https://www.youtube.com/watch?v=nuCgiIs4VAs> and "The Office—The Faces of Jim": <https://www.youtube.com/watch?v=YMNvzQQMe_E>.

15. Hight has usefully outlined the deployment of televisual space in mockumentary.

TV audience. Jim frantically gestures to the cameras to move away from the car, but they persist, so Karen spots them and, following their gaze, sees Jim in his preposterous fake mustache. Part of the humor in this scene rests on the implication that the cameras are so obtrusive, so obviously *there* in that parking lot, that Karen can't help but notice them. Karen's look at and Jim's gestures toward the cameras are examples of how metanarration serves the hyperrealist effect with continual reminders that the equipment and operators are always there. Phyllis sparks a similarly metanarrational moment when she says privately to Dwight on having discovered his renewed affair with Angela (who is now engaged to Andy), "You know I know. You know *they* know," with a glance toward the camera.[16] Phyllis knows that the evidence of infidelity visible to her has also been visible to "them." "They" are the camera crew present during this otherwise confidential conversation, but by extension of the narrative address, "they" are also *us*, the actual audience interpellated by Phyllis's glance at the camera. "*We*" know what Dwight and Angela have been up to, because faithful viewers of the series get the benefit of the camera operators' ever-watchful presence.[17]

Reality Effect 2: Addressing the Camera

Metanarrational moments in *The Office* are funny, the way they are in Laurence Sterne's eighteenth-century spoof of protorealist narration, *Tristram*

---

16. Season 5, episode 4, "Crime Aid." Phyllis and Dwight are seated near each other in a confidential pose. Dwight is whittling.

> PHYLLIS: [sigh] What are you making?
> DWIGHT: A knife.
> PHYLLIS: You're making a knife with a knife?
> DWIGHT: You got a better way?
> PHYLLIS: You want to talk about it?
> DWIGHT: About what?
> PHYLLIS: You know I know. [Glances towards the cameras.] You know they know.
> DWIGHT: I know none of that. If I did, you'd be the last to know.

17. The series' eighth-season denouement establishes the characters' previous unawareness that the crew has been surreptitiously filming them when they thought their microphones were turned off and their actions were invisible. The series finale answers the implicit question "What would happen if your most secret activities were all recorded on videotape?" by assigning consequences that are generically comedic. For instance, Stanley's wife learns of his infidelities, but he turns out to be much happier after she has divorced him; Angela is appalled to learn that Oscar has been sleeping with her gay husband, but the Senator's blithe exploitation of Angela and Oscar during his re-election campaign ends up strengthening the co-workers' friendship despite the betrayal, and so on.

Shandy, or in postmodernist fiction from Nabokov's *Pale Fire* to Rushdie's *Midnight's Children,* and—as I have mentioned above—according to received narrative theory, they ought to disrupt the formal realism of the show as they interrupt the mimesis for reference to the diegesis. Indeed, this is what happens in single-camera sitcoms that satirize the mockumentary genre— including *Arrested Development, Parks and Recreation,* and *Modern Family*— examples of "instances which seem to suggest that the narratee can be some kind of inanimate object, for example a recording device (as when the interviewees in *Sex and the City* speak directly to the camera)" (Allrath, Gymnich, and Surkamp 19).[18] But in mockumentary, as I have been arguing, addresses to the camera can have a hyperrealist effect that is missing in reality-TV shows like *The Real Housewives.* During action sequences, the "housewives" do not acknowledge the presence of the cameras; during interview segments, too, they continue to behave as if the cameras were not there. Following reality-TV conventions, the interviews consist of autobiographical speech, in which the speaking subject uses narrative as a means of creating and sustaining a self he or she can call "I." I believe that the relative degree of the reality effects in these shows depends not just on whether the characters acknowledge the presence of the virtual persons holding the cameras, but also on the formal representation of the characters' acts of autobiography. Closely related to metanarration is direct address to the camera and, by extension, to the viewing audience.

The trope of the individual speaking privately to a camera or an interviewer is common to most reality-TV shows. The "confessional" is integral to the structure of *The Real World,* where the show's subjects have always been required each week to spend time in an isolated space, speaking directly to a video camera as though they were confiding in the actual viewer. Televisual convention usually reserves speaking directly into the camera for persons in positions of authority, such as news reporters and anchors, or game-show

---

18. Mills and Thompson have separately proposed the term "comedy *vérité*" for sitcoms that use mockumentary styles without pretending to be documentaries. I want to emphasize that sitcoms in this category such as *Modern Family, Parks and Recreation,* and *Arrested Development* do not pretend to be documentaries, but regularly use the actor's direct gaze at the camera; interview sequences where the actor speaks to an invisible person next to the camera; and subjective shots through bushes, shuttered windows, or partially closed doorways. (The pilot of *Parks and Recreation* used mockumentary techniques such as actors' directing comments and questions to the camera crew, but after the first episode that pattern disappeared.) These sitcoms, unlike *The Office,* make such heavy use of shot / reverse shot and shifts between long, medium, and close-up shots, that the illusion of documentary is dissipated. The characters in these shows do not so much address the camera crew as they do the audience, in what has become a familiar subjective treatment for the purpose of drawing the viewer into the tight communities of family or co-workers being represented.

hosts. Subjects on *The Real World* are thus implicitly granted authority to speak about their own impressions and feelings, and therefore to hail the viewer. In reality-TV shows like *The Real Housewives,* however, the characters do not directly address the camera when they are speaking about themselves. Here as in many other reality shows, the characters speak to a virtual interviewer implicitly seated just next to the person holding the camera, and if they ever actually happen to glance at the camera, those glances get edited out. In this way the interview sequences on *The Real Housewives* imitate the visual structure of interviews on news and information programs, where the subject speaks to an interviewer who is offscreen but not holding the camera. The actual viewer is not directly addressed and therefore, I am arguing, not interpellated, but excluded from the interaction; the so-called housewife is always looking away from the actual viewer.

By contrast, *The Office* repeatedly departs from this pattern. Characters being privately interviewed can speak directly to the camera, flicking their eyes between the space where the implied interviewer would be sitting and the place where the camera operator sits.[19] Because the camera operators and interviewers are always silent and invisible both in fly-on-the-wall reality TV and in mockumentary, and because this convention of direct address gives the characters of *The Office* a systematic opportunity to return the camera's gaze, these mock-interview moments transform the mockumentary's audience into interlocutors, not just viewers. The characters seem to reach through the fourth wall to address the actual viewers, as if the characters were participating in a genuine exchange with the individual members of their viewing audience. In a character-establishing scene from the pilot of the U.S. version, for example, Steve Carrell's Michael appears unable to resist including the camera in his gaze while he brags about the reasons he considers himself to be the best boss his employees have ever had because he is "so hilarious." In the final ten seconds of a twenty-five-second speech directed to the invisible interviewer, Michael glances at the camera three times while he displays a "World's Best Boss" mug he says he found at Spencer Gifts. This shifting glance might have appeared just to be a tic in Steve Carrell's acting style, but we can see how calculated the effect is if we look at the original British version of the same speech. In this version, only twelve seconds long, Ricky Gervais's David waits until he finishes speaking about being the best boss, but likewise includes the camera—and the viewing audience—in a final glance into the lens. Clearly Gervais—who directed the U.S. pilot—instructed Carrell to demonstrate the character's self-serving compulsion to engage the camera people

19. See TV Tropes: <http://tvtropes.org/pmwiki/pmwiki.php/Main/ConfessionCam>.

in his self-congratulatory act, as they are stand-ins for the addressee who is supposed to be impressed. In reality TV, these glances would be edited out, severing the effect of direct address from character to actual audience.

Reality Effect 3: Constructing the Incoherent Subject

In all the iterations of *The Real Housewives* these interview moments are heavily edited not just to promote a narrative line but also to establish the subjects as excessively coherent individuals clearly distinguishable from one another. The TV Tropes website suggests that this is how characterization always works on reality-TV shows, but I think the misogyny of *The Real Housewives* requires a heavier-than-usual hand in what TV Tropes calls "manipulative editing." Because these Botoxed and lip-enhanced women all are similarly coiffed and made-up in keeping with the programs' presentation of them as excessively wealthy, interchangeable females, their personalities need to be more distinct than their appearances are. This is true even when the "real housewives" are marked by racial difference, as they are in the Atlanta series. In the original cast of *The Real Housewives of Atlanta,* only one of the main characters is white while the others are all African American (NeNe, Sherée, and DeShawn) or mixed-race (Lisa, whose maiden name is Wu and whose features combine Asian and African American looks). Kim claims in early episodes that she is "a black woman trapped in a white woman's body," although the others do not hesitate to invoke racial difference when they get into fights with Kim.[20] Beyond the fact that Kim wears big blonde wigs and the others have dark hair and complexions, the characters are mainly defined by their various delusions: Kim is the one who believes she can sing (she sets out to become a country singing star even though she is unable to carry a tune), Sherée is the one who believes she is a clothing designer (she holds an elaborate fashion show where there are no clothes, only life-size sketches of clothes), DeShawn is the one who believes she is a philanthropist and social reformer (she hosts a disastrous benefit gala for young African American women who need to learn to use makeup in order to raise their self-esteem), and so forth. Each of the women's statements in interview sequences clearly and unambiguously reinforces this sense of herself, while scenes of gossip among the other women serve to point up the absurdity of the delusion, as

---

20. In a particularly rancorous fight on Kim's tour bus, NeNe tells her, "You better watch your tone and how you speak to people, specially when you're talking to a sister." She goes on to accuse Kim of treating her African American assistant as a "slave." See <http://www.bravotv.com/the-real-housewives-of-atlanta/season-3/videos/the-full-bus-fight>.

when everyone else says that DeShawn has no idea how to set up a benefit gala, or when NeNe says she has never in her life known Kim to sing or even so much as to hum, or when the fashion show with no clothes gets thoroughly trashed in a funny but nasty postmortem exchange in a beauty salon between NeNe and her sassy gay male friend Dwight, who is one of the very few male characters featured in interview sequences.[21]

To tune in to any episode of *The Real Housewives* and watch any of the interview sequences is to see the unambivalent, unambiguous, absolutely righteous certainty with which "real housewives" on these shows are always portrayed as speaking to the interviewer about themselves, their feelings, and their experiences. Eyes dramatically widened, hands gesturing emphatically, voice slightly raised, they are always portrayed as positively sure about what they are saying. In a fan's remix of sequences from *Atlanta* where characters discuss NeNe's supposed attempt to choke Kim, both players speak to the interviewer without ambivalence about the righteousness of their own actions.[22] Similarly, in the scenes from *The Real Housewives of New York* revolving around the feud between Bethenny and Kelly, the two women have entirely different recollections of a fight Kelly picked with Bethenny in a bar, and each is equally emphatic in telling the offscreen interviewer that the other's account of the incident is false.

Usually the so-called housewives are speaking from the first moment of the interview sequence to the last, but sometimes for a brief instant they will be quiet. On *The Office,* as in the "best boss" sequences featuring David and Michael, the moment after a character stops speaking to the invisible interviewer can present an opportunity for the character to glance self-consciously into the cameras. By contrast, when a "real housewife" stops talking she continues looking pointedly away from the camera. One interview with NeNe in *The Real Housewives of Atlanta* shows a gesture toward the character's interiority that is rare on these programs, and telling in its conversational dynamics. At the end of a monologue where NeNe reflects on her certainty that she never could go back to her hometown of Athens, Georgia, and that she never *should* go back to Athens, Georgia, she briefly looks away from her invisible interlocutor and down as she says "Lord, have mercy!," turning her head as if to refuse for a moment the interchange with the interviewer and to

---

21. Surely it is no coincidence that Dwight's gender performance is effeminate (he wears elaborate eye makeup, for instance). In early seasons of *The Real Housewives of New York,* the male character who is most often featured in the interviews is Alexis's husband, Simon, whom many of the other characters say they suspect is "gay." The subject position inscribed in *The Real Housewives* series is consistently inscribed as not-masculine.

22. See <http://www.youtube.com/watch?v=ZFPAsUcR-Vk>.

be alone with her thoughts. Significantly this fleeting visual assignment of an interiority does not bring NeNe into virtual contact with the actual viewer. She could look at the camera, at us, and become a self in relation to ours the way the characters in *The Office* seem to do with their self-conscious glances in our direction, but she does not. Her momentary "self" does not take shape intersubjectively, but as a turning inward and away, not just from the unseen interviewer but from the actual audience. Like all the other "real housewives," she evidently believes she is absolutely certain who she is, in and of herself. By showing what a misfit small-town girl NeNe actually is in the wealthy urban society she now inhabits, the show repeatedly implies that her certainty is another delusion, indeed that her volatile temper, her shouting and name-calling and hair-pulling, might really belong not in the haute bourgeois regions of Atlanta but in that too-small town from which she came.

If you begin noticing how consistently the so-called housewives avoid glancing at the camera, these repeated scenes of indirect address to the interviewer can come off as uncanny, not just because the women's comments about themselves have been edited to give the impression that they are thoroughly convinced by their self-representations despite the show's elaborate presentation of evidence of their falseness, but also because that editing always produces narratives of the self that are simply too coherent to be really real. Judith Butler's study of the ethics of intersubjectivity, *Giving an Account of Oneself*, sheds some light on the situation of enunciation that I claim can produce this uncanny effect in reality TV. Butler likens "the demand for self-identity or, more particularly, for complete coherence" in one's interlocutor to "a certain ethical violence," because inevitably, "when we claim to know and to present ourselves, we will fail in some ways that are nevertheless essential to who we are" (42). I don't think "violence" is too strong a word for *The Real Housewives'* insistence on demanding complete coherence in the so-called housewives' self-presentation. For Butler the inevitable "failure" inheres in the gap between the temporality of discourse about one's own self and the present constitution of the speaking "I." Thus, counterintuitively enough, "If the identity we say we are cannot possibly capture us . . . then *any effort 'to give an account of oneself' will have to fail in order to approach being true*" (42; emphasis mine). Here, then, lies the heart of reality TV's failure to seem really real. Whether or not the individual women ever actually experience the obvious disjuncture between their life experiences and their accounts of themselves, the program's structure ensures that no glimmer of that awareness makes its way into the final edited version of the interview sequences.

Butler's analysis can also help illuminate the way reality TV's rendition of its subjects reflects the brand of vulgar psychoanalysis that animates so much of post-Freudian popular culture. As Butler observes,

> Some have argued that the normative goal of psychoanalysis is to permit
> the client to tell a single and coherent story about herself that will satisfy the
> wish to know herself, moreover, to know herself in part through a narrative
> reconstruction in which the interventions by the analyst or therapist contrib-
> ute in many ways to the remaking and reweaving of the story. (51)

The structure of indirect address in reality TV's off-kilter interview sequences
places the viewer in the position of the psychiatrist to whom the patient—
lying on the couch and looking away from the doctor's face—is always speaking. The viewer, therefore, is virtually placed in the position to diagnose and
evaluate the speaker's self, although the viewer, unlike the analyst, plays no
active part in the remaking and reweaving of the subject's story about herself.
In reality TV, the editing does that for us. The exchange of glances that could
seem to put the actual viewer and the so-called housewife on the same ontological plane, if only momentarily, is prohibited by the show's structure.

By contrast, in both its British and American versions, *The Office* stages
its characters' awareness of the gaps between their accounts of themselves
and those parts of the self that resist or evade narration, that is to say, the
unconscious.[23] Tim and Jim, in two versions of the same scene from the
British and American pilot episodes, make similar though not identical
responses to the interviewer's implicit question about their work. Neither
Tim nor Jim glances at the camera, but their lines contrast with their body
language to suggest the gap between the story they are telling about their
professional lives—almost preposterously straightforward—and their own
conflicted sense of who they are. Out of their mouths come details about
selling copier paper, while their faces suggest the desire to please the interviewer, the embarrassment of finding themselves in this dead-end job, the
hope that they are too good for what they are doing, the fear that they might
not be, and the desperate courage with which they both conclude by admitting "I'm boring myself, just talking about this." The reality effect inheres in
the actors' imitation of the incoherent subjectivity every actual viewer inhabits. This makes the characters, as undergraduates like to say, "relatable" in a
way that the so-called housewives cannot be.

Not all the characters in *The Office* evince the self-consciousness that Tim
and Jim's addresses to the camera signify—which is one important reason
why the Tim/Jim figure takes shape as the protagonist in the serialized storyline of both the British and American versions. Indeed, the other characters' lack of self-awareness is the source of most of the comedy and all of

---

23. See Royal's application of a similar argument to Woody Allen's mockumentary films.
Royal argues that Allen uses voice-over and other "metacinematic" effects to comment on the
constructedness of all narrative as well as to attempt to make a self out of fragments of story.

the discomfort of watching *The Office,* which resembles the uneasiness of watching real reality TV, but actually deconstructs the narrative source of that uneasiness. Every time he speaks to the camera, the character of the boss—portrayed virtually identically in the pilot episodes by Ricky Gervais in the British version and Steve Carrell in the American version—embodies the discomfiture of the autobiographical "I" that Butler has outlined. Around the edges of both bosses' verbal response you can see the ambivalence, the contrast between self-image and self-awareness, and all the many contradictions endemic to autobiographical speech, played out in their facial expressions and body language. To watch Carrell's Michael respond to the silent interviewers' questions is to see Butler's model of ambivalent subjectivity acted out. Butler again:

> Indeed, if we require that someone be able to tell in story form the reasons why his or her life has taken the path it has, that is, to be a coherent auto-biographer, *we may be preferring the seamlessness of the story to something we might tentatively call the truth of the person,* a truth that . . . might well become more clear in moments of interruption, stoppage, open-ended-ness—in enigmatic articulations that cannot easily be translated into narrative form. (64)

To be sure, there is no "truth of a person" that we could attribute to a purely fictional TV character. And yet it's *The Office*'s mimetic representation of speakers' moments "of interruption, stoppage, open-endedness" that makes this fiction feel so much more "true" than the reality shows do.

In another set of parallel scenes from both pilots, for example, the boss of each office talks about not being afraid of the woman from "corporate" who supervises him. Gervais's David smiles while he tells the invisible interviewer the boss's name is Jennifer Taylor Clark. "We call her 'Camilla Parker Bowles,'" he continues through the smile, then after an infinitesimal pause: "Not to her face [still smiling, then a short pause]—not that I'm afraid of her." As these last words leave his mouth his expression briefly shifts to the classic universal face of fear: eyebrows raised, eyes widened, and mouth slightly open. The camera cuts to the next scene after lingering only long enough to register the contradiction between David's words and his final expression. Carrell's rendition of the same speech alternates more rapidly between jokiness and fear. Telling the interviewer about the boss, he makes an American version of David's lame joke: "I call her Hillary Rodham Clinton—[brief pause] well, not to her face—[another brief pause] because, well, not because I'm scared of her—[much longer pause] because I'm not—[still longer pause] and [pause] yeah." My point is not that the character's true feeling about Jan is fear, or that he is covering up his real feelings with the joke. To read the scene that way would be, as Butler says, to "prefer the seamlessness of the story" over "something we might tentatively call the truth of the person"—in this case, the truth of mixed feelings. Once again Gervais has directed Carrell to interpret the lines almost exactly as he himself had spoken them: viewing the two scenes together serves as a reminder that this naturalistic representation of self is itself artificially produced by performative and narrative means.

Such metanarrative reminders are also, as I have mentioned, part of what makes *The Office* so funny, along with the pratfalls, practical jokes, personal idiosyncrasies, insults, and other staples of situation comedy that characterize the show. Again (and amazingly) Butler:

> So if, at the beginning—and we must laugh here since we cannot narrate that beginning with any kind of authority, indeed, such a narration is the occasion in which we lose whatever narrative authority we might otherwise enjoy—*I am only in the address to you,* then the "I" that I am is nothing without this "you," and cannot even begin to refer to itself outside the relation to the other by which its capacity for self-reference emerges. (82)

If this manifestation of deixis is true for people relating to one another in the material world, how much more true is it for fictitious characters! "I *am* only in the address to you." The characters of the office narrate an "I" that exists *only* in relation to the "you" who is the audience for whom the camera operators stand in. The reality effect emerges out of the representation of this link between autobiographical narration and the performance—which is to say the constituting—of the self.

No narratologist herself, Butler distinguishes between narrative, on one hand, and the exchange between a speaker and an addressee, on the other. For her, the rhetorical connection pulls against narrative:

> I would suggest that *the structure of address is* not a feature of narrative, one of its many and variable attributes, but *an interruption of narrative*. The moment the story is addressed to someone, it assumes a rhetorical dimension that is not reducible to a narrative function. It presumes that someone, and it seeks to recruit and act upon that someone. Something is being done with language when the account that I give begins: it is invariably interlocutory, ghosted, laden, persuasive, and tactical. It may well seek to communicate a truth, but it can do this, if it can, only by exercising a relational dimension of language. (63; emphasis mine)

Unusual as it may be to say such a thing about an idea of Judith Butler's, this distinction is too simple. To think of "the structure of address" as "an interruption of narrative" is to revert to the old formalists' aversion to "narrative intrusions" upon the "illusion of reality." From Bakhtin's dialogics to Seymour Chatman's model of narrative transmission to Jim Phelan's and Peter Rabinowitz's work on the rhetoric of narration, the exchange between a speaker and interlocutor has long been recognized as central to narrative form. ("Who is speaking? To whom? In what circumstances?"—these are, as I have said, the basic questions to ask about narrative voice.) The motivation for the rhetorical move, the acknowledgment of ambivalence and ambiguity in the exchange with another self, is what gets edited out of *The Real Housewives* and dramatized in *The Office*. The autobiographical self occupies that gap between the occasion of speaking the "I" and the speaker's sense of what that pronoun's referent might be, or how it might exceed and contradict what the "I" is saying. The brilliance and originality of *The Office* inheres in the series' acknowledgment of this "truth about the self" and its incorporation of that truth into its narrative structure, a structure made possible only by the existence of the reality shows it mocks.

Both male and female characters on *The Office* embody the hyperrealism afforded by the show's acknowledgment of the ambivalent, divided self. And yet it is not surprising that the characters in *The Office* who stand out during the first five seasons as having the most fully elaborated relationship with the cameras and the most frequent opportunities to express ambivalence are men, namely Jim and Michael. In the U.S. version, Pam could be cited as an exception, but for every glance she directs at the camera, her suitor/husband Jim has perhaps a dozen more. Once they have become a couple, Pam and Jim are usually interviewed together, while Jim continues his own special relationship with the cameras in action scenes. Pam's represented subjectivity is without a doubt subordinated to Jim's, and Jim's is consistently the most ambivalent—hence the most seemingly incoherent and complex—of all the show's characters. As for *The Real Housewives,* its representation of newly wealthy females as excessively coherent subjects contributes—in a way *The Office* does not—to mainstream culture's stubborn insistence that women are not fully human. What is performed as "true" about these faux-real "housewives" reflects back on real heterosexual American women of all races, ages, and classes, whatever their personal relationships to the identity of "housewife" might be.

Works Cited

Alber, Jan, and Rüdiger Heinze, eds. *Unnatural Narratives–Unnatural Narratology.* Berlin & Boston: deGruyter, 2011.

Allrath, Gaby, Marion Gymnich, and Carola Surkamp. "Introduction: Towards a Narratology of TV Series." *Narrative Strategies in Television Series.* Ed. Gaby Allrath and Marion Gymnich. London: Palgrave Macmillan, 2005. 1–43.

Barthes, Roland. "The Reality Effect." *The Rustle of Language.* Trans. Richard Howard. New York: Hill and Wang, 1986. 141–48.

Booth, Wayne. *The Rhetoric of Fiction.* 2nd ed. Chicago: U of Chicago P, 1983.

Butler, Jeremy. *Television Style.* New York: Routledge, 2010.

Butler, Judith. *Giving an Account of Oneself.* New York: Fordham UP, 2005.

Chatman, Seymour. *Story and Discourse: Narrative Structure in Fiction and Film.* Ithaca: Cornell UP, 1980.

Genette, Gérard. *Narrative Discourse: An Essay in Method.* Trans. Jane E. Lewin. Ithaca: Cornell UP, 1980.

Herman, David, James Phelan, Peter Rabinowitz, Brian Richardson, and Robyn Warhol. *Narrative Theory: Core Concepts and Critical Debates.* Columbus: The Ohio State UP, 2012.

Hight, Craig. *Television Mockumentary: Reflexivity, Satire, and a Call to Play.* Manchester: Manchester UP, 2011.

Lee, Michael J., and Leigh Moscowitz. "The Rich Bitch: Class and Gender on *The Real Housewives of New York City.*" *Feminist Media Studies* 13.1 (2013): 64–82.

Malina, Debra. *Breaking the Frame: Metalepsis and the Construction of the Subject.* Columbus: The Ohio State UP, 2002.

McCabe, Janet, and Akass, Kim, eds. *Quality TV: Contemporary American Television and Beyond.* New York and London: Tauris, 2007.

Mills, Brett. "Comedy Vérité: Contemporary Sitcom Form." *Screen* 45.1 (2004): 63–78.

Mittell, Jason. *Complex TV: The Poetics of Contemporary Television Storytelling.* New York: NYU P, 2015.

———. "Narrative Complexity in Contemporary American Television." *The Velvet Light Trap* 58 (2006): 29–40.

Neumann, Birgit, and Ansgar Nünning. "Metanarration and Metafiction." *The Living Handbook of Narratology.* Ed. Peter Hühn et al. Hamburg: Hamburg UP. <http://hup.sub.uni-hamburg.de/lhn/index.php ?title=Metanarration and Metafiction &oldid=1924>. Accessed 21 Mar. 2013.

O'Sullivan, Sean. "Broken On Purpose: Poetry, Serial Television, and the Season." *Storyworlds* 2 (2010): 59–77.

Royal, Derek Parker. "Falsifying the Fragments: Narratological Uses of the Mockumentary in Woody Allen's *Husbands and Wives* and *Sweet and Lowdown.*" *Post Script: Essays in Film and the Humanities* 31 (2012): 54–66.

Thompson, Ethan. "Comedy Vérité? The Observational Documentary Meets the Televisual Sitcom." *Velvet Light Trap* 60 (2007): 63–72.

PEGGY PHELAN

Hypothetical Focalization and Queer Grief[1]

The critical paradigm we call "queer" insists that the identity it names is always *in relation to,* a conviction that finds its theoretical roots in Lacanian psychoanalysis.[2] The term queer can be used as a noun or an adjective, and increasingly has morphed into a verb, as in *queering narratology.* The term's diffuseness reminds us that queer continually names and performs a relation to something other than itself. By emphasizing the social and performance aspects of sexual identity, queer, as a critical concept, makes claims that are collective, contingent, and multiple, rather than singular, absolute, or rooted in an individual psychic subject. While much of the affective force of "being" queer—a being made manifest through performance—is, of course, reflected in individual lives and narratives, the ideological and social force

1. The signature is mine but the ideas and feelings expressed herein have many sources. In addition to the citations formally included in the text, I would like to acknowledge the help of Lauren Berlant, Ann Carlson, Sue Lanser, Celeste Goodridge, Angela Farr Schiller, Monika Greenleaf, Melissa Boyde, Amanda Lawson, and Peta Tait. Frederick Luis Aldama led a rich seminar at the 2011 Project Narrative Conference devoted to the first version of this essay and I am grateful to him and to all participants for that inspiring discussion.

2. Lacan's most significant contribution to psychoanalysis is his contention that the psychic subject is necessarily a social subject, and therefore a split subject. See Juliet Flower Mac-Cannell, *Figuring Lacan: Criticism and the Cultural Unconscious* (Lincoln: U of Nebraska P, 1986) for a concise summary of this aspect of Lacan's work.

of the critical term queer derives from its capacity to function as a response to a collective call. The self-appellation queer derives from a perpetual two-step between disidentification with heteronormativity and identification with other queer persons and objects.[3] Since queer names something discovered and encountered in relation to, it dramatizes the ongoing improvisational performance that constitutes identity-making *tout court*.

The emphasis on collective identity, and its attendant conception of social-sexual identity as performance, has made the fit between queer theory and narrative theory uncomfortable. The narratives often extolled by narratologists often concern individual quests and are often shaped by singular voices, and narrative theory has sought to discover and discern concepts that apply to fixed, even at times universal, narrative structures. Emphasizing formal structures rather than thematic content, narrative theory's dedication to discerning and disentangling concepts such as discourse and story, author and reader, character focalizer and narrator focalizer, is itself in some ways antithetical to the collective, contingent, and relational force of queer thinking more broadly. Influenced by both poststructuralism's focus on the blurring of subject positions and psychoanalysis's rigorous validation of affect as meaning-maker, queer theorists are sometimes skeptical of the arduous effort made by narratologists to pursue systematic precision and fine parsing of structural concepts.

In her 2001 essay on narrative ethics, Lynne Huffer contends, "One of the hallmarks of queer theory is its rejection of traditional narrative in favor of a more liberatory performativity" (6). Huffer cites Judith Butler's provocative speculation that "performance may preempt narrative as the scene of gender production" (Butler, "Gender Trouble" 339). Butler's argument is rooted in a Lacanian psychoanalytic axiom that sexuality, the aspect of subjectivity most intimately tied to the unconscious, exceeds "any definitive narrativization" (Butler, "Imitation" 315). These are turbulent waters and worthy of far more attention than I will give them here.[4] But suffice it to say that Butler's philosophical interest in performance has led some queer theorists to assume that narratology, with its emphasis on the heterodynamic structure of narrative, is not a promising topic for the advancement of queer thought.[5] But those who

3. For more on the performance epistemology at the heart of queer disidentifications, see José Esteban Muñoz, *Disidentifications: Queers of Color and the Performance of Politics* (Minneapolis: U of Minnesota P, 1999).

4. For a fuller discussion of narrative and sexuality see Judith Roof, *Come As You Are: Sexuality and Narrative* (New York: Columbia UP, 1996) and D. A. Miller, *Narrative and Its Discontents: Problems of Closure in the Traditional Novel* (Princeton: Princeton UP, 1989).

5. Huffer takes pains to complicate a too sturdy opposition between queer thinking and narrative theory and praises the work of Butler and Sedgwick in particular. But she also

study queer performance and those who study narrative have some mutual interests, although on the surface these may seem less strategic than unwitting. Indeed, it seems to me that the concept of performance has particular valence for forging queer narratology.

Take, for example, Susan Lanser's "Sexing the Narrative," a reading of Jeanette Winterson's 1992 novel, *Written on the Body*, one of the earliest and most promising attempts to link narratology and queer theory.[6] Lanser notes that Winterson's decision to leave the narrator's gender unmarked raises significant questions about the ways in which gender and sexuality function as narrative markers within narratives more broadly. Winterson's narrator is deeply in love with Louise (a woman), who is married to Elgin (a man). The reader may, therefore, read the narrator as a straight man or as a lesbian woman. But as Lanser points out, the introduction of the narrator's boyfriend Crazy Frank in the second half of the novel disallows the first two hypotheses about the narrator's gender and sexuality. The narrator can neither be an exclusively straight man nor an exclusively lesbian woman. Lanser spells out some of the consequences for narrative theory:

> Might we now have to include in narratology *two* markers (or absence of markers) of the narrator's identity—sex and sexuality—along with the marker of gender that mediates these two? [. . .] My point in raising these various possibilities [. . .] is not to suggest that narratology can decide these questions [. . .] My point is that gender, sex, and sexuality constitute narratologically significant elements. (89–90)

I agree with Lanser, but I also believe that these narratological markers are, fundamentally, contingent.[7] That is to say, Lanser's contention that gender "mediates" the reader's interpretation of the narrator's sex and sexuality is also a claim that presupposes the belief that erotic expression performs and makes meanings that exceed carnal acts as such. Indeed, the narrator's shifting affec-

---

concludes, "Nonetheless, despite the complexity and ambiguity of these exemplars of the queer, queer theory has solidified into a legitimate discursive and academic field over the course of the last decade, and has therefore become more fixed (as all legitimated discourses do) in its claims to self-definition. Thus a metanarrative has developed in which the fluid, destabilizing queer performance stakes out its difference from that which came before by setting up a stable, fixed feminist narrative as its nonqueer, identitarian other" (7). For a discussion of the heterodynamic structure of narrative see Roland Barthes, *S/Z: An Essay*, trans. Richard Miller. New York: Hill and Wang, 1974), the commentaries on it by D. A. Miller in his *Narrative and Its Discontents*, and Judith Roof in her *Come As You Are*.

6. A revised version of this essay appears in Kathy Mezei, ed., *Ambiguous Discourse: Feminist Narratology and British Women Writers* (Chapel Hill: U of North Carolina P, 1996).

7. I mean contingent here in the sense of "dependent upon."

tive and erotic performances are what mediate the reader's shifting hypotheses about the narrator's gender and sexual identities. Winterson's narrator's gender and sexual identities can only be decided in relation to the heteromorphic gender difference between Louise and Frank. If the narrator's only erotic entanglements were with Louise, the reader could reasonably assume the narrator is either a lesbian woman or a heterosexual man. But the introduction of the narrator's erotic relationship with Frank, as Lanser rightly claims, "erases the possibility of [reading the novel's plot as] a straight heterosexual male in love with a married woman, and hence the standard age-old scenario of Western literature" (90). Equally, the introduction of the narrator's erotic relationship with Frank disallows the possibility of reading the plot as lesbian romance. It is the gender difference between Louise and Frank that dramatizes the interrelationship between gender and sexuality that determines how to interpret both the gender and sexuality of the narrator. While one might argue that *Written on the Body* has multiple narrators, the similarity in narrative voice and focalization throughout the novel makes that possibility unpersuasive.[8] Rather than creating multiple narrators, Winterson creates a narrator whose gender and sexual identities emerge in relation to heteromorphic erotic objects. And this is what makes *Written on the Body* an exemplary queer narrative. Winterson's novel enacts the ways in which queer gains meaning only in relation to characters and things other than itself.

I.

I noted above that the narrator's focalization does not change in *Written on the Body*. But it is wise to retrace this comment and to put it within the context of focalization's broader story within narrative theory. The concept of focalization was introduced by Gérard Genette in 1972. Genette's new concept was meant to disentangle the frequent conflation of the perspective of the narrator and the character. By creating the critical category of focalization, Genette called important attention to a discernible difference between seeing and speaking in narrative. Some characters saw and therefore knew things that other characters did not. Genette elucidated three types of focalization: zero, multiple, and internal; he argued that focalizers were independent of narrator types because, at least initially, he did not attribute focalization to

---

8. For a good discussion of the various proposals to "solve" the problems raised by Winterson's unmarked narrator, see Jago Morrison, "'Who Cares About Gender at a Time Like This?': Love, Sex and the Problem of Jeanette Winterson," *Journal of Gender Studies* 15.2 (2006): 169–80.

narrators at all (see 185–211). Following Genette, Seymour Chatman and Gerald Prince insist that narrators are never focalizers because they are elements of discourse, whereas focalization belongs only to story.[9] James Phelan and Mieke Bal (among others) argue that both characters and narrators can be focalizers.[10] These arguments are more than local skirmishes. They help illuminate the difficulty, and perhaps even the impossibility, of disentangling seeing from saying. For within written narratives seeing is also saying—even if what one sees is that one cannot say. Although Genette attempted to sharpen the distinction between point of view and focalization by restricting focalization to answering the question "who perceives?," these tweaks did not solve the larger problem with the concept as a whole.[11] Monika Fludernik points out that the "extensive debate on focalization has really demonstrated that the category is an interpretive one and *not* exclusively a textual category" (258). I agree and further suggest that, *pace* Genette, focalization exposes the deeply entwined relationship between perceiving and saying in written narrative.

Recognizing the trouble with focalization as Genette and his adherents employ it, but still interested in the general issue of doubt produced by discrepancies in perception across a written narrative, David Herman introduces the term hypothetical focalization (HF) as a "(partial) classification of the ways uncertainty can enter narrative discourse via focalization" (244). HF, Herman argues, "entails the use of hypotheses, framed by the narrator or a character, about what might be or have been seen or perceived—if only there were someone who could have adopted the requisite perspective on the situations and events at issue" (231).

While the critical reception of Herman's concept has focused on whether or not it is helpful or redundant—some suggest that hypothetical focalization is the same as Genette's zero focalization, or that zero focalization enables HF—less attention has been given to Herman's motivation to find a term for what he calls a "grammar of doubt."[12] Insofar as narratology is dedicated to meta-understanding, to describing how it is we come to understand narra-

---

9. Patrick O'Neill, *Fictions of Discourse: Reading Narrative Theory* (Toronto: Toronto UP, 1994), offers a concise summary of these positions.

10. For Chatman and Prince see Willie van Peer and Seymour Chatman, eds., *New Perspectives on Narrative Perspective* (Albany: State U of New York P, 2001). For character focalization see James Phelan, *Living to Tell About It: A Rhetoric and Ethics of Character Narration* (Ithaca: Cornell UP, 2005), especially pages 98–131; and Mieke Bal, *Narratology: Introduction to the Theory of Narrative* (Toronto: U of Toronto P, 1997).

11. See Gérard Genette, *Narrative Discourse Revisited,* trans. Jane E. Lewin (Ithaca: Cornell UP, 1988).

12. See, for example, Burkhard Niederhoff, "Focalization," *the living handbook of narratology,* ed. Peter Hühn et al. (Hamburg: Hamburg UP). < http://www.lhn.uni-hamburg.de/article/focalization>. Accessed 8 May 2012. Narrative Dictionary online.

tives, it necessarily comports with the *might have been* that haunts reading fiction as a mode of cognitive and affective action. Queer theorists, to speak very broadly, have been all about the epistemological and affective consequences of doubt and uncertainty: indeed, some of the most subtle and influential work in the field concerns shame, trauma, optimism, love, and grief, emotional fields that emerge primarily through grammars of affective doubt.[13]

Moreover, I register a provocative wistfulness in Herman's definition of HF: "the use of hypotheses, framed by the narrator or a character, about what might be or have been seen or perceived—if only there were someone who could have adopted the requisite perspective on the situations and events at issue" (231). Herman's use of the word "requisite" suggests that HF brings us close to an omniscient perception that could have occurred had everything fallen into place.[14] Hypothetical focalization, therefore, seems particularly valuable for reading queer autobiographies, especially those concerned with childhood. Indeed, coming-out narratives often recount the drama by which a hypothetical perspective about sexuality becomes a requisite one for the narrator.[15] The idea that queerness might have been correctly recognized if only a hypothetical focalizer had been there to notice it is itself a common trope in such narratives. Equally potent is the "if only I had been straight" hypothetical focalization that often makes queer memoirs comic.[16] In both tropes,

13. The list of works devoted to affect and queer theory is long. Some of the most influential include Douglas Crimp, "Mourning and Militancy," *October* 51 (Winter 1989): 3–18; Eve Kosofsky Sedgwick and Adam Frank, "Shame in the Cybernetic Fold: Reading Silvan Tomkins," *Critical Inquiry* 21.2 (1995): 496–522; Ann Cvetkovich, "Public Feelings," *South Atlantic Quarterly* 106.3 (2007): 459–68; Anne Anlin Cheng, *The Melancholy of Race* (New York: Oxford UP, 2001); David L. Eng and Shinhee Han, "A Dialogue on Racial Melancholia," *Loss: The Politics of Mourning*, ed. David L. Eng and David Kazanjian (Berkeley: U of California P, 2002), 343–71; and Eve Kosofsky Sedgwick, *Touching Feeling: Affect, Pedagogy, Performativity* (Durham: Duke UP, 2003).

14. This sense of wistfulness is enhanced by Herman's reading of Bing Crosby's 1934 hit, "Santa Claus Is Coming to Town." Herman ignores Crosby's masterful vocal performance and focuses instead on Haven Gillespie's lyrics. Herman is particularly interested in this line from the chorus: "He sees you when you're sleeping." Herman argues that this line indicates that "we are in a condition of being focalized by Santa" (240). The reading of the song adds to the wistfulness I find in the concept.

15. See Roof, *Come As You Are*, 104–13 for a fuller discussion of coming-out narratives and narrative theory. It is probably worth underlining that some of the attention to requisite perspective on sexuality stemmed from a political moment in which strategic representation of the lives of gays and lesbians was still very new. As transgender and genderqueer political strategies emerge, my hunch is that the grip on requisite perspectives on and about sexual/gender identity will loosen and hypothetical perspectives will come to the fore.

16. Some exemplary queer memoirs that illustrate these tropes include Terry Galloway, *Mean Little Deaf Queer: A Memoir* (Boston: Beacon, 2009); Dorothy Allison, *Two or Three Things I Know For Sure* (New York: Plume, 1996); and Judith Barrington, *Lifesaving: A Memoir* (Portland, OR: The Eighth Mountain Press, 2000).

hypothetical focalization is, in part, a function of retrospection, the departure point for memoir generally. Queer memoirists often suggest that if his or her "true" sexuality had been recognized and accepted, if only hypothetically, it may have been lived and narrated in a better key. This kind of reading demonstrates the ease with which focalization slips between interpretive and textual levels, as Fludernik argued.

II.

> We're undone by each other. And if we're not, we're missing something. This seems so clearly the case with grief, but it can be so only because it was already the case with desire. [. . .] As a mode of relation, neither gender nor sexuality is precisely a possession, but, rather, is a mode of being dispossessed, a way of being *for* another or *by virtue of* another.
> —Judith Butler, "Violence, Mourning, Politics"

If memoirs, especially those that concern childhood, illuminate one important affinity between HF and queer narrative, eulogy illuminates another crucial alignment. Butler's insistence on the strong link between grief and desire also reminds us that just as we wish for a "requisite" perception, so too might we wish for a liberation from the cognitive and affective labor of such fullness. Eulogies and elegies often suggest the many social deaths and microbiological processes that render biological human death an ongoing act, rather than a single event with a clear beginning and end.[17] Perhaps for this reason eulogies have been especially potent genres for the elaboration of HF's performative reach. Take, for example, W. H. Auden's eulogy for W. B. Yeats. Auden's narrator remembers Yeats's "last afternoon as himself" and imagines it as if he had the "requisite perspective on the situations and events at issue":

> But for him it was his last afternoon as himself,
> An afternoon of nurses and rumours;
> The provinces of his body revolted,
> The squares of his mind were empty,
> Silence invaded the suburbs,
> The current of his feeling failed; he became his admirers. (245)

---

17. For more on death as a repeatable act, see Peggy Phelan, "Andy Warhol: Performances of Death in America," *Performing the Body / Performing the Text,* ed. Amelia Jones and Andrew Stephenson (London: Routledge, 1999), 223–37.

This becoming at the end of the line registers the monumentality of Yeats's death in a clause. Yeats becomes his admirers and Auden underlines the ever-shifting dialogue between reader and writer, which can ricochet between the erotic and the cannibalistic. The intermingling of reader and writer, of *you* and *me*, constitutes one of the central performances of written narrative and, as with any radical *jouissance*, this porousness erodes the security of the proprietary relation between us. I take up the part of the writer and you are cast as the reader. But I read this as I write it, and you, no doubt, rewrite it, improve it, make it your own as you encounter it here and there. Psychically, the erosion of this hold on subject position is often treacherous and painful. For this reason, Freud linked falling in love with suicide in his famous essay "Mourning and Melancholia" (1917), describing them both as events in which the ego is overwhelmed by the encounter with the other (see 251–55). There is something of this same process in the practice of passionate reading and writing; an inhabitation, however hypothetical, of the voice and sensibility of the other. For the reader, the other has the writer's name; for the writer the other is often simultaneously an interior and exterior addressee. This mutual, albeit temporary, inhabitation produces both grief for its inevitable ending and a powerfully immediate resistance to the proprietary claims of singular subjectivities.[18] During the first crest of the AIDS crisis in the United States in the 1980s, gay men in particular wrote searing elegies that theatrically enacted both this grief and this resistance.[19] It was this work, deeply passionate and deeply personal, that drove the first generation of queer theorists to imagine a discursive critical responsiveness to the facts of queer lives and deaths, actually and imaginatively.

III.

The particular inflection of the term queer in contemporary thought is indebted to Eve Sedgwick's critical and autobiographical work. In her two

---

18. I am using the term "inhabitation" here, rather than "introjection," or "incorporation," because I am interested in the resonance between the former term and pregnancy. To be pregnant with the writing voice, for both the reader and the writer, is to become continuous with it very much in the manner of the merging of two bodies in pregnancy. I am also trying to counter the logocentric preoccupations of a discourse that routinely privileges dissemination, penetrating analyses, and so on.

19. Exemplary texts in this genre include Paul Monette, *Love Alone: Eighteen Elegies for Rog* (New York: St. Martin's, 1988); Thom Gunn, *The Man with Night Sweats: Poems* (London; Boston: Faber and Faber, 1992); *Tongues Untied*, VHS, dir. Marlon Riggs, 1989 (San Francisco, CA: Frameline [distributor], 1989); and David Wojnarowicz, *Close to the Knives: A Memoir of Disintegration* (New York: Vintage, 1991). And a bit later, George Haggerty, "Love and Loss: An Elegy," *GLQ: A Journal of Lesbian and Gay Studies* 10.3 (2004) 385–405.

groundbreaking books, *Between Men* and *Epistemology of the Closet*, Sedgwick wrote passionate essays about male characters in fiction who were in love with each other, sometimes wittingly, sometimes not. But my own interest in Sedgwick's work stems from the ways in which she infused critical writing with queer autobiography.

Her 1987 essay "A Poem Is Being Written" returns to Sigmund Freud's essay "A Child Is Being Beaten," to forge links between poetry, rhythm, and sexuality. One of Freud's lasting legacies is the use of oneself as a case study; he made it acceptable to build a theory from one's own desires, jokes, and dreams. This model of theory building was crucial for the early formation of queer studies, and Sedgwick's work was compellingly adept at enacting the potency of self as case study. In part 1 of "A Poem Is Being Written," Sedgwick argues that carnal and metric responsiveness share the same psychic and creative root. Part 2 meditates on why anal eroticism seems to be an inconceivable aspect of women's sexuality. Reading this today, the idea that repeating metrical rhymes and repeated spankings attune a child to the rhythms of erotic life seems, if not exactly commonplace, certainly plausible. But Sedgwick's call, in part 2 of the essay, to broaden cultural recognition of women's anal eroticism has hardly been borne out. What interests me about Sedgwick's essay here, however, is the way in which it pivots between the past and the future and thereby establishes a double voice that alerts us to the voice within or beneath the voice written on the page. The first part of the essay is essentially a memoir: Sedgwick the scholar reads her childhood verse from her professorial point of view. She is concerned with trying to reconstruct her mood, thoughts, and style as a young student and hypothetically imagines herself anew as a writer who is still writing within the voice of the text we are reading. Sedgwick's essay, then, is a writing that nominates itself a rewriting, a wistful attempt to pay respect to her much-missed younger self. (And I now write of these two Eves, Kosofsky and Sedgwick, in my own wistful attempt to enliven, once more, her now deceased selves.) Sedgwick's opening proposition exemplifies Fludernik's point that hypothetical focalization is both interpretive and structural:

> This essay was written late: twenty-seven years late, to the extent that it represents a claim for respectful attention to the intellectual and artistic life of a nine-year-old child, Eve Kosofsky. But it would be fairer to admit (and I can testify to this, since my acquaintance with the person named has been continuous) that her claim for attention to her intellectual and artistic life has in fact, exceptionally, persisted through every day of these twenty-seven

years and more, as unremittingly and forcefully as self-respect would permit
and very often a good deal more so. What comes late, here, is then not her
claim itself, which both deserves and was denied respect *because of its very
commonplaceness,* but the rhetorical ground on which alone it can be made
audible, which is unfortunately and misleadingly the ground of exception.
She is allowed to speak, or I to speak of her, only here in the space of professional success and of hyperconscious virtuosity, conscious not least of the
unusually narrow stylistic demands that hedge about any language that treats
one's own past. ("A Poem Is Being Written" 110)

Admitting that her "requisite perspective" on the events detailed in nine-
year-old Eve Kosofsky's poetry has come about because of her professional
success as a literary critic, the thirty-six-year-old literary critic goes on to
hypothesize a life as a mature poet, a life she both did and did not live under
the name "Eve Kosofsky Sedgwick." At the time she wrote the essay, Sedgwick was not then writing poetry "professionally." The present participle of
the essay's title, "A Poem Is Being Written," testifies to the act of writing that
is the center of the essay's performance: the essay we read (re)animates nine-
year-old Kosofsky's poetry by bringing Sedgwick's professional expertise as
a literary critic (and not as a poet) to it. Thus, the performance of "requisite
perspective" here derives from both Sedgwick's authority as literary critic and
her continuous relationship with the nine-year-old poet whose text she reads
(and rewrites).

"A Poem Is Being Written" marks a critical turn in Sedgwick's work from
a clear border between writer and object of study to a messier meditation on
herself in relation to the object of study. Sedgwick's essays are robust inquiries into intersubjectivity, one fostered for her primarily by her love for specific people and texts. Some of her work, as is often the case for writers who
publish a lot and often under deadline, feels at times uneven, perhaps even
oddly misshapen, meandering, not fully persuasive. As Sedgwick continued to
write, her focus moved from considering a particular topic (Henry James, Eve
Sedgwick) for a particular audience (oneself, one's classmates, one's peers),
toward the performance of Writing as primary subject, object, and addressee.
In Sedgwick's later work, she dedicated herself to imagining Writing as a vital
performance close to breathing; she crafted arguments carried as much by
body as by mind. In her *Dialogue on Love,* published in 1999, Sedgwick created a prose poem that imagines writing as rhythmic and melodic as breath's
own in and out (7–12). One consequence of this approach was an erosion
of her own position as singular author: the dialogue contains some of her

therapist's notes written at the time of their encounter.[20] Influenced by Buddhist practice and thought, the text also contains halibun, short haiku-like poems traditionally used to describe travel, and these, as well as her therapist's case notes, work against the implicit narrative shape of the psychoanalytic dialogue. Trying to resist the definite pleasures of the teleological successful therapy story, Sedgwick continually underlines her ambition to forge an addressee interested in writing toward Writing, an addressee with the capacity and interest to read for shape, sound, and rhythm; the text is a record of Sedgwick's decisions about where and how to shape the word that takes its place in the ocean of sentences to come, decisions determined by the echo of sounds that precede that tide.

IV.

One of Sedgwick's last published essays "about" a writer was her eulogy for Lynda Hart. In it, she remarked:

> The last work of Lynda's that I saw was the notebook of quotations that she assembled, in her careful handwriting, and asked the people who were caring for her in her illness to read to her as a kind of continuing ground of meditation. Although the writing was drawn from diverse spiritual traditions, rather than being Lynda's own, it was still her book in completely unmistakable ways. [. . .] It had a relation to truth, to truthfulness and to truth-telling, that was clearly of the greatest importance to Lynda herself and to those of us who loved her, and yet never tried to mobilize the Truth into one thing. It was more like a flowing river of truthfulness, and in that sense—in that sense only—it was also a river of consolation. ("Eulogy" 235)

I was both moved and puzzled by Sedgwick's description of Hart's last work. By the time of Sedgwick's eulogy for her, Hart and I had written a book together, many essays, various dialogues, some published some not, and a score of letters, emails, poems, shopping notes.[21] In some ways our writing was the most vital part of our connection and in other ways our writing kept

---

20. For a smart reading of the therapist's notes in particular, see Elizabeth Stephens, "Queer Memoir: Public Confession and/as Sexual Practice in Eve Kosofsky Sedgwick's *A Dialogue on Love*," *Australian Humanities Review* 48 (May 2010): 31–40.

21. Among other texts we published as named co-authors, see Lynda Hart and Peggy Phelan, eds., *Acting Out: Feminist Performances* (Ann Arbor: U of Michigan P, 1993), and "Queerer than Thou: Being and Deb Margolin," *Theatre Journal* 47.2 (1995): 269–82.

us apart. Our reading–writing relation was such a rich river because we made little distinction between writing and reading. If I read something I liked, or something I didn't, I'd scrawl something on it and mail it to her, or, after she moved in, simply leave it on the table for her. When we were apart she'd often fax me the marginalia from pages she had read with the published text all redacted; we'd play a game in which I'd have to guess to what text the marginalia belonged. So yes, Eve was correct to note that Lynda's meditation book was decidedly "hers," but how could it be otherwise? Why, I wondered, would Sedgwick feel that was something worth pointing out? It was her book in the way it was our communication, a giving and taking that did not trouble overmuch about what was hers, what was ours, what was now, what was then. Or at least not then when we believed in the ocean of sentences to come. But now, now that she's gone and I have all these papers and books and notes and letters, I sometimes cannot tell which ones are hers, which mine, which are responses, which are initiatives. Our writing was and is sometimes a river of consolation and sometimes a river of grief without end. (A lamentation, a keening, a song.) A writing that was, a writing that is, in relation to each other, but also more fundamentally in relation to acts of reading and writing that obviated the distinction between each act and between each of us.

Lesbians often suffer from "boundary issues," or so the clinical literature suggests. And yet many lesbians and queers are so accustomed to experiencing the predominantly straight patriarchal world "as if" we are both in it and to the side of it that this blurring itself may be said to produce a constant hypothetical focalization of one's own queer autobiography. Thus the porosity of "boundaries" may well be a form of potent literacy, a hypothetical focalization that moves the autodiegetic I from the "as if" or subjunctive tense into the indicative, *we are*. And it may also be the case that falling in love is itself an act in which one hypothesizes that the beloved might have the capacity to adopt "the requisite perspective on the events at issue" in the ongoing drama of autodiegetic narrative.

V.

As a girl, my siblings and I often went down to the small creek that ran behind the school yard. It was mainly a muddy and moist trickle, but we respected it and stayed curbed by its bank. One day, frustrated and lonely, I ventured to the bank alone. There I saw two rocks that were completely, almost theatrically, dry. Lit by the noon sun, the orange yellow stone just under the surface of the dingier brown flickered and flamed. When I picked the rocks up, I felt a thin membrane of dew on the bottom of both rocks and noticed that the one in my right hand filled my palm entirely, while the one in my left stopped short of my finger-tips. I made sure there were no bugs on them and then I took them back into the school yard and sat at a table and began to rub them together. I was determined to make them spark. It was so much labor: I was grunting and sweating, the sun was in my eyes. The rocks had lost their original appeal, but I carried on. Then finally after what felt like hours but must not have been, a tiny flame leapt between them. Startled, I jumped up and dropped them instantly.

This memory expresses, materially rather than metaphorically, something of what I mean here by "in relation to." Each rock remained itself as I pressed and panted and forced them into fire but I was nonetheless startled, despite my determined effort, by the fact of the flame they made. The rocks were "dead" but they became alive with the energy of burning when the work of my fevered palms lit them. Perhaps most writing about the dead beloved stems from the belief that if pressed hard enough the tomblike present might be made to coax the heat of their vitality to burn again within the surviving writer. The grieving writer takes up two different modes of consciousness—one in which the beloved is dead and one in which she is not dead. The latter may well be an expression of the wished for and the might have been, but it is also perhaps a version of inhabiting the requisite perspective that only death allows, and thus one that can only be grasped belatedly. ("This essay is late: twenty seven years late . . ." begins Sedgwick's "A Poem Is Being Written.") The genre of eulogy often traces the struggle to grasp the consolation within this "requisite perspective" on the dead person's life.

For both Sedgwick and Hart, the twin experiences of love and grief prompted them toward autobiographical essay writing. Both of them came of age professionally in the shadow of AIDS and both of them had breast cancer. Both women loved both men and women but neither of them considered themselves bisexual. Both of them loved literature, and much of their writing was motivated by the desire to think through the connection between erotic desire and subjectivity. And both came to write their own work as if writing itself might be reparative, if only in a temporary sense.[22] And they both turned from writing the literary criticism that was the core of their graduate training, to writing and art-making informed deeply by their Buddhism. Lynda prepared for her death by consciously framing it as an encounter with the *bardo*, a way of writing and living a transition that perhaps prose cannot fully allow or convey.

---

22. See Eve Kosofsky Sedgwick, "Paranoid Reading and Reparative Reading, Or, You're So Paranoid, You Probably Think This Essay Is About You," *Touching Feeling: Affect, Pedagogy, Performativity* (Durham: Duke UP, 2003).

While Sedgwick's first books impressed me with their brilliance, looking back I can see that part of what shook me about them was how precisely she balanced the traditional skills of literary analysis, close reading, with the emerging politics of queer sexuality. In her celebrated essay "White Glasses," Sedgwick chronicles a complicated transition from the one who writes to the one who reads. That transition is prompted by a double health crisis. She began writing the talk about four months before she presented it at CUNY's Gay and Lesbian Studies Conference in May 1991. It was intended to pay tribute, and perhaps eulogize her beloved friend, the writer and scholar Michael Lynch, who had decided to stop all treatment for HIV. She begins her talk with the recollection of a previous talk, one she heard Michael Lynch give as chair of a panel she had organized for the MLA in 1986, where she met Lynch for the first time. And therein begins her remarkable testimony to Lynch, to his white glasses, to their great love affair, and to their mutual grappling with death's relentless unlocatability.

In section 4, Sedgwick's essay turns from writing to and for Lynch to writing to and for herself:

> When I decided to write "White Glasses" four months ago, I thought my friend Michael Lynch was dying and I thought I was healthy. Unreflecting, I formed my identity as the prospective writer of this piece around the obituary presumption that my own frame for speaking, the margin of my survival and exemption, was the clearest thing in the world. In fact it was totally opaque: Michael didn't die; I wasn't healthy: within the space of a couple of weeks, we were dealing with a breathtaking revival of Michael's energy, alertness, appetite—also with my unexpected diagnosis with a breast cancer already metastasized to several lymph modes. ("White Glasses" 255)

Jane Gallop has masterfully read the complex temporality at work in Sedgwick's essay (see especially 87–114). My own interest, though, is in the collapse of the proprietary relationship between healthy author and ill subject; the intermingling of the sick and well chronicled and captured in Sedgwick's essay speaks to the difficulty of discerning who says from who speaks. Sedgwick enters her own illness narrative in relation to her intimacy with Lynch's. Sedgwick's original motivation to write "White Glasses," which stemmed from a hypothesis that cast her as the healthy survivor who would speak lovingly of the dying Lynch, is undone as she stumbles across a different, richer, more complicated set of facts. She receives a diagnosis of breast cancer, and she reads the collectively written logbook of Lynch's caregivers. When Sedgwick visits the surprisingly healthy Lynch the week before she delivers her paper, and a few months after her cancer diagnosis, she takes "a few minutes to look through the logbook kept by Michael's care team. I leafed back to February, to the time of my diagnosis and mastectomy, and was amazed to find that one caregiver's shift after another had been marked by the restlessness, exhaustion and pain of Michael's anxiety about what was going on with me in Durham" ("White Glasses" 267). Gradually Sedgwick realizes that what she had taken to be Lynch's near-miraculous return to health was a kind of command performance of love, a love that had him "at my ear daily with hours of the lore, the solicitude, the ground level truth-telling and demand for truth-telling that I simply had to have" (267). What "White Glasses" performs then is the intricacy and complexity of truth and the quite often spectacularly counterintuitive, indeed queer, flow between the ill and the well. Lynch, ostensibly dying, in fact nurtures Eve as she encounters her cancer diagnosis, but his guidance and love comes at the cost of his own health. Or maybe Lynch is, like Henry James's Milly Theale, simultaneously spectacularly well and dreadfully ill. Sedgwick's essay traces the shifting layers of love's truth and treats it as fundamentally conditional and nonabsolute. Need here, as everywhere, is paramount. To be Eve's witness to truth, Michael concealed his own suffering and pain. Maybe this is what all true love requires, the lie that enables another('s) truth. While we do not have Lynch's account of his response to Sedgwick, her record of his solicitude animates something of his love for her. Sedgwick's essay now reads as a eulogy for both writers, who are also readers. Indeed, movements between acts of reading and writing are continually blurred in the essay.

When Lynda was dying, Eve came and sat with her, long after other people who were seemingly closer to Lynda had left. I was impressed with her capacity to sit, to just be, without draining Lynda in any way. I sometimes watched her reading the meditation book, and so when she wrote about her reading in her eulogy for Lynda, I was not surprised. But I think Sedgwick's remarks have stayed with me for so long because underneath the actual words I sensed Sedgwick proposing a radical conception of both belonging-to ("it was still completely her book in completely unmistakable ways") and becoming ("a flowing river of truthfulness"). My immediate sense that it was odd to point out that the book was Lynda's may reflect my own resistance to the echo I hear across Sedgwick's eulogy for Hart and "White Glasses." For even as Eve was declaring the notebook Lynda's, she was also reading it in relation to her own belief in truth-telling, a belief she established and defined when she wrote about reading Lynch's caregivers' logbook. In other words, while I think that Sedgwick's remark about all the different ways of composing, signing, and authoring a book is wonderfully open, the echo I hear across Sedgwick's description of Lynch's logbook as a source for truth-telling and Hart's last book as a source for truth leads me to believe that even while Sedgwick was declaring Lynda's book Lynda's, she was also rendering it her own.

Moreover, because Sedgwick further claims that this notion of truth-telling was something "clearly of the greatest importance to Lynda herself and to those of us who loved her," I feel an almost reflexive desire to push against Sedgwick's claim. Fiction was a central love in Lynda's professional and personal life. She boasted of her theatricality and self-dramatization and took great pride in her capacity to fake it until she could make it. But more than simply saying "ah but look at this and this, it's more complicated . . . ," I think my overall resistance to Sedgwick's naming the book so decisively Lynda's stemmed from my fear that her pronouncement of whose book it was impinged on my own investment in being Lynda's co-author and perpetual addressee.

VI.

In recollecting these echoes after the deaths of Lynch, Sedgwick, and Hart, I place my own narrative voice back in a context that inevitably extends the border of the term "last book." For there were more books after the one Sedgwick named last, and some of these contain the words of Lynch, Sedgwick, and Hart in complex temporal and political frameworks. Insofar as queer autobiography seeks a narrative form exemplifying the *in-relation-to*, it never fully forms; therefore it resists becoming the last book, the final word, the singular death. Nor can such a queer autobiography be fully or finally or authoritatively signed—the most one can proffer is a performance that enshrines the signature as a ritualized performance.[23] As this text slides between surnames and first names—"Lynda," "Hart," "Eve," "Kosofsky," "Sedgwick," it seeks to mark the multiple readers and writers still composing queer autobiography.

"White Glasses" is divided into thirteen sections of different lengths. Sections 7 and 8 are composed entirely of quotations. Section 7 begins with a quote from Butler, who is in turn quoting Lacan. I will now quote Sedgwick, quoting Butler: "Judith Butler in *Gender Trouble*: 'Lacan remarks that "the function of the mask dominates the identifications through which refusals of

---

23. For more on the performance of signatures, see Jacques Derrida, "Signature Event Context," *Margins of Philosophy*, trans. Alan Bass (Chicago: U of Chicago P, 1982), 308–30; and Peggy Phelan, "P. S.," *Khoraographies for Jacques Derrida, on July 15, 2000*, special issue of the online journal *Tympanum* 4, guest ed. Dragan Kujundzic and gen. ed. Peter Woodruff <http://www.usc.edu/dept/comp-lit/tympanum/4/phelan.html>.

love are resolved." In a characteristic gliding over pronominal locations, Lacan fails to make clear who refuses whom'" ("White Glasses" 252). The Butler quote continues, and without commenting on it in any way, Sedgwick follows it with a quote from Michael Moon, who comments on Butler's reading of Lacan. Sedgwick's writing, in other words, theatricalizes her reading. In these two sections of "White Glasses," writing and reading become an instance of tracking proliferating citation. Intermingling voices, feelings, pronouns, narratives of the sick and the well, Sedgwick's writing toward Writing blurs the distinction between the beloved and the lover so deeply that it produces a self-effacement to the point of lying, to the point of dying.

What Sedgwick called Lynda's "last book" was a book of citations, passages that helped Hart enact her own passage from life to death. Most were written in Lynda's hand, but some pages were copied out for her by me and by others. Michael Lynch's logbook, entirely written by others, was the book that revealed to Eve, who thought herself his intimate, that Michael's return to health was a fiction, one Eve may have needed to misread and so did. In suggesting that Sedgwick is the author of both Lynch's and Hart's "last books" I am not accusing her of overwriting them somehow and inscribing them with her signature. I am, rather, acknowledging that the appeal of queer writing comes from the porosity between the reader and the writer, and indeed between the slippage between misreading and reading "right"/write. This approach to queer reading and writing may offer narratology a more complicated challenge than it has focused on to date. While Herman's concept of HF, and the field's larger interest in the grammar of doubt, holds much promise for queer narratology, it is worth noting that a methodology that has taken clarity and precision as its goals may have significant blind spots in regard to these messier and blurrier textual performances. While pursuing clarity is, of course, useful and valuable, it is not the only task narrative theory might undertake.

Coda

Sedgwick's eulogy for Hart was the first of two eulogies offered at Lynda's memorial service in January 2001, and it was published later in the "Lynda Myoun Hart Memorial Issue" of the journal *Women and Performance*. I gave the second eulogy and was asked to publish it as well. But I could not. For me, the eulogy was meant to be spoken and heard, not to be read. And since I had long been associated with the defense of the live and ephemeral against the published text no one found it odd. But not wanting to be left out, and not wanting my refusal to publish my eulogy, which was always her eulogy, to be misread as a refusal to give tribute to Lynda, which is the purpose of a special issue dedicated to someone who will never read it, I decided to publish another essay in the volume. I called it "Tenderness." It included a short coda about Lynda, the last line of which is "*Tender is death's deep sore, tenderness its salve and more*" (26). But the essay itself is mainly about "Sea and Poison," a performance by the Chicago-based ensemble Goat Island. They dissolved the company in 2009 and that ending, coupled with Sedgwick's death a few months later, led me back to Lynda's death, and more particularly, to the last months of our time together in the flesh. One of our most potent arguments concerned the title of one of her books. I lost that argument, and many others, and therefore her third published book is called *Between the Body and the Flesh*. After her death, I wondered if she had been writing a space for death in its spine, a death that was known before it arrived.

The day we heard Lynda's cancer had returned was the first day I was allowed to walk unpatched, after a difficult eye surgery. To celebrate, I went to Lynda's for lunch. As I walked the short distance from our homes, the streets of New York shifted in and out of focus. One eye was fairly clear; the other though was weeping, squinting, weak from the bright light. Once arrived, I collapsed on her couch. While she was cooking, the phone, which was next to the couch, rang and Lynda asked me to pick it up. It was the doctor and so I beckoned Lynda to come from the kitchen and take the call. The doctor told Lynda that the chemotherapy and radiation she had undergone had not succeeded in destroying the cancer cells. Lynda did not respond verbally; instead, she thrust the phone back into my hand. Startled and off guard, I asked the doctor to repeat what she had told Lynda. Lynda sat next to me on the couch furiously writing on yellow sticky-notes and shoving them at me, making me ask the doctor all the things she wanted to know but could not voice herself. I could not read Lynda's notes very well: both the venom of her fear and the bruised and swollen veins in my surgically repaired eye made it impossible for me to focus on her writing. But I can still see the swirl of her arm, can still feel the angle of her fingers pressed against her pen and the thrust of her arm as she delivered the sticky-notes across my lap. And I still feel the slow fall of them falling to the floor: derelict confetti, whispering grief.

As I squinted at the lines, squiggles more than words, I remembered the drawings I saw in some caves in Uluru, the outback of Australia. Lynda and I started our walk in the desert together, but were soon fighting about one thing or another and Lynda walked into the hot brisk wind and I retreated toward a cave, which strikes me now as symptomatic of most of our responses to conflict. When I saw the cave drawings, made with stone or rock that still exerted a pressure centuries later, I thought about the ache involved in expression, the will to be heard, understood, felt. And in the memory of Uluru's dry desert the memory too of the two rocks I found near the creek at my school as a child was also nestled. The heat that scared me into dropping those rocks seemed to have stayed with me and was now burning my ear as the doctor delivered her deplorable diagnosis.

More than representing something "as old as time" the Uluru drawings seemed to me to be a pure expression of time itself, the achievement of duration. As I listened to the doctor explaining Lynda's cancer to me on a phone in New York in August 2000, I wanted to be like those pictures in the cave. To be not "on" or "in" time—mortal or immortal, finite or infinite—but somehow *of* time, part of its unwavering beat. The drawings on the caves in Uluru were probably not created with the idea that they would last for centuries. And probably what I saw was "curated," at least to a limited extent. And yet the drawings somehow remain visible in the general flow of time, registering still as some granulated sands deliberately shaped and set in a wave that keeps flowing.

But that day in New York on the phone with the doctor I was acting as Lynda's voice, mouthing the words in a script I could not read but could somehow decipher from the energy of her arm and from the love she had written all over me so many times before. I asked the questions I thought she wanted to know the answers to, even though she could not actually bear to hear a word the doctor said. Neither one of us acknowledged any mistakes— she kept writing and I kept pretending to read. The doctor's words poured into my ear and I flashed on the Mouse Trap from *Hamlet*—the poisoned death being poured into my ear. But I also thought of the story of the Virgin Mary, impregnated through the ear by the Holy Spirit, who later speaks in tongues. Lynda and I had had so many conversations about maternity, about getting pregnant, about adoption, about domesticity. But we also were in love with writing and reading and with something that flowed between us because of those acts. Like most privileged white women in late twentieth-century U.S. culture, we worried about the relationship between that potency and pregnancy, the relationship between the psychic and material demands of our work in relation to the surety of the demand within the maternal call. All this is in me as I watch Lynda write her sticky-notes that afternoon. She wrote so as not to listen; I pretended to read while not being able to see; and the doctor acted as if we'd all be fine.

Three months later Lynda was dead and my eye was healed although deeply, permanently, scarred. That scar is my gauze, the broken gaze that ruptured the form of expression of my love for Lynda. Even now, all these years later, I cannot claim to have the "requisite perspective" or even to be a reliable focalizer. All I can claim is that when we both were body and flesh we loved one way, and now that she is "between the body and the flesh" we love some other ways. I was lucky for a time to share her heart.

Lynda Hart: her name is what I offer to you now, a performative signature that is not mine to take or give. Or at least not in the economy of truth-telling most of us recognize. But I do it anyway, while inviting you to take it or give it too, as you like, as you love, as you breathe.

Works Cited

Auden, W. H. "In Memory of W. B. Yeats." *Collected Poems.* Ed. Edward Mendelson. New York: Vintage, 1991. 245.

Butler, Judith. "Gender Trouble, Feminist Theory, and Psychoanalytic Discourse." *Feminism / Postmodernism.* Ed. Linda J. Nicholson. Routledge 1990: 324-40.

———. "Imitation and Gender Insubordination." *The Lesbian and Gay Studies Reader.* Eds. Henry Abelove, Michèle Aina Barale, and David M. Halperin. Routledge, 1993: 307-20.

———. "Violence, Mourning, Politics." *Studies in Gender and Sexuality* 4.1 (2003): 9-37.

Fludernik, Monika. *Towards a "Natural" Narratology.* New York: Routledge, 1996.

Freud, Sigmund. "Mourning and Melancholia." (1917). *The Standard Edition of the Complete Psychological Works of Sigmund Freud.* Ed. and trans. James Strachey. London: Hogarth Press, 1966. 14: 243-58.

Gallop, Jane. *The Deaths of the Author: Reading and Writing in Time.* Durham: Duke UP, 2011.

Genette, Gérard. *Narrative Discourse: An Essay in Method.* Trans. J. E. Lewin. Ithaca; London: Cornell UP, 1980.

Hart, Lynda. *Between the Body and the Flesh: Performing Sadomasochism.* New York: Columbia UP, 1998.

Herman, David. "Hypothetical Focalization." *Narrative* 2.3 (1994): 230-53.

Huffer, Lynne. "'There Is No Gomorrah': Narrative Ethics in Feminist and Queer Theory." *differences: A Journal of Feminist Cultural Studies* 12.3 (Fall 2001): 1-32.

Lanser, Susan S. "Sexing the Narrative: Propriety, Desire, and the Engendering of Narratology." *Narrative* 3.1 (Jan. 1995): 85-94.

Phelan, Peggy. "Tenderness, For Lynda Hart." *Women and Performance: A Journal of Feminist Theory* (Lynda Myoun Hart Memorial Issue) 13.1: 25 (2002): 19-26.

Sedgwick, Eve Kosofsky. *A Dialogue on Love.* Boston: Beacon, 1999.

———. "Eulogy." *Women and Performance: A Journal of Feminist Theory* 13.1: 25 (2002): 233-35.

———. "A Poem Is Being Written." *Representations* 17 (1987): 110-43.

———. "White Glasses." *Tendencies:* Durham: Duke UP, 1993: 247-60.

Winterson, Jeanette. *Written on the Body.* New York: Knopf, 1993.

PART II

*I*ntersectional Narrative Theories

SUSAN STANFORD FRIEDMAN

Religion, Intersectionality, and Queer/Feminist Narrative Theory

The *Bildungsromane* of Ahdaf Soueif,
Leila Aboulela, and Randa Jarrar

> One could even say that intersectionality is the most important
> theoretical contribution that women's studies, in conjunction
> with related fields, has made so far.
>
> —Leslie McCall, "The Complexity of Intersectionality"

*L*eslie McCall claims central importance for intersectionality in a 2005 essay in *Signs*, arguably the most prominent journal in interdisciplinary feminist studies in the United States. Where, then, is intersectionality in queer/feminist narrative theory? At a forum on narrative theory at the 2010 Modern Language Association conference, Susan Sniader Lanser challenged narrative theorists to engage more substantially with the feminist concept of intersectionality for its rich potential for narratology in general and for queer/feminist narrative theory in particular.[1] Intersectionality is a key concept in locational feminist theory that emphasizes the differences among women resulting from the interactions of multiple systems of oppression. As a concept, it has greatly influenced feminist criticism, including the study of literary narratives. What Lanser asks for, however, is that narrative theory *per se* adapt intersectionality for examining the interaction of narrative form and content, for theorizing the *how* along with the *what* of literary narrative, the *discourse* as well as the *story*.

---

1. I adopt, throughout, this volume's linking of queer/feminist narrative theory, knowing that the distinctions are worth exploring but are beyond the scope of this essay.

I hope to answer Lanser's call within the context of a broader consideration of intersectionality. Why, I ask, has intersectionality as a theoretical concept and methodology in queer/feminist studies left out religion as a constitutive part of identity? As feminist theory, criticism, and activism evolved since the 1970s, gender analysis has gradually and often with much struggle expanded to include such other dimensions of identity as race, class, sexuality, nationality, postcolonialism, disability, and age. Religion is typically missing from this familiar list, which often ends with the proverbial "etc." or "and so forth" to indicate its potential for seemingly infinite growth.[2] But rather than simply adding religion, I argue that consideration of religion reveals a problem in intersectional theory more generally—namely its emphasis on systems of oppression in the formation of identity. In my view, it is no mere oversight that religion seldom appears in the iconic lists of intersectional axes of power. While religion often functions as a system of oppression, it also figures as a source of identity, community, and spirituality. This potentially positive dimension of religion is particularly evident in the female *Bildungsroman,* where religion can appear not just as another structure of women's subordination but as a generative dimension of the *Bildung* plot. Rethinking intersectionality through the lens of religion provides a potential pathway for queer/feminist narrative theory to engage more substantially with intersectional analysis of narrative.

To lay the groundwork for this potential, I begin with a brief discussion of intersectionality and religion, move to a provisional framework for understanding religion, and turn to the female *Bildungsroman* as a genre with which to test the incorporation of religion into an intersectional queer/feminist theory. A brief discussion of Ahdaf Soueif's *The Map of Love* (2000) precedes an intersectional reading of Leila Aboulela's *The Translator* (1999) and Randa Jarrar's *A Map of Home* (2008). These diasporic, Muslim *Bildungsromane,* I conclude, point the way toward integration of religion into an intersectional queer/feminist narrative theory and also a reconsideration of intersectionality's privileging of oppression as the primary focus of analysis.

Feminist Intersectionality and Religion

The legal scholar Kimberlé Crenshaw coined the term *intersectionality* in 1989 to characterize the dynamic interaction of racism and sexism as these

---

2. For an exception, see Wadsworth's discussion of intersectionality and religion in her specialized study of same-sex marriage controversies in California. Without reference to intersectionality, Fiorenza integrates religion into an intersectional analysis and Crowley and Maparyan call for attention to religion and spirituality.

structures of oppression shape the lives of black women. Her neologism crystallized the insistence by feminists of color since the late 1960s that gender oppression never exists in isolation from other axes of power like race and class. Influenced by such feminist theorists as Audre Lorde, Barbara Smith, the Combahee River Collective, and June Jordan, U.S. feminist theory by the 1980s had developed concepts of multiple oppression, locationality, and positionality to account for the differences among women produced by the intersections of different structures of oppression. The term *intersectionality* caught on like wildfire to signify both a theory and a methodology for feminist analysis, one that incorporates but goes well beyond Crenshaw's original focus on black women and women of color. As feminist postcolonial studies, disability studies, queer theory, and transnational studies developed in the 1990s, more categories were added to the intersectional matrix. Now widely used across the disciplines, intersectionality is touted as providing a flexible model for understanding the dynamic, relational, and situational formation of individual and collective identities within multiple and interactive structures of oppression.[3] The editors' introduction to the 2007 special forum of *Politics and Gender* on intersectionality articulates the prevailing view in feminist theory that *intersectionality* allows us to "confront interlocking systems of oppression . . . [by placing] special emphasis on the simultaneity of oppression . . . and the need to move beyond simple, additive models" (264–65).

An expansive and ever-expanding *intersectionality* has become what Kathy Davis calls a "a feminist success story" and, as such, a "buzzword" that is ambiguous and open-ended.[4] *Intersectionality*'s very success revved the engines of critique in feminist theory's persistent drive for self-reflexive reinvention. The term's spread led to charges of vagueness, confusion, expansionism, and tokenism. Some believe it conflates or inadequately considers individual identity and social structures. Others question whether it involves an additive or a genuinely integrative approach. Some query whether it is a paradigm, heuristic, process, strategy, or methodology. Others charge that it has no methodology and is particularly unsuited for empirical research. Still others find it static, tending to conflate the differences between racism,

---

3. See for example the special issues on intersectionality of *The European Journal of Women's Studies* (2006) and of *Politics & Gender* (2006) and the Routledge book series "Routledge Advances in Feminist Studies and Intersectionality." On the centrality of intersectionality, see Berger and Guidroz; Hawkesworth; Lykke; May in Orr, Braithwaite, and Lichtenstein, pp. 183–202; and Smith. Robyn Wiegman's *Object Lessons* provides an extended genealogy of the term and debates about it (239–300).

4. For other substantive discussions of intersectionality, see for example Choo and Ferree; Hancock; Ludvig; McCall; and Yuval-Davis.

sexism, and class as structures of oppression. And still others debate whether it should be limited to race, class, and gender or expanded to include other oppressions.[5]

None of these critiques, however, mentions the overwhelming absence of religion from discourses of intersectionality. And none probes the possible limitations of the concept's privileging of oppression as the foundational component of intersectional analysis. Feminist scholars, theologians, and activists have not, of course, ignored religion; vibrant studies of gender and religion have existed for decades, frequently in tandem with dramatic advocacy for institutional change within and across religions.[6] What is missing is systematic consideration of religion in theories and practice of intersectionality. Nina Lykke's "broad, umbrella-like definition" of intersectionality in *Feminist Studies: A Guide to Intersectional Theory, Methodology, and Writing*, for example, is as significant for what it leaves out as for what it includes:

> According to this definition, intersectionality can, first of all, be considered as a theoretical and methodological tool to analyze how historically specific kinds of power differentials and/or constraining normativities, based on discursively, institutionally and/or structurally constructed socio-cultural categorizations such as gender, ethnicity, race, class, sexuality, age/generation, dis/ability, nationality, mother tongue and so on, interact, and in so doing produce different kinds of societal inequalities and unjust social relations. (50)

Religion is perhaps implicitly included in Lykke's "and so on," but uneasily so because religion as a component of communal or individual identity cannot so easily be confined to "power differentials" or "normativities"—in short, to structures of inequality and injustice, or narratives of oppression and resistance. Religion is the elephant in the room of intersectionality.

Religion has often been deployed to oppress groups of people such as women, racial or ethnic minorities, or members of other religions. Conversely, religion has often played a vital role in resistance to oppression. But issues of religion are not *always* about power. Religion is often a site of complex negotiation that isn't fully explained by a binarist model of oppression/resistance. In particular, the spiritual, psychological, and even bodily dimensions of religious belief, practice, and communal belonging are significantly different from, though entangled with, other constituents of identity such

---

5. For critiques or discussions of attacks on *intersectionality*, see especially Davis 68–69, 75–76; Lykke 8; Ludvig 246–48; McCall 1772–73; Phoenix and Pattynama 187–89; Wiegman 239–300; and Yuval-Davis.

6. For a sampling, see for example Castelli's *Women, Gender, Religion: A Reader*.

as race, class, sexuality, or national origin. Analysis of these *axes of power* in intersectional analysis is important, but an exclusive focus on oppression potentially suppresses more positive dimensions of religious identity. I suggest that we develop a discourse of the intersecting *axes of difference* in thinking about the entanglements of multiple dimensions of identity (individual and communal). And I suggest we do so in a transformational rather than additive way. To echo a familiar feminist dictum: you can't just add religion to the intersectional pot and stir. Consideration of religion potentially changes the pot. More broadly, it shifts intersectionality's theoretical emphasis on oppression to recognize the creative agencies inherent in identity.

A Provisional Framework for Thinking about Religion

What is religion, and how should we think about it? An intersectional queer/feminist narrative theory incorporating religion requires a provisional framework for inquiry about religion *per se,* one that includes more than one given religion or disciplinary approach. I find it useful to posit that all religions have three interlocking, yet distinctive aspects—the theological, the cultural, and the institutional—each of which changes over time, varies by region, and contains heterogeneities within. By *theological,* I mean the particular beliefs, creeds, and doctrinal tenets of a religion, often embedded in sacred texts, oral traditions, music, and dance; often subjected to much commentary, interpretation, and contestation. By the *cultural,* I mean the communal rites, rituals, and practices of a religion that take part within the larger collective of people who identify or can be identified with the religion. By the *institutional,* I mean the political, economic, educational, and spatio/temporal manifestations of a religion, incorporating the hierarchies within a given religion as well as the conflict between or cooperation of one with other religions. The theological, cultural, and institutional aspects of religion take shape in relation to each other—dynamically and interactively, hardly separable in actual instances of religious belief, practice, or institutional formation. Ideally, we need an interdisciplinary framework for thinking about religion's part in feminist intersectionality.[7]

Consideration of the theological, cultural, and institutional aspects of religion gains greater precision in the context of what I provisionally designate as ten key dimensions of religious formations worldwide and through time. I

---

7. For other overviews of religion, see Asad; Braun and McCutcheon; Strenski; Taylor; Wilcox. For sociological, psychological, and anthropological approaches to religion, Durkheim, Freud, and Geertz have been foundational.

suggest that we remain alert to these dimensions, using them as touchstones for a feminist intersectionality incorporating religion and consequently for a queer/feminist narrative theory.

1. Most—if not all—religions assume or promote belief in or adherence to a set of ideas and practices, often involving one or more spiritual forces that influence human life and embody a sense of the sacred to which people may appeal for help, guidance, or protection or toward which people feel love, passion, or fear. Such belief systems typically incorporate a defining ethos, morality, and/or rules for how to live, die, behave, and relate to others in daily life. This aspect of religion takes on distinctive shapes in both "high" or official culture and "low" or popular culture—the one performed by religious authorities in prescribed settings; the other, by ordinary people in their everyday lives.

2. Religions rely upon specific linguistic, representational, and expressive forms that embody the theologies of the sacred and engage the human imagination, mind, and senses. These may be narrative, symbolic, lyric, dramatic; oral, visual, written, performed; and kinetic, touch or taste related. Religion, in short, engages the representational and the symbolic at the same time that it is experienced through the body.

3. Religions designate certain people as religious authorities, putting them in charge of religious community, sites, rituals, education, and theological interpretation of sacred texts, oral traditions, and sacred objects.

4. Religions typically treat certain spaces as sacred, establishing practices or rules about them; they theorize time in linear, cyclical, or transcendent modes.

5. Religions are not static, monolithic, or homogeneous, however much they might claim to be. They are heterogeneous, fluid, ever-changing, typically exhibiting a dynamic tension between continuity and change, traditionalism and reform.

6. Religions are syncretist, absorbing elements of earlier religions or blending beliefs and practices from other religions or cultural values.

7. Religion is a contradictory site of community and perpetual conflict— sometimes violent, sometimes peaceful. Contestation between religions as well as within any given religion appears to be inevitable, if not constitutive. Individuals or subgroups within a religion often practice or believe in the religion differently. Such variations account for much conflict but are also part of religion's dynamism and capacity to change, as well as the agency of people within it.

8. While religion is practiced primarily in local and communal settings, it is also variously translocal, transnational, or even global in scope. Some religions link multiple communities into a larger religious identification; some take form as diasporic dispersions; and some promote conversion worldwide, aiming for a transnational community of members.

9. Religion often has a particular relationship to state power, even as it might transcend national borders. States—from the imperial to the autocratic or the democratic—often associate themselves with a particular religion or deploy religion as a rationalization for or mechanism of rule.

10. The world religions—with the possible exception of Animism—produce a range of orthodoxies and heterodoxies with a spectrum between extremes along which individuals and communities place themselves or are placed. One such spectrum runs between the fundamentalist, legalistic, and literalist pole on one hand and the personal, symbolic, and mystical on the other. The fundamentalist pole establishes an inside/outside of believers/infidels, or believers/apostates, a binary policed by religious authorities and based on an assertion of one religion as the sole source of spiritual truth and salvation. The mystical pole emphasizes direct experience of the spiritual, often unmediated by religious authorities and willing to accept the legitimacy of other religious pathways to the divine.

Religion, the *Bildungsroman,* and Ahdaf Soueif's *The Map of Love*

How then do the theological, cultural, and institutional formations of religion as I have sketched them assist in the development of an intersectional queer/feminist narrative theory? For sure, I do not mean to sideline attention to narrative structures of oppression and resistance by integrating religion into intersectionality. Religion as institutionalized oppression or the cultural practice of resistance has generated many agonistic narrative forms. Toni Morrison's *Beloved,* for example, contrasts the slave-owners' theologically and institutionally sanctioned use of Christianity to justify the dehumanization of African Americans with the slave and former slave's defiant retention of West African religious practices to enable their survival and healing. But integrating religion into the intersectional matrix of identities requires thinking beyond an exclusive focus on power relations—power over and power against.

The *Bildungsroman* offers a specific testing ground for an intersectional queer/feminist narrative theory in which religion generates narrative structures well outside the agonistic patterns of oppression and resistance. The *Bildungsroman* featuring a woman protagonist, it should be remembered, was a rich resource for early feminist narratology, which emphasized the difference gender makes in the *Bildungsroman*'s developmental plots, particularly the genre's conventional patterns of male initiation into adult sexuality and vocation and eventual integration into family, community, and nation. Subsequently, queer/feminist narrative theory moved from a focus on gender in *Bildung* plots to its intersection with other constituents of identity such as race, sexuality, class, nationality, migration, and disability.[8] I suggest here that queer/feminist narrative theory examine the difference religion makes to intersectional approaches to *Bildung* plots.

Religion as a component of *Bildung* requires more than the addition of theological, cultural, and institutional power relations to an intersectional analysis of the narrative. Instead, religion plays a potentially complex and contradictory role in the protagonist's developing identity—that is, her sexual, vocational, and spiritual growth as well as her sense of new belonging in family, community, and nation. In conjunction with other components of identity, different aspects of religion might inhibit her *Bildung*; others might generate or enable it.

Contemporary Muslim migration *Bildungsromane* provide a telling case in point, especially because of the complex mix of geopolitics, racialization, and gender issues that swirl around the issue of Islam in the twenty-first century. Binarist oppositions based predominantly on power relations—for example, East/West, Islam/secularism, modernity/tradition, patriarchy/feminism—don't explain the *Bildung* plots. Writing against Western stereotypes of Islam as singularly oppressive for women, Muslim authors often highlight religion as a central element of *Bildung*, engaging with gender inequities but never reducing religion to questions of power, and seldom rejecting it entirely. Instead, religion—especially a modified practice of religion—is generative; it provides the *Bildung* plot's kinetic movement as it intersects with other dimensions of communal and individual identity.

Consider briefly Ahdaf Soueif's *The Map of Love*, a Man Booker Prize finalist published in 2000 with over a million copies sold and translated into

---

8. For three early influential studies, see *The Voyage In* (Abel et al.); *Writing Beyond the Ending* (DuPlessis); and *Unbecoming Women* (Fraiman); see Fuderer and Millard for more recent overviews. For studies of the genre integrating gender analysis with race, ethnicity, class, and diaspora, see Bolaki; Feng; Jain; and Mullaney. See also Esty; McWilliams; and Moretti on the *Bildungsroman*.

many languages.[9] As a narrative that reconstructs historical memory as the foundation for *Bildung,* the novel features American and Egyptian cousins in the present day uncovering their forgotten family history of intermarriage—English–Egyptian; Christian–Muslim—against the backdrop of the British Empire in Egypt, the Ottoman Empire, the Egyptian Independence movement of the late nineteenth- / early twentieth-century, and contemporary East–West conflict. Three interconnected female *Bildung* plots structure the novel: the American Isabel searching for her Anglo-Egyptian roots; her newly discovered Egyptian cousin Amal uncovering forgotten family history; and their shared English ancestor, Anna Winterbourne, moving from the restrictions of Edwardian widowhood to the freedom of marriage to a Muslim Egyptian. It is Anna's story in the early twentieth century that Isabel and Amal reconstruct.

A focus on gender oppression within religion would yield little understanding of *The Map of Love.* But the intersections of religion with gender, class, and colonialism are central. Anna's early twentieth-century *Bildung,* for example, involves her willing conversion to Islam, acceptance of veiling and seclusion to the women's quarters, and recognition of the paradoxically greater freedoms and political involvements open to her in Egypt than she had in England as the upper-middle-class war widow of a colonial agent. Instead of focusing on women's oppression within Islam, Soueif's narrative explores the complex role of gender in the emergent modernity of colonial Egypt. We learn as Anna learns how British colonizers justified their rule as civilizing agents through their condemnation of the veil at the same time that Egyptian reformers pushed for both independence and education for women. The novel also engages with many aspects of religion for which gender remains a part of the story, but not centrally so. Personal, political, and religious allegories of a transnational and religiously syncretist love appear as central both to the advancing modernities of women in England and Egypt and to the lives of their descendants in the late twentieth century. *The Map of Love* is suffused with a feminist sensibility, but one of a particular kind in which religion figures centrally and positively.

The novel's major trope—a three-paneled tapestry that Anna completed before she left Egypt with her young daughter after the assassination of her husband Sharif—embodies the significance of religion in the *Bildung* plot that reunites the diasporic family and assists in the reconstruction of familial and

---

9. Born and educated in Cairo, Soueif got her Ph.D. in Britain, where she now lives and works as a writer, translator, and organizer for Amnesty International, the Caine Prize in African literature, and the Palestinian Festival of Literature.

national histories. Symbolizing the divisions of families, nations, and religions as the legacy of empire, the tapestry's three parts are separated after the murder of Sharif. The first panel, which Isabel inherited from her mother, features Isis; the second, which Amal's brother Omar got from their mother (Layla, Anna's sister-in-law), depicts Osiris; and the third, representing their son Horus, disappears mysteriously, secretly preserved by the family's Ethiopian maid. Each panel contains part of a verse from the Qur'an: "From the dead come the living," a verse that blends the Isis religion with Islam and Christianity. In the novel's magic-realist denouement, Isabel mysteriously finds the third panel in her camera bag amidst the faint smell of orange blossoms, enabling her to unite the tapestry and read its full Isisian-Islamic-Christian message of rebirth.

The religion that enables Isabel's *Bildung* plot exists outside the institutional confines and dogma of orthodoxy, a cultural practice of religion signaled by the novel's privileging of Sufism, the mystical dimension of Islam. Isobel believes that the reunion of the sundered parts of the tapestry results from her visit to a Sufi shrine at Anna's old home, where a woman in blue who smells of orange blossoms leads her to a young mystic saint. When Isabel takes Amal back to the shrine, they find it sealed, but Isabel believes that the woman in blue put the third panel of Horus in her camera bag. The syncretist blending of religious theology, practice, and mysticism in the story of the tapestry signals the fulfillment of the complex, interlocking *Bildung* plots. In *The Map of Love*, religion drives the narrative, not as one of many intersecting oppressions, but as a spiritually enlightening dimension of *Bildung*s that are thoroughly entangled with issues of colonialism, nationality, gender, and class.

Bildung in Leila Aboulela's *The Translator* and Randa Jarrar's *A Map of Home*

Islam figures centrally in the *Bildung* plots of two other diasporic Muslim novels: Aboulela's *The Translator* and Jarrar's *A Map of Home*. A staged dialogue between them demonstrates how very different diasporic Muslim sensibilities—one pious, the other queer—share an exploration of religious identity as a generative component of *Bildung* within an intersectional matrix of gender, sexuality, migration, class, national identity, and religion.

Aboulela was born and educated in Khartoum, migrated to Aberdeen, Scotland, and published her first novel *The Translator* in 1999, and now lives mostly in Dubai.[10] Of Palestinian, Egyptian, and Greek heritage, Jarrar was

---

10. Aboulela published *Coloured Lights* (short stories) in 2001, *Minaret* (novel) in 2005, and *Lyrical Alley: A Novel* in 2011. Her short story "The Museum" in *Coloured Lights* won the

born in Chicago, grew up in Egypt, Kuwait, and New York City and published her first novel *A Map of Home* in 2008. Like Soueif's *The Map of Love,* the *Bildung* plots of these novels do not use religion to designate gender oppression but rather represent a particular relationship to religion as the linchpin of narrative development.

Aboulela's *The Translator* features Sammar, a Sudanese woman working as a translator in Aberdeen. She begins the novel in a state of complete emotional paralysis, frozen by the sudden death of her cousin-husband, a medical student from the Sudan who died in a car accident in Aberdeen five years before; the novel ends with her awakening as an independent woman. As we learn from Sammar's fragmentary memories, she had taken her husband's body and their baby son to her aunt/mother-in-law in Khartoum. In the face of her mother-in-law's recriminations and controlling behavior, she had returned to Aberdeen, where she now lives a lonely, hallucination-ridden, death-in-life for which Aberdeen's drear climate serves as objective correlative. Signaled by the return of colored head-scarves to her life, Sammar's awakening comes through the convergence of the courtship and conversion plots. Sammar and the non-Muslim professor for whom she translates Arabic texts gradually fall in love. Developing modestly on the phone, through sound without sight or touch, this new love unfreezes past memories, allowing Sammar's new growth to unfold through retrospective accounts to the professor of her past life (and his to her). Since Islam forbids women to marry outside the religion, she asks him to convert so that they can marry. But he refuses, and she angrily returns to Khartoum to a deadened life under her mother-in-law's corrosive rule. The professor's sudden appearance in Khartoum as a newly converted Muslim resolves the courtship plot, and the two set off for a married life in Aberdeen, where each recommits to being a translator of sorts and where they will touch for the first time. Like Soueif's *The Map of Love,* the intermarriage uses intimacy between two people to signify allegorical meanings about the relation between Islam and the West.

Jarrar's *A Map of Home* exhibits many of the narrative patterns of the classic female *Bildungsroman.* Where Sammar's future growth is partly retrospective, *A Map of Home* opens with the birth and naming of its protagonist, Nidali, and tracks her emergence out of the cocoon of family towards a life on her own in which she will fulfill her ambition to become a writer by penning the novel we are reading. Contrasting with Aboulela's tale of circular migration between two homes, *A Map of Home* recounts multiple migrations, conditioned first by Nidali's father's leaving Palestine for Egypt and his marriage to her mother, the daughter of a Greek Christian woman and a Muslim Egyp-

Caine Prize for African Literature, and her novels have been listed for the Orange Prize.

tian father. Nidali herself is born in Boston, but moves to Egypt, then Kuwait, then Egypt again, and finally Texas—each move determined by her father's status as a Palestinian refugee, at home nowhere, seeking education and economic opportunity in the face of statelessness and repeated expulsions. Over her mother's protestations, her father gave her a boy's name, Nidal, which means "resistance," forced her to have a boy's haircut, demanded that she aim her life toward getting a Ph.D., but beat her badly on numerous occasions, especially when he caught her with a boy or faced her disobedience. Her father's mixed messages on gender and sexuality are complemented by her mother's gift of Wonder Woman decals and her intermittent resistance to her husband, which most importantly takes the form of her obsessive piano playing. With an identity constantly on the move, Nidali comes to regard her "map of home" as a "blank page," a "whiteness on the page" (193) that she herself will fill, through syncretic mixing of the different cultures where she has lived. Her rebellious love–hate relations with her parents drive the narrative and underlie her experimentations with bisexuality and her ambitions to be a writer.

Islam is central to both *The Translator* and *A Map of Home*. But on the face of it, the novels could not be more different in their engagements with religion. Never challenging the theology or institutions of Islam, *The Translator* expresses a devout, highly observant Muslim perspective with its tale of heterosexual longings kept modestly offstage. *A Map of Home*, in contrast, violates the religious proprieties *The Translator* preserves as it presents a Muslim identity that exudes a secular spirit of irreverence, rampant desire, masturbatory pleasure, and bisexual experience narrated in graphic detail. *The Translator's* free indirect discourse centers in the mind of Sammar, punctuated by brief periods of dialogue. The novel's imagistic narrative symbolically relies on the sun, heat, cold, snow, and drought to render or comment upon the characters' interior states of mind. Its style is decorous, lyrical, imagistic, and at times surreal. *A Map of Home* relies on its first-person, naïve child narrator to produce a tone of outrageous excess, raunchy humor, and biting satire from which no group is immune, including pious Muslims. Jarrar's refusal of Muslim advocacy contrasts sharply with Aboulela's conversion narrative, which allegorically implies that Islam will bring spirituality to a sterile West. Whereas Nidali moves through a succession of male and female, Muslim and Christian adolescent lovers representing a queer, syncretist cultural stew, Sammar refuses to go out alone in public with the professor, unquestioningly believes in the Qur'an as divine revelation, and accepts the Islamic law that while Muslim men can marry outside the faith, Muslim women cannot.

The religious sensibilities of the novels are so different that they occupy quite distinctive points along a spectrum ranging from a secular Muslim identity to advocacy of Islam as a set of orthodox beliefs and religious practices determined by religious authority. These differences between the novels align quite predictably with a spectrum of views toward Islam among Muslim feminists. Jarrar, for example, is closer in spirit than Aboulela to the self-defined "Muslim Refusnik," Irshad Manji, the Canadian journalist and TV personality who wrote *The Trouble with Islam Today: A Muslim's Call for Reform in Her Faith.* As an immigrant to Canada from Uganda of South Asian heritage, Manji writes, "Most of us Muslims aren't Muslims because we think about it, but rather because we're born that way. It's 'who we are'" (16). Not a pure secularist, however, Manji wants her religion to reform its outdated and authoritarian practices, to make room for lesbians and feminists like herself, and to recognize the Qur'an as a text open to diverse interpretations.[11] Aboulela, on the other hand, is more attuned to the views of Zainah Anwar, a leader of a feminist group in Malaysia called Sisters in Islam. As observant Muslims, they advocate for women by taking up issues like education, employment, family practices, and violence against women. Above all, they insist upon women's right to interpret the Qur'an for themselves. "We are more convinced than ever that it is not Islam that oppresses women, but interpretations of the *Qur'an* influenced by the cultural practices and values of a patriarchal society that regards women as inferior and subordinate to men" (Anwar 238).

As different as Manji and Anwar are in relation to Islam, they share a belief in the significance of the *umma,* the worldwide collectivity of Muslims, they want women to have a more equitable place within the *umma,* and they challenge the male hierarchy of Islam to insist on the right of women to interpret and reinterpret the Qur'an in their own ways. Like many Muslim feminists, they reinvigorate the early Islamic tradition of *ijtihad;* that is, the reasoned interpretation of the Qur'an contrasted with readings based on tradition and authority.[12] This common ground between otherwise quite different Muslim feminists like Manji and Anwar helps bring into focus what *The Translator* and *A Map of Home* share. In short, both novels make key aspects of Islam defining moments in the *Bildung* of their protagonists. And both challenge a legalistic, authority-based view of Islam to insist that women directly engage with the spirit of Islam, not just its ritual practices or authorities.

---

11. Manji and Jarrar refer to Islam's sacred book as the Koran; Soueif and Aboulela follow the alternate convention of referencing the Qur'an, as do I.

12. See Anwar; Barlas; Wadud.

The Translator, Islam, and the Marriage Plot

As the *Bildung* plot unfolds, *The Translator* narrates the individual's relationship to Islam by opening up an ironic gap between Aboulela, the writer, and Sammar, whose past and present reveal an insecure woman whose life others have always controlled. She has much to learn about not defining her worth solely through marriage, a *Bildung* plot that hinges centrally on her relationship to Islam. As a widowed woman and migrant, Sammar is carefully observant of Islamic law and practices, but to grow as a woman she must learn the importance of a personal, spiritual relationship to Allah, the Five Pillars of Islam, and the Qur'an. The resolution of the conversion plot and the marriage plot depends upon Sammar's greater understanding of Islam's spiritual dimension, an understanding that can develop only with her learning to become an independent woman, not solely dependent on marriage for fulfillment.

The key scene that encapsulates these issues narrates Sammar's plea that the professor, aptly named Rae Isles, convert to Islam so that they can be married. As a professor of Middle East studies, Rae knows all about Islam, but has kept his distance from the religion, believing that his work explaining the Middle East will have more credibility if he remains "objective" and "detached" (114). Sammar is outraged by this distanced relationship, claiming that he puts himself "above all of this, above me, looking down" when he knows very well that Islam "is for everyone . . . not just Arabs" (114). What he denies by refusing to convert, in her view, is a recognition that the Qur'an "was the miracle that Muhammad, peace be upon him, was sent with. And it's different from the miracle of the other Prophets because it's still with us now" (111). What Sammar alludes to is Islam's recognition of the Jewish and Christian prophets before Muhammad, but the belief by some Muslims, particularly those on the orthodox side of the spectrum, that Islam represents the perfected endpoint of the Abrahamic religions, and thus the only religion with the supreme truth.[13] Sammar wants Rae to convert because she believes that the Qur'an is divinely inspired and that Islam is the one, true religion. Sammar's faith in the absolute truth of Islam becomes evident as she explains to Rae the *shahadah,* the first of the Five Pillars of Islam, a scene in which the ironic gap between Sammar and Aboulela is at its widest. Taken from the *Hadith,* the sacred texts recording the sayings of Muhammad, the *shahadah*

---

13. See, for example, the self-styled Islamic "traditionalist," but not fundamentalist, Seyyed Hossein Nasr, whose influential overview of Islam ambivalently expresses a commitment to interfaith dialogue and yet certainty that Islam represents the superior fulfillment of the earlier Abrahamic religions.

alludes to the statement of belief that Muslims are required to make in prayer, a statement that also accomplishes conversion if said publicly and with sincerity. As Sammar explains to Rae, "It's two things together, both beginning with the words, 'I bear witness.' . . . There is no god except Allah, nothing else is worthy of worship. That's the first thing . . ." (111; second ellipsis in original). "Then the second thing . . . ," she continues. "I bear witness that Muhammad is His messenger" (111; ellipsis in original). At her request that he say the *shahadah,* he refuses, clearly in distress, saying, "It's not in me to be religious" (113). Sammar then asks Rae to just go through the motions, just say the words without believing them so that they can marry. Their exchange ironizes Sammar's relationship to Islam and uses Rae's response as a non-Muslim to point out the relationship to Islam she must learn to acquire:

> "If you say the *shahadah* it would be enough. We could get married. If you just say the words . . ."
>
> "I have to be sure. I would despise myself if I wasn't sure."
>
> "But people get married that way. Here in Aberdeen there are people who got married like this . . ."
>
> "We're not like that. You and I are different. For them it is a token gesture."
>
> She thought, it is clear now, it is so clear, he does not love me, I am not beautiful enough. I am not feminine enough. . . . (115; ellipses in original)

Sammar's desire for marriage at all costs and her belief that Rae's refusal to convert is a rejection of her womanhood not only perverts the spiritual meaning of the *shahadah* but also demonstrates her dependence on marriage for legitimation. Ironically, in refusing to convert without sincerity, Rae demonstrates a relationship to religion, one based on personal belief and honesty, that Sammar needs to learn. That she cruelly curses him to live a life forever alone and lonely reinforces Aboulela's point that in insisting on the letter of Islamic law without its spirit, Sammar has lost her way as both a Muslim and a woman. Aboulela's critical stance toward her protagonist at this moment of the narrative identifies the author's position on the spectrum of Muslim feminisms: advocating for the independence of women who submit not to men or marriage but to Allah as a devout Muslim attuned to the spirit of the law.

Sammar's *Bildung,* and the resolution of the marriage/conversion plot, unfolds after her return to Khartoum. There, she faces the same recriminations from her aunt/mother-in-law, keeps longing for a letter from Rae, experiences dreams and hallucinations, and sleepwalks through the days and nights in a state of anguish and paralysis—all uncanny repetitions of her life in Aberdeen before Rae came into it. What moves Sammar beyond this state of repetition is memories of conversations with Rae and their growing love. These recapitulations enable her to see her request that he say the *shahadah* in a new light. Her plea was not about Rae and the state of his soul, she realizes, but all about her need to be someone's wife:

> She had never, not once, prayed that he would become a Muslim for his own sake, for his own good. It had always been for herself, her need to get married again, not be alone. If she could rise above that, if she would clean her intentions. . . . She would do it now from far away without him ever knowing. (160)

It is this realization that eventually leads her out of the morass, into a second awakening. Accepting herself as a woman without marriage in this life, she thinks of Paradise: "What kept her going day after day: he would become a Muslim before he died. It was not too much to want, not too much to pray for. They would meet in Paradise and nothing would go wrong there, nothing at all" (168). In becoming the kind of Muslim the novel privileges, a woman whose relationship to God is based in the spirit of Islam, Sammar has fully awakened as a woman and a believer. The narrative rewards this personal mode of religion by having Rae recite the *shahadah* with sincerity and then seek her in Khartoum.

A Map of Home, the Qur'an, and the *Bildung* Plot

In contrast to *The Translator*, *A Map of Home* plays with the trope of the veil to violate Islamic principles of female modesty—as a book, it explicitly uncovers the female body and desire, including masturbatory, lesbian, and bisexual desire. As such, it queers the kind of pious relationship to Islamic theology, cultural practice, and institutional authority that *The Translator* advocates. Nonetheless, *A Map of Home* does not represent a purely secular position on the spectrum of Muslim feminisms. The Qur'an frequently appears in the narrative as a positive source of meaning, with different *suras* or verses directly cited or echoed. More centrally, portions of the Qur'an play a causal role in the *Bildung* plot, especially in the framing chapters of the novel.

Chapters 1 and 2, entitled "Our Given Names" and "Comfort," feature interwoven stories about Nidali's name, baby brother, parents' courtship, "boy" haircut, and early questions about religion. The centerpiece of these stories is a narrative that unites the theological, cultural, and institutional dimensions of religion: Nidali's determination to win the Qur'an recitation contest at the Kuwait City Boys School, restricted by convention though not by religious law to boys. To participate, she agrees to cover her hair, even though her father screams, "Forget those retarded idiots! You must be cleansed to read the Koran, but no one ever said you had to be covered" (48–49). Studying with her father angers him even more, leading him to mock her mistakes and whip her with a hanger in a frenzy of anger at her imperfection (50).

The story so far, with its echo of the Qur'an's legitimation in *sura* 4:34 of men beating women, appears to reinforce the notion of Islam as a religion that oppresses women. But Jarrar swerves away from this view as the story continues. At the contest, Nidali recites her *sura* without mistakes and with great feeling—"as though I was singing" (50–51). "Thank you, sister," said the iman, as he "bowed his head" (51). Not only does she win the contest but the last lines of the *sura* she recites also represent one of the novel's core values: "*For with every hardship there is ease. With every hardship there is ease. When your prayers are ended resume your toil, and seek your lord with all fervor*" (51). This *sura* provides Nidali comfort and ballast to the unfolding stories of hardship from wars at home and between nations.

The novel's final moment returns again to the Qur'an, this time in connection with Nidali's conviction of her future as a writer as she defiantly leaves for a college far from her parents. Here, Islam and vocation conjoin to compel Nidali to write, but to write without forgetting her "map of home," defined in the diasporic plot of the novel as a site of memory and imagination rather than a geographical place. As she packs, her mother brings her a bundle of papers, everything that Nidali had ever written, and says: "These are your writings. . . . These are your words. You will be a writer, no? You must keep all this for posterity. I want you to write" (289; ellipses in text). Nidali understands that she has inherited her mother's commitment to art in the face of all who would silence her, most especially Baba. Her mother's request enjoins her, "Don't you ever, ever, in your life, *umrik*, ever, ever . . . ever forget us" (289; ellipses in text). Jarrar's possible echo of Sandra Cisneros's *House on Mango Street* recalls the one-eyed old woman who tells Esperanza, also a writer in formation: "When you leave you must remember to come back for the others. A circle, understand? . . . You must remember to come back. For the ones who cannot leave as easily as you" (105). But where Cisneros's appeal to the young writer to remember her culture and family is entirely secular, Jarrar swerves without segue from the lines paralleling Cisneros into the Qur'an, citing the opening of the 31st *sura* known as The Pen or the *Luqman* verse: "By the pen, and what they write, you are not mad: thanks to the favor of your Lord!" (288). The pen reminds Nidali of an indestructible pen that a woman gave Baba on a flight from Amman to Kuwait. Over his protestations, Mama was sure the pen was a spy pen, but when beating the pen with a hammer left it intact, the family drove into the woods together to throw it away. The novel concludes with these lines:

> Baba recited from *Luqman*, "If all the trees on the earth were pens, and the sea, replenished by seven more seas, were ink, the words of God could not be finished still."
> Mama reached over and threw the pen out the window.
>
> I catch the pen now and listen to all our stories. (290; spacing in original)

The indestructible writer's pen, with which Nidali will write the stories that map her home, is a pen bequeathed by her mother and father and is resonant with a Qur'anic passage on God as a wielder of pen and ink, making a world that is still in the process of creation. As catcher of the pen, Nidali is not so much God's replacement—the artist as God—but rather God's instrument, a pen, a specifically female pen contributing her part in the larger process of God's unending creation of the universe. Intersecting with this theological resonance is the association of the artist's pen with the phallus, evident in Sandra M. Gilbert and Susan Gubar's famous question about phallocentric poetics: "If the pen is the metaphorical penis, with what organ can females generate texts?" (7). As a queer protagonist in a female body with a boy's name and haircut, Nidali appropriates the phallic pen to write, legitimated through the lines of the *Luqman sura* from the Qur'an. Consistent broadly speaking with Muslim feminists' appropriation of the concept of *ijtihad,* Jarrar's use of the Qur'an in the *Bildung* plot emphasizes Nidali's personal engagement with the sacred text that she makes her own.

Different as the novels are, both *The Translator* and *A Map of Home* show how the *Bildung* narratives of their female protagonists emerge out of the entanglements of religion with family, sexuality, vocation, class, and migration. For both, the sacred texts and practices of Islam and the transnational community of the *umma* have a continuing importance to growth. For both, the narrative emphasis is on a woman's independent and personal relationship to those texts and to God, a relationship that is not mediated by male clerics or by *shari'a.* Jarrar's novel certainly stretches Islam far more than Aboulela's and retreats from daily ritual observance. We can imagine Sammar and Rae praying five times a day, for example, but not Nidali. Jarrar's Islam resists the strictures of female modesty while Aboulela's affirms them in both story and performative discourse. And that difference is significant. Equally striking is the tolerance of other religions in *A Map of Home* in contrast to the privileging of Islam in *The Translator*. These novels belong at different points on the spectrum between orthodox and heterodox, between fundamentalism and secularism, that I outlined above. The protagonists engage differently with theological, cultural, and institutional dimensions of their religion, contrasting stances toward religion that alter the meaning of community, exile, and migration in the *Bildung* plot.

Conclusion

Queer/feminist narrative theory, I have argued, needs to incorporate intersectionality as concept, heuristic, and methodological strategy, particularly as it deals with narratives of communal and individual identity. In doing so, it should include religion in the intersectional matrix of other identity components whenever the entangled theological, cultural, or institutional aspects of religion enter the story. The *Bildungsromane* of three contemporary diasporic Muslim writers demonstrate the difference religion can make to an intersectional queer/feminist narrative theory and by extension to the concept of intersectionality itself. As different as Soueif's *The Map of Love*, Aboulela's *The Translator*, and Jarrar's *A Map of Home* are in their engagements with religion—mystical and syncretist; piously Islamic; and queerly Muslim—each shows that religion can function as a causal component of narrative becoming, not solely as a restrictive axis of power. Taken together, they demonstrate how *Bildung* plots integrate the complex, often contradictory components of identity into narratives of becoming, how intersectional identities (individual and plural) generate patterns of mobility and resolution that are variously teleological or open-ended.

Queer/feminist narrative theory and feminist intersectionality more generally will benefit from bringing into visibility that elephant in the room—namely religion (as well as the secularism that forms in relation to it). While the significance of religion for Muslim *Bildungsromane* published within a decade of 9/11 hardly needs defense, I want to argue more broadly for a thorough integration of religion into intersectional analysis because religion—whether for good or evil—has so often in human history been a major touchstone for communal and individual identities, for human spirituality and cultural practice, for societal structures and ethos, for war and peace. As such, queer/feminist narrative theory—whatever its period or region—needs to develop systematic ways of integrating religion into its intersectional analysis. Even more broadly, the introduction of religion into intersectionality suggests that the term's heavy, if not exclusive, emphasis on oppression needs rethinking in relation to other dimensions of identity. "Race" is not *always* about racism, any more than Judaism is always about anti-Semitism, or "queerness" is always about heteronormativity, or "gender" is always about sexism. Whether individual or communal, identity is never constituted solely through oppression. Putting "religion" into intersectionality's unfilled slot of "etc." and "so forth" helps us see the need for a fundamental shift in the concept of intersectionality itself, a shift in which interlocking oppressions remain an issue, but not exclusively so.

Works Cited

Abel, Elizabeth, Marianne Hirsch, and Elizabeth Langland, eds. *The Voyage In: Fictions of Female Development.* Hanover: UP of New England, 1983.

Aboulela, Leila. *Coloured Lights.* London: Polygon, 2001.

———. *Lyric Alley.* New York: Grove Press, 2011.

———. *Minaret.* New York: Grove Press, 2005.

———. *The Translator.* 1999. New York: Grove Press, 2006.

Anwar, Zainah. "Sisters in Islam and the Struggle for Women's Rights." *On Shifting Grounds: Muslim Women in the Global Era.* Ed. Fereshteh Nouraie-Simone. New York: Feminist Press, 2005. 233–47.

Asad, Talal. *Genealogies of Religion: Discipline and Reasons of Power in Christianity and Islam.* Baltimore: Johns Hopkins UP, 1991.

Barlas, Asma. *"Believing Women" in Islam: Unreading Patriarchal Interpretations of the Qur'an.* Austen: U of Texas P, 2002.

Berger, Michele Tracy, and Kathleen Guidroz, eds. *The Intersectional Approach: Transforming the Academy through Race, Class, and Gender.* Durham: U of North Carolina P, 2010.

Bolaki, Stella. *Unsettling the Bildungsroman: Reading Contemporary Ethnic America.* Amsterdam: Rodopi, 1994.

Braun, Willi, and Russell T. McCutcheon, eds. *Guide to the Study of Religion.* London: Cassell, 2000.

Castelli, Elizabeth A., ed. *Women, Gender, Religion: A Reader.* New York: Palgrave, 2001.

Choo, Hae Yeon, and Myra Marx Ferree. "Practicing Intersectionality in Sociological Research: A Critical Analysis of Inclusions, Interactions, and Institutions in the Study of Inequalities." *Sociological Theory* 28.2 (June 2010): 129–49.

Cisneros, Sandra. *The House on Mango Street.* New York: Vintage, 1989.

Crenshaw, Kimberlé. "Demarginalizing the Intersection of Race and Sex: A Black Feminist Critique of Antidiscrimination Doctrine, Feminist Theory and Antiracist Politics." *University of Chicago Legal Forum* 4 (1989): 139–67.

———. "Mapping the Margins: Intersectionality, Identity Politics, and Violence Against Women of Color." *Stanford Law Review* 43.6 (July 1991): 1241–99.

Crowley, Karlyn. "Secularity." Orr, Braithwaite, and Lichtenstein. 283–302.

Davis, Kathy. "Intersectionality as Buzzword: A Sociology of Science Perspective on What Makes a Feminist Theory Successful." *Feminist Theory* 9.1 (2008): 67–85.

DuPlessis, Rachel Blau. *Writing Beyond the Ending: Narrative Strategies in Twentieth-Century Women Writers.* Bloomington: Indiana UP, 1985.

Durkheim, Émile. *The Elementary Forms of the Religious Life.* 1912. Trans. Carol Closman. New York: Oxford UP, 2001.

Esty, Jed. *Unseasonable Youth: Modernism, Colonialism, and the Fiction of Development.* Oxford: Oxford UP, 2011.

European Journal of Women's Studies. Special Issue on Intersectionality 13.3 (2006).

Feng, Pin-chia. *The Female Bildungsroman by Toni Morrison and Maxine Hong Kingston: A Postmodern Reading.* New York: Peter Lang, 1997.

Fiorenza, Elisabeth Schüssler. *Wisdom Ways: Introducing Feminist Biblical Interpretation.* Maryknoll, NY: Orbis, 2001.

Fraiman, Susan. *Unbecoming Women: British Women Writers and the Novel of Development.* New York: Columbia UP, 1993.

Freud, Sigmund. *The Future of an Illusion.* 1928. New York: Broadview, 2012.

Fuderer, Laura Sue. *The Female Bildungsroman in English: An Annotated Bibliography of Criticism.* New York: Modern Language Association of America, 1990.

Geertz, Clifford. "Religion as a Cultural System." *Anthropological Approaches to the Study of Religion.* Ed. M. Blanton. London: Tavistock, 1966. 1–46.

Gilbert, Sandra M., and Susan Gubar. *Madwoman in the Attic: The Woman Writer and the Nineteenth-Century Literary Imagination.* New Haven: Yale UP, 1979.

Hancock, Mange-Marie. "When Multiplication Doesn't Equal Quick Addition: Examining Intersectionality as a Research Paradigm." *Politics & Gender* 5.1 (March 2007): 63–79.

Hawkesworth, Mary. "Intersectionality." *Feminist Inquiry: From Political Conviction to Methodological Innovation.* New Brunswick: Rutgers UP, 2006. 207–48.

Jain, Anupama. *How To Be South Asian in America: Narratives of Ambivalence and Belonging.* Philadelphia: Temple UP, 2011.

Jarrar, Randa. *A Map of Home.* New York: Penguin, 2008.

Lanser, Susan Sniader. "Feminism's Masterplots." Modern Language Association Conference, January 2011. Address.

Ludvig, Alice. "Differences between Women? Intersecting Voices in a Female Narrative." *European Journal of Women's Studies* 13.3 (2006): 245–58.

Lykke, Nina. *Feminist Studies: A Guide to Intersectional Theory, Methodology and Writing.* London: Routledge, 2009.

Manji, Irshad. *The Trouble with Islam Today: A Muslim's Call for Reform in Her Faith.* 2003. New York: St. Martin's, 2005.

Maparyan, Layli. *The Womanist Idea.* London: Routledge, 2012.

May, Vivian M. "Intersectionality." Orr, Braithwaite, and Lichtenstein. 183–202.

McCall, Leslie. "The Complexity of Intersectionality." *Signs* 30.3 (Spring 2005): 1771–800.

McWilliams, Ellen. *Margaret Atwood and the Female Bildungsroman.* New York: Ashgate, 2009.

Millard, Kenneth. *Coming of Age in Contemporary American Fiction.* Edinburgh: Edinburgh UP, 2007.

Moretti, Franco. *The Way of the World: The Bildungsroman in European Culture.* London: Verso, 1987.

Morrison, Toni. *Beloved.* New York: Knopf, 1987.

Mullaney, Julia. *Postcolonial Literatures in Context.* London: Continuum, 2010.

Nasr, Seyyed Hossein. *Islam: Religion, History, and Civilization.* San Francisco: HarperSanFrancisco, 2005.

Orr, Catherine M., Ann Braithwaite, and Diane Lichtenstein, eds. *Rethinking Women's and Gender Studies.* New York: Routledge, 2012.

Phoenix, Ann, and Pamela Pattynama. "Intersectionality." *European Journal of Women's Studies* 13.3 (2006): 187–92.

Politics & Gender. Forum on Intersectionality 3 (2007): 229–80.

Smith, Bonnie G. *Women's Studies: The Basics.* New York: Routledge, 2013.

Soueif, Ahdaf. *The Map of Love.* New York: Anchor, 2000.

Strenski, Ivan, ed. *Thinking about Religion: A Reader.* Oxford: Blackwell, 2006.

Taylor, Mark C., ed. *Critical Terms for Religious Studies.* Chicago: U of Chicago P, 1997.

Wadud, Amina. *Inside the Gender Jihad: Women's Reform in Islam.* Oxford: Oneworld, 2006.

———. *Qur'an and Woman: Rereading the Sacred Text from a Woman's Perspective.* New York: Oxford UP, 1999.

Wadsworth, Nancy D. "Intersectionality in California's Same-Sex Marriage Battles: A Complex Proposition." *Political Research Quarterly* 64.1 (2011): 200–16.

Wiegman, Robyn. *Object Lessons.* Durham, NC: Duke UP, 2012.

Wilcox, Melissa M. "Tilting at Windmills: Defining and Predicting Religion." *Religion in Today's World: Global Issues, Sociological Perspectives.* Ed. Melissa M. Wilcox. New York: Routledge, 2013. 1–16.

Yuval-Davis, Nira. "Intersectionality and Feminist Politics." *European Journal of Women's Studies* 13.3 (2006): 193–209.

SUZANNE KEEN

Intersectional Narratology in the Study of Narrative Empathy

This essay seeks to explore why further understanding narrative empathy requires adoption of an *intersectional narratology*, a method that can accommodate the different directions and locations of a rich set of texts, contexts, and identities while framing global observations about the workings of narrative in the world. Since exploration of narrative empathy takes place at an interdisciplinary crossing point (of literary studies and psychology), a communication challenge deriving from competing definitions of the term "empathy" often arises. The legitimacy of the kind of intersectional research I propose in this essay depends upon baseline terminological clarity, a clarity that rarely exists when scholars from different disciplinary contexts discuss empathy. To reach that end of greater clarity about the disparate phenomena discussed under the label of empathy, I discuss here psychologist C. Daniel Batson's authoritative description of different concepts called empathy. Because Batson, a preeminent figure in the field of empathy research, does not comment on empathy for nonexistent beings, I further extend each concept to gloss its application to the study of narrative empathy. Further communication across disciplinary lines can be improved if parties know which version of "empathy" we mean when we write and speak about it.

Two other terms demand immediate attention: *intersectional* and *narratology*. Robyn Warhol has urged feminist critics to "take what Kimberlé

Crenshaw named an 'intersectional' approach because white privilege, class privilege, heteronormativity, and other positions of relative power complicate hierarchies of gender."[1] Though Warhol makes a strong case that feminist narratology has already branched out to "include race, sexuality, nationality, class, and ethnicity as well as gender, the components of intersectional analyses" ("Feminist Approach" 9), she prefers the term "narrative theories" to narratology because it "still connotes for many a theoretical approach cut off from questions of history and context" (9). I pitch my tent on the ground of postclassical narratology, which opens "the fairly focused and restricted realm of narratology to methodological, thematic, and contextual influences" (Alber and Fludernik 9). Postclassical narratology has been profoundly shaped by feminist narrative theory. Its transdisciplinary embrace of cognitive and affective theories of narrative also makes it accommodating to a developing theory of narrative empathy. As I have earlier defined it, narrative empathy involves "the sharing of feeling and perspective-taking induced by reading, viewing, hearing, or imagining narratives of another's situation and condition. Narrative empathy plays a role in the aesthetics of production when authors experience it . . . in mental simulation during reading, in the aesthetics of reception when readers experience it, and in the narrative poetics of texts when formal strategies invite it" (Keen, "Narrative Empathy"). In this essay I suggest how an intersectional narratology necessarily complicates research questions about narrative empathy, in the end strengthening conclusions we may draw about its formal techniques, its impact on readers, and its effect on real-world changes in attitudes and behavior.

Though my prior work on narrative empathy has made contributions to rhetorical narratology, it has taken a focused approach to specific roles in a communication model, emphasizing (for example) varieties of authors' empathy involved in inviting feeling responses from nearer and more remote audiences.[2] When one turns to actual readers and their experiences of narrative empathy, I have argued, one finds a great diversity of responses, including individuals who respond in an emotionally disengaged fashion to works that many others find intensely moving.[3] This can be accounted for in part by differences among readers, differences in experience, identity, and temperament or disposition.[4] Intersectionality, a feminist concept examining "the relationships among multiple dimensions and modalities of social relations and

---

1. See Warhol, "A Feminist Approach to Narrative" 9.
2. For my broadest narratological discussion, see Keen, "Narrative Empathy"; on authors' empathy, see Keen, "Strategic Empathizing."
3. See Keen, *Empathy and the Novel* 65–99.
4. See Keen, "Readers' Temperaments and Fictional Character."

subject formations" (McCall 1771), meshes well with a narrative poetics that is open to diverse effects of narrative techniques in various texts, contexts, and modes, following Meir Sternberg.[5] Like intersectional analyses of discrimination (Crenshaw), for which the concept was first formulated, my version of intersectional narratology seeks to understand why certain positions and concepts are privileged while others suffer from inattention or disparagement. In her foundational rendering of feminist intersectionality for narrative theory, Susan S. Lanser emphasizes the discernment of the way "systemic, structural, and institutional 'traffic' . . . operates to the advantage or disadvantage of individuals and groups according to their social positioning" (34). This means, in my extension, that intersectional narratology need not aim primarily at uncovering discriminatory representations, but may also focus on the status of the representational vehicles carrying meanings. It thus extends the feminist project of scrutinizing non-mainstream texts to complicate observations based on a limited canon.

In its application to narrative empathy, intersectional narratology enables discussion of the complex overlays of narrative form, contexts of creation and reception, and identity that work together to provoke diverse responses to narrative, among divergent readers of a wide variety of texts. It complicates rather than schematizing, and it risks proliferation of axes rather than insisting on neat taxonomies. It still remains narratology as long as it seeks evidence of impact of narrative techniques, manifestations of theme in form, and as long as it discerns dominant, residual, and emergent forms in historical contexts. As Lanser writes, intersectional feminism "can now map and be mapped by narrative patterns across time and space, accounting for vectors of difference to create a narratology that is deeply locational and therefore cross-cultural and historical" (32). An intersectional narratology would skeptically examine beliefs in universal impacts of narrative techniques, but it would embrace evidence that examines narrative arts' contribution to an expanded circle of empathy, especially if that extension benefited vulnerable members of disadvantaged peoples. For when narrative empathy reaches across boundaries of difference, geographical and temporal distance, to evoke shared feeling, what—if anything—happens as a result? Propositions, derived from the science of real-life empathy, include changed attitudes, greater tolerance, reduced fear of the other, and increased helping behavior or altruism.

An intersectional narratology brought to bear on narrative empathy extends rhetorical narratology's interest in transactions between authors

---

5. On the "Proteus Principle" as it applies to the effects of narrative techniques, see Sternberg.

and readers, makers and audiences, emphasizing the challenges to theorizing of substantial differences among real human beings. Yet it also accommodates a sense of shared human experiences derived from the behavioral sciences, where much of the empirical work on empathy has been carried out. The psychology of narrative impact examines ranges of possibilities, discovers clusters of frequent experiences, and records outliers among readers' responses to emotionally evocative texts. These empirical techniques support intersectional narratology's project of discerning differences stemming from multiple competing axes of identity and experience in subjects. I concur with Lanser that "the *articulation* of women—and men—into distinct pluralities opens multiple new avenues for historical, cross-cultural, and intra-cultural inquiry" (Lanser 33; emphasis in original). Intersectional narratology enables the theorist to employ markers of identity, technique, or impact derived from contextual, feminist, and queer narrative theories, rather than sticking to a single binary contrast. The emergent queer narratology has already usefully complicated the binary starting point of much early feminist narrative theory. Further openness to the multiple intersecting axes of readers' subject positions and the protean possibilities of narrative techniques (Sternberg) characterizes intersectional narratology. This makes it especially adaptable to the study of narrative empathy. Just as empathy involves both affective and cognitive responses, the study of narrative empathy inquires how the blend of affective *feeling with* and cognitive accuracy in mind-reading relates to multiple aspects of readers,' characters' and authors' identities.

Empathy: What It Is and What It Does

In contemporary discourse, empathy has many definitions, components, and roles to play in accounts of human emotional responsiveness, communication, social behavior, and altruism. It is one of the factors, for instance, attributed to the decline of violence against women (Pinker 409–15) and gays (447–54) in the latter part of the twentieth century and in the early decades of the twenty-first century. C. Daniel Batson, one of the most influential authorities on empathy in psychology, has recently highlighted eight of the possible phenomena known as empathy, as the term is currently used in psychology and to a lesser degree in philosophy.[6] His essay represents an important disentangling of competing meanings that imply different research methodologies

---

6. For a history of the term going back to its origins in late nineteenth-century German psychological aesthetics, see Lauren Wispé.

and assumptions about empathy's real-world impact. Here as in subsequent paragraphs, I extrapolate from Batson's real-world empathy between human subjects to narrative empathy, where some of the agents involved are made out of words. Discussions of narrative empathy ought to establish firmly to which version of empathy they correlate, and this discussion should make that definitional task easier for intersectional narrative theorists to accomplish. Although only some of the phenomena listed by Batson are obviously involved in narrative empathy, where the eliciting prompt of empathetic feeling is a construct or effect of narrative (including fictions) rather than another actual person in the real world, a review of the phenomena using Batson's categories freshens our sense of their links to literary response as well as their inherent complexity. This complexity encourages the development of an intersectional narratology, especially as it pertains to narrative's impact on vulnerable populations. An intersectional narratology would skeptically examine claims for universal impacts of narrative techniques, but it would welcome evidence that shows the narrative arts contributing to an expanded empathetic circle.

Batson's overview of the eight psychological states that correspond to different versions of empathy begins with a cognitive definition, "Concept 1: Knowing Another Person's Internal State, Including His or Her Thoughts and Feelings" (4). Sometimes called cognitive empathy, this phenomenon has been studied by William Ickes for its degree of successful mind-reading, or "empathic accuracy" (Ickes 57), since most humans estimate with relative ease what a person close to them is thinking or feeling, in everyday mind-reading. For narratologists, knowledge of internal states correlates with matters of narrative situation and narratorial reliability or unreliability. An intersectional narratologist might investigate whether the age, gender, ethnicity, and literary experience of a reader makes a difference in the response to a first-person narrator such as Katniss Everdeen in Suzanne Collins's *Hunger Games* trilogy (2008–10). In a recent discussion, an eleven-year-old girl resonated with the emotions of narrativity, especially curiosity and suspense. She took Katniss's narration at her word. An eighteen-year-old young woman in the same conversation felt no sympathy, distrusted Katniss's self-reports, and reported a cooler response to the narration. The eighteen-year-old was alert to the gaps in Katniss's (a consonant narrator's) own self-knowledge, which had a distancing effect for her. Would an olive-skinned reader, or one who had lost a parent in an industrial accident, recognize Katniss's internal states more readily? A larger and more diverse sample of readers could help an intersectional narratologist test some of the many existing suppositions about conditions that increase the likeliness of cognitive empathy.

For narratologists concerned with form, questions about cognitive empathy and narrative technique often suppose differing impacts of first- and third-person narration. In narrative empathy for fictional constructs, I have argued, empathic accuracy for characters can be vouchsafed by third-person narrators' representation of characters' consciousness (*Empathy and the Novel* 136). When a narrator generalizes in a reliable fashion about a character's thoughts and feelings, using psycho-narration, readers have little reason to doubt it. Similarly, in fiction employing either quoted (interior) monologue or narrated monologue (free indirect discourse), in which the words of the characters' thoughts appear, narrative empathic accuracy will be high. However, the potential that Batson acknowledges, that "you could be wrong, at least about some nuances and details" (4), increases radically in less reliable first-person-narrative situations (*Empathy and the Novel* 137), or when readers bring their individual preferences, memories, experiences, predictions, fantasies, and feelings to the task of co-creating fictional characters by filling in the gaps (Keen, "Readers' Temperaments" 295–96). Thus experiences of narrative empathy, which cannot be verified by cross-checking with real people about their actual feelings, involve greater likelihood of what I have named *narrative empathic inaccuracy*, the strong conviction in reader's empathy that divergently attributes emotion or state of mind to a fictional persona, at cross purposes with an author's apparent intentions (*Empathy and the Novel* 137).

Batson's second concept, "Adopting the Posture or Matching the Neural Responses of an Observed Other" (4), refers to the rapid, automatic, and unconscious mimicry of others' bodily or facial positions. Some psychologists believe that the neural substrates of this widespread animal behavior underpin other more cognitive, conscious forms of empathy in humans, though not necessarily to higher-order concern, sympathy, or altruism.[7] Motor mimicry in an audience certainly occurs during dramatic productions, in film viewing (such as facial close-ups or action sequences of acrobatic parkour), and probably in response to graphic narrative representations of nonhuman characters (Keen, "Fast Tracks" 135, 137). As Batson comments, "the problem of anthropomorphism arises precisely because we humans have the ability—and inclination—to make such inferences" about what others think and feel, "even about other species" (5). It is possible that descriptions of characters' disposition in space in imagined locations of prose or verse fictional storyworlds call upon readers' motor mimicry. Reports of painful bodily experiences or descriptions of dysphoric facial expressions, even of fictional

---

7. Blair and Blair report, "There are no current data relating motor empathy to moral or social rule development" (139).

characters, can elicit physical responses in the reader's own body (Warhol, *Having a Good Cry* 62–63). Though often regarded as a behavior of sentimental women responding to affecting stories (Radway), such experiences are also reported by male readers. When my husband read John Muir's account of Mr. Young hanging from a cliff in Alaska with dislocated arms (40–41), he grunted aloud and adjusted his own shoulders to make sure they were still in their sockets. Does a gender difference between reader and protagonist alter the degree of motor mimicry experienced when reading a novel such as *The Hunger Games*? When Collins manipulates the pace of her narration, employing expansion as Katniss stands immobilized on the metal circle at the start of the games for sixty seconds (148–49), do readers' differing axes of identity, including experiences of timed athletic contests, alter their degree of motor mimicry? Pace of reading, heart rate, sweating, and visible signs of bodily posture alteration could all be studied with the assistance of a psychologist.

Concept 3 of Batson's survey addresses the more affective element of emotion-matching and emotion-catching: "Coming to Feel as Another Person Feels" (Batson 5). Identifying this well-documented aspect of human behavior as *emotional contagion* suggests that the same feeling spreads from person to person, whereas the older terminology of sympathy, dating back to David Hume and Adam Smith's influential eighteenth-century accounts, does not demand an exact match in feelings. (Hume and Smith do also describe instances of motor mimicry under discussion of sympathy, compassion, and fellow feeling). Since empathy in some contexts appears as a virtual synonym of sympathy, this concept clearly has a literary history (Keen, *Empathy and the Novel* 39–55). The version of emotion-catching and matching that Batson describes comes closer to empathy as theorized by the neuroscience of mirror neurons, comprising a shared manifold for intersubjectivity (Gallese 171). Mirror neurons work quickly, giving an onlooker a fast physiological version of the observed subject's action, expression, or feeling. That is, if humans have a mirror neuron system like other primates, then witnessing or even hearing about another's feelings may prompt fast emotion-matching and catching without an extensive educational process. This kind of empathy and its narrative correlate could be studied by adepts in neural imaging. To what degree biological differences among subjects, let alone social and cultural aspects of identity, alter this affective emotion-matching is an open question. Intersectional narratology could focus on contentions that appear in essentialist binary formulations, such as the argument that female readers are more empathetic than men.[8]

---

8. The culturally promulgated assumption that women are more empathetic than men (Baron-Cohen 1–2) is not borne out when physiological measures of empathy are employed

The remaining concepts enumerated by Batson more obviously corre-late with aspects of narrative empathy. Batson's concept 4 draws on the origi-nal meaning of empathy as a translation of *Einfühlung*, as theorized by late nineteenth- and early twentieth-century aesthetics: "Intuiting or Projecting Oneself into Another's Situation," as Batson describes aesthetic empathy (6). Batson pushes the definition towards human perspective-taking, lightly gloss-ing the target of *Einfühlung* as "some inanimate object, such as a gnarled, dead tree on a windswept hillside" (5). Aesthetic empathy remains an important effect of fictional storyworlds. Fiction readers and writers know that setting can evoke narrative empathy, both through its connection with a human per-spective and through a feeling for the landscape, buildings, rocks, and trees. Suzanne Collins opens the last novel of her trilogy, *Mockingjay* (2010), with a prompt to *Einfühlung*:

> I stare down at my shoes, watching as a fine layer of ash settles on the worn leather. This is where the bed I shared with my sister, Prim, stood. Over there was the kitchen table. The bricks of the chimney, which collapsed in a charred heap, provide a point of reference for the rest of the house. How else could I orient myself in this sea of gray?
>   Almost nothing remains of District 12. (3)

The disorienting ruins of the firebombed house and its surrounding min-ing town employ the association of a human-built environment with human culture (hearth and home), as well as with the missing people. Though the passage alludes to family, Collins directs the reader's attention to the fate of destroyed objects. Although a reader who has gone through a house fire or aerial bombardment would possess empathetic reference points for this scene, the gray ash alludes to the televised scenes of the aftermath of the Towers' collapse in the 9/11 attack. (In 2001, Collins's original readers were between five and ten years old.) Do readers who remember 9/11 more readily make this poetic connection? As Rae Greiner has recently argued, the "the formal protocols of empathy align with those of poetry" (420), actively relating the *unalike* human perceiver and inanimate object of perception, analogously with metaphor: "With its fusion of subject and object, empathy accomplished the work of metaphor, while sympathy, with its emphasis on context—

(Lennon and Eisenberg 197, 203). Cognitive science on gender difference in empathy affirms that men and women have equal empathic capacities, and acknowledges that sufficient motiva-tion accurately to read others' thoughts and feelings alters performance, which accounts for perceptions of gender differences in empathy if females are more motivated by cultural expecta-tions than most males (Ickes et al. "Gender Differences" 219).

one's adjacency to or distance from others with whom one does not merge— calls the attributes of metonymy to mind" (421). It will take a serious effort to resuscitate psychologists' interest in the early twentieth-century version of aesthetic empathy.[9] Batson dismisses it: "Such projection is rarely what is meant by empathy in contemporary psychology" (6). However, for literary studies, *Einfühlung* has a specific literary history, from Vernon Lee's early theorizing to the mid-twentieth-century work of romanticist Richard Harter Fogle to recent work by Greiner.[10] Congruently, in contemporary neuroscience, the study of brain response to verbal directional prompts may provide a basis for understanding how empathy for things and others rests on a foundation of physical orientation (Zwaan and Taylor). This has a bearing on some of the most vivid effects of fictional storyworlds on aesthetic empathy in immersion reading.[11]

Deliberate perspective taking, or in Batson's terms for concept 5, "Imagining How Another Is Thinking and Feeling" (7), involves sensitivity to another's point of view. Related to the aesthetic projection of *Einfühlung* (concept 4), but moving away from inanimate targets, the "imagine other" condition of empathy involves one person's "feeling into" another's thoughts and feelings. This definition of empathy focuses on the other person, with an awareness of the separate being of that individual. Rather than experiencing emotional fusion with the other, the empath who engages in perspective taking employs observation of the other and knowledge of that person. Empathy in this sense is a more obviously cognitive operation that depends on having a theory of (another's) mind (ToM). For narrative theorists exploring the phenomenon of character identification, this mode of empathy transposes quite neatly to the kind of narrative empathy that follows on effortful attention to a fictional character's actions, circumstances, speech, represented thoughts, and reported or inferred motives. Much (but not all) of the philosophy of empathy refers to perspective taking.[12]

The closely related concept 6, "Imagining How One Would Think and Feel in the Other's Place" (Batson 7), also receives emphasis in philosophi-

---

9. For my effort to discover how aesthetic empathy contributes to Thomas Hardy's strategic empathizing in poems such as "The Convergence of the Twain," see my "Empathetic Hardy" 354–56, 363–65.

10. Greiner persuasively argues that the realist novel's representational aims accord more with *sympathy* than with empathy.

11. Studies of the effects of video games suggest that moving in the three-dimensional space of the game may activate spatial orientation mirror neurons. See Tajerian.

12. For a comprehensive collection of recent philosophy of empathy, see Coplan and Goldie. "Special Section: Empathy" in *Emotion Review* (2012) also contains contributions from philosophers, psychologists, cognitive neuroscientists, and literary critics.

cal accounts of empathy, in part because of its appearance in Adam Smith's *A Theory of Moral Sentiments* (1759) under the older term sympathy. This version of empathy is also cognitive (since it involves active imagining), but it is rooted in role-taking (putting oneself in the shoes of another) rather than taking the perspective of that person. It answers the question *How would I feel?* rather than *How does s/he feel?* Batson notes that the "imagine-self perspective is in some ways similar to the act of projecting oneself into another's situation" (concepts 4 and 5), but asserts that the two stances should not be confused, as "the self remains more focal here than in aesthetic projection" (7). Like perspective-taking empathy, role-taking empathy is likely to be involved in readers' experiences of narrative empathy. Indeed, many readers reporting strong sensations of character identification phrase their experiences in terms of how they would feel themselves in the position of the character. Some theorists of narrative empathy regard this form of empathy as more "categorical," more dependent on matches with the self and group identity, and therefore less other-directed and less likely to lead to the ethical expression of compassion than "situational" empathy (Hogan 134–36), which is closer to perspective taking (Batson 7, concept 5). An intersectional approach to experimental design might well be able to examine these possibilities, which have been theorized but not subjected to empirical testing.

If role taking is more egotistical than perspective taking, personal distress is more self-focused than either. Personal distress is an empathic reaction that focuses on one's own sensations to the point of diverting attention from the suffering other's experience. As concept 7, Batson describes it as "Feeling Distress at Witnessing Another Person's Suffering" (7). As Batson explains it, personal distress expresses not feelings *for* (sympathy) or feelings *like* the other's feelings (empathy as defined by concepts 1–6), but "feeling distressed *by* the state of the other" (Batson 8; emphasis in original). Personal distress as described by developmental psychologist Nancy Eisenberg is an aversive emotional response that leads to avoidance. It can have little to tell students of narrative empathy, since true aversion leads to cessation of the reading or viewing that evokes the response (Keen, *Empathy and the Novel* 4–5). Many younger readers of Suzanne Collins's *Hunger Games* abandoned *Mockingjay*, the third novel of the trilogy, in which representations of violence escape the game arena and take over the primary fictional world. Collins's interrogation of just-war theory and her unsparing account of the costs of violent resistance to an unjust regime drive many of her young readers away. If the ability to be transported by fiction is one of the key precursors to narrative empathy, then proneness to personal distress rather than other-oriented empathy may become an obstacle to immersion reading. The effects of personal distress continue when the reading is not abandoned. Educational circumstances that compel reading of an upsetting fiction or viewing of a distressing film to continue in the face of an aversive response can block the impulse to get away from the stimulus, but they cannot dictate a spirit of receptiveness or openness in readers and viewers.

Batson's eighth and final concept will be familiar to literary scholars, for it is best known as sympathy, with an emphasis on the feeling component rather than the cognitive knowing another's perspective described in concept 6. "Feeling for Another Person Who Is Suffering" (Batson 8), or for the fictive equivalents of persons in narrative, has been discussed under the older terms pity, compassion, fellow feeling, and sympathy. Related to empathy in some social psychology as the concerned outcome of an other-oriented feeling *for* another, empathic concern expresses an appropriately "congruent" emotion that needs to match the other's feeling exactly: feeling sorry for a frightened person or gratified for a joyful person would exhibit sympathy. Many philosophers regard sympathy as an ethical expression of what begins as empathy, a more mature and other-directed concern than the motor mimicry, emotional contagion, or feeling-matching that Batson describes in concepts 1 through 3. As a goal of fictive representation, sympathy has had a prominent role to play in literature, with important statements in its favor by Henry Home, Lord Kames, Percy Bysshe Shelley, and George Eliot (Keen, *Empathy and the Novel* 44–55) and historic exhibits in the narratives of George Eliot, James Joyce, Harper Lee, Doris Lessing, Maya Angelou, Toni Morrison, and hundreds if not thousands of other novelists. Some influential commentators on the social impact of the realist novel persistently refer to its *empathy*-inducing qualities (Hunt 27–34; Nussbaum 90; Pinker 177). It must be acknowledged, however, that to the perpetual bedevilment of those who would distinguish empathy from sympathy, the terms have often been conflated or reversed. As Keith Oatley, an expert guide to the emotions involved in fiction reading, remarks, in his *Such Stuff as Dreams: The Psychology of Fiction*, "In modern usage, sympathy is generally taken as separate from empathy (feeling with), and usually means feeling for someone in their predicament" (118). Oatley associates literary experiences of character identification with empathy, and readers' recollection of emotional memories with sympathy (126), and I concur with that difference, although I think that character identification does not inevitably lead to empathy (or vice versa).

Strangely, Batson does not address fantasy empathy. One of the most widely used empathy scales is Mark Davis's Interpersonal Reactivity Index, or IRI (Davis, "Multidimensional" 85). Davis's multidimensional scale includes subscales measuring personal distress, empathic concern, perspective-taking, and fantasy empathy. The fantasy empathy subscale measures subjects' "tendency to imaginatively transpose" themselves "into fictional situations" (Davis, *Empathy* 57). David acknowledges that fantasy empathy exhibits congruence with perspective taking (58) but rightly insists that the questions elicit experiences of "imagining oneself in the place of *fictitious* characters appearing in books, movies, and plays" (58; emphasis mine), a key difference often glossed over in discussions of narrative empathy's relation to altruism or prosocial behavior.[13]

If we are to understand how narrative empathy works in human subjects, then the difference between fiction and nonfiction narrative should not be disregarded. An intersectional narratology can attend to generic differences among other axes. I have argued that a perception of fictionality (whether the source is truly made up or simply presented as fiction) enhances the likelihood of empathic response by releasing readers or viewers from any sense of obligation to help real people in the real world (or the expectation of reciprocity) (Keen, *Empathy and the Novel* 16). Fictionality may intensify readers' empathy without necessarily causing altruism. This contention has not yet been tested, and readers of the many popular memoirs on the contemporary literary scene doubt it. However, the relation of fiction to empathy has been affirmed in several ways. There is some evidence that people of high-empathy dispositions enjoy fiction more than people of low-empathy (or no-empathy) dispositions (Esrock; Mar et al., "Bookworms"); lack of enjoyment of fiction is a diagnostic trait for high-functioning autism (Wing). The Raymond Mar lab in Toronto has recently demonstrated that readers with a preference for nonfiction score lower on social abilities associated with empathy than readers who prefer fiction (Mar et al., "Bookworms"). The Mar group has also investigated the impact of exposure to fiction on readers' ability to interpret emotional facial cues and on their verbal ability, in contrast to nonfiction reading (Fong and Mar). The additional complication of fictional versus nonfictional narrative prompts combine with the existent dichotomies in empathy research: the affective and cognitive; the automatic response and the learned behavior; the self- and other-directed forms of imagining; the neural and the moral.

---

13. While Martha Nussbaum asserts that experiences of narrative empathy (with the right kind of novels) will produce good world citizens (90), other theorists find examples of the prosocial impact of empathy in fiction itself. For example, see Hoffman 225, where he uses the actions of fictional characters engaged in altruistic acts to demonstrate the efficacy of empathy.

Theoretical Intersections in Narrative Empathy

Batson's disentangling of empathy-related concepts reveals the complexities of empathy research. Even under the big umbrella of "psychology," the study of empathy can involve expertise in both affect and cognition. The neural substrate and chemical bases of empathic responses have been studied by neuroscientists, while social and developmental psychologists have charted much of empathy's roles in social behavior and moral development. Philosophers in a variety of traditions (ethics, moral sentimentalism, utilitarianism, aesthetics) have theorized empathy, sometimes in collaboration with cognitive scientists or developmental and social psychologists. The study of empathy is automatically interdisciplinary, even if not all empathy researchers undertake the task of answering questions and posing problems that navigate disciplinary boundaries. As relative latecomers (or belated returners) to the scientific and scholarly conversation about empathy, literary theorists find some assumptions congenial and some alien, some conclusions predictable and some startling, some running counter to our own disciplinary commitments, some affirming our beliefs, and some challenging our deepest convictions. Developing an intersectional narratology will assist researchers in the discovering and disseminating findings about narrative empathy in an interdisciplinary field.

For instance, while studying narrative empathy as a feature of immersion fiction reading, junctions of narratology, feminism, affective studies, and cognitive science could help us answer how, under which circumstances, and in response to which techniques, individuals as distinct from one another as we are can experience the emotional fusion and intense recognition of shared feeling. Introspective testimony from readers and viewers who have experienced narrative empathy (or not!) in response to an emotionally evocative text should receive our respectful attention, but we should not make the error of mistaking our own intense reading experiences for universal or predictive phenomena. They are instead starting points for an intersectional narratology of narrative impact. Thus variable cultural contexts, individual differences among people, readers' temperamental dispositions, as well as their gender and sexual orientation, would emerge from the brackets into which classical narratology placed all evidence about actual audiences. Though this procedure would render the convenient construct "the reader" irreducibly complex, fluid, and extremely resistant to simplification and schematization, it would encourage confidence in future discoveries about narrative empathy.

Intersectional narratology participates in the extension of feminist narratology's project, responding to Ruth Page's challenge: "To make a more convincing discussion of the ways in which gender might intersect with the characteristics of narrative form, considerably more empirical data are needed, about the tellers and receivers as well as the tales themselves" ("Feminist Narratology?" 52–53). This data originates from many sources, including the work of David S. Miall, Melanie Green, Raymond Mar, and their collaborators. Literary scholars have begun and should continue the project of communicating their empirical findings, as well as collaborating with researchers in other disciplines. So, for instance, empathetic effects of narrative have been evaluated by means of experiments in discourse processing, in the psychology of narrative impact, and through philosophical introspection, but the conflicting data on gender and empathy have not yet been systematically investigated with respect to either literary responses of female and male audiences or gendered narrative forms.[14]

Among other questions, the relation of narrative empathy to altered attitudes and prosocial action in the real world, often theorized by philosophers such as Martha Nussbaum, deserves the respect of experimental scrutiny. Research in neuroscience, cognitive science, developmental psychology, and discourse processing has advanced our knowledge of both empathy and narrative empathy, but much remains to be discovered. Regarding narrative, Fong and Mar remark, "empirical research investigating the social outcomes of reading is in its infancy" (61). Regarding empathy, two of the neuroscientists who have extended our understanding of its neural substrate enumerate the gaps: "A second big issue is the link between empathic brain responses and sympathy or compassion, that is, feeling *as* and feeling *for* the other. Thirdly, it is an open question how empathic brain responses relate to prosocial motivation and behavior and finally, almost nothing is known about the plasticity of the empathic brain, that is, about the trainability of empathy and compassionate motivation, all issues that should have considerable practical impacts on society" (Hein and Singer, "I Feel" 157). Note that these scientists point out what is *not known* about the chain of responses reputed to exist between empathy and sympathy and empathy and altruism, let alone how those relations change when empathy, in psychology's empathy-altruism relation, is replaced by *narrative* empathy. Literary scholars and reception theorists can add nuance to the discussion of empathy-inducing texts, which have often been hedged about with canonical barriers that suggest only the most high literary narratives can have ethical effects. What if escapist reading also benefits readers by shifting perspectives, opening up attitudes, and prompting more generous feelings and actions toward others? The answers to

---

14. More common in psychology is the opposite effort, to control for gender rather than contrasting male and female responses.

these research questions about narrative empathy will be of immediate interest to many, including feminist and queer theorists, who hope to show how narrative literature, broadly defined, can expand the empathetic circle in the real world.

A conjunction of cognitive narratology, feminism, and affective studies occurs when studying narrative empathy: whenever we ask how, under which circumstances, and in response to which techniques, beings so different from one another as we are can experience the emotional fusion and intense recognition of shared feeling mediated by fiction. As many of the contributors to this collection demonstrate, narrative empathy felt and exercised by makers (novelists, graphic narrative artists, filmmakers, the amateur videographers of the "It Gets Better" project) motivates fictional and nonfictional utterances aimed at specific target audiences. This strategic narrative empathy may be focused in its direction, announcing and forming a text's intended audience (Keen, "Strategic Empathizing"), though texts may certainly have multiple audiences, as Brian Richardson has theorized. Furthermore, the divergent evidence of actual readers' various responses to individual narratives motivates a layering of methodologies. As I argue in *Empathy and the Novel*, no one narrative text evokes empathy from all readers, nor does any specific narrative technique reliably produce the spontaneous shared feeling and perspective taking that are the hallmarks of empathy as conceived by contemporary psychology and philosophy (92–99).

Matters of identity, experience, and context combine with the possibilities enabled by readers' and viewers' embodied minds to condition potential responses to the invitations of narrative technique (Keen, "Readers' Temperaments"). In novels, stories, and film fictions, narrative empathy overarches narratological categories: a range of techniques might be operating at once to produce the likelihood of empathy. It can involve fictional characters; point of view and narrative situation; handling of pace, duration, and seriality; and storyworld features such as settings. An intersectional narratology begins with some contextual premises: the willingness to combine inquiry about a narrative technique—for instance use of a second-person "you" narration—with data from outside the text. Does familiarity with the conventions of 1930s documentary films, which commonly address the viewer, train a reader to accept a "you" role as an addressee? Does a habit of playing Xbox Live with friends make a reader of fiction more flexible about the overlap in addressee and avatar in "you" narratives? In co-creating a "you" narration, does a queer reader feel more or less likely than a straight reader to naturalize it representationally into a "he" or "she," or do other experiences and aspects of identity complicate a queer/straight binary? Does a female and feminist reader accustomed to cross-reading books for boys more easily sustain the sense of "you" as narratee? Do any of these differences correlate with—or cause—heightened or diminished sensations of narrative empathy?

While classical narratology typically focused its attention on forms, techniques, taxonomies, and communication models, feminist narratology reevaluates these theories in light of gender. This matters to a theory of narrative empathy not because empathy is an exclusively or especially female trait: it is not tied to biological sex. Males and females show similar ranges of empathic responsiveness on physiological measures (Lennon and Eisenberg 197, 203). Cultural contexts, however, can motivate the expression of empathic concern by females more than by males. The gendering of genre plays a role in reaching readers that have been acculturated to regard experiences of emotional fusion as desirable or as a response to be suppressed. This in turn has a bearing on the marketing and reception of emotionally evocative fiction. Gendered conventions that appeal to the ostensibly female, feeling reader or a male excitement-seeking reader thus make up a culture-bound component of narrative empathy. To return to my example of second-person narration, if gender is one of the axes of identity that orients readers' co-creation of fictional worlds, do female (or feminist) readers make feeling readers prone to identify with characters who look like, feel like, dress like, speak like "you"? Or is the word "you" enough all by itself to erase barriers of difference? A feminist narratologist, in cooperation with an analyst of discourse processing, or a psychologist of narrative impact, could design a study to find out. To my mind, devising those studies is preferable to simply believing that we already know the answers.

You might think, for instance, that commentary about readers' empathy would foreground the women readers who purchase most of the fiction bought in stores and check out the majority of novels borrowed from libraries, the popular genres and middlebrow fiction aimed at them, and the tradition of women writers seeking to educate their readers' sympathetic imaginations, but you would be wrong. Commentators on the edifying effects of literary novel-reading often attempt to dignify the novel's ethical project by ruling out ordinary women readers' common experiences of feeling with fiction (e.g., Robinson 413). My own work on narrative empathy has pursued a feminist critical agenda by arguing that the disparagement of women's middlebrow and escapist reading by writers on narrative ethics undermines broad claims made about the impact of "the novel" on readers (Keen, *Empathy and the Novel* 102–5). Which novels do they mean? Only canonical, realist, literary fiction written primarily by men prior to 1925? A theory of the impact of readers' empathy will only benefit from extension to a greater and more representative range of narratives. If we want to understand how novels alter readers' perceptions of others, we should not begin by ruling out most of the novels read because they are popular with women (Oprah books) or that belong to denigrated subgenres (romances, mystery novels). For despite the work of feminist literary critics who have expanded the range of valued texts and kinds of reading experiences (Radway; Warhol, *Having a Good Cry*), exclusion of all but the most canonical and high literary texts typifies commentary on readers' empathy. We should ask what role gender plays in reader response to narrative techniques, modes, and genres rather than using prejudiced categorization as a means to eliminate diverse readers and texts from the scope of our studies. Following Ruth Page's caution, techniques and effects of narrative empathy should not be expected to map onto gendered modes of narrativity such as *écriture féminine* ("Feminist Narratology?" 43). We should be alert to the publishing market's response to book purchasers' gender, and biases that still show in the greater number of novels written by men reviewed in the influential weekly book reviews, reviews still (in 2011!) mainly authored by male reviewers.[15]

Once the range of narratives has been opened up to include what diverse readers actually read or watch—including *telenovelas*,[16] graphic narratives,[17] Oprah books,[18] multi-authored fan-fiction,[19] fictions created for the Internet,[20] Booker-prize shortlisted novels—I believe we will discover a great array of techniques and representations that invite emotional engagement and evoke narrative empathy. However, the effect of real-life empathy on altruism (or the less stringent standard of prosocial helping behavior) does not necessarily carry over in predictable outcomes of narrative empathy, though imaginative role-taking for fictional characters has been shown to shift perceptions of outgroups (Hakemulder 146–47). More favorable perception of despised group members is a significant outcome, but it differs from real-world helping of representatives of those or similar group members. The evidence for

---

15. Male reviewers outnumber female reviewers, and books by women are reviewed less frequently than those by men. See the research aggregated by VIDA, Women in Literary Arts.

16. Keep an eye out for the work of Theresa Rojas on *telenovelas*.

17. I have written about the strategic empathy employed by graphic narrative and comic book authors in "Fast Tracks to Narrative Empathy."

18. As I argue in *Empathy and the Novel*, Oprah Winfrey makes empathy a linchpin of her aesthetics, as evidenced by her televised book club discussions (115–16).

19. See Ruth Page on the narrative poetics of participatory storytelling projects (*Stories and Social Media*).

20. A superb online novel with many opportunities for responses of narrative empathy is Geoff Ryman's *253: A Novel for the Internet about London Underground in Seven Cars and a Crash*.

altruism induced by narrative empathy is scanty though the cultural faith in the benefits of narrative empathy is strong.[21] Seeing what isn't working the way we expect can lead to alternative explanations. So, for instance, the cultivation of the sympathetic imagination through rendered perspectives of fictional characters is a linchpin of narrative ethics. Yet cognitive scientific efforts to verify this theory by studying the empathetic impact of role-taking instructions during fiction reading have not yielded robust results. Cognitive science surprises us by showing instead that exercises in *visualizing mental imagery* more reliably produce empathetic effects and (short-term) helping behavior. In other words, a more vivid and absorbing storyworld, visualized in the mind's eye, may intensify the ethical effects of reading where the injunction to "walk in the shoes" of a character may not (Johnson 150–55). Joining a fictional world as a temporary visitor may involve effects as robust as those often attributed to character identification.

One possible yield of experimental scrutiny could be the challenge to re-evaluate previously disparaged aspects of reading (such as escapism and fantasizing) as an aspect of narrative empathy. We could ask whether an experience of narrative empathy facilitates cross-reading over generic categories that usually imply a gendered readership, or other barriers to imaginative access to fictional worlds. We could discover whether narrative empathy felt for a minor character opens a path for critical resistant reading. We could extend the fascinating work begun by psychologist Shira Gabriel, in which she and her graduate student Ariana Young demonstrate that immersive reading of fantasies such as Stephanie Meyer's *Twilight* (2005) and J. K. Rowling's *Harry Potter* books (1997–2007) gives children the experience of belonging and thereby enhances empathy: "The current research suggests that books give readers more than an opportunity to tune out and submerge themselves in fantasy worlds. Books provide the opportunity for social connection and the blissful calm that comes from becoming a part of something larger than oneself for a precious, fleeting moment" (Gabriel and Young 993). While *amae*[22] and empathy are linked in some psychological studies of Japanese subjects, Gabriel and Young are the first to suggest the link as an effect of fiction reading. Their finding challenges hierarchies of literary quality and taste that

---

21. See Keen, *Empathy and the Novel* 16–26, 145–46 for my critique of the application of psychology's empathy–altruism relation to narrative empathy. For the empathy–altruism hypothesis regarding real-life empathy and prosocial action, see Batson, ed., *The Altruism Question*.

22. Not widely known outside of the psychology of emotion, the term *amae* describes the comforting feeling of attachment and belonging that receives more emphasis in collective cultures than in individualistic societies (Doi).

would regard *Twilight* and *Harry Potter* as unlikely sources of socially beneficial reading experiences. An intersectional narratology could ask if the temporary shedding of identity that occurs when readers intermingle with fictive
beings in fantasy worlds opens readers to empathy across social difference by
way of *amae*. Freed from the strictures of representational identity aesthetics,
we could admit that fans of *Twilight* include middle-aged moms and adult gay
men as well as thirteen-year-old girls, and that they seek not images of themselves but to get out of this world.[23]

The goal of such research projects would not to be to defend *Twilight* as
art, but to understand what happens when such diverse members of the actual
readership of a novel experience social connection, satisfaction, and positive
feelings while reading a series of novels that reverses the conventional horror at vampires. This calls upon the would-be intersectional narratologist to
suspend some of her own categorical presuppositions, derived from her own
axes of identity. As a literary critic I dislike *Twilight*'s tedious prose style. As a
middle-aged feminist I am dismayed by the popularity of a romance for teenagers and tweens that features such explicit representations of violent sexuality
(*Breaking Dawn* [2008]). As an English professor I tip my hat to any popular
novelist whose work encourages voracious reading. As a non-LDS gentile I
wonder why a Mormon novelist would choose to represent immortal marriage in terms of conversion to vampirism, which I associate with soul death.
As a former watcher of *Kolchack: the Night-Stalker* (1974–75), I resist the allure
of vampire Edward Cullen, preferring the warm-blooded Native American
werewolves. I am on Team Jacob. My gay brother-in-law is on Team Edward.
What's up with that? Clearly a large number of readers of the *Twilight* books
are getting a big charge out of character identification and empathy with Bella.
Isabella, announces *Parenting* magazine, was the number one name for baby
girls in 2010, after a forty-year period of rarity (Goodin). I would be an irre-
sponsible student of narrative empathy if I ignored this cultural phenomenon, with its evidence of widespread impact. If we want to understand how
narrative empathy works, and to investigate whether these experiences lead
to changes in the real world, then we should not ignore *Twilight* and *Harry
Potter*. But how do we go about discovering the role that empathy plays in
creating the groundswell of popularity that leads to a bestseller? The crowd-
sourcing of reader response may be necessary.

Reports from diverse readers make any discoveries about shared experiences or predictions about impact more persuasive. One critic's introspec-

---

23. See Blackford for the case that girls seek reading experiences about fictional worlds
different from their social worlds and about characters distinct from themselves.

tion about narrative impact on herself may begin the process of analysis, but one reader's impressions should not inevitably be construed as *the* reader. Thus, in applying intersectional narratology to narrative empathy, reports from more readers than one should be analyzed. This would obligate narrative theorists to attend to readings that may strike professional literary critics as erroneous. When the movie of *The Hunger Games* (2012) came out, a subset of young viewers objected in tweets to the film's Rue, played by a young black actress ("Hunger Games Cast Subjected to Racist Attacks"). They had read Rue as white, having misread, skipped, or forgotten the clear descriptions in the novel that render Rue as having "bright, dark eyes and satiny brown skin" (*Hunger Games* 98). Their sympathy for the character, to whose death Katniss responds humanely and subversively, was disrupted by the accurate representation of her race. Intersectional study of this failure in strategic narrative empathy could address readers' and viewers' age, gender, race, reading level, skimming and skipping, and disposition to fantasy empathy. The condemnation of the evident racism of the young viewers' tweets does not help us understand how the novel permitted an empathetic response while the film blocked it.

Formalist analysis can and ought to intersect with accounts of the experiences of actual and various readers. Gender and sexual identity are among the conditioning factors that contribute to readers' collaboration in fictional worldmaking, but so are underlying temperaments and individual life experiences (Keen, "Readers' Temperaments" 296). I recall here Eve Sedgwick's first axiom, "*People are different from each other*" (22; emphasis in original). Sedgwick saw women and queer and effeminate men as especially adept at "the refinement of necessary skills for making, testing, and using unrationalized and provisional hypotheses about what kinds of people there are to be found in one's world" (23). This observation suggests that feminist and queer readers (as well as women writers and gay and lesbian authors) cultivate skills of interpretation that can contribute to an intersectional narratology. Individual male straight readers, too, should be recognized as possessing differences that escape what Sedgwick castigated as "inconceivably coarse axes of categorization that have been painstakingly inscribed in current political and critical thought" (22). We *are* all different from one another, but in our embodied humanity we also share the narrative habit: stories are part of the natural habitat that we spin out of ourselves as we respond with emotion and calculation, moodily and rationally, to a world populated with other beings. Narratives are extraordinarily effective devices for opening the channel of fellow feeling and breaking through barriers of difference thrown up by distance, time, culture, experience.

Works Cited

Alber, Jan, and Monika Fludernik. "Introduction." *Postclassical Narratology: Approaches and Analyses*. Columbus: The Ohio State UP, 2010. 1–31.

Baron-Cohen, Simon. *The Essential Difference: The Truth about the Male and Female Brains*. New York: Basic Books, 2003.

Batson, C. Daniel. "These Things Called Empathy: Eight Related but Distinct Phenomena." Decety and Ickes 3–16.

———, ed. *The Altruism Question: Toward a Social-Psychological Answer*. Hillsdale, NJ: Erlbaum, 1991.

Blackford, Holly Virginia. *Out of This World: Why Literature Matters to Girls*. New York: Teachers College P, 2004.

Blair, R. J. R., and Karina S. Blair. "Empathy, Morality, and Social Convention: Evidence from the Study of Psychopathy and Other Psychiatric Disorders." Decety and Ickes 139–52.

Collins, Suzanne. *Catching Fire*. New York: Scholastic, 2009.

———. *The Hunger Games*. New York: Scholastic, 2008.

———. *Mockingjay*. New York: Scholastic, 2010.

Coplan, Amy, and Peter Goldie, eds. *Empathy: Philosophical and Psychological Perspectives*. Oxford and New York: Oxford UP, 2011.

Crenshaw, Kimberlé W. "Mapping the Margins: Intersectionality, Identity Politics, and Violence against Women of Color." *Stanford Law Review* 43.6 (1991): 1241–99.

Davis, Mark. *Empathy: A Social Psychological Approach*. Boulder: Westview, 1994.

———. "A Multidimensional Approach to Individual Differences in Empathy." *JSAS Catalog of Selected Documents in Psychology* 10 (1980): 85.

Decety, Jean, and William Ickes, eds. *The Social Neuroscience of Empathy*. Cambridge: MIT P, 2011.

Decety, Jean, and Claus Lamm. "Empathy versus Personal Distress: Recent Evidence from Social Neuroscience." Decety and Ickes 199–213.

Doi, Takeo. "The Concept of Amae and Its Psychoanalytic Implications." *International Review of Psycho-Analysis* 16 (1989): 349–54.

Eisenberg, Nancy. "The Development of Empathy-Related Responding." *Moral Motivation through the Life Span*. Ed. Gustavo Carlo and Carolyn Pope Edwards. Lincoln and London: U of Nebraska P, 2005. 73–117.

Esrock, Ellen J. *The Reader's Eye: Visual Imaging as Reader Response*. Baltimore: Johns Hopkins UP, 1994.

Fogle, Richard Harter. "Empathetic Imagery." *The Imagery of Keats and Shelley: A Comparative Study*. Chapel Hill: U of North Carolina P, 1949. 139–83.

Fong, Katrina, and Raymond A. Mar. "Exposure to Narrative Fiction versus Expository Nonfiction: Diverging Social and Cognitive Outcomes." *De stralende lezer; wetenschappelijk onderzoek naar de invloed van het lezen. [The radiant reader; scientific research concerning the influence of reading]*. Ed Frank Hakemulder. Delft, Netherlands: Eburon Academic, 2012. 55–68.

Gabriel, Shira, and Ariana Young. "Becoming a Vampire Without Being Bitten." *Psychological Science* (2012): 990–94.

Gallese, Vittorio. "The Roots of Empathy: The Shared Manifold Hypothesis and the Neural Basis of Intersubjectivity." *Psychopathology* 36.4 (July–August 2003): 171–80.

Goodin, Kate. "Top 10 Girl Baby Names of 2010." *Parenting*, n.d. Web. Accessed 30 Jan. 2012.

Green, Melanie. "Transportation into Narrative Worlds: The Role of Prior Knowledge and Perceived Realism." *Discourse Processes* 38 (2004): 247–66.

Greiner, Rae. "Thinking of Me Thinking of You: Sympathy versus Empathy in the Realist Novel." *Victorian Studies* 53.3 (Spring 2011): 417–26.

Hakemulder, J. F. "Imagining What Could Happen: Taking the Role of a Character on Social Cognition." *Directions in Empirical Literary Studies*. Ed. Sonia Zyngier, Marisa Bortolussi, Anna Chesnokova, and Jan Aurarcher. Amsterdam: Benjamins, 2008. 139–53.

Hein, Grit, and Tania Singer. "I Feel How You Feel But Not Always: The Empathic Brain and Its Modulation." *Current Opinion in Neurobiology* 18.2 (2008): 153–58.

Hoffman, Martin. *Empathy and Moral Development: Implications for Caring and Justice*. Cambridge: Cambridge UP, 2000.

Hogan, Patrick Colm. "The Epilogue of Suffering: Heroism, Empathy, Ethics." *SubStance* 30.1–2 (2001): 119–43.

Hume, David. *A Treatise of Human Nature*. Ed. L. A. Selby-Bigge. Oxford: Clarendon P, 1978.

"Hunger Games Cast Subjected to Racist Attacks in Shocking Tweets." *US Weekly*. 26 Mar. 2012. http://www.usmagazine.com/entertainment/news/hunger-games-fans-have-racist-debate-over-stars-playing-rue-thresh-2012263. Accessed 16 July 2012.

Hunt, Lynn. *Inventing Human Rights: A History*. New York and London: Norton, 2007.

Ickes, William. "Empathic Accuracy: Its Links to Clinical, Cognitive, Developmental, Social, and Physiological Psychology." Decety and Ickes 57–70.

Ickes, William, P. R. Gesn, and Tiffany Graham. "Gender Differences in Empathic Accuracy: Differential Ability or Differential Motivation?" *Personal Relationships* 7 (2000): 95–110.

Johnson, Dan R. "Transportation into a Story Increases Empathy, Prosocial Behavior, and Perceptual Bias toward Fearful Expressions." *Personality and Individual Differences* 52 (2012): 150–55.

Keen, Suzanne. "Empathetic Hardy: Bounded, Ambassadorial, and Broadcast Strategies of Narrative Empathy." *Poetics Today* 32.2 (Summer 2011): 349–89.

———. *Empathy and the Novel*. Oxford and New York: Oxford UP, 2007.

———. "Fast Tracks to Narrative Empathy: Anthropomorphism and Dehumanization in Graphic Narratives." *SubStance* #124 40.1 (2011): 135–55.

———. "Narrative Empathy." *The Living Handbook of Narratology*. Ed. Peter Hühn. Hamburg: Hamburg UP. http://wikis.sub.uni-hamburg.de/lhn/index.php/Narrative_Empathy. Accessed 14 Jan. 2012.

———. "Readers' Temperaments and Fictional Character." *New Literary History* 42.2 (Spring 2011): 295–314.

———. "Strategic Empathizing: Techniques of Bounded, Ambassadorial, and Broadcast Narrative Empathy." *Deutsche Vierteljahrs Schrift* 82.3 (Sept. 2008): 477–93.

Lamm, Claus, Jean Decety, and Tania Singer. "Meta-analytic Evidence for Common and Distinct Neural Networks Associated with Directly Experienced Pain and Empathy for Pain." *NeuroImage* 54 (2011): 2492–502.

Lanser, Susan S. "Are We There Yet? The Intersectional Future of Feminist Narratology." *Foreign Literature Studies* 32.4 (2010): 32–41.

Lee, Vernon. [Violet Paget]. *The Beautiful: An Introduction to Psychological Aesthetics*. Cambridge: Cambridge UP, 1913.

Lennon, Randy, and Nancy Eisenberg. "Gender/Age Differences in Empathy/Sympathy." *Empathy and Its Development*. Ed. Nancy Eisenberg and Janet Strayer. Cambridge: Cambridge UP, 1987. 195–217.

Mar, Raymond A., Keith Oatley, Jacob Hirsh, Jennifer dela Paz, and Jordan B. Peterson. "Bookworms versus Nerds: Exposure to Fiction versus Non-fiction, Divergent Associations with Social Ability, and the Simulation of Fictional Social Worlds." *Journal of Research in Personality* 40 (2006): 694–712.

Mar, Raymond A., Keith Oatley, and Jordan B. Peterson. "Exploring the Link between Reading Fiction and Empathy: Ruling Out Individual Differences and Examining Outcomes." *Communications* 34 (2009): 407–28.

McCall, Leslie. "The Complexity of Intersectionality." *Signs* 30.3 (2005): 1771–800.

Meyer, Stephanie. *Breaking Dawn*. Boston: Little, Brown, 2008.

———. *Twilight*. Boston: Little, Brown, 2005.

Miall, David S. "Neuroaesthetics of Literary Reading." *Neuroaesthetics*. Ed Martin Skov and Oshin Vartanian. Amityville, NY: Baywood, 2009. 233–47.

Muir, John. *Travels in Alaska*. 1915. Rpt. Penguin Nature Library. Ed. Richard Nelson. Harmondsworth: Penguin, 1997.

Nussbaum, Martha C. *Cultivating Humanity: A Classical Defense of Reform in Liberal Education*. Cambridge: Harvard UP, 1997.

Oatley, Keith. *Such Stuff as Dreams: The Psychology of Fiction*. Malden, MA: Wiley-Blackwell, 2001.

Page, Ruth E. "Feminist Narratology? Literary and Linguistic Perspectives on Gender and Narrativity." *Language and Literature* 12.1 (2003): 43–56.

———. *Stories and Social Media: Identities and Interaction*. London: Routledge, 2012.

Pinker, Steven. *The Better Angels of Our Nature: Why Violence Has Declined*. New York: Viking, 2011.

Radway, Janice. *Reading the Romance: Women, Patriarchy, and Popular Literature*. Chapel Hill: U of North Carolina P, 1984.

Richardson, Brian. "Singular Text, Multiple Implied Readers." *Style* 41.3 (2007): 257–72.

Robinson, Jenefer. *Deeper than Reason: Emotion and Its Role in Literature, Music, and Art*. Oxford and New York: Oxford UP, 2005.

Ryman, Geoff. *253: A Novel for the Internet about London Underground in Seven Cars and a Crash*. 1996. <http://www.ryman-novel.com/>. Accessed 30 Jan. 2012.

Sedgwick, Eve Kosofsky. *Epistemology of the Closet*. Berkeley: U of California P, 1990.

Smith, Adam. *The Theory of Moral Sentiments*. 1759. Ed. D. D. Raphael and A. L. Macfie. Volume 1. *Glasgow Edition of the Works and Correspondence of Adam Smith*. Oxford and New York: Oxford UP, 1976.

"Special Section: Empathy." *Emotion Review* 4.1 (2012): 3–97.

Sternberg, Meir. "Proteus in Quotation-Land: Mimesis and the Forms of Reported Discourse." *Poetics Today* 3.2 (1982): 107–56.

Tajerian, Maral. "Fight or Flight: The Neuroscience of Survival Horror." *Gamasutra: The Art and Business of Making Games*. http://www.gamasutra.com/view/feature/172168/fight_or_flight_the_neuroscience_.php. Accessed 13 July 2012.

VIDA, *Women in Literary Arts*. "The 2011 Count." http://www.vidaweb.org/the-2011-count/. Accessed 2 July 2012.

Warhol, Robyn. "A Feminist Approach to Narrative." *Narrative Theory: Core Concepts and Critical Debates*. David Herman, James Phelan, Peter J. Rabinowitz, Brian Richardson, and Robyn Warhol. Columbus: The Ohio State UP, 2012. 9–13.

———. *Having a Good Cry: Effeminate Feelings and Pop-Culture Forms*. Columbus: The Ohio State UP, 2003.

Wing, Lorna. "Asperger's Syndrome: A Clinical Account." *Psychological Medicine* 11 (1981): 115–30.

Wispé, Lauren. "History of the Concept of Empathy." *Empathy and Its Development*. Ed. Nancy Eisenberg and Janet Strayer. Cambridge: Cambridge UP, 1987. 17–37.

Zwaan, Rolf A., and Lawrence J. Taylor. "Seeing, Acting, Understanding: Motor Resonance in Language Comprehension." *Journal of Experimental Psychology* 135.1 (2006): 1–11.

SUE J. KIM

Empathy and 1970s Novels by Third World Women[1]

In addition to the overall questions motivating this volume, two questions—one general and one more specific—inspired this essay. First, in
the wake of poststructuralist and other critiques of Eurocentric, bourgeois
feminisms, cross-cultural feminist solidarity remains a thorny question: to
what extent can feminists share allegiances "across cultures"? As we know,
our often compulsory performances of gender, sex, and subjectivity do not
express something wholly ontologically prior to that expression but rather
help constitute it; even if human beings share biological potentialities, not
only our cultural understandings but also our emotional and cognitive processes and material realities are conditioned by history and culture. One way
to think in terms of both universality and difference, then, is through the ways
in which narratives draw on shared potentialities while also producing different outcomes in different historical contexts. A second, related question is one
raised by Suzanne Keen: To what extent does empathy aroused by novel reading result in "prosocial action"? In contrast to some optimistic views about

1. I would like to thank all the participants of the Queer and Feminist Narrative Theory
Symposium, as well as my co-panelists and audience participants when I presented earlier versions of this paper at ASAP/3 in October 2011 and MLA in January 2012, particularly Meghan
Marie Hammond. Thanks also to Jennifer Ho, Betsy Huang, Paul Lai, and Stephen Hong Sohn
for their invaluable feedback, support, and general wisdom.

the moral effects of novel reading, Keen examines evidence that suggests that, historically, reading novels does not necessarily produce ethically desirable results. Nonetheless, Keen maintains that "*both authors' empathy and readers' empathy have rhetorical uses*," and she calls for further study on empathy and narrative, particularly on postcolonial novels (140; emphasis in original).

In this essay, I explore these two questions by examining an instance when narrative empathy did arguably produce notable social change by crossing and changing existing borders between different groups of women. I first review some discussions of empathy and its relation to narrative, ethics, and subjectivity. I then discuss the terms "Third World women" and "women of color," both of which I use in this essay, and I examine ways in which, in the 1970s, postcolonial and ethnic women writers—including Anita Desai, Buchi Emecheta, Bessie Head, Merle Hodge, Maxine Hong Kingston, and Toni Morrison—employed specific narrative strategies in part to explore and map out the kinds of oppressions, repressions, and erasures that women of color shared across ethnic and national boundaries. I examine not only how these instances of narrative empathy worked, but also what this case can show us about the possibilities and limits of empathy and other emotional responses to reading, particularly in later decades in the context of an increasingly flexible, voracious, and fetishizing global capitalism.

Empathy

As is the case with many basic affective and cognitive processes, empathy is familiar yet difficult to define. Empathy is generally described as a process in which a subject experiences the emotions of what he/she believes another person to be feeling. Basic empathy is described as an immediate reaction—for instance, the empathy of babies who cry when other babies cry (Keen 17)—but empathy becomes more complex, cognitively, affectively, and somatically, producing a variety of effects depending on context. For instance, the social position of the empathizer to the person being empathized with can mediate the reaction, as does the empathizer's aversion to personal distress, disagreement with the assumptions underlying the emotions, and so on. Some scholars, such as Amy Coplan, argue for a narrow definition of empathy, while others, such as Martin Hoffman, argue for a broader definition that does not necessarily involve volitional or complex psychological understanding.[2]

---

2. For an overview of the various genealogies of empathy, contemporary multidisciplinary research on empathy, and reassessments of empathy's relationship(s) to literature, see Hammond and Kim.

Partially motivating recent interest on empathy are its perceived moral and ethical potentials. In the widespread "empathy–altruism" hypothesis, novel reading produces moral growth on the part of the reader, who understands others more fully and engages in "prosocial" actions. But Suzanne Keen points out that, given the dearth of evidence that novel reading actually translates into social action or into erasing biases based on familiarity, such an emphasis on the power of empathy may be not just illusory but actually dangerous. For example, "failed empathy" can result in disillusionment, withdrawal, and apathy (Keen 54–55). Richard Delgado describes false or superficial empathy as the liberal fantasy of believing one knows the other while in fact simply reproducing power hierarchies by imposing the self on the other.[3] In short, such debates ask, what is the relationship of empathy to *justice*?

One way we can explore empathy's relation to justice is by interrogating the dynamics of difference and sameness. Some accounts of empathy, particularly those espousing empathy as producing prosocial behavior, hinge on the argument that empathy helps make the "other" into the "same" through the shared emotion. Liberal individualist accounts hold that empathy between different persons reveals their sameness and produces altruism, charity, volunteerism, and so forth. Even more sophisticated accounts of empathy privilege sameness; for instance, Hogan privileges "situational empathy," or empathy based on shared experience, particularly of suffering, over "categorical empathy," or empathy based on shared identity, because the former serves to bridge ostensible differences between subjects and groups (150). While I would not wholly discount the ethical potential of empathy, standard accounts of empathy that privilege sameness over difference can be problematic for two reasons. First, accounts of empathy that hinge on shared emotion underestimate the potential normative function of ideology in such experiences of empathy. In other words, a perceived empathic process of "making the other into the same" may actually participate in a complex, multifaceted ideological apparatus that in effect forces the other to be the same in order to count as a subject. Second, some accounts of emotion underestimate the complexity of subjectivity itself by focusing on individuals as atomized and discrete rather than dialectically related to groups and systems and, relatedly, by insufficiently considering the different definitions of a subject. In such cases, a perceived emotional sameness may serve to mystify and perpetuate hierarchal differences.

---

3. Such "false" empathy roughly describes the literature of subjectivity tourism/fetishism that I will discuss later in the essay.

Empathy can serve a normative function that not only prescribes what one should feel but also defines who can feel, or who constitutes a subject capable of feeling. For instance, Remy Debes, who considers narratives as integral to producing empathy, argues that empathy is by definition normative. He differentiates the intelligibility of another's emotion from a legitimation of the appraisals that produce that emotion. If we did not agree with the interpretations, explanations, and value systems of another person, we would not necessarily feel the same way. This approval may be tacit or unwilling, and the empathizer may not necessarily recommend this path to everyone. Nevertheless, Debes claims, "to empathize as the result of narrative is not just to identify the 'why' of the emotion, it's to accept the emotion in light of the 'why'—in light of the reasons offered in a narrative. And it's to accept those reasons just because one feels the same way as the narrator" (224). Instances of empathy, then, can be examined for the implicit (or explicit) ideological and/or ethical norms embedded in the shared emotions. Furthermore, overly narrow accounts of empathy may implicitly prescribe who constitutes a thinking, feeling subject.[4]

Another approach to empathy and justice is to consider that feeling between individuals may insufficiently account for different kinds of subjects in multiple, simultaneous systems. Even if we understand others as "capable of feeling" as we do, or if we imagine that we feel the emotions of others, the feeling subject is not necessarily equivalent to the political, economic, or legal subject; they are connected but not identical. Barbara Johnson makes the useful distinction that "lyric and law might be seen as two very different ways of instating what a 'person' is"; the "lyric" subject is "emotive, subjective, individual," whereas the "legal" subject is "rational, rights-bearing, institutional" (550). For instance, as Susan Lanser argues, the eighteenth-century novel that helped develop a modern sense of subjective interiority licensed a lyric subject at the expense of the legal subject. Lanser writes, "The very dynamic of the novel that gives speaking voices their efficacy may also be encouraging a separation between the psychological and the political" (497). Novels thus played a key role in developing a notion of the human that privileged the affective and obscured the legal, economic, and political subject.

---

4. For instance, Ralph Savarese argues vigorously against the commonplace notion that autistic people do not experience empathy. Savarese points out that research into the cognitive process of autistic people as well as examination of texts written by autistic authors demonstrate that some autistics experience a greater range of empathy beyond narrow and normative "neurotypical" conceptions of affect and cognition. Savarese argues for "neurodiversity," which would approach cognition as happening in a variety of ways, and "neurocosmopolitanism," which calls on neurotypicals to work towards understanding unfamiliar ways of thinking and being to the same extent that, for example, autistic people have had to do (284, 288).

We might add to the lyric and legal subjects a third term or category: the "embodied" subject, which includes elements of the subject that are neither "individual" as generally recognized nor "institutional," but rather unrecognized and/or perceived as nonvolitional. This embodied subjectivity may include elements of identity that have been discussed over the past several decades: gender, race, queerness, cognition, disability, emotion, and performativity (in the Butlerian sense). In terms of empathy, the embodied subject may refer to aspects of subjectivity that commonly accepted models of the lyric or the legal fail to account for. For instance, examples of embodied subjects who put pressure on definitions of the "lyric" and "legal" subject may include autistics who are seen as less capable of empathy (and/or less human) because they do not *feel* the same way as neurotypicals, or women of color, whose bodily marked intersections of gender and race historically rendered them less legible as either psychologically complex or political, rights-bearing subjects.[5]

In other words, not just our experiences of but also—and perhaps more importantly—our definitions of empathy play a key role in articulating and demarcating group boundaries, including the border between "person" and non-person, or whom we consider subjects. While recognizing our common possibilities as feeling, thinking beings can serve the ends of justice, conceptions of empathy that privilege an individual lyric subject, while occluding aspects of personhood that are legal and/or embodied, risk legitimizing existing hierarchical orders and concealing the ideological functions of empathy. That is, notions of empathy that are limited to the lyric individual run the risk of exacerbating structures of oppression and exploitation by failing to locate the sufferings of others in those structures and histories, and by failing to recognize the distinctions as well as the connections between the lyric, legal, and embodied subjects. So the fact that altruism may not be produced by empathy via novel reading is almost beside the point. Empathy in reading literature can produce meaningful social change when it is linked to an understanding that ostensibly individual emotions are tied to cognition, ideology, and social structures, as well as to social-political movements beyond the text, but to which the text refers and in which it participates. When the contexts change, the same strategies meant to evoke readerly empathy will not necessarily produce the same results.

---

5. That is, everyone has gender and race, but the minority term is marked; e.g., women "have" gender whereas men are presumed not to.

"Women of Color"

The novels I deal with here include Anita Desai's *Clear Light of Day* (1980); Buchi Emecheta's *Second-Class Citizen* (1974), *The Bride Price* (1976), and *The Joys of Motherhood* (1979); Bessie Head's *When Rain Clouds Gather* (1968), *Maru* (1971), and *A Question of Power* (1974); Merle Hodge's *Crick Crack, Monkey* (1970); Maxine Hong Kingston's *Woman Warrior* (1975); and Toni Morrison's *The Bluest Eye* (1970) and *Sula* (1974). While the specific con-texts of their production, publication, and reception vary widely, these texts share ideological concerns and aesthetic strategies at a moment marked by political mobilizing among non-white feminists across ethnic and national boundaries.[6] In the United States, Great Britain, and postcolonial nations, such texts became the de facto "representative" literary voices in English of Third World women. Furthermore, despite variations in the contexts of the texts, they share an explicit critique of gendered and racial oppression. These texts are significant as the works that attained publication (several through Heinemann), indicating a level of conformity to publishing and literary standards. Written within and against the tradition of novels in English, these novels pose a particularly interesting intellectual challenge for narra-tive theory. The literary strategies and political concerns of these novels are also shared by writers in the 1980s, including Alice Walker, Sandra Cisneros, and Tsitsi Dangarembga, as well as writers in the 1990s and later. Moreover, the common aesthetic strategies of these novels are more noticeable when contrasted to the work of other women of color / Third World women writ-ers in the 1970s—such as Theresa Hak Kyung Cha, Jessica Hagedorn, Gayl Jones, and Nicholasa Mohr—that, although dealing with similar issues, did not garner critical attention from feminist and ethnic studies scholars until a generation later.

These writers emerge at a moment in which, as has been well documented, Third World women were becoming politicized by both the experience in political mobilizing in anticolonial, Civil Rights, antiwar, cultural national-ist, and second-wave feminist movements, as well as internal critiques of

---

6. For instance, Maxine Hong Kingston became an instant literary celebrity, while fu-ture Nobel Prize winner and public intellectual Toni Morrison's first novel, *The Bluest Eye*, received mixed reviews and sold relatively few copies. South African / Botswana writer Bessie Head was well received by British and American reviewers, even being invited to the presti-gious University of Iowa International Writers Program—although her experience there was complicated—but her novels never sold in large quantities. Head's experiences in the English publishing and the literary worlds provide fascinating insight into the vicissitudes of being a "woman of color" writer in this moment; see Eilersen as well as Nazareth's reply to Head's ac-count of her visit to Iowa, "Path of Thunder: Meeting Bessie Head."

sexism, homophobia, racism, and bourgeois assumptions. The 1970s sees a relative flourishing of feminist organizing in, for example, the First National Chicana Conference in 1971; the publications of *Asian Women* in 1972 and the Combahee River Collective Statement in 1974; the 1975 UN Conference on Women's Issues in Mexico City; the 1977 National Women's Conference in Houston, TX, where the term "women of color" was coined as a political designation, and so forth. In the context of decolonization and worldwide student movements, many of these discussions were explicitly and self-consciously transnational. Further theorizing about "women of color" comes in the 1980s with publications by Angela Davis, bell hooks, Audre Lorde, Gloria Anzaldúa, Mitsuye Yamada, and others, several through Kitchen Table: Women of Color Press, founded by Barbara Smith in 1980. Chandra Talpade Mohanty famously intervened in homogenous constructions of "Third World woman" in 1984, and critics such as Chela Sandoval, Geraldine Heng, Grace Hong, and others have variously taken up Third World and/or women of color feminism in the following decades. While some uses run the risk of essentialism, most theoretical discussions of "women of color" and "Third World women" explicitly state that they are *political* designations meant to elucidate a subject position that points outward to social structures, rather than inward toward biology or essence.

While the terms "women of color" and "Third World women" have sometimes been used interchangeably, debates over the terms, as well as "postcolonial feminism," have been numerous.[7] I do not want to gloss over the complexities of the terms; in fact, part of my focus is on how these heterogeneous groups of women somehow became a historically and ideologically marked group. The salient point here is that the category or group of "Third World women" or "women of color" was not in common usage prior to the 1970s when women of color began organizing across racial, ethnic, and national boundaries.[8] These women shared a critique of white middle-class

---

7. For just a few examples, see Sangari; Mohanty; Suleri; and Rajan and Park.

8. For example, despite differences between Japanese, Chinese, Korean, Filipina, Vietnamese, and other Asian American women, a pan-Asian American feminist identity was forged through shared experiences of U.S. racial formations as well as of patriarchy and heteronormativity. As the editors of 1971's *Asian Women* write, "Asian-American women are faced with a double contradiction—their struggle as a Third World people in a racist nation and their role as women in a sexist society . . . . Third world women in the United States understand the double jeopardy of color and sex"; moreover, they argue, "We must not be divided from other Third World women" (129). Similarly, Cherríe Moraga notes in the introduction to the foundational 1984 *This Bridge Called My Back* that the feminists in the collection "identify as Third World women and/or women of color" (xxiv). In the foreword to the second edition, however, Moraga notes, "In the last three years I have learned that Third World feminism does not provide the kind of easy political framework that women of color are running to in droves" (n.p.).

feminism, nationalist and cultural nationalist patriarchy, colonialism and neo-imperialism, and also often capitalism and homophobia.[9]

Furthermore, the terms "women of color" and "Third World women" have been applied to all of the writers I am discussing (e.g., Head, Kingston, Desai, Morrison). Part of my argument is that the very narrative strategies that the novels use to evoke empathy in readers played a role in constituting this group and articulating its politics.[10] In these texts, empathy is invoked not only through identification with the characters, but also through an exploration of the social systems producing yet limiting that character. A key narrative strategy to create this double-layered empathic experience is the use of split internal perspective, creating a space between the ideological naïveté of the protagonist(s) at the diegetic level and the more complex analysis of the narrator or implied author. These narrative strategies produce a double-layered empathy that seeks to explore the subject as both lyric, or individual and feeling, and legal, or institutional and political. The reader is invited to empathize with the emotions of the lyric subject, but the texts also show how the lyric subject is reproduced by the legal subject's situation. Moreover, the texts illuminate how the relative powerlessness of the legal subject is tied to the women of color's embodiment as raced and sexed beings.

In mapping out these shared experiences and social oppressions, these 1970s novels did not simply appeal to already existing communities of readers; rather, in facilitating empathy, the novels played a part in identifying certain subjectivities, experiences, and situations as gendered and raced across national and ethnic boundaries, and thereby constituting new communities through reading. This process involved not only shared emotions but also—and crucially—a shared recognition and critique of intersecting systems of power based on conceptions of the body. In Hogan's terms, this group of readers moved from "situational empathy" to "categorical empathy." That is, a

---

9. "Race" is inflected variously in the texts, as variously and complexly as it functions in the world. Colonial racial regimes are distinct from racial formations of the United States, and the particular inflections of ethnic groups within the United States are also varied (e.g., "model minority" myth). But while the specific histories and ideologies are different, what ties the Western minority and the postcolonial together is the project of worldwide white supremacy, which historically produced the very concept of racial minorities and makes race so ubiquitous and complex an ideological monster for us to deal with today. Thus, "race" today often refers both to ethnic minorities in the West and to people of Third World nations—as well as "whiteness" as a historical construction—whose modern experience has been shaped by colonialism and neo-imperialism.

10. Moreover, individual writers have complex relationships to different kinds of feminisms; for instance, Chikwenye Okonjo Ogunyemi notably leaves Buchi Emecheta out of her genealogy of womanism, although others have questioned this omission. See Ogunyemi; Sougou; and Haraway.

certain set of historically produced social systems shaped a set of experiences shared by these writers, whose novels deploy common narrative strategies to evoke empathy in readers. Readers of all kinds could and did empathize, but some readers shared experiences evoked in the novels because they were located in a similar social position. This particular set of readers defined a new group—"women of color" or "Third World women"—based not only on those shared experiences but also on the critique of the social systems that produced their shared experiences.[11]

"Neither White nor Male"

Suzanne Keen has described three kinds of strategic empathy employed by authors. First, *"bounded strategic empathy"* functions "with an in-group, stemming from experiences of mutuality and leading to feeling with familiar others" (xiv). Second, *"ambassadorial strategic empathy* addresses chosen others with the aim of cultivating their empathy for the in-group" (xiv). Third, *"broadcast strategic empathy* calls upon every reader to feel with members of a group, by emphasizing common vulnerabilities and hopes through universalizing representations" (xiv). The writers I examine here employ both "ambassadorial" empathy—in the sense of calling out to specific others not hitherto identified as part of their own group—as well as "broadcast" empathy in pointing out systemic injustices, in which everyone is complicit and which everyone should recognize as unjust. Nevertheless, because the systems they were writing about cohere around certain raced and gendered bodies, the stories and characters may have been more familiar and more readily empathizable to readers who shared that nexus of social identifiers (i.e., race

---

11. I am not saying that the novels were the *only* things bringing together women of color. But the writing played a key role in the development of this particular group that while diverse had much in common structurally and experientially, and these commonalities are what helped develop later development in women of color, Third World, and postcolonial feminisms. Furthermore, these women of color were not the only ones to have used these narrative techniques, which are used by all kinds of writers; rather, my emphasis is on the confluence of a group of writers, texts, and readers responding to and in a particular historical moment. Also, the empathy-evoking features of the texts are not their only or even primary features; rather, I am interested in how these texts worked in an overall historical process, and what this process can show us about empathy. Finally, when talking about literature and society, causality is not always measurable or traceable, but in addition to examining narrative strategies and effects on readers, we can also look at larger social and ideological changes. In this case, I would argue that "social change" means not only on-the-ground political mobilizing *but also* the articulation of a political identity based on a political analysis, or changes in the shape and definition of social groups.

and gender), whose readerly empathy played a role in creating a "category" based on these shared social locators. Or, to return to Keen's terms, the in-group audience for "bounded strategic empathy" was an ongoing product of the intersection of narrative strategies that were also meant to elicit ambassadorial and broadcast empathy. To induce such reactions, these texts tend to employ either first-person and/or third-person limited perspective through a particular character or characters. As Keen points out, the use of internal perspective, through either first-person character narration or third-person narration that shows us a character's perspective, tends to encourage character identification and promotes readerly empathy (96). This third-person narration can be either *fixed* in one character's viewpoint throughout a text, or *variable*, shifting between characters' points of view (96). Techniques like free indirect discourse, interior monologue, and psychonarration also promote this internal perspective.

Furthermore, in these novels empathy is invoked not only via identification with the characters but also through an exploration of the social systems producing yet limiting that character. The reader is invited to empathize with the text or with the implied author's critique of and sometimes anger at the system. A key narrative strategy to create this double-layered empathic experience is the use of split internal perspective, creating a space between the ideological naïveté of the protagonist(s) at the diegetic level, and the more complex analysis of the narrator or implied author. This split perspective tends to appear in three forms: (1) a narrator of "now" and a younger protagonist (often a child) of the action; (2) two female characters (or more) in and out of which the narrative perspective alternates; and (3) between a third-person narrator and a character. I will sketch out some of the ways this split perspective works.

First, the distance between the child narrator and the adult narrator allows the text to reflect on the ideological forces at work on the child narrator, particularly those having to do with race/ethnicity and gender. *Crick Crack, Monkey* and *Woman Warrior* are pointed examples of this. In *Crick Crack*, we can identify at least three distinct—although not entirely separate—voices of the first-person narrator "Tee": an adult narrator, the initial child narrator, and the older child's voice (in the second part of the novel). She has many names—her formal name, Cynthia; her nickname, Tee; and the name of her fair "proper me," Helen—that reflect the different ideological directives of her childhood, her education, and her class mobility. Likewise, many moments in *Woman Warrior* are split between the intense emotions of the child narrator and the overt or covert reflections of the adult narrator; for example, the child narrator's initial understanding of her mother's stories contrasts with the adult narrator's interpretation of them. The reader is invited to share in the child narrator's experiences and emotions *as well as* the older narrator's analysis of and emotions about the situation.

Second, in some texts, internal perspective alternates between two doubled female characters, usually with one character who obeys some cultural rules, and another who does not follow the rules or, rather, follows different rules. This doubling allows the text to highlight conflicting interpretations of ideological injunctions while also exploring the shared structural limits on each woman's freedom. Examples of this include Bim and Tara in *Clear Light of Day;* Claudia and her sister as well as Claudia and Pecola in *The Bluest Eye;* the narrator and her mother in *Woman Warrior;* and Nel and Sula in *Sula.* This doubling in a sense allows one woman to try on different paths, attitudes, and so on, and in many instances to experience the limits imposed on her by the constrictions of gender, class, and race. For example, in *Sula,* Nel follows the rules—she gets married, has children and a house, and does all the things that her mother wants her to do—while Sula goes to college, has affairs, lives alone, and is insufficiently filial to her mother. In the novel, we hear both their perspectives via their internal thoughts as well as through pointed conversations. When Sula asks, "Why? I can do it all, why can't I have it all?" Nel replies, "You *can't* do it all. You a woman and a colored woman at that. You can't act like a man. You can't be walking around all independent-like, doing whatever you like, taking what you want, leaving what you don't" (142). Despite their different choices, Nel ends up alone and angry, and Sula ends up discontented, shunned, and dead. Ultimately, at the end of the novel Nel realizes she was missing not her husband Jude but rather Sula; the divergent paths of the two women ultimately serve to highlight their loss in not banding *together* against shared structural forces that delimit them by race and gender.

The third recurrent example of this split internal perspective is between a third-person narrator and a character to whom that narrator has been closely tied. Bessie Head does so quite often, sometimes adopting a disconcertingly metaphysical tone; both *A Question of Power* and *Maru* have third-person narrators closely tied to the protagonist, yet the narrator often inserts evaluative comments. Likewise, in Buchi Emecheta's *Second-Class Citizen,* the narrator steps back from close identification with Adah to comment on the situation, sometimes with a direct address to the reader. Toni Morrison is the master of all three techniques. Most of *The Bluest Eye,* for example, is narrated in first person by Claudia. At the start of the novel, an older Claudia-narrator ruminates with comments like "We thought, at the time . . ." and "It was a long time before my sister and I admitted to . . ." (5–6). The first section, "Autumn," shifts between the nine-year-old Claudia narrating in present tense and the adult Claudia narrating in past tense. The novel ends with the narrator in the "now," criticizing herself and her peers for achieving a self-definition by contrasting themselves to Pecola. The Claudia adult narrator tells us: "All of us felt so wholesome after we cleaned ourselves on her" (205). In addition, Claudia and Pecola are contrasted to see what possibilities and limitations are available to women of color. The younger Claudia, with a modicum of class privilege and family stability, can destroy blonde dolls, while Pecola has few resources to defend herself from the assaultive power of dominant ideals of goodness and beauty. Claudia and Pecola share the weight of a hegemonic blonde, blue-eyed femininity from which they are categorically excluded.

Other parts of the novel focus on Pecola's perspective via the third-person narrator (40, 44–58). The third-person narrator, however, steps back from Pecola's internal perspective in order to highlight the systemic problems that produce her suffering. For example, when Pecola goes to Mr. Yacobowski's store to buy candy, the narration alternates between Pecola's thoughts, Yacobowski's perspective, and the narrator's metacommentary. On one hand, Pecola experiences feelings that she does not yet have the language to express, feelings that the narrator explains emerge from her subconscious sense of the man's "total absence of human recognition" for her. On the other hand, the narrator asks us, "how can a fifty-two-year-old white immigrant store-keeper with the taste of potatoes and beer in his mouth . . . his sensibilities blunted by a permanent awareness of loss, *see* a little black girl?" (50). Here, the narrator invites us to empathize not only with Pecola and even Yacobowski, but also with the narrator's distress at the dehumanizing racial and gendered systems in which they are both caught. The use of present tense throughout this scene further troubles the difference between diegetic and narrative time, between the "past" of Pecola and the "now" of the storyteller, suggesting that the implications of the scene extend beyond that one moment in time. The narrator then suggests how we should feel not simply with the characters but about the situation: Leaving the store, Pecola experiences a fleeting moment of rage—but shame quickly takes over again. The narrator then interjects, "Anger is better. There is a sense of being in anger. A reality and a presence. An awareness of worth. It is a lovely surging" (50). In other words, we are invited not only to experience Yacobowski's blindness and Pecola's humiliation and rage but also the narrator's assessment that anger is the more appropriate response to this situation. In other words, the novel shows that Pecola as a lyric subject—a feeling individual—is tied to her as a legal subject—institutionally defined—because of her embodiment as black and female (and young).

Likewise, in *Sula,* the third-person narrator steps outside Nel and Sula's perspectives to comment directly on their overall situation. In what is sometimes called "psychonarration," the narrator describes the characters' states of mind:

> So when they [Nel and Sula] met, first in those chocolate halls and next through the ropes of the swing, they felt the ease and comfort of old friends. Because each had discovered years before that they were neither white nor male, and that all freedom and triumph was forbidden to them, they had set about creating something else to be. Their meeting was fortunate, for it let them use each other to grow on. Daughters of distant mothers and incomprehensible fathers . . . , they found in each other's eyes the intimacy they were looking for. (52)

The various novels also use minor characters to offer perspectives that differ pointedly from those of the protagonist and/or character-narrator, with implicit or explicit evaluations of these contrasting views by the narrator-I. The kinds of characters who figure largely in these tales include husbands and brothers, mothers and aunts, and various socially marginal figures (old bachelors, prostitutes, etc.). These characters promulgate patriarchy, nationalism, or cultural nationalism, and/or exist distinctly outside communally sanctioned boundaries and thereby draw attention to these boundaries. In terms of setting and place, the texts include minimal direct reference to or explanation of public historical-national events. In contrast to the self-conscious historiographic metafiction of, for example, Salman Rushdie's *Midnight's Children,* in which the lyric subject is arguably subordinated to the legal subject (and the body primarily a metaphor for the state), Desai's *Clear Light of Day* narratively subordinates the 1947 partition of India and Pakistan to the domestic dynamics of Bim and Tara. *Clear Light of Day* is not any less political than *Midnight's Children*; rather, what affects Tara and Bim at that historical moment is patriarchy in the shape of their brother Raja's frustrated desire to be a poetic or political hero, and whether or not they can inhabit available roles of femininity and masculinity. In many senses, these novels are domestic fictions, in which the texts share a heightened awareness of and narrative attention to private spaces and the body, not only in terms of skin color, beauty regimens, classed and raced standards of beauty, and the policing of sexuality, but also in relation to food preparation and consumption, illness and neurosis, and other everyday, intimate bodily functions.

However, while class and sexuality are central to the theorization of women of color feminism, these issues do not figure as centrally in the novels

I am focusing on here—or rather, these issues figure differently. While much women of color feminism has foregrounded lesbians and poor women, many of the texts formally naturalize a middle-class, heterosexual point of view. For instance, the narrative strategies of several novels invite the reader to empathize with the middle-class protagonist, not the poor. Even in stories of poverty, such as *The Bluest Eye*, the reader is prompted to identify with the adult middle-class Claudia, rather than the poor, mad Pecola. Pecola may be the ostensible subject of the novel and the title, but because the evaluation and description of the narration comes through Claudia, the novel invites us to identify with Claudia-as-narrator instead of Pecola. Similarly, even though Margaret in *Maru* is a Masarwa (derogatorily referred to as "Bush" people) and therefore deemed inferior to the Batswana, she is educated by and named after a white missionary. These texts also tend to be heterocentric. While there are degrees of female intimacy, there are few lesbians. The absence of lesbians is striking in contrast to, again, the work of women of color theorists, or the fiction of Gayl Jones and Nicholasa Mohr.

These absences are in some ways written into what become the accepted terms, "women of color" and "third world women"; both terms foreground gender and race. In part, these women-of-color writers were less concerned with subverting a prescriptive middle-class, hetero femininity because they were trying to interrupt a white/Western middle-class femininity that was, in many ways, defined against them. But in contrast to early women-of-color feminist theory, this group of novels focuses more readerly empathy on the embodied subject of gendered and racial regimes than the legal subject in economic or sexual regimes. Thus the figure of the "woman of color" as lyric subject in these novels runs the risk of becoming recuperable and/or complicit with a straight and bourgeois yet raced femininity. In the next section, I argue that this is in part the trajectory that takes place in later decades.

Empathy, Feminism, and Narratology

In later decades (and even in the 1970s), the identity category "women of color" and even "Third World women" can and has been appropriated into late capitalism's consumerist, individualist multiculturalism, partly due to the narrative configurations of empathy, subjectivity, and ideology outlined in the previous section, but partly regardless of the specific narratives. As has been well documented, the 1980s in particular saw a backlash against social movements around the world. Concomitantly, the logics of culture and the marketplace rapidly transformed into more flexible, mobile, and "cosmopolitan" forms. Ostensibly, the non-white woman fits into this cosmopolitan consumerist world as both subject and object. She fits into this new world order as literal subject; take, for example, the Asian woman shown flying business class in an advertisement in *The Economist*. The advertisement invites women not to deny their gender and non-whiteness but to embrace it. Yet a few pages later, we may also see advertisements featuring an exotic Asian stewardess, or an exhortation to make use of the nimble, pliant labor of Third World women in free trade zones. Within this contradictory context, the Third World woman can also function in the literary marketplace as an object of empathy. Today, liberal multiculturalism and cosmopolitanism are not seen as antithetical to but in many ways compatible with and even necessary for global capitalism, and a tenet of this sort of multiculturalism is that one ought to empathize with cultural others. In other words, consumption of novels by Third World women can and does constitute a certain kind of cultural capital for the middlebrow and/or educated cosmopolitan reader, even and perhaps especially in the university classroom as one key training site for neoliberal subjects.

One telling example of this commodification of women of color's subjectivities can be seen in the new editions of several of these women's novels from the 1970s and 1980s. Whereas the first editions featured some kind of abstract drawing, a child, a picture of a place, or some image otherwise suggested in the text, editions in the 1990s and 2000s frequently feature a photograph of a woman on the cover, sometimes quite glamorously made up. Such bodies appear on newer editions of *Nervous Conditions; Dictée; Crick Crack, Monkey; Woman Warrior* (prominently featuring the almond-shaped eye); and *Clear Light of Day*, and this fetishization applies to both women in Third World nations and minority women in the West.[12] Similar changes have not occurred with newer editions of *Midnight's Children, Invisible Man,* or *Gravity's Rainbow*; we do not see draped across the cover of *Things Fall Apart* an exotic male model whose body we might link to both the protagonist and the author. In other words, the same texts that can invite narrative empathy for both lyric and legal subjects can also be mobilized in service of the consumerist liberal multicultural logic of late capitalism. These covers illustrate a fetishized aesthetic that transcends any individual cover designer; the packaging and objectifying of Third World women's bodies speaks to the market for their "humanity" via a dominant, naturalized conception of empathy in terms of the atomized, discrete lyric subject.[13]

---

12. I have not cited the specific editions here because my goal is not to vilify one particular publisher or editor; rather, my interest here is in an aesthetic and ideological trend.

13. In this context, the ideological and aesthetic interventions of the work of Cha, Jones,

These novels—and their particular narrative strategies for inviting readerly empathy—have been and are being conscripted into the general production of a limited, normative notion of subjectivity as lyric (feeling, individual) and legal in certain ways (race, gender, nation), but not in others (economic, sexual). This commodification of empathy for the Other constitutes a kind of subjectivity fetishism and tourism. The middle-class woman of color can be targeted as a new cosmopolitan consumer subject to be marketed to, as well as an object of consumption for others. This object of readerly empathy is a figural "woman of color" who appears to wield the newly desirable cultural capital of "difference" but is actually the same—lyric and limited versions of the legal subject of neoliberalism—and can be used to obscure the conditions of women of color—particularly poor and/or lesbian women of color—by obfuscating economic and sexual regimes. The apparent empathy induced by these novels on the multicultural marketplace to some extent actually mystify their commodification, because they are marketed and read as bearing the aura of "the human" in lyric terms (Coykendall). The individual's readerly empathy may be real, and a reader may experience genuine emotion at the sufferings of a protagonist in very different circumstances. But if that empathy remains at the level of lyric subject, at the expense of the legal subject or certain varieties of legal subjectivity (e.g., gender vs. class), then the readerly empathy not only fails to bridge differences but also participates in licensing and exacerbating the hierarchical, exploitative legal, economic, and political systems that produce those differences.

The empathy from the novels I discuss here can be productively contrasted to other novels from the 1970s and 1980s, including *Corregidora* and *Dictée*. *Corregidora*'s protagonist Ursa resists the empathy of a typical middle-class reader; the violent sexuality of the history that produces her is so foregrounded that the novel is often described as "brutal." Similarly, critics in the 1990s and after embraced *Dictée* for its critique not only of imperialism and patriarchy but also of the very processes of ideological subject formation.[14] Nicholasa Mohr's novels feature poor women and a variety of sexualities (hetero, homo, pan), but because their target audience is young adults, the narratives function very differently. They do not produce as deep a sense of the lyric subject's interiority in quite the same way as, say, Kingston's or Morrison's, but they do relentlessly highlight the sexual and economic regimes that shape the lives not only of poor women of color but also of their communi-

---

and Mohr become even more interesting. While modernist aesthetics can also be commodified and fetishized, narrative empathy would work differently or perhaps not exist as empathy per se.

14. See Kim and Alarcón as well as Lowe.

ties. These different approaches, however, do not prevent these novels from also being appropriated and instrumentalized in late capitalist multicultural consumerism; book covers of new editions of *Dictée* and *Corregidora* similarly foreground the woman of color's body. But their complication of conventional readerly empathy makes these texts slightly more difficult to consume easily, although, as literary tastes change—again, often through the medium of the university classroom—and the exigencies of capitalism change, they may also become familiarized and commodified.

IN THE 1970S, narrative strategies of empathy in these novels helped articulate a group across existing boundaries, partially through an insistence on the subject as both lyric and legal, and, moreover, whose legal subjectivity was impinged upon due to certain elements of embodiment. In later decades, the marketing of women of color (e.g., the women's bodies on the book cover to market her story within) draws on this lyric notion of the subject and certain aspects of legal subjectivity (particularly patriarchy and racism as located in the past[15]), but, in its instrumentalization in fostering the hegemony of consumerist individualism and the fetishization of difference, may obscure other aspects of legal subjectivity, such as class and sexuality.

So, to return to the first questions of this paper: When questions arise about the differences between cultures, the conversation often relies on an implicit notion of groups as fixed, discrete, autonomous. For instance, categorical empathy is seen as the less ethically desirable outcome because it is based on an in-group and thus on exclusion. But the preference for situational empathy over categorical empathy does not take into account that most modern group categories arose—at least at some distant point in the past—out of a sense of situational commonality. Today, the most marked, politically charged identity group categories—including nationalisms—arise out of historical systemic processes (colonialism and neo-imperialism, patriarchy and heteronormativity, capitalism and labor flows) that shaped the unmarked norm ("Western white male") as much as the Other, and certainly narratives, particularly novels since the eighteenth century, have had a central place in articulating those categories. To return to the second question: empathy produced by reading—and the myriad political, affective, cognitive, and other results of this reading experience—may effect social change, but this potential depends in large part on the conceptions of empathy and subjectivity and the

---

15. Note that "the past" can be projected in terms of space, as in other cultures/places being less modern than the West.

historical context in which these concepts are operative. In other words, both empathy and subjectivity are complex, historically and institutionally embedded concepts.

In this sense, expanding our conceptions about empathy is consonant with broadening the field of narrative theory to engage feminist and queer theory, which is inextricably interwoven with the fields and concerns of ethnic, postcolonial, disability, and Marxist studies. To echo Robyn Warhol's *Gendered Interventions,* in understanding narrative empathy, narrative theory can help us elucidate a poetics, but contextualizing and historicizing are necessary accompanying processes. This inextricable relationship between history, narrative form, and the ethics of reading is why narrative theory must continue to widen the field of literary, historical, and theoretical texts that it examines and incorporate the insights garnered from examinations of these texts in order to continue as a living, vibrant field.

Works Cited

Asian Women's Coalition. *Asian Women.* Berkeley: University of California, 1971.

Cha, Theresa Hak Kyung. *Dictée.* 1982. Berkeley: Third Woman Press, 1995.

Coplan, Amy. "Will the Real Empathy Please Stand Up? A Case for Narrow Conceptualization." *The Southern Journal of Philosophy* 49 (2011): 40–65.

Coykendall, Abby. "Re: cultural capital." Message to the author. 16 May 2011. Email.

Debes, Remy. "Which Empathy? Limitations in the Mirrored 'Understanding' of Emotion." *Synthese* 175 (2010): 219–39.

Delgado, Richard. "Rodrigo's Eleventh Chronicle: Empathy and False Empathy." *California Law Review* 84 (1996): 61–100.

Desai, Anita. *Clear Light of Day.* New York: Harpercollins, 1980.

Eilersen, Gillian Stead. *Bessie Head: Thunder Behind Her Ears.* Cape Town: James Currey, 1996.

Emecheta, Buchi. *The Bride Price.* 1976. New York: Braziller, 1980.

———. *The Joys of Motherhood.* 1979. Portsmouth: Heinemann, 1994.

———. *Second-Class Citizen.* 1974. New York: Braziller, 1983.

Hammond, Meghan Marie and Sue J. Kim, eds. *Rethinking Empathy Through Literature.* New York: Routledge, 2014.

Haraway, Donna. "Reading Buchi Emecheta: Contests for Women's Experience in Women's Studies." *Inscriptions* 3–4 (1988). <http://culturalstudies.ucsc.edu/PUBS/Inscriptions/vol_3-4/DonnaHaraway.html>. Accessed 15 Jan. 2013.

Head, Bessie. *Maru.* Portsmouth: Heinemann, 1971.

———. *A Question of Power.* Portsmouth: Heinemann, 1974.

———. *When Rain Clouds Gather.* Portsmouth: Heinemann, 1969.

Hodge, Merle. *Crick Crack, Monkey.* Portsmouth: Heinemann, 1970.

Hoffman, Martin L. *Empathy and Moral Development: Implications for Caring and Justice.* Cambridge: Cambridge UP, 2001.

Hogan, Patrick Colm. *The Mind and Its Stories: Narrative Universals and Human Emotion.* Cambridge: Cambridge UP, 2003.

Hong Kingston, Maxine. *Woman Warrior: Memoirs of a Girlhood Among Ghosts.* New York: Vintage, 1975.

Johnson, Barbara. "Anthropomorphism in Lyric and Law." *Yale Journal of Law and the Humanities* 10.2 (1998): 549–74.

Jones, Gayl. *Corregidora.* Boston: Beacon Press, 1975.

Keen, Suzanne. *Empathy and the Novel.* New York: Oxford UP, 2007.

Kim, Elaine, and Norma Alarcón, eds. *Writing Self, Writing Nation.* Berkeley: Third Woman, 1994.

Lanser, Susan. "The Novel Body Politic." *A Companion to the Eighteenth-Century English Novel and Culture.* Ed. Paula R. Backscheider and Catherine Ingrassia. Malden, MA; Oxford: Blackwell, 2006. 481–503.

Lowe, Lisa. *Immigrant Acts.* Durham: Duke UP, 1996.

Mohanty, Chandra Talpade. "Cartographies of Struggle: Third World Women and the Politics of Feminism." *Third World Women and the Politics of Feminism.* Ed. Mohanty et al. Bloomington: Indiana UP, 1991. 1–47.

Moraga, Cherríe, and Gloria Anzaldúa. *This Bridge Called My Back: Writings By Radical Women of Color.* New York: Kitchen Table / Women of Color, 1984.

Morrison, Toni. *The Bluest Eye.* 1970. New York: Knopf, 2000.

———. *Sula.* New York: Plume, 1982.

Nazareth, Peter. "Path of Thunder: Meeting Bessie Head." *Research in African Literatures* 37.4 (Winter 2006): 211–29.

Ogunyemi, Chikwenye Okonjo. "Womanism: The Dynamics of the Contemporary Black Female Novel in English." *Signs* 11.1 (1985): 63–80.

Rajan, Rajeswari Sunder, and You-me Park. "Postcolonial Feminism / Postcolonialism and Feminism." *A Companion to Postcolonial Studies.* Ed. Henry Schwarz and Sangeeta Ray. Malden, MA; Oxford: Blackwell, 2005. 53–71.

Sangari, Kumkum. "The Politics of the Possible." *The Nature and Context of Minority Discourse.* Ed. Abdul JanMohamed and David Lloyd. New York: Oxford UP, 1990. 216–45.

Savarese, Ralph. "Towards a Postcolonial Neurology: Autism, Tito Mukhopadhyay, and a New Geo-poetics of the Body." *Journal of Literary & Cultural Disability Studies* 4.3 (2010): 273–90.

Sougou, Omar. *Writing Across Cultures: Gender Politics and Difference in the Fiction of Buchi Emecheta.* New York: Rodopi, 2002.

Suleri, Sara. "Woman Skin Deep." *Critical Inquiry* 18.4 (1992): 756–69.

Warhol, Robyn. *Gendered Interventions: Narrative Discourse in the Victorian Novel.* New Brunswick: Rutgers UP, 1989.

PART III

Lifewriting, Gender, Sex

ALISON BOOTH

Screenshots in the *Longue Durée*

Feminist Narratology, Digital Humanities, and
Collective Biographies of Women

"*D*igital humanities" (DH), or computational research in the humanities, is rapidly evolving in an environment that has undergone several geological events in recent decades, including the seismic shift of feminist
studies. In this new millennium, I along with others who work on women,
gender, literature, history, and related matters have been inducted into DH,
with its tools that recondition practice and in turn challenge both old and new
theories and aims.[1] DH has changed how I spend my time and has led me to
collaborate with librarians, programmers and designers, research assistants,
and far-flung professors of history as well as literature (including Classicists
and Medievalists). A digital project feels as much like building or quilting as
like writing and editing; we create a terminus of many routes, a web—poetic
figures dominate the technological as much as the interpretative, shaping the
very infrastructure of inquiry.[2] I'm not pushing a utopian vision that would

---

1. In the past decade, voices have been raised to challenge digital projects' apparent blindness to diversity and theoretical critique (race, gender and sexuality, postcolonial, and disability
studies). See Martha Nell Smith, "Frozen Social Relations," 403–10, citing her own and others'
previous interventions on identity politics in DH.

2. There is, after all, a language of programming code which a computer is said to read;
data exist as such only after they are labeled. Ryan, in "Cyberage Narratology: Computers,
Metaphor, and Narrative," considers the metaphors in narratology and computer technology
(113). I have experienced DH as a process of learning new nouns and verbs (how to *commit* to

leave behind longstanding inquiries. Rather I hope to illustrate a project that is more of an expansion than a departure from the project of feminist narratology. My Collective Biographies of Women project (CBW), begun as an online annotated bibliography, has also become a digital prosopography and an experiment in narrative theory. What I mean by these terms will I hope become clear in the following pages.

Feminist literary studies, narrative theory, and DH, three fields that intersect in CBW, would benefit from more interaction and user-friendly communication with outsiders. I introduce aspects of the CBW project, and in particular our detailed analyses of short biographies of women, for the sake of furthering such influence and collaboration. Postclassical narratology can behave as if it has heard everything that feminist and queer theories have to say. Digital humanities can be preoccupied with new tools without taking stock of theoretical challenges within historical disciplines. Yet DH practitioners often have more engagement with so-called Theory and critique of representation than colleagues in humanities departments give them credit for (Bauer). Narratology, computer science, and engineering or design all have high thresholds for the uninitiated to join the conversation; even those who write about the culture or poetics of new media can be hazy on the nuts and bolts of computer programming or markup (the work with software that instructs computers how to read our data). Narrative theory has concentrated on fiction (in print or film), largely overlooking what is distinctive in nonfiction, and the Web presence of this work tends to consist of encyclopedias or digitized articles. The considerable activity today in computational models of narrative structure (relating to artificial intelligence), big-data textual analysis or topic modeling (as in digitization of the novel in English), or born-digital narratives (as in hypertext collaborative narratives or videogames) has so far offered little for a historical inquiry into the life narratives of women that have circulated in print.

Although in early days of feminist theory computation seemed a masculine, technocratic domain, and there are still signals that the hacker or gamer is presumed heterosexual white or Asian male, DH as an international community strives to see itself as blind to embodied or economic differences. There have been successful feminist digital projects such as Orlando and the Women Writers Project (formerly at Brown University). CBW, too, is a literary study with a database of historical women. Yet unlike comparable or larger projects, CBW is not limited to women writers nor is it a collection of

subversion is a daily procedure, not a call to social action). DH also has a funhouse effect on time, slowing it down and speeding it up: any phase of a project can take many person-hours over years, and technology supersedes a process before it is fully implemented.

edited digitized texts. The printed biographical collections accessed in CBW, written by men as well as women, feature famous and obscure women, from many nations and historical contexts and representing most possible occupations. CBW began with a bibliography of all the English-language books published during the period 1830–1940 that include biographies of three or more women (we record many texts before and after), for a total of 1,270 collections. CBW collects information about short nonfiction narratives in these collections—a rich corpus upon which to build a model of nonfiction and add to the few existing theoretical or formal studies of biography. Instead of an edition, CBW is a study of trends in the representation of historical women in groups, and a study of a narrative genre in relation to social networks and ideology of gender, class, and other social difference. Collective biographies or prosopographies of women can reveal conceptual or practical networks among women of various kinds, and revise our retrospective interpretations. Instead of deriving our pictures of gender ideology from the pronouncements of Sarah Ellis, John Ruskin, Margaret Fuller, or Charlotte Perkins Gilman, we might find unexpected alternatives in the narratives reproduced in these books.

The wealth of contradictory models, as well as the multiple versions of the same historical persons and events, makes this a fascinating dataset for women's biographical history, measuring trends in gender ideology from within the horizons of Anglo-American literate or upper classes. Among some 8,000 women and more than 13,400 chapters (including numerous versions of the same individual and some multisubject chapters), we find some diversity of race, nationality, and sexuality, and some address to working-class audiences. Women who love women or women who self-fashion as masculine did infiltrate the lists because of their achievements in war, the arts, or literature. In many (but not all) of the collections, an implied young female audience or an implied Protestant corporate authorship have their normative effects. Taking account of the revision some historical women actually made in expected life trajectories, nineteenth-century biographical collections can be more flexible than mainstream fiction at the time, so that Rosa Bonheur, Harriet Hosmer, and Charlotte Cushman, for instance, are openly honored artists without denial or censure of their performed masculinity or lesbianism. Biographies do have a limited number of plots or ideological scripts, but nonfiction treatments of historic individuals also exceed the emplotment of the good daughter, wife, or mother, the virago, or the tragic lover.

CBW has a range of distinctive features that should be especially interesting to those engaged in feminist studies, narrative theory, or both. The longstanding feminist initiative to recover women's biographies and histories can be revitalized with deeper and broader study of publications in the print era, informed by critical examination of our terms of inquiry. Structural narratology can be revived in a morphology of a nonfiction genre, across national and historical boundaries, because new mediation allows us to make really big generalizations and qualify them at the same time.[3] Among the many features of CBW, in this essay I shine light on the sample corpora or documentary social networks focused on certain persona types, and the markup schema that we have devised for interpreting the variations within the conventions of these clustered narratives about women's lives. Our work with the sample corpora and the Biographical Elements and Structure Schema (BESS), very much in progress, hopes to foster dialogue among feminist studies, narrative theory, and digital innovation.

After introducing a general view of prosopography and a more inside view of CBW's ongoing study of biographical narrative, I will return to the implications of scale and method for a digital feminist narratology. Questions of method and professional affiliation touch on the matters of agency, recognition, and collectivity at the heart of a feminist or queer narrative theory. Digital projects, for all their gleaming thresholds, only warrant the labor of building them if they accommodate living inquiry on an unprecedented scale. From another angle, the technology can yield spectacular information that has no salience if our projects have not been designed with attention to the ongoing dialogues of criticism and theory in the disciplines in the humanities—as if providing answers to pointless questions. That's where a thorough grounding in the humanities comes in, to keep the digital side of the equation on its mettle.

Sample Archives and a New Narrative Analysis

While documenting a forgotten genre, my book *How to Make It as a Woman* (2004), and hence its digital sequel, sought to trace a history of categorization and comparison of representative figures and clustered types, from Joan of Arc, Queen Victoria, Madame Roland, and Isabella Bird to some obscure minister's wife who helped to settle Oklahoma.[4] In the Scholars' Lab, we initi-

---

3. Vladimir Propp's *Morphology of the Folktale* (1928) derived a morphology of 31 elements or functions (further developed by Greimas) that recur in Russian folktales. Mark Alan Finlayson at MIT claims to confirm Propp's model on natural-language texts using Analogical Story Merging on his Workbench, an annotation tool.

4. It seems inevitable now that the annotated bibliography, too large for the printed book, came to flourish in its searchable and accessible form on the University of Virginia Library's server (Booth, "The Collective Biographies of Women: Preface"). The bibliography is accessible at http://womensbios.lib.virginia.edu. Every year more of the world's libraries are

ated steps toward studies in a narrative genre, as our open-source project links to Google Books and to WorldCat (the database of library catalogs), with more immediate access to page images and portraits. Along with an inter-active chart of the most popular subjects and types, we developed Featured Subjects (incorporating students' research) as starting points for research on individual women. More recently we have concentrated narrative analysis on subsets of the bibliography's list, sample corpora of the collections that include a certain woman and the networks of other personae associated with her. (A sample corpus consists of a set of about 9 to 25 books in the form of page images, TEI [Text Encoding Initiative] files of the prose, and our separate files of analysis of the narratives [in XML, or Extensible Markup Language].)

We centered the first two sample corpora on two antithetical Victorian women, Sister Dora and the adventuress Lola Montez, chosen in part because there is no overlap—no book that holds Sister Dora ever includes Lola Mon-tez. Sister Dora, or Dorothy Wyndlow Pattison (1832–78), a clergyman's daughter from Yorkshire, became internationally renowned as a version of Florence Nightingale, a modern Saint Theresa or precedent for Mother Teresa. Becoming an expert in surgery and treating wounds, she ran small hospitals for victims of industrial accidents or smallpox epidemics near Birmingham in the 1870s. She was revered for some fifty years—in nineteen collective biog-raphies of women between 1880 and 1930—and then dropped out of sight (in one collection of 1993).[5] In what circumstances did her kind of career become possible and then lose its appeal? How did the treatments of her life recon-cile her performance of a saintly type with mundane evidence, in the age of newspapers, photography, and railroads, and with witnesses who knew her in daily life? What kinds of collections included Sister Dora? Her life is retold in collections of "Noble Workers," as I call them, from a title by Jennie Chap-pell. Noble Workers (the 141 women who one or more times share a volume with Sister Dora) defy the oxymoron of status in this phrase; they are ladies engaged in social work of some kind, often taking responsibility for the souls,

---

available online. CBW was peer-reviewed by Networked Infrastructure of Nineteenth-Century Electronic Scholarship (NINES) in 2007. I worked with Bethany Nowviskie and Joe Gilbert in the Scholars' Lab; in 2009, I started as a fellow of the Institute for Advanced Technology in the Humanities at UVA, collaborating with Worthy Martin and Daniel Pitti. The current database is accessible at http://cbw.iath.virginia.edu/cbw_db/ and a new design (in progress) can be seen at http://cbw.iath.virginia.edu/public/index.php. Rennie Mapp has been Project Manager from 2013 to 2014.

5. She garnered a couple of full-length biographies almost a hundred years apart, by Lon-sdale and Manton, and a TV miniseries. For more on Sister Dora, beyond our Featured Subject treatment, see Booth, "Recovery." The versions of her life in collective biographies show little interest in Victorian social context and never focus on her brother, Mark Pattison, the Oxford don associated with George Eliot's *Middlemarch*. This introduction to Sister Dora and Lola Montez overlaps with Booth, "Prosopography."

appetites, and discipline of the poor, often with an attachment to regimentals or orders: in one collection of 1898, a composite frontispiece (see fig. 8.1) unites Frances Willard of the Women's Christian Temperance Union; Agnes Weston, the Sailor's Friend; Catherine Booth in the Salvation Army, and Sister Dora (Booth and Dora adopt uniforms of sanctity).

A strikingly different constellation of types of personae appears in the second corpus, which we call "Women of the World," fourteen collections that include Lola Montez (250 other women accompany Montez in these books, some several times).[6] The Oxford *Dictionary of National Biography* (ODNB) labels Lola Montez (who was born in Ireland in 1821 and died in New York in 1861) with the occupational term "adventuress."[7] She was also a world-traveled performer: a self-styled Spanish dancer famous for her spider dance. In a brief star turn, she became the mistress of Ludwig I of Bavaria, who created her Countess of Landsfeld; her anticlerical influence and popularity among the students led to a revolution in 1848. In collections in CBW, she finds herself classified with other wild beauties born in Ireland, with pretty horsebreakers of Mayfair or with hard-living entertainers in the gold rush of Australia or California (settings of her various triumphs and scandals). In *How to Make It as a Woman*, I noted that the collection of "bad" women largely goes underground during the nineteenth century; an eighteenth-century relish for French and English courtesans and adventuresses resurfaces around the 1890s. The 1920s were a heyday of such volumes as *Gallant Ladies* by Cameron Rogers, which featured women from Mata Hari to Calamity Jane.[8] Like

---

6. In 2014, we have extended our samples to books that include the scientist Caroline Herschel, the novelist Frances Trollope, Cleopatra, and the French assassin Charlotte Corday, with numerous other women. The CBW database assigns types both to collections and to persons based on the argument of tables of contents and narratives themselves as to the biographies' relevance: women of the Bible, mothers or wives of leaders, and so on. Investigation of networks and texts in the sample corpora will reveal less manifest typological relationships among personae (versions of life narratives). Statistics are in flux in any active database.

7. Apparently, she is one of five women so designated in the ODNB, though many a mistress, wife, or ancestor of a famous man, as well as a range of writers and performers, are alleged to be adventuresses within their biographies in the ODNB (the word appears twenty-one times). The exact word does not delimit the type. There are 66 returns for a search of "courtesan" in the ODNB, including multiple references to famous individuals; "mistress" 1,473 (including the "demi-mondaine" Montez); "adulteress" is a term applied seven times (including to Montez). "Dancer" is an appellation used 474 times, and it includes a high proportion of men and gay lovers as well as women or wives of famous men. "Performer" appears 566 times but is not used in reference to Montez. Some men appear under the vocational type "rogue" or "adventurer."

8. Some pieces are reprinted from *The Pictorial Review*. "The very term 'Gallant Ladies' connoted carnal misdemeanors and bawdy overtones deserving of condemnation and deletion," though Rogers begins by noting that male adventurers get an easier pass and insists that regarding his own heroines, "the word 'gallant' denotes not sexual aberration, but courage, resource

FIGURE 8.1. Frontispiece Uniting Sister Dora with Frances Willard, Agnes Weston, and Catherine Booth

other digital studies of archives, we can trace chapter and book titles to capture different social values. Lola Montez and Sister Dora, with their adopted professional names and costumes, were British contemporaries (Lola Montez died in New York in 1861, Sister Dora in Walsall in 1878), and books promoting Noble Workers overlap with the years of publication of books of Women

and character," the issue of chastity being more "no more consequential" in their lives than it would be in the narratives of Odysseus or John Paul Jones (11–12).

of the World. Nevertheless, Lola Montez, famous and much written about, only surfaced in biographical collections after 1897, since her story cannot be shaped into a positive model of femininity. If Sister Dora appears in her white starched cap, Lola Montez wears black lace and wields a whip.

To analyze the assorted narratives in such sample corpora, we developed an editorial system called Biographical Structure and Elements Schema (BESS). Comparative evaluation is imbedded in collected life narratives, and our editorial schema, using a large set of controlled vocabulary (more on this later), records the textual location (the numbered paragraph) of kinds of events, social encounters, rhetoric, and other features. The computer can then retrieve and collate any passages in all twenty versions that represent the event type *recognition,* for example, as in the statue erected in memory of Sister Dora, and align it with this event type in other women's biographies. Or we can compare versions that deploy the standard rhetoric of *analogy* among models, as when Sister Dora is likened to Florence Nightingale, to Saint Theresa (Baring-Gould), or even to Christ (Green-Armytage 117). A book that includes Sister Dora, such as Rosa Nouchette Carey's *Twelve Notable Good Women of the XIX Century* (London and New York, 1899), also features the prison reformer Elizabeth Fry alongside lives of a similar type, female philanthropists such as Angela Burdett-Coutts (each with her own *recognition* or *analogy,* and so on). What then can we make of all the versions of Fry over time; the rise and fall of interest in Burdett-Coutts; the common ground or variation among chapters in the same volume; and the assorted networks of representation formed by collections of similar or different types across this genre?

We are beginning to flesh out a morphology of biography (based on our model of short, collected biographies of women). In this brief essay I cannot elaborate on the poetics of third-person life narrative that I will develop elsewhere. Suffice it to say that the key distinctions from standard narrative theory that we find in third-person narratives about real people fall under four headings: the author-narrator role; referentiality and verifiability; the status of versions; and construction of the audience.[9] As in many forms of nonfiction, the person named on the title page, the voice of the preface, the implied author, and the teller of the tales are so similar that the distinctions have little use. Unlike fiction, the discourse of biography arranges a story that is presumed to be true (rather than the reader's reconstruction of imagined events), and hypothetically any number of versions could attempt an accurate reference to those extratextual matters of fact. (Writing one's own life makes

---

9. A few studies of the difference of nonfiction have been helpful, notably Eric Heyne's, and most recently, a fine synthesis by Monika Fludernik. Yet these have overlooked biography, whether single or collective.

a truth claim but does not invite anyone else to have an equal say.) It's a sign of nonfiction that all versions of a known life (or historical events) potentially could be verified or improved by further research (they are not more or less faithful adaptations of a fairy tale or a novel).[10] Finally, biographies unlike political histories present themselves in the mode of communication between flesh-and-blood author and reader about a real individual, in the often-explicit expectation that the audience identifies with a flesh-and-blood person and pursues similar experiences in the real world. The method and design of BESS will improve as we interpret different types of sample corpus. Formal studies of a genre require more than the data mining of masses of digitized texts. We hope to show that our method of digital analysis at midrange scale, beyond close reading of a few canonical works, can be adapted to other narrative genres and contexts.

Prosopography, Documentary Social Networks, and the BESS Schema

Modern conceptions of life narrative privilege the unique, self-fashioning individual (Booth, "Prosopography"). Yet the uses of biography should alert us to a positive ethics of sharing identities. Feminist, queer, postcolonial, and other perspectives have favored a conception of the subject as constructed from intersecting positions. Collections of life narratives, from pantheons and hagiography through printed books, exhibit lives in overlapping contexts and roles, placing even more than the usual pressure on all life narrative to assimilate personal details into narratable forms. Any biography shapes the profile according to social and generic conventions that guide audience response. Collections of brief lives enhance this collocation and colloquy. Even today, with distrust of authority and inauthenticity, we respond to lives as models more or less positive or negative, from Facebook pages to reality television to biopics and the Biography channel.

A comparative rhetorical network is common to biographies in all formats, but especially those that sort and collect persons by social category, as in the books incorporated in Collective Biographies of Women. The longstanding conventions of biography in the West were reinforced, since the Reformation, by Protestant martyrologies and, with the growth of capitalism and literacy, by lives of worthies or writers and by self-help auto/biographies.

---

10. Many legends such as Faust or Cinderella migrate in various versions (and characters such as Dracula escape their original texts to function in new versions). But biography has a particularly interesting relationship between the ur-text of an actual person and the various personae presented in various representations of the life.

In CBW, these narrative conventions encounter prescriptions about women's lives and an array of affiliations and aims that motivate a particular volume. The underlying concept of my research is prosopography, which has been defined as collective biography, as I generally use it. Social histories, movements, and commemoration, in print and other media, turn to selections of names and life narratives.[11] *Prosopon,* from ancient Greek, indicates the face or personal appearance, and *graphy* of course refers to writing. Although at one time prosopography referred to describing a single person's appearance, it became a term for a scholarly method of representing plural *personae,* locating and reconstructing the life histories of members of certain social groups, usually from eras before printing and public record-keeping were well established.[12] In addition to its multiple-personae form, its rhetoric tends to be elegiac as well as exemplary. A few persons must stand in for hidden faces among the ancestors. Each persona is thus a metonymic figure for a social role. Over time and across many texts, the same individual receives many different discursive treatments, adding to the sense of subjectivity as a field of sliding signification rather than identity.

In CBW's bibliography, for example, A. J. Green-Armytage's *Maids of Honour* (1906) gathers twelve short biographies (with portraits) to demonstrate achievements of unmarried women in a range of careers. In such a book, a well-known woman will be assessed in comparison to other eminent women, to her sex in general, or to men of achievement. To understand such documentary or constructed social networks, we design searches and displays of "degrees of separation" between individuals, for instance to show how any of the eleven women with "one degree" of separation from Sister Dora in *Maids of Honour* might be assorted in other volumes (the possible combinations quickly reach the thousands).[13] These virtual associations of women (*docu-*

11. Digital prosopographies flourish, for example Prosopography of Anglo-Saxon England (http://www.pase.ac.uk). Berkeley Prosopography Services (http://berkeleyprosopography.org), funded by NEH Office of Digital Humanities, are "applying techniques from the fields of Natural Language Processing (NLP) and Social Network Analysis (SNA) to extract the names and basic familial relationships of people mentioned in texts, and then to assemble the social network of the people based upon the activities described" (Schmitz). Notably, these texts tend to be difficult (as in cuneiform texts in Akkadian) and unyielding of the complete biographical representation we expect in the print era. See also People of the Founding Era (http://pfe.rotunda.upress.virginia.edu/), a more inclusive social history culled from the digitized "papers" of Founding Fathers and Dolley Madison.

12. The method of prosopography insistently focuses on individuals only for the purpose of studying groups. K. S. B. Keats-Rohan's research program eschews modern-era collective biography, claiming prosopography as a quantitative method of aggregating standardized profiles of individual lives (see Keats-Rohan).

13. In Figure 8.2, we have selected collections that belong to both "good character or deeds" *and* "reformers, social workers" types, in order to limit the results for legibility on a

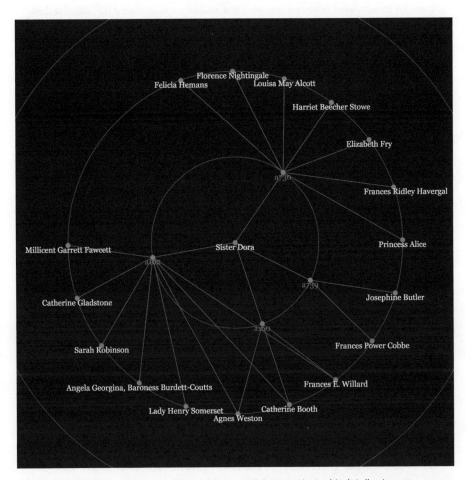

FIGURE 8.2. R-Graph of Selected Siblings of Sister Dora in Four Biographical Collections

mentary social networks because constructed, without necessary interaction during their lifetimes) will be correlated with data such as time or place. The publications show very little concern for intellectual property; they offer a kind of literate, crowdsourced folklore, recirculating previous versions and conventions of biographical narrative. Nevertheless, some fidelity to the documented events in individual lives makes the narratives diverge from prescrip-

radial graph. The graph shows seventeen women appearing in four collections with Sister Dora. Agnes Weston, Catherine Booth, and Frances Willard appear in two collections with Dora, a160 and a162, both by Chappell.

tions of gender and other templates for a socially conditioned life. Material of this scope and complexity begs for a digital platform.

The more innovative experiment in the CBW project is a contribution to narrative theory, an XML stand-aside markup schema called Biographical Elements and Structure Schema or BESS, designed in collaboration with Worthy Martin, Daniel Pitti, and Suzanne Keen. With small teams of graduate research assistants, I have been analyzing the 20 versions of Sister Dora's life and the 14 versions of Lola Montez's life, and have branched out to the other subjects in these 34 collections, the Noble Workers and Women of the World. Thus we can measure variations among versions of one person and among multiple lives narrated by the same author. The formal techniques of biographical narrative resemble those of fiction, and they embed recurrent motifs or ideological scripts as well as "action macrostructures" (García Landa) that—so far—require human interpretation.[14] Each BESS XML file becomes a kind of abstract outline associated with the numbered paragraphs of the text.

One of our key elements is "Stage of Life," *before, beginning, middle, culmination, end,* and *after.* These named stages resemble the Aristotelian idea of the beginning, middle, and end, and the Freytag triangle of the rising and falling action, and allow us to outline the discourse of the short biography in relation to the historical chronology of the person's life. Biographies, especially in factual summaries or short form, tend to be chronological, yet narrative discourse may vary this order for different effects. Suzanne Keen emphasizes narrative theory's concepts of pace as well as the order/disorder of the story/discourse distinction: where do we find expansion or digression, gaps, pauses, foreshadowing or retrospection?[15] A biography often inserts future or posthumous events as reflections on the development or impact of the subject's life. The first paragraph of some biographies includes all stages of life in a summary, and this seems more common if the story is controversial as well as eventful on the world stage. Some biographies omit narration of ancestry

---

14. BESS is a system of standardized conceptual elements and a vocabulary of "controlled values," using the Extensible Markup Language or XML coding language. To identify the type of each element that appears in a specific paragraph of text, we insert the appropriate value or term in the element tags within a separate XML document. This annotation of what appears in each paragraph of a text can then be measured and compared to other versions of the biography or to many other biographies in the corpus.

15. Emma Kafalenos has contributed to structural analysis of narrative in terms of Greimasian functions, and in "Not (Yet) Knowing" she contributes to ways to detect narrative in action. In BESS, we often translate the terms of narratology into more accessible language, given that we rely on a team of editors. DH often captures significant omissions or disruptions in repetition, as narratology may highlight the not-narrated or "disnarrated" (Dannenberg 305).

or birth (*before* or *beginning*), and many later nineteenth-century collections represent living members of societies or causes without anticipating *end* or *after*. In our terms, *beginning* includes birth, education, possibly marriage, and may extend well into middle age for some who find career late in life. *Middle* consists of recurrent activity in the persona's recognized role, be it motherhood or recording data from a telescope or exploring Africa. *Culmination* is our term to avoid the narrower terms "climax," "crisis," or "triumph"; to be tagged as this stage of life, paragraphs must narrate a specified event in time and place that in some way tests human powers, begins with an uncertain outcome, or transforms further events. In spite of the triangle of plot, *culmination* can happen early or often in a persona's life. A biography might consist almost entirely of *culmination,* as some chapters about a named individual record only a "noble deed" or emergency episode (female heroism in a shipwreck rescue or in combat are favorites of this sort). Still other kinds of chapters represent groups, networks, or movements rather than individual chronicles, as in anonymous characterization of Women of the East or galleries of the beauties of Versailles. The variety of pace and order in the emplotment of women's collective biographies correlates with different types of personae and collection, as our project can demonstrate.

Like all studies of narrative, BESS focuses on *events* (including actions) and *agents* (our term for *actants,* from people to weather). A life story, we expect, is made up of events and agents in real times and places, in various relations to the focal individual. Here are three paragraphs (9–11) from the *beginning* stage in a version of Sister Dora's life (a185.bi002):

> 9 Once, when Dorothy was away from home, one of the village boys fell ill with typhoid fever. His one wish was to see "Miss Dora," as he called her, and the poor child listened anxiously every day for her carriage wheels. At last she came, and he was the first to hear her. "There's Miss Dora! There she is!" he cried, and, exhausted by the effort, fell back on his pillow.

> 10 She went to him at once and remained to the end, nursing him with loving care, and cheering him with her bright smile and comforting words. This was the first time she had done anything of the sort, and even then she was more influenced by the desire to be kind than by the child's suffering.

> 11 She was now growing tall and strong like her father, and beautiful of face like her mother. She delighted in games of all kinds, but particularly those best suited to boys. Nothing gave her so much pleasure as a good gallop across the moors, or a ride to hounds with her brothers. Whatever she did,

whether work or play, she did with her whole heart: there were no half measures with Dorothy Pattison; if a thing were worth doing, she did it well. (a185 bi002)

A sample of the event markup in BESS may be efficient here:

```
<event>
    <textUnitRangeReference>
      <start>9</start>
      <end>10</end>
    </textUnitRangeReference>
    <type>illness, nonfamily individual</type>
    <type>nursing, local amateur</type>
    <agentType>male patient, poor</agentType>
    <agentType>boy, unrelated, unnamed</agentType>
</event>
```

Events in BESS allow more than one type and various so-called *child elements* or subentries; most notably, if the text specifies someone or something interacting with the persona or protagonist, we mark AgentType. Our vocabulary for agents is designed to bring out the social structure: what sorts of events correlate with what social roles in the narratives of which type of persona?

The bare-bones account of a life has certain determining cruxes, "kernel" events necessary to any version of the story, as well as factual details not transferable to another person. Seymour Chatman develops the narratological distinction between kernels and "satellites," the intervening events that devolve from kernels and are less necessary to the causality of the story (54–55). We can demonstrate how various versions of a single life select, omit, or arrange the typical and unique, the ubiquitous kernels and optional satellites. Having analyzed all versions of Sister Dora's life, the team has named and given unique ID numbers to recurrent events; her story has ten *kernels*, rarely if ever omitted; ten common *satellites* or embellishments inessential to her unique narrative; and seven rare satellites, including this one, "Dying Village Boy Waiting for Dora's Return" (E00020); analysis of a corpus of versions of a historical life allows us to build a theory of narrated events in terms of frequency rather than causality.[16]

---

16. Precise counts of rates of the named events in all versions will be forthcoming. In other versions, this *childhood anecdote, talent predicted* is supplanted by a story (E00021, a rare satellite) that she stayed out one night to nurse a dying old woman and was told by her angry family

In an interesting shift of tone, paragraph 11, above, calls for analysis in these BESS terms: Event types: *riding; games, playing; hunting;* Topos type: *physical prowess, athletics; family, genetic heritage of persona;* PersonaDescription types: *physically strong; beautiful; skilled, masculine leisure activity; skilled, athletic; energetic or untiring;* Discourse types: *summary, more, much or all life in less prose; iterative, repeating or persistent.*[17] This paragraph's events are neither kernels nor satellites that develop Sister Dora's narrative but recurrent activities that we do not tag with ID numbers and names. Her brothers are the agent types in these events; the location is *open country.* Arguably the aim of the above paragraphs (9–11) is to characterize the persona in youth, in a kind of forecast of her vocation. The ministering angel at the bedside becomes surprisingly vigorous, a tomboy. Obviously our vocabulary must omit some details and qualities for the sake of comparative economy. The reward will come in contrasting the distribution, presence, and absence of various element types according to the type of persona (nurse vs. adventuress) and the type of collection, correlated with date of publication and religious, political, regional, or other affiliations. We can also trace the "style" of different biographers, who may have repertoires of persona description, discourse, or topoi, applied to very different subjects in a collection.

Along with the events and persona description, these narratives are dedicated to various social values and discursive effects that still require human interpretation. I have already given some impression of the element topos, a spatial concept for the structures of feeling and/or habitual social interaction beyond the explicit level of observed action. The biographies in CBW inevitably share topoi with biographies in general. Thus in these three paragraphs, we encounter *dying or deathbed* (TextUnitRange 9–10) and another topos, *family, genetic heritage of persona* (TextUnit 11), important to any biography. Similarly, another key element in BESS, discourse, traces textual effects common to many kinds of narrative. Thus for example paragraph 9 deploys *focalization,* when the dying boy listened and "was the first to hear" the carriage bringing

---

not to come home till summoned. Named events, linked to data about time and geo-location, will form part of interactive timelines revealing historical networks among the women studied in our sample corpora.

17. See http://cbw.iath.virginia.edu/exist/cbw/dual/a185/bio02 for an html display of the text and BESS markup. A prototype tool for visualizing BESS analysis with text is accessible at http://cbw.iath.virginia.edu/cbw_db/bess.php. We can elicit patterns of co-occurrence such as the Topos "duty," PersonaDescription "humble," and Discourse "evaluation" in paragraphs in different stages of the life of Caroline Herschel. "Duty" is a topos that never appears in a life of Lola Montez. Force-directed graphs can visualize the comparisons of clustered or mutually exclusive terms in groups of texts.

Sister Dora back to care for him. Narratives in the Florence Nightingale line tend to exploit the Dickensian sentiment of the patient's perspective.[18]

In the vocabulary for the element "discourse," we identify quotations of various kinds, in this case *quotation, agent's speech, unique,* because these are guides to narrative levels, as when the biographer invents dialogue or copies from an interview or autobiography. In contrast with the *scene* in paragraphs 9–10, we flag *summary* and *iterative* discourse in paragraph 11, as indications of pace. We find differing discourse according to different persona types, which naturally attract different terms of persona description. For example, narrators of Lola Montez's life often adopt *irony* in a sophisticated tone and style suited to an adult, modern audience such as men in their clubs. Women of the World discourse includes more *evaluation* (expressed judgment of behavior), more *emphasis in typeface, punctuation* (can you believe she did this!), and more doubt: *versions of story compared, disputed.* Sister Dora is *self-sacrificing,* not so Lola; the magnificent Montez is *violent* and *wild,* Dora never is.

Such patterns will emerge as we tag these elements in the versions of women's lives in various networks. The potential micro-interpretation, familiar from the techniques of close reading a single poem or paragraphs in a novel, underlies the BESS analysis at every phase. The digital interpretation tagging elements to paragraphs is that much more laborious than a good close reading. The cost of that labor must be assessed against the value of quantifiable comparison in support of a new vision of the networks of representation of women in this context, and a new model for narrative theory in digital terms. The texts are always there to be reread for the details, and other editors can always reinterpret them. Printed prosopographies provide a rich opportunity for systemic interpretation because they build in comparative modulation of conventions while striving to adhere to some degree of fact. Are some narrative devices and structures specific to one network or one period of biographical representation? Do others "travel" remarkably consistently across gender and other categories of identity?

Within any cohort, variants are telling, and further probing reveals that individuals might belong to other persona types or cohorts. The astronomer

---

18. As I've said, we're interested in documenting the distinction of nonfiction. In nonfiction, it is no solecism to introduce an unnamed person who never reappears; Dickens, for example, would not squander the opportunity of this boy as a character. What becomes of narrative theory applied to a biographical and historical discourse such as this? What of Mieke Bal's terms, for instance, for fabula, story, and text? From a version that we read, do we reconstruct the historical person as we reconstruct the fabula of fiction? In practice, though biographical texts are referential, the past is another country and we *can't* fully verify other than through other documentation.

Caroline Herschel, for example, shares a volume with Sister Dora three times. Herschel, known for being the sister of the famous astronomer William Herschel (rather than a self-appointed religious "sister"), also has twenty-five books to her name, among 268 women of widely different eras, nationalities, and occupations. Herschel began life in Hanover (then ruled by England), and at the end of her life resided there; she died in 1848, just at the time of the revolution in Munich sparked by Lola Montez. But Herschel is known for domestic service and scientific learning rather than cosmopolitan venture. The most renowned scientist in the CBW archive, Herschel implied women's worthiness for higher education. Her virginal, self-sacrificing persona would look foolish among the Women of the World, and Herschel never shares a book with Lola Montez. Yet at one phase of her life Herschel was a successful musical performer (and housekeeper) while her astronomer brother made his living as a musician in Bath. Sister Dora and Caroline Herschel, unmarried, are consistently portrayed as heroic in self-denial and hard work, day and night. Beautiful, autocratic Sister Dora repeatedly overcame epidemics and industrial disasters; homely, submissive Caroline Herschel repeatedly discovered comets. In contrast, the repetitions in Lola Montez narratives are less about service or achievement than romance and scandal: redundant marriages (including bigamy) and adulteries, debuts on stage, violent episodes, and exile. The portraits of Sister Dora always show her in the self-designed uniform, and are often the same profile image, seated, from the waist up—many based on the same photograph. I have seen only a handful of engraved portraits of Caroline Herschel in CBW books or elsewhere. Lola Montez appears in a wide array of images, including photographs and caricatures, as her celebrity spread around the world. Nurse reformer, scientist, adventuress—the substance and manner of their written lives must vary. And so does the kind of collection in which they appear.

Studies of genre and theories of narrative have always been concerned with the recurrence and variation within conventions. Our in-depth comparison of versions of different personae and collection types will bring out the effects of gender ideology; CBW and projects like it can also coordinate literary analysis with biographical, historical, and geospatial data. Users should be able to ask questions and search and sort our data in ways that we don't yet predict. Visualizations may reveal patterns generated by our analysis that challenge inferences drawn from poring over a shelf of books. The tools of digital inquiry, conversely, need critical and theoretical insight if they are going to answer questions worthwhile to humanists, whether or not these are the questions we are already in the habit of asking. The findings through the use of the schema should benefit both studies of life narrative and feminist literary history. It's unwarranted here to tell you all about Sister Dora, Lola Montez, or Caroline Herschel, but I can illustrate the potential interpretation with a few examples of typical scenes in the life of Sister Dora. Take a common satellite event that we have called "Sister's Arm" (E00014 in the database): once, Sister Dora defied a surgeon who determined that a young workman's right arm, crushed by machinery, must be amputated to save the man's life. She said she would take responsibility for trying to save the arm, in spite of the risks, and the surgeon angrily gave in. For days she watched over and tended to the arm. In the end it healed and she saved the arm and the patient's life and livelihood. "She called it *her* arm"; and when she in turn lay ill, the worker "would ring at the hospital door to inquire how she was, . . . 'Tell Sister it's *her arm* that pulled the bell!'" (Green-Armytage 105; Lonsdale 73; Manton 189; Chappell, *Four Noble Women* 105). Another common satellite event (E00013) dramatizes one of her countless house calls to smallpox patients in the slums. In a cottage one night she found a man on his deathbed, abandoned by his family and friends. A woman whom she had sent to buy another candle never returned, and she sat alone with the suffering man with his seeping sores. He begged, "Sister, kiss me before I die." She embraced him and remained all night, in the cold dark after the candle burned out, with the dying man in her arms. In the morning he was dead (Lonsdale 68; Manton 202; Foster 145; Chappell, *Four Noble Women* 105). The experience of such an event must have been harrowing, but as a story, necessarily originating with the survivor herself, it becomes iconographic. We call this recurrent scene "The Case of the Man Who Died in the Dark." Both these named scenes deal in the topos *physical contact with man,* permitted because of the threat of death. If a feminist scholar happened to read all the biographies of Sister Dora, she or he might notice that all versions feature these or other anecdotes of intimate nurture of working men in defiance of conventional medical practice.[19] From another angle, a digital humanist might have set up a program to search for frequencies or proximities of words or phrases related to "arm" or "die" or "man." But such discoveries are improbable without an interpretative schema designed for this archive and prepared to detect gender and class and psychosexual implications, informed by theoretical paradigms of the body and representation.

---

19. Both Lonsdale and Ridsdale reported Pattison's obvious preference for men: "she disliked the sole company of women" (Ridsdale quoted in Manton 158) and primarily nursed male victims of industrial accidents (Lonsdale 85). Usually the only motive for reading many versions of one life is to prepare for another version; a biographer of Sister Dora would collate authoritative versions and try to confirm the original events, narrating the life once more.

There is another aspect to the "Man Who Died in the Dark" episode, involving a pattern of imagery of *dark* or *light* (we identify such figures or images under the element "discourse") associated with the social spaces and class and gender roles of philanthropy. One biographer, Wilmot-Buxton, refers to the need for "moral as well as actual sunshine" in the zones of industrial poverty (275), and many note that Dorothy Pattison's nickname as a child was "Little Sunshine." In the CBW narratives, a lady often figures as a beacon or source of light entering the darkness of streets or impoverished homes. Digital tagging can now trace this imagery to specific kinds of events or activities, settings, and types of collection or persona. The underlying typology or topos of such scenarios we have called *lady braving dark space*. Word searches can take us only so far; contexts and correlated values bring out more of the rhetorical design. For example, I examined references to "night" and "work" in narratives about Sister Dora and Caroline Herschel, realizing that both the nurse and the astronomer work at night, but for the latter it is an entirely positive condition for observing celestial rather than human bodies. I laughed to realize that Lola's performance of menacing sexuality also could be regarded as working at night. Her attribute is a whip, not a telescope or a bandage. Biographers explicitly censure Montez, "a woman who, in the full *light* of the nineteenth century, renewed all the scandals that disgraced the Middle Ages," showing that "vice can sometimes triumph" before "a fall" (Wyndham; emphasis mine).

Implications for Feminist Narratology in a Digital Age

In digital humanities as well as feminist studies, it is not uncommon to retell how we or I got here.[20] The history of my digital project reveals stages in the development of gender-inflected humanities as well, like screenshots of a *longue durée*. Invited to contribute reflection on the history and future of feminist and queer narrative studies, I had the unsettling sense of leaping toward a new horizon while reaching back over two hundred years. This divided movement is not merely a consequence of the fraught interaction of the three fields I noted at the beginning: feminist studies, narrative theory, and DH. It is also because technology has stirred up old desires for universal

---

20. Conference panels in DH can be overtaken by show and tell, and it's hard not to be preoccupied with narrating what happened in transformative innovations in research. We can make allowance for this as similar to the poster sessions or exhibitions at meetings in health professions, sciences, or social sciences, calling for timeliness and applied research.

or global models. My graduate training coincided with the rise of feminist theory, women's history, and flourishing studies of Victorian literature and culture, in the 1980s—all instilling distrust of universals (though not, in practice, eschewing heroic biography). But as personal computers and the Internet transformed research methods in the 1990s, I shifted into bibliography, a field I once considered dreary and untheoretical. Digitization of texts and online access to library archives made it possible to investigate the history of print in unprecedented ways, and a Web-based bibliography invited expansive use and new functions. Meanwhile I was also influenced by narrative theory as it intersected with poststructuralist ideological criticism in the 1980s and 1990s. At Narrative conferences I joined panels with queer theorists, feminist critics of Victorian novelists, narratologists studying race in contemporary film or graphic novels—the rich array of what with Rita Felski and others I would call strategic formalism.[21] In an era that distrusted formalism as an evasion of ideology, our strategy was to conjoin poststructuralist approaches to textuality, narratological and aesthetic approaches to written texts, and feminist and ideological critiques of texts, culture, and history. I would never have undertaken bibliography of a print genre without digital resources and without the shared precept that narratives perform cultural work as fundamental as the construction of gender, class, and race. A potential corpus of all narratives in all genres and contexts, in print or born digital, would—some say it already has—transform what it means to read or interpret narrative.

Susan Lanser, in her classic 1986 essay "Toward a Feminist Narratology," rightly claimed that till that point narratology and feminist studies had ignored each other (674). Significantly, she commended a "'sociological poetics,'" "abstract and semiotic" but also "concrete and mimetic" for relevant feminist critique (Lanser). It was a topos of that time to end an essay with a hopeful sidestep from the dead end of poststructuralist feminist theory, an appeal to *both/and* rather than *either/or*; feminist narrative studies, accordingly, called for both the "-ism" and the "-ology," both political and formal commitments. At the symposium, Lanser proposed a similar balance of goals, but I heard a shift in the emphasis for our global, digitized era: we need an inductive, particular method that also reaches out to the scale of Franco Moretti's literary histories. In a quarter century, feminist narrative studies have thrived as the "-ology" has been muted: all sides have eschewed "scientistic . . . high structuralism" with its "terminology and . . . taxonomies," as David Herman puts it. More positively, Herman and others develop a post-

---

21. The idea is comparable to Gayatri Spivak's strategic essentialism, a claim of coherent and shared identity (such as gender or race) for political and historical purposes. Strategic formalism provisionally brackets the hermeneutics of suspicion or critique.

classical narratology uniting "formal and functional" models to address "new questions about (the relations between) narrative structure, its verbal, visual or more broadly semiotic realization, and the contexts in which it is produced and interpreted" (Herman 3, 8, 9). A postclassical feminist narratology joins poetics and rhetoric, the *parole* of usage and the *langue* or extensible system. There is all the more vitality in a renewed structuralism because of the capability of digital study to encompass masses of minute particulars, by both human curation and unsupervised learning, as we say. We can reveal both subtle and huge patterns invisible to the human being reading a small set of texts. The risk might be a reinstatement of scientistic, universalizing perspectives. Instead, I urge that we remember, as this retrospective invites us to do, the reasons for a feminist critique of structuralist normative models.

Not that feminist literary studies have always gotten it right in the past. In spite of the drive to expand the archives under consideration, histories of women's writing or narrative and gender have been too narrow. One of my goals is to loosen the novel's grip on narrative theory of all kinds and to enhance theories of nonfiction, specifically biography. You might say there has been plenty of feminist narrative theory devoted to lifewriting; the symposium included a range of examples of it within the framework of individual and group recognition and self-expression. In both history and literary studies, attention to autobiography and memoir far exceeds consideration of biography or prosopography (exceptions include Caine and Hill). To a large extent discussion of biographies of women have focused on a single person or text, or generalized about the privacy or tragedy of women's lives. In the first volume of the journal *Narrative* (1993), Linda Wagner-Martin, biographer of Plath and Stein, deplored the prescriptive plots for female biography in the 1990s: "the only biographies of women that will sell are those of the aberrant, the misfit, the sensationalized," rather than "another domestic story" (266–67). Disregarding the collective biographies that kept being printed by trade publishers throughout this period, Wagner-Martin overlooks thousands of female biographies that conform to the masculine individualist model as she describes it: a narrative that presupposes "that the subject has led an exemplary life, that this life is best treated chronologically and pegged on historical events external to the subject, that the subject's internal life is not intrinsically significant" (267–68).[22] Carolyn Heilbrun, in her influential *Writing a Woman's Life* of 1988, had similarly segregated the entrenched gender plots of biography, suggesting that "only in the last third of the twentieth century"

---

22. In a book first published in 1994, Wagner-Martin observes that a surge in biographies of women by women has begun to "shift" the "conventions for biography" (Wagner-Martin, *Telling Women's Lives* 159).

might a woman's life be written as an ambition plot (60). In *How to Make It as a Woman* I challenge the standard feminist histories of life narrative, and I don't need to repeat the refutation now. Presuppositions about gender and biography have been based on a handful of monographs about famous individuals, primarily writers. Comprehensive studies like CBW can uncover far wider variation in gender and genre.

Recuperative work in any field of advocacy, including race, gender, and sexuality, tends to foreshorten the history of representation. There were varied models of women's lives available well before second- or third-wave feminism and we cannot presuppose their difference from men's biographies, and still less their reductive similarity to each other. The quantity and variety of print-era collective biographies of women is still news. In 2010 it gets scant notice in Barbara Caine's overview, *Biography and History*, a contribution to a Palgrave series, Theory and History.[23] After several academic generations in which biography has been frowned upon as a method or topic in both history and literature departments, it remains crucial in the humanities. We can brace ourselves against the illusions of transparency or hero worship. Narrative theory needs to acknowledge the vast range of writing in referential or nonfiction modes, and feminist studies should encompass a wide spectrum of representation in the print era rather than perpetuate the belletristic definition of literature and a narrow focus on women poets or novelists.[24]

A history of feminist narrative studies is no simple story of progress; I have already remarked on the shifting dimensions of time in reflections such as this. It was in 1994 that Margaret Homans rightly warned against presuming that "narrative and social structures are cognate" (9). Homans nevertheless shared the feminist poststructuralist suspicion of "linear narrative and history"; "'beginning, middle, and end' . . . and . . . the unified consciousness of a 'hero who acts as the subject'" (12) cannot be adapted for the narratives of Other experience. For better or worse, linear plots of triumph over adversity, heroic action, and public recognition are narratable and often prospectively useful in prosopographies as well as single biographies of marginal subjects. Narrative and social structures are not cognate. A biography of Lola Montez may replicate her nonlinear, shape-shifting adventures in its structure,

---

23. Caine notes a few "collective biographies devoted entirely to women" since the eighteenth century, and devotes short sections to prosopography (which she associates with the 1920s and restricts to nonbiographical analysis of data about aggregates of individuals [58]) and group biography, "one of the most significant new developments . . . since the 1970s" (61). Her account is plausible if you overlook several recent studies including my own; it repeats the rhetorically useful notion that the records of women have gone missing.

24. Feminist studies in early modern or medieval periods do attend to diaries, letters, ecclesiastical writings, and histories.

yet rhetorically elicit sophisticated contempt or male heterosexual desire for sexual rough play. The study of printed biographical collections in relation to a database of historical persons provides an experimental setting for better understanding of the social contexts of narrative, in this instance, Anglo-American women's history and biography.

Digital scholarship and techniques of reading may reveal the fine-grained and the worldwide significance of this body of Victorian life narratives, much as Google Earth flies in or out, from the spinning globe through layers of national histories to the unique coordinates. I have suggested that our method combines close and distant readings, in a middle range. Franco Moretti's "comparative morphology" traces literary forms through history and across the globe in what he calls "distant reading." Wai Chee Dimock retains a commitment to the text itself; the literary field "needs to maintain an archive that is as broad-based as possible, as fine-grained as possible" because there will never be a totalizing "law of literary evolution" as Moretti believes (Dimock 79). In another dimension, Stephen Best and Sharon Marcus argue for surface reading as a corrective to the customs of Jamesonian critique or symptomatic reading that plumbs what the text represses; surface reading includes bibliography and poetics, as the CBW project does. The computer doesn't supersede various ways to read. Female prosopography is suitably vast, varied, visual, and collaborative for online presentation. Within this expansive global horizon, CBW also remains committed to the microscale of close and surface reading of texts and book designs, while it updates comparative studies of folklore or archetypes with current transnational concepts of "traveling genres" developed by Dimock, Margaret Cohen, and others.

Feminist and queer narrative theorists have learned that the ideological uses of aesthetic forms or discourses cannot be prejudged. Moreover, we know that older or newer approaches may be taken in directions impossible to map as strictly progressive or the reverse. I suggest that my discoveries of the variety and recurrent patterns in the printed versions of women's lives are only apparently at odds. The systems and networks can attend to conditions of individual lives that queer the categorical binaries. A postclassical narratology helps us deploy digital tools to magnify and expand our readings. If literature has been the quintessential apparatus for the discovery of the individual, it has always also constructed adaptable roles and types. Prosopographical approaches acknowledge the intricacies of literature, individual without being individualist, collective without being universalizing, in networks of intersectional representation. Users of CBW may build their own analyses of parallel lives across different social sectors or of multiple versions of one life, of publication history, historical developments and geographical distributions, and of conventions of biographical narrative. Without putting ourselves in the position of the readers of these books as originally published, we nevertheless can participate in the social exchange as well as diverse narrative potential generated by the expansive conventions of prosopography.

Works Cited

Bal, Mieke. *Narratology: Introduction to the Theory of Narrative.* 3rd ed. Toronto: U of Toronto P, 2009.

Baring-Gould, Sabine. *Virgin Saints and Martyrs.* London: Hutchinson, 1900.

Bauer, Jean. "Who You Calling Untheoretical?" *Journal of Digital Humanities,* March 9, 2012. Web. Accessed 10 October 2014.

Best, Stephen, and Sharon Marcus. "Surface Reading: An Introduction." *Representations* 108.1 (2009): 1–21.

Booth, Alison. "The Collective Biographies of Women: Preface." *Collective Biographies of Women.* University of Virginia Library. <http://womensbios.lib.virginia.edu>. Accessed 13 Feb. 2012.

———. *How to Make It as a Woman: Collective Biographical History from Victoria to the Present.* Chicago: U of Chicago P, 2004.

———. "Prosopography and Crowded Attention in Old and New Media." *On Life-Writing.* Ed. Zachary Leader. Oxford: Oxford UP, forthcoming.

———. "Recovery 2.0: Beginning the Collective Biographies of Women Project." *Tulsa Studies in Women's Literature* 28.1 (2009): 15–35.

Caine, Barbara. *Biography and History.* Hampshire: Palgrave Macmillan, 2010.

Carey, Rosa Nouchette. *Twelve Notable Good Women of the XIXth Century.* London and New York: Hutchinson, 1899.

Chappell, Jennie. *Four Noble Women and Their Work.* London: Partridge, 1898.

———. *Noble Workers.* London: Partridge, 1910.

Chatman, Seymour. *Story and Discourse: Narrative Structure in Fiction and Film.* Ithaca: Cornell UP, 1978.

Cohen, Margaret. *The Novel and the Sea.* Princeton: Princeton UP, 2010.

Dannenberg, Hilary P. "Gerald Prince and the Fascination of What Doesn't Happen." *Narrative* 22 (October 2014): 304–11.

Dimock, Wai Chee. *Through Other Continents: American Literature Across Deep Time.* Princeton: Princeton UP, 2006.

Finlayson, Mark Alan. "Deriving Narrative Morphologies Via Analogical Story Merging." 2009. <http://www.mit.edu/~markaf/doc/finlayson.kokinov.nbupress.2009.137.pdf>. Accessed 10 October 2014.

Fludernik, Monika. "Factual Narrative: A Missing Narratological Paradigm." *Germanish-Romanische Monatsschrift* 63.1 (2013). 117–34.

Foster, Warren Dunham. *Heroines of Modern Religion.* New York: Sturgis & Walton, 1913.

García Landa, José Ángel. "Action Macrostructures." *Structural Narratology.* 2005. Web. Accessed 10 Feb. 2012.

Green-Armytage, A. J. *Maids of Honour.* London; Edinburgh: Blackwood, 1906.

Heilbrun, Carolyn G. *Writing a Woman's Life.* New York: Ballantine, 1988.

Herman, David. "Introduction." *Narratologies.* Columbus: The Ohio State UP, 1999. 1–30.

Heyne, Erik. "Where Fiction Meets Nonfiction: Mapping a Rough Terrain." *Narrative* 9.3 (2001): 322–33.

Hill, Kate, ed. *Museums and Biographies: Stories, Objects, Identities.* Suffolk: Boydell Press, 2012.

Homans, Margaret. "Feminist Fictions and Feminist Theories of Narrative." *Narrative* 2 (1994): 3–16.

Kafalenos, Emma. "Not (Yet) Knowing: Epistemological Effects of Deferred and Suppressed Information in Narrative." *Narratologies.* Ed. David Herman. Columbus: The Ohio State UP, 1999. 33–65.

Keats-Rohan, K. S. B. "Biography, Identity and Names: Understanding the Pursuit of the Individual in Prosopography." *Prosopography Approaches and Applications: A Handbook,* 139–81. *Prosopographica et Genealogica* 13. Oxford: Occasional Publications UPR, 2007.

Lanser, Susan. "Toward a Feminist Narratology." *Feminisms.* Rev. ed. New Brunswick: Rutgers UP, 1997. 674–93.

Lonsdale, Margaret. *Sister Dora, a Biography.* Boston: Roberts Brothers, 1880.

Manton, Jo. *Sister Dora: The Life of Dorothy Pattison.* London: Methuen, 1971.

Moretti, Franco. *Distant Reading.* New York: Verso, 2013.

Ridsdale, Ellen. *Sister Dora: Personal Reminiscence of Her Later Years.* Walsall: Griffin, 1880.

Rogers, Cameron. *Gallant Ladies.* New York: Harcourt, Brace, 1928.

Ryan, Marie-Laure. "Cyberage Narratology: Computers, Metaphor, and Narrative." *Narratologies.* Ed. David Herman. Columbus: The Ohio State UP, 1999. 113–41.

Schmitz, Patrick. "Using Natural Language Processing and Social Network Analysis to Study Ancient Babylonian Society." *UC Berkeley iNews.* March 10, 2009. Web. Accessed 10 October 2014.

Seymour, Bruce. "Lola Montez (1821–1861)." *Oxford Dictionary of National Biography.* May 2008. Web. Accessed 5 Feb. 2012.

Smith, Martha Nell. "Frozen Social Relations and Time for a Thaw: Visibility, Exclusions, and Considerations for Postcolonial Digital Archives." Digital Forum. *Journal of Victorian Culture* 19:3 (2014): 403–10.

Wagner-Martin, Linda. "Notes from a Women's Biographer." *Narrative* 1 (1993): 266–73.

———. *Telling Women's Lives: The New Biography.* New Brunswick: Rutgers UP, 1994.

Wilmot-Buxton, E. M. *A Book of Noble Women.* Boston: Small, Maynard, 1907.

Wyndham, Horace. *The Magnificent Montez: From Courtesan to Convert.* Project Gutenberg. New York: Hillman-Curl, 1936.

HILLARY CHUTE

The Space of Graphic Narrative

Mapping Bodies, Feminism, and Form

t is striking that at a symposium filled with scholars of queer and feminist theory and narratology, such a huge proportion of the critics present are engaged with graphic narrative. "Graphic narrative" refers to work composed in the medium of comics—a form in which the fundamental narrative procedure is one of turning time into space on the page through frames on the page. (Graphic Narrative is also the title of a special issue of *Mfs: Modern Fiction Studies* I co-edited in 2006, in which I was interested in expanding the terminology of "graphic novel" to be more inclusive of nonfiction.) At least *one quarter* of the scholars who presented papers at the 2011 Queer and Feminist Narrative Theory Symposium has done scholarly work on comics. Robyn Warhol has an essay on Alison Bechdel's *Fun Home* in *College Literature*; Valerie Rohy published on *Fun Home* in *GLQ*; Ann Cvetkovich published an essay on *Fun Home* in the *Women's Studies Quarterly* special issue on Witness, co-edited by Irene Kacandes; and Julia Watson wrote on *Fun Home* in *Biography*.[1] Susan Stanford Friedman has written on Marjane Satrapi's *Persepolis* and cosmofeminism; Sidonie Smith writes on human rights and comics in the recent anthology *Graphic Subjects*; Rebecca Wanzo, as she announced

---

1. See Warhol; Rohy; Cvetkovich (this issue of WSQ has a three-essay section whose title, "Graphic Narrative as Witness," is borrowed from the original title of my contribution there on Marjane Satrapi); Watson.

at the symposium, has a second book project examining "representations of African American citizenship in comic art"; Frederick Aldama has edited two volumes about comics, *Your Brain on Latino Comics* and *Multicultural Comics*, the latter of which includes an essay by James Peterson on the cartoonist Aaron McGruder; and David Herman's book *Basic Elements of Narrative* offers a long section on Daniel Clowes's graphic novel *Ghost World*.[2] Graphic narrative, which has emerged only in the past few decades as an area of scholarship, brings to the forefront a form in which we see an overlap of intellectual questions that occupy feminist, queer, and narratological studies: namely, I believe, the issue of *narrative space* and embodiment.

I am going to touch on how I understand comics proposes these connections, and what kind of questions and issues it brings up for thinking, particularly, about the shape of lifewriting today. For me, a burning question for feminist narrative theory is connected to the large number of feminist life narratives in the form of comics.[3] My own recent book *Graphic Women* is on feminism and life narrative—specifically, on comics and life narrative: it examines the work of Aline Kominsky-Crumb, Phoebe Gloeckner, Lynda Barry, Marjane Satrapi, and Alison Bechdel.[4] Among symposium participants gathered at The Ohio State University, we had represented in the conference hall over *half* of the extant critical scholarship on Alison Bechdel's *Fun Home: A Family Tragicomic*, a 2006 graphic memoir that quickly ignited academic inquiry.[5]

---

2. See Friedman, "Cosmopolitanism"; Smith, "Human Rights and Comics"; Aldama, *Your Brain on Latino Comics* and *Multicultural Comics*; Peterson; and Herman. Wanzo, in addition to the forthcoming book, has published several essays and book chapters on comics, including in *Multicultural Comics*. Further, Sidonie Smith, a past president of Modern Language Association, gave her 2011 Presidential Address on "Narrating Lives" and discussed the work of Bechdel and cartoonist Art Spiegelman (*Maus*).

3. Although here I focus broadly on feminisms and comics narratives, there are many specifically queer comics, and these have been and will continue to be of interest for feminist and queer theorists and narratologists.

4. Following Nancy K. Miller's 2007 *PMLA* essay on "entangled selves" in lifewriting, I use *autobiography, memoir,* and *lifewriting*—or, as I prefer, *life narrative*—more or less interchangeably in this essay, although useful distinctions are spelled out, as Miller points out, in Smith and Watson's *Reading Autobiography,* as they also are on the first page of Yagoda, and in Couser (18). Lifewriting scholars (Miller, Smith and Watson, Marianne Hirsch, Gillian Whitlock, Linda Haverty Rugg, Bella Brodzki, and Leigh Gilmore, among others) have been interested in comics, as have narrative theory scholars (the journal *Narrative* has published interesting and important essays on comics over the past fifteen or so years, such as Jeanne Ewert and Erin McGlothlin's essays on *Maus,* from 2000 and 2002, respectively).

5. *Fun Home* has continued to generate scholarship. See, for instance, Gardiner; I have heard discussions around a proposal for an MLA volume on *Approaches to Teaching "Fun Home"* (which would join their current volume on *Teaching the Graphic Novel,* which came out in 2009).

FEMINIST AUTOBIOGRAPHICAL comics were first published in the early 1970s—and antecedents of all sorts, especially in the form of the artists' book, can be traced back earlier—but in the past twenty or so years there has been a veritable explosion of significant feminist, and queer, works in comics form.[6] Howard Cruse's semi-autobiographical *Stuck Rubber Baby* (1995), about homosexuality and racism in the Civil Rights Movement, is a major comics work of the 1990s—and a new edition appeared in 2010. (Cruse founded the influential comic book series *Gay Comix* in 1980, spurring the careers of figures like Bechdel.) *Stuck Rubber Baby* appeared in the wake of the groundbreaking success of Art Spiegelman's *Maus: A Survivor's Tale* (1986 and 1991), a two-volume biographical, and autobiographical, comics work about Spiegelman's father's experiences in Poland during World War II. The *Maus* series, widely acclaimed, won a Pulitzer Prize, and cleared the way for increased attention to "comics as a medium as self-expression," as Spiegelman put it.

A year after Cruse's book, *Seven Miles a Second,* the comics autobiography of celebrated queer artist David Wojnarowicz, who collaborated with cartoonists James Romberger and Marguerite Van Cook, appeared: it was published posthumously, became a cult classic and was reissued in 2013. A few years later, famed writer and critic Samuel Delany, with Mia Wolff, published the autobiographical comics love story *Bread & Wine* (originally published in 1999, it is also to be reissued this year). Even more recently, in the past ten years, the substantial critical focus on Bechdel's *Fun Home*, a memoir about the gay daughter of a closeted father that meditates on identifying and defining queerness, has generated, as I discuss here, attention from a wide range of scholars and cartoonists alike. Comics works like Bechdel's *Fun Home* and Marjane Satrapi's international bestseller *Persepolis* (2003), about growing up as a young girl in Tehran in the 1970s and 1980s, have shifted up the field of life narrative.[7] These authors have followed up, too, with further works that

---

6. For a brief history of feminist and queer autobiographical comics, see *Graphic Women*. There is also a rich range of queer and feminist comics work that is not autobiographical. Attention to queer/gay comics on the whole is increasing, as is evident in the 2012 anthology *No Straight Lines: Four Decades of Queer Comics,* which sold out its first printing by publisher Fantagraphics. Other well-known and relevant queer comics works include Diane DiMassa's series *Hothead Paisan,* Roberta Gregory's *Bitchy Butch,* and Alison Bechdel's comic strip *Dykes to Watch Out For,* which ran for twenty-five years. For lesbian comics specifically see the collection *Dyke Strippers.*

7. *Persepolis* came out in four volumes in France starting in 2000; in the United States two volumes appeared in 2003 and 2004. In 2007 Satrapi and fellow comics artist Vincent Paronnaud directed a feature-length black and white animated film adaptation of the same name, which won a prestigious award at the Cannes Film Festival and was nominated for Best Foreign Film at the Academy Awards.

explicitly address feminism and queerness, as we see in Bechdel's *Are You My Mother? A Comic Drama* (2012), and Satrapi's *Embroideries* (2005). Other feminist/queer comics in the autobiographical vein include those by Barry (*One Hundred Demons*), Gloeckner (*A Child's Life; Diary of a Teenage Girl*), Kominsky-Crumb (*Love That Bunch; Need More Love*), Diane Obomsawin (*On Loving Women*), Michelle Tea (*Rent Girl*), Ellen Forney (*Marbles*), Ariel Schrag (*Awkward; Definition; Potential; Likewise*), and A. K. Summers (*Pregnant Butch*). Some recent shorter works, among a large proliferation, include pieces by Jennifer Camper in her *Juicy Mother* series.

In their complex word and image form these graphic narratives call fresh attention to the broad category of "narrative" and its direct connection with feminism. Feminist narratologist Robyn Warhol and I have disagreed in the past about the value of what "word and image" as a descriptor of comics makes legible for analysis. I acknowledge her position, which focuses on describing comics as composed of three rather than two separate channels that carry forward the narration, although I continue to use "word and image" here.[8] Warhol and I agree, however, that "the new genre of graphic memoir stretches narratological understanding of how storytelling works," as she articulates it ("The Space Between" 13).[9] One of the benefits of the recent prominence of graphic narrative is that interest in the form has focused attention on the intersection of the long tradition of word and image studies (and visual theory and culture studies) and narratology—or what Warhol calls postclassical narratology.

Further, comics narratives are meaningfully broadening academic discourse across departments and disciplines. As a narrative form that is both

8. Warhol, "First-Person Graphic in Bechdel's *Fun Home*," a 2008 MLA Convention session; and "The Embedded Looker: Charting Narration in Graphic Memoir," a 2010 MLA Convention session. See Warhol 2011 for further articulations. Warhol's essay "The Space Between: A Narrative Approach to Alison Bechdel's *Fun Home*" describes, as in her earlier papers, her preferred schema as the three narrative levels intradiegetic, extradiegetic, and images (3). Although Warhol understands my definition, first articulated in *PMLA*, as too binary, as I explain in *Graphic Women* and elsewhere, I am deeply interested in the empty spaces and gaps of comics, as Warhol is too; our interests are actually quite similar although I do not focus in the way that she does, after Genette, on the two diegetic locations of the prose dimension of comics.

9. Warhol states that postclassical narratology can help comics theory push past the dual model ("Space Between" 5). Postclassical narratology is and will continue to be very useful to scholars thinking about how the form of comics functions. However, I believe Warhol's model doesn't account for the flexibility with which many scholars put the "word and image" rubric to use. Many comics scholars and cartoonists, myself included, consider "word and image" an only putatively binary formulation—one that opens up into other dimensions, many of them, like the gutter, productively awkward or unclassifiable. See, for instance, my chapter on *Fun Home* in *Graphic Women*, particularly the sections "The Gap Between Sentence and Symbol" and "Gaping."

visual and verbal, comics rests uneasily between disciplinary or departmental locations, but this slipperiness is part of what makes its study so productive. In spring 2012, for example, Alison Bechdel and I co-taught a theory and practice mixed graduate and undergraduate course at the University of Chicago called "Lines of Transmission: Comics and Autobiography." "Lines of Transmission" was cross-listed with Gender Studies, English, Creative Writing, Art History, and the Department of Visual Art.[10] Our course focused extensively on "narrative" as a category of analysis, and, along with several key works of structural linguistics, the classic 1981 volume *On Narrative* was a significant reference point. (I remember before our collaboration, years ago, seeing a marked-up copy of Hayden White's "The Value of Narrativity in the Representation of Reality," from that volume, on Bechdel's studio desk.) We taught Bechdel's own work—the two graphic memoirs *Fun Home* and *Are You My Mother?*—along with other primary works of graphic autobiography, and essays on the history and theory of autobiography; students wrote a final analytical paper and produced "minicomics"—self-published editions of their own autobiographical comics. Comics's cross-discursive form necessitates analysis that crosses boundaries: we had art and art history students focus on narrative theory, and literature students focus on reading the space of images, attending to line and composition.

Perhaps the most truly basic, yet to me crucial assertion I could make about comics is that it calls important attention to form and formalism—a formalism that is enabling. Comics is a medium that wears its form on its sleeve, so to speak: it is patently artificial, juxtaposing hand-drawn boxes, meant to represent moments of time, on the page. And each page of a graphic narrative functions as a discrete unit, where the size, shape, and arrangement of panels and tiers and balloons and text boxes and gutters dictate narrative pace and suggest meaning. Comics has a different relationship to mimesis than photography and film; it never suggests transparency. Unlike film and theater, comics does not unfold *in time*. And, unlike most narrative prose, comics is conspicuously site-specific: it cannot be "reflowed" like the text of a novel can be. Readers of comics are left to "decode" (as Spiegelman put it) the relationship of lines on a page. In 2003, as a graduate student thinking through how to write a dissertation about nonfiction comics, I remember seeing W. J. T. Mitchell's "Theories and Methodologies" piece in *PMLA* about form, titled "The Commitment to Form, or, Still Crazy After All These Years," and thinking, *aha*. The explosion of gripping, narratively intricate, sophisti-

---

10. Bechdel and I had students from nine different departments in our 27-person class: Anthropology, Art History, Comparative Literature, English, Gender and Sexuality Studies, International Studies, Psychology, Sociology, Theater and Performance Studies.

cated graphic narratives in the late twentieth and early twenty-first centuries seemed exactly to demonstrate what he framed as a renewal of form when he wrote, "The modernist moment of form, whether modeled on organism, perceptual gestalten, or structural coherence, may be behind us, but that only means that some new notion of form, and thus a new kind of formalism, lies before us" (324). I was also particularly interested at the "Post.45" annual conference in 2011 to hear Brian McHale and Amy Elias on a panel titled Rethinking Formalism(s).[11] McHale's "Against Historicism? Or, Can We Imagine the Present?" proposes the importance of Russian formalism, a movement whose lexicon, including defamiliarization, has been useful to considering the moves that comics works make—Spiegelman even cites Viktor Shklovsky in his recent work of comics about comics, *Portrait of the Artist as a Young %@&·*!*. In Elias's "Dialogics and the Avant-Garde," the different dialogics she analyzed seem to potently combine in comics.[12] In my view, comics is a form that is *internally,* conspicuously dialogic, or cross-discursive, across its words and images. The words and images in comics do not match, or synthesize. It is not a redundant form in which illustration repeats the words, but rather one in which both images and words move the narrative through a constant, active, uneasy back-and-forth: comics stages a dialogism in its basic narrative processes, where words and images work in relation to each other but necessarily never blend. (This notion might also be clarified in Lyotard's discussion of the *différend.*)[13] Further, comics is *externally* dialogic, drawing its readers *in* to construct meaning in the spaces of the gutters between the panels that constitute its most fundamental narrative grammar.

It is this participatory aspect of comics that Seymour Chatman took up in 1978 in *Story and Discourse,* when in a four-page section called "A Comic Strip Example" he analyzed a ten-frame Sunday newspaper comic strip, demonstrating how the reading of comics is a kind of "reading out" as opposed to ordinary reading because it "[leaves] the burden of inference to the reader" (38).[14] Comics weaves what I think of as *interstice* and *interval* into its constitutive grammar, and it provokes the participation of readers in those interpretive spaces that are paradoxically full and empty. To the extent that the formal

---

11. Amy Elias, "Dialogics and the Avant-Garde," and Brian McHale, "Against Historicism? Or, Can We Imagine the Present?," session on "Rethinking Formalism(s): The Association for the Study of Arts of the Present," Post.45 Conference, 30 Apr. 2011, Cleveland, OH.

12. For Elias on dialogics, see "The Dialogical Avant-Garde."

13. See Chute, "History and Graphic Representation in *Maus.*"

14. Chatman analyzes a syndicated comic strip from 1970, "Short Ribs" by Frank O'Neal, which appeared in the *San Francisco Chronicle.* In Chatman's view, "reading out" is qualitatively different from ordinary reading, though so familiar as to seem natural (41).

proportions of comics put into play what we might think of as the unresolvable interplay of elements of absence and presence, we could understand the gutter space of comics to suggest a psychic order outside of the realm of symbolization—and therefore, perhaps, a kind of Lacanian Real.[15]

Stepping back, what does this description of comics form have to do with feminism? In my opinion, everything. My interest here is not *necessarily* in feminist "content" in narrative, although that can, of course, be relevant, but rather in *how comics texts model a feminist methodology in their form,* in the complex visual dimension of an author narrating herself on the page as a multiple subject. The proliferation of different bodies and voices of an author (say, a child body, an adult body, and separate adult narratorial voices in speech and in overarching narration) existing in the space of a single page, for example, collapsing or protracting temporal dimensions, is a feature of autobiographical comics that is hard to replicate in other mediums. We can see this, to name just one example, in the figure by Phoebe Gloeckner, an image to which I will return—it is an image of the adult author kissing her own child self. In the introduction to *Graphic Women* I write, "Graphic narrative brings certain key constellations to the table: hybridity and autobiography, theorizing trauma in connection to the visual, textuality that takes the body seriously. I claim graphic narratives, as they exhibit these interests, 'feminist'" (4). For me this means that even work without explicit, stated feminist content—for example, Art Spiegelman's *Maus*—is a work we can consider feminist. (Of course, it is possible for there to be misogynistic comics; comics form must not necessarily always express feminist concerns. But I am interested in emphasizing how, say, positionality, location, and embodiment—key feminist issues—are part of the basic grammar of comics form.) The form of comics powerfully addresses itself to the linkages between lifewriting and feminist theory. In locating iterations of their earlier bodies in space on the page—and in making these bodies, perhaps, interact and overlap—cartoonists force us to confront a non-overdetermined materiality of the body and the proliferation, or multiplicity, of selves that are both driving concerns of feminist narrative.

A central preoccupation of feminism—and of narrative and sexuality studies in general—is embodiment (the briefest definition from the *OED* is yet useful: Corporeal inhabitation).[16] In particular, the embodiment that we

---

15. Alan Sheridan describes Lacan's Real in language apposite to the gutter: "the ineliminable residue of all articulation, the foreclosed element, which may be approached, but never grasped" (280).

16. See *Oxford English Dictionary,* s.v. "embodiment," 2.a.: "The corporeal 'vesture' or 'habitation' *of* (a soul)."

get in comics, indicated by the mark of the hand as an index of the body, and also represented by a proliferation of narrating bodies in space on the comics page, demonstrates why the form is so urgent for expressing life stories, particularly stories of development, of trauma, and of hybrid subjectivity. What does it mean for an author to literally reappear, in the form of a *legible, drawn* body on the page, at the site of her own trauma, for example—what I think of, following Lynne Huffer, as at the site of "her inscriptional effacement"? Comics life narrative establishes what I think of as an expanded *idiom of witness,* a practice of testifying that sets verbal languages with and against visual language in order to embody individual and collective experience, to put contingent selves and histories into form.[17] Leigh Gilmore's formulation of the public and political dimensions of speech is useful: she writes of "the nexus of trauma and gender as the terrain of political speech, even when that speech explicitly draws on a rhetoric of private life" ("Jurisdictions" 715). With comics, this important conceptualization of speech is even further amplified and accounts for both the verbal and the visual elements of the narrative. Drawing your body can be an act of political speech. In their provocatively titled "The Trouble with Autobiography: Cautionary Notes for Narrative Theorists," autobiography scholars Smith and Watson underscore the materiality of narrative—how autobiography insists on "the inextricable connection of narrative and the materiality of the body" (367). There is, perhaps, at least in the world of print, no place this is more clear than in the form of comics. A comics autobiography is drawn by hand—so that we are always aware of the presence of the body of the maker; it is a haptic form that proposes the materiality of the body on every page. Further, a comics autobiography calls our attention to key issues of perspective and positionality: the location of bodies in space, within frames: the view frames take, the kinds of bodies that are located within them (often, powerfully, in recent work, the author's own child body).[18] Comics makes literal and active in narrative self-constitution the crucial feminist concern that Adrienne Rich identified as "the politics of location."

THE VISUAL REGISTER of comics need not be understood as necessarily trafficking in the putatively easy, affectively powerful legibility of the visual— or, on the other hand, the I/eye of surveillance and disembodied power. The visual can sometimes be, critically, conflated with an uncomplicated representational politics of visibility, as in the important but commonplace feminist

---

17. See *Graphic Women* 3–4 for a similar and more detailed discussion; see also Huffer 4.
18. See, for example, Gilmore and Marshall's essay "Girls in Crisis" in *Feminist Studies.*

trope of "making the hidden visible." I claim instead the capaciousness of comics's visual form as an ethical and troubling visual aesthetics, or poetics— a complex literary location for theorizing embodiment and narrative. (By "troubling," I do mean to indicate that the way comics is able to be spectacular can sometimes feel uncomfortable, although I wager this discomfort can also be productive, especially in the realm of feminist and/or queer politics, where comics is able to take on many views and to inhabit ambivalent perspectives.) As Donna Haraway opens her important 1988 essay "The Persistence of Vision": "I would like to proceed by placing metaphorical reliance on a much maligned sensory system in feminist discourse: vision. Vision can be good for avoiding binary oppositions. I would like to insist on the embodied nature of all vision, and so reclaim the sensory system that has been used to signify a leap out of the marked body" (677).[19] In comics we are constantly confronted with the "embodied nature of all vision"—an issue that is suggested by the author's visualization of his or her past through handmade marks on the page, and is further highlighted by the conspicuous, self-reflexive frames of comics form. And in comics, in particular, we see *the mapping of bodies in space.* In comics data moves over space as well as over time, even if the movement is recursive, backtracked, or palimpsested.[20] Bechdel has said, "Cartoons are like maps to me, and *Fun Home* is a pretty accurate map of my life" ("PEN/ Faulkner" 4). We see this clearly too in a page from *Are You My Mother?* in which Bechdel charts her years from 25 onwards through a spatialized chart of changing therapists and girlfriends (see fig. 9.1). A colleague in Art History, Niall Atkinson, who works on Italian Early Renaissance urban space recently said to me, discussing contemporary digital construction of maps of Renaissance cities, "When data is plotted spatially it constructs different kinds of knowledge." This applies to the data of the self and it is, centrally, what the form of comics brings to the table at the intersection of feminist and narrative studies.

The kinds of knowledges that come from mapping a life in time and in space are "situated knowledges," to draw on a central feminist concept also named by Haraway in "The Persistence of Vision." One of the key descriptions of comics form is that its procedure *is to turn time into space,* what we can think of as "choreographing and shaping time" through the sculpting of the page into panels and tiers—*boxes of time* that are framed and spatially juxtaposed

---

19. "The Persistence of Vision" has been excerpted, twice—in Conboy et al. and in Mirzoeff's *Visual Culture Reader.* It initially appeared as part of a longer essay titled "Situated Knowledges: The Science Question in Feminism and the Privilege of Partial Perspective" in *Feminist Studies.*

20. See Chute, "Comics Form," for further elaborations of the importance of comics's mapping abilities, especially in the work of Bechdel and Joe Sacco.

FIGURE 9.1. Page from Alison Bechdel, *Are You My Mother?* (Boston: Houghton Mifflin, 2012; Unpaginated [22]). Used by permission of Alison Bechdel / Houghton Mifflin.

on the page.[21] Conventionally, comics panels are each supposed to represent one punctual moment, one temporality. The way we see authors *layer* temporalities—sometimes literally crushing them up against each other—in the space of the panel is key to understanding how the form expresses complex, proliferated subjectivities for the self. Many scholars, including ones present at the Queer and Feminist Narrative Theory Symposium, have previously indicated the importance of *spatiality*, not only as a dominant modality of the postmodern, something we see across many canonical works of criticism, but further as a central rubric for life narrative. In their book *Women, Autobiography, Theory* (1998), for example, in a section on "Prospects for Theorizing Women's Autobiography," Sidonie Smith and Julia Watson, following Susan Stanford Friedman, suggest "spatiality, rather than temporality, as a focus of critical reading practices" (39).[22] In comics, a spatially site-specific form much like concrete poetry or the artists' book, we see an amplification of the importance, theoretical *and* material, of the stuff of space for life narrative. The attention to bodies in space, bodies producing space, and bodies taking up space that comics proposes is about situating the self, to evoke the title of Seyla Benhabib's classic feminist study—and it also makes legible how autobiographers constitute themselves in the very process of creating life narrative. It is striking to me that so much of the conversation at the Queer and Feminist Narrative Theory Symposium was about *temporality*. And particularly, say, in analyses of *Fun Home,* we see the notion of a productively antihistoricist "queer time" or "queer temporality," but much less emphasis on *Fun Home*'s recursive spatiality, and on how the narrative offers the *space of the page* to showcase the protagonist's role not only as subject but additionally as an active archivist and curator of her own life.[23]

I will conclude with a very brief discussion of an image from cartoonist Phoebe Gloeckner's 1998 book *A Child's Life and Other Stories*—an image I wrote about in my dissertation in 2006, and in my book in 2010, and which continues to exemplify something for me (see fig. 9.2). This image enacts, conceptually and materially, what many comics texts accomplish in mapping the bodies that populate, and generate, their narratives. *A Child's Life* offers a full-page picture of a child being kissed on the face, sensually, by an adult woman who grasps her face. We can see two earrings in the woman's left ear,

---

21. Art Spiegelman states that comics works most fundamentally "choreograph and shape time" ("Ephemera" 4).

22. For an important view of space and mapping, see Friedman, *Mappings* and "Locational Feminism."

23. See, for instance, Cvetkovich and Rohy. The space of the comics page allows for the incorporation and repurposing of archives.

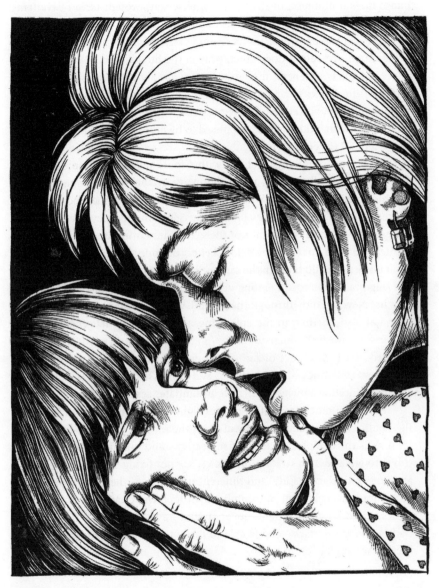

FIGURE 9.2. Page from Phoebe Gloeckner, *A Child's Life and Other Stories* (Berkeley: Frog / North Atlantic Books, 1998). Used by permission of Phoebe Gloeckner.

one dangling; and the white shirt of the child patterned with dark hearts. This image does not appear in the book's otherwise thorough table of contents, and its absence, paradoxically, appears to underscore its importance. Its title, as we see on the page itself, is "A Child's Life," as is the title of the book in which it appears, but it does not appear in the book's own listing of its contents. Its logic is so central, it seems, that it floats above (or seamlessly threads through) the book. The adult's open lips touch the child's cheek; she looks both aggressive and tender; predatory, even, yet also protective.[24] Gloeckner has explained that the image is supposed to be herself as an adult kissing herself as a child (Orenstein 29).

This image seems to match up with Gloeckner's dedication to her second book—"for all the girls when they have grown"—and we can see it as succinctly expressing Freud's idea of *Nachträglichkeit*.[25] Gloeckner's claim of addressing girls when they have grown carries both the delayed effect of sexual experience—the cognizance of the sexual dimension of experience—and the delayed effect of trauma, a delayed effect of understanding. By putting her adult body and child body in the same space, contiguous on the page, Gloeckner stages a conversation among versions of self—a conversation we recognize happens not only through the graphic visibility of different selves on the page but also, further, in the collapsing of temporality that enables such a tender—or invasive?—intersubjective (and non self-same) relation. What gets mapped here is this space of ambiguous desire *and* disavowal of the past. The bodiliness of comics—both *pictured,* and expressed *in form*—is a powerful site of exploration in which narrative instantiates sexuality.

There is so much interest in comics right now, from quarters focused on the politics of form, and those focused on the form of politics, because comics reveals the complex creation of subjectivity and unfinished selves. It does this through attention to locating bodies, but not fixing them, in space: older and younger selves collide, and different iterations of the "I" can be literally contiguous, available but not stabilized. In its form, comics adopts so many topics that drive feminist and queer studies—even the idea of pathologized bodies *taking up space*—and is able to make these politics and propositions literal and tangible on the page.

---

24. For more on Gloeckner and this image, see my *Graphic Women* chapter "Phoebe Gloeckner's Ambivalent Images."

25. Thank you to Tom Gunning for proposing this idea.

Works Cited

Aldama, Frederick Luis. *Multicultural Comics: From Zap to Blue Beetle*. Austin: U of Texas P, 2010.

———. *Your Brain on Latino Comics: From Gus Arriola to Los Bros Hernandez*. Austin: U of Texas P, 2009.

Barry, Lynda. *One Hundred Demons*. Seattle: Sasquatch, 2002.

Bechdel, Alison. *Are You My Mother? A Comic Drama*. Boston: Houghton Mifflin, 2012.

———. *Fun Home: A Family Tragicomic*. Boston: Houghton Mifflin, 2006.

———. "PEN/Faulkner Event with Lynda Barry and Chris Ware." Washington, DC. 9 Nov. 2007. Transcript.

Camper, Jennifer, ed. *Juicy Mother*. New York: Soft Skull, 2005.

Chatman, Seymour. *Story and Discourse*. Ithaca: Cornell UP, 1978.

Chute, Hillary. "Comics as Literature? Reading Graphic Narrative." *PMLA* 123.2 (2008): 452–65.

———. "Comics Form and Narrating Lives." *Profession* 2011: 107–17.

———. *Graphic Women: Life Narrative and Contemporary Comics*. New York: Columbia UP, 2010.

———. "'The Shadow of a Past Time': History and Graphic Representation in Maus." *Twentieth Century Literature* 2 (2006): 199–230.

———. "The Texture of Retracing in Marjane Satrapi's *Persepolis*." *Women's Studies Quarterly* 36.1–2 (Summer 2008): 92–110.

Couser, C. Thomas. *Memoir: An Introduction*. New York: Oxford UP, 2012.

Cruse, Howard. *Stuck Rubber Baby*. New York: HarperPerennial, 1995.

Cvetkovich, Ann. "Drawing the Archive in Alison Bechdel's *Fun Home*." *Women's Studies Quarterly* 36.1–2 (Summer 2008): 111–28.

Delany, Samuel R., with Mia Wolff. *Bread & Wine*. Seattle: Fantagraphics, 1999.

Elias, Amy J. "The Dialogical Avant-Garde: Relational Aesthetics and Time Ecologies in *Only Revolutions* and *TOC*." *Contemporary Literature* 53.4 (2013): 738–78.

Forney, Ellen. *Marbles: Mania, Depression, Michelangelo, and Me*. New York: Gotham, 2012.

Friedman, Susan Stanford. "Locational Feminism: Gender: Cultural Geographies, and Geopolitical Literacy." *Feminist Locations: Global and Local, Theory and Practice*. Ed. Marianne DeKoven. New Brunswick: Rutgers UP, 2001.

———. *Mappings: Feminism and the Cultural Geographies of Encounter*. Princeton: Princeton UP, 1998.

———. "Wartime Cosmopolitanism: Cosmofeminism in Virginia Woolf's *Three Guineas* and Marjane Satrapi's *Persepolis*." *Tulsa Studies in Women's Literature* 32.1 (2013): 23–52.

Gardiner, Judith Kegan. "Queering Genre: Alison Bechdel's *Fun Home: A Family Tragicomic* and *The Essential Dykes to Watch Out For*." *Contemporary Women's Writing* 5.3 (2011): 188–207.

Gilmore, Leigh. "Jurisdictions: *I, Rigoberta Menchú, The Kiss*, and Scandalous Self-Representation in the Age of Memoir and Trauma." *Signs: Journal of Women in Culture and Society* 28.2 (2003): 695–718.

Gilmore, Leigh, and Elizabeth Marshall. "Girls in Crisis: Rescue and Transnational Feminist Autobiographical Resistance." *Feminist Studies* 36.3 (Fall 2010): 667–90.

Gloeckner, Phoebe. *A Child's Life and Other Stories*. Berkeley, CA: Frog, 1998.

———. *The Diary of a Teenage Girl*. Berkeley, CA: Frog, 2002.

Hall, Justin. *No Straight Lines: Four Decades of Queer Comics*. Seattle: Fantagraphics, 2012.

Haraway, Donna. "The Persistence of Vision." *Writing on the Body: Female Embodiment and Feminist Theory*. Ed. Katie Conboy, Nadia Medina, and Sarah Stanbury. New York: Columbia UP, 1997. 283–95.

———. "Situated Knowledges: The Science Question in Feminism and the Privilege of Partial Perspective." *Feminist Studies* 14.3 (Fall 1988): 575–99.

Herman, David. *Basic Elements of Narrative*. Malden, MA: Wiley-Blackwell, 2009.

Huffer, Lynne. "'There is no Gomorrah': Narrative Ethics in Feminist and Queer Theory." *differences: A Journal of Feminist Cultural Studies* 12.4 (2001): 1–32.

Kominsky-Crumb, Aline. *Love That Bunch*. Seattle: Fantagraphics, 1990.

———. *Need More Love*. London: MQ, 2007.

Miller, Nancy K. "The Entangled Self: Genre Bondage in the Age of the Memoir." *PMLA* 122.2 (2007): 537–48.

Mitchell, W. J. T. "The Commitment to Form, or, Still Crazy After All These Years." *PMLA* 118 (2003): 321–25.

Obomsawin, Diane. *On Loving Women*. Trans. Helge Dascher. Montreal: Drawn & Quarterly, 2014.

Orenstein, Peggy. "Phoebe Gloeckner Is Creating Stories about the Dark Side of Growing Up Female." *New York Times Magazine* 5 Aug. 2001: 26–29.

Peterson, James Braxton. "Birth of a Nation: Representation, Nationhood, and Graphic Revolution in the Works of D. W. Griffith, DJ Spooky, and Aaron McGruder et al." Aldama, *Multicultural Comics* 105–19.

Rohy, Valerie. "In the Queer Archive: *Fun Home*." *GLQ* 16.3 (2010): 341–63.

Satrapi, Marjane. *Embroideries*. Trans. Anjali Singh. New York: Pantheon, 2005.

———. *Persepolis: The Story of a Childhood*. Trans. Mattias Ripa and Blake Ferris. New York: Pantheon, 2003.

———. *Persepolis: The Story of a Return*. Trans. Anjali Singh. New York: Pantheon, 2004.

Schrag, Ariel. *Awkward and Definition: The High School Chronicles of Ariel Schrag*. New York: Touchstone, 2008.

———. *Likewise*. New York: Touchstone, 2009.

———. *Potential*. New York: Touchstone, 2008.

Sheridan, Alan. "Translator's Note." *Four Fundamental Concepts of Psycho-Analysis*. By Jacques Lacan. New York: Norton, 1978. 277–82.

Smith, Sidonie. "Human Rights and Comics: Autobiographical Avatars, Crisis Witnessing, and Transnational Rescue Networks." *Graphic Subjects: Critical Essays on Autobiography and Graphic Novels*. Ed. Michael A. Chaney. Madison: U of Wisconsin P, 2011. 61–72.

———. "Narrating Lives." 2011 Presidential Address. The Modern Language Association Annual Convention. Los Angeles, CA, 6 Jan. 2011. <http://www.mla.org/pres_address_2011> Accessed 30 June 2012.

Smith, Sidonie, and Julia Watson. "Introduction." *Women, Autobiography, Theory*. Ed. Smith and Watson. Madison: U of Wisconsin P, 1998. 3–52.

———. "The Trouble with Autobiography: Cautionary Notes for Narrative Theorists." *A Companion to Narrative Theory*. Ed. James Phelan and Peter Rabinowitz. New York: Blackwell, 2005. 356–71.

Spiegelman, Art. "Ephemera vs the Apocalypse." *Indy Magazine* Autumn 2005.

———. *Maus: A Survivor's Tale: And Here My Troubles Begin*. New York: Pantheon, 1991.

———. *Maus: A Survivor's Tale: My Father Bleeds History*. New York: Pantheon, 1986.

Summers, A. K. *Pregnant Butch*. Berkeley, CA: Soft Skull Press, 2014.

Tea, Michelle. *Rent Girl*. San Francisco: Last Gasp, 2004.

Wanzo, Rebecca. "Black Nationalism, Bunraku and Beyond: Articulating Black Heroism and Cultural Fusion in Comics." *Multicultural Comics: From Zap to Blue Beetle*. Aldama, *Multicultural Comics* 93–104.

———. "Narrativizing the Nexus of Difference, Disability, and State Control in Female Genital Cutting Memoirs." Ohio State's Project Narrative Symposium: Queer and Feminist Narrative Theory. Hyatt Regency Hotel, Columbus, OH. 12–14 May 2011. Conference Presentation.

Warhol, Robyn. "The Space Between: A Narrative Approach to Alison Bechdel's *Fun Home*." *College Literature* 38.3 (Summer 2011): 1–20.

Warren, Roz, ed. *Dyke Strippers: Lesbian Cartoonists from A to Z*. San Francisco: Cleis Press, 1995.

Watson, Julia. "Autographic Disclosures and Genealogies of Desire in Alison Bechdel's *Fun Home*." Biography 31.1 (2008): 27–58.

Wojnarowicz, David, with James Romberger and Marguerite Van Cook. *Seven Miles a Second*. New York: Vertigo, 1996.

Yagoda, Ben. *Memoir: A History*. New York: Riverhead, 2009.

WENDY MOFFAT

The Narrative Case for Queer Biography[1]

*T*o speculate on the future of queer theory, it's fruitful to begin by examining its ancestry. Like New Historicism and feminist inquiry, queer theory was born of a desire to "do justice to difference (individual, historical, cross-cultural), to contingency, to performative force, and to the possibility of change" (Sedgwick, *Touching* 93). In the late 1970s, scholars began to "puncture" the *grands récits* of criticism and history.[2] They wanted to *get real* and to do so they invoked particularly personal kinds of truth-claims, examining both the textured events of real lives and their own political position as critics, narrators, and historians. Dismantling and exposing cultural assumptions, their project became a critique of subjectivity itself. Their tool of inquiry was theory, which Jonathan Culler defines with elegant simplicity as "writing with effects beyond its original field." (3) Culler's definition reveals the inherent attraction to an *other* in the function of the form. Interdisciplinarity is itself a form of desire.

---

1. A portion of section 3 was published in a slightly different form as "E. M. Forster and the Unpublished 'Scrapbook' of Gay History: 'Lest We Forget Him,'" *English Literature in Transition* 55.1 (2012): 19–31. I am grateful for permission to include it here. Thanks to Emma Kaufman for a thoughtful reading of an earlier manuscript, and concrete good advice.

2. The word *puncture* comes from Catherine Gallagher and Stephen Greenblatt's *Practicing New Historicism* (49). I take up a longer consideration of their argument later in this chapter.

It's a particular irony that despite queer theory's focus on real bodies and material culture, it cut itself off from some of its richest evidence. From my liminal position as biographer and reader of queer theory I've found little dialogue between queer theory and gay social history, though both have been rich resources in my work. Having written a biography of E. M. Forster, a gay man who is sometimes deemed to have been insufficiently queer, I'm convinced that lifewriting could be the best ground to explore queer subjectivity. In this chapter, I'll explore how we got here, and suggest a way forward. My narrative case for queer biography addresses both the story of disciplinary tensions and the particular promise of narrative theory in returning the queer to the promise of "the possibility of change."

Cross Dressing: Or, Temporality and Disciplinarity

Notions of time have always been at the heart of the queer. Queer theory's project helped to dismantle the myth of transcendent time and sequential time that had shaped humanist criticism for a generation. Scholars engaged in this task understood they were embedded in time; they felt the thrill of this critical moment. Almost immediately the smartest theorists began to think about the relations among these new questions in a temporal frame. In 1990 Eve Kosofsky Sedgwick acknowledged the "almost irremediably slippery" relations between feminist and queer inquiry.[3] She did so, tellingly, by situating the inquiry in a temporal narrative frame:

> The study of sexuality is not coextensive with the study of gender; correspondingly, antihomophobic inquiry is not coextensive with feminist inquiry. But *we can't know in advance* how they will be different. (Sedgwick, *Epistemology of the Closet* 27; emphasis mine)

Here Sedgwick anticipates the future of queer critical work. Her locution "antihomophobic inquiry" may sound a bit dated to our ears, tied as it is to the concept of gay identity. It does not have the rangy, capacious force of the queer, with its resistance to a hetero/homo binary, which opens the way to

---

3. The moment is ripe for such genealogies. The groundbreaking work in both queer and feminist inquiry is old enough to be our mother. It's been twenty years since Susan Lanser's "Toward a Feminist Poetics of Narrative Voice" was first published. In May 2011 Project Narrative sponsored the prescient Queer and Feminist Narrative Theory Symposium that engendered this book. The Winter 2012 issue of *New Literary History* queries the future of postcolonial studies. Heather Love's most recent works returns to Erving Goffman; Sharon Marcus's to Clifford Geertz.

nonnormative identities beyond the sexual. But Sedgwick's figuration is prophetic in a different key. This passage warns those of us who care about the future of the queer to resist normativity in our framing of the story that is to come. She conceives of this danger as a narrative problem.

The latent queerness of this theoretical moment is visible in hindsight in a second example. In recounting the origins of the journal *Representations,* Catherine Gallagher and Stephen Greenblatt describe fierce discussions among scholar-friends as a "spectacle," a kind of queer performance:

> The group came to understand, that there was, in interdisciplinary studies, a tendency to invoke, in support of one's own positions, arguments that sophisticated thinkers in those disciplines *had in fact been calling* into question. We had, as it were, been complacently dressing ourselves in each other's cast-off clothes . . . The spectacle was not entirely grotesque: some of the intellectual hand-me-downs looked surprisingly good on our friends. (3; emphasis mine)

The pluperfect progressive tense of Gallagher and Greenblatt's tale hints at a different temporal anxiety. Even at the beginning, it's all over, framed as teleology, embedded in time.

Even couched in a tone of wry bemusement, Gallagher and Greenblatt's words betray anxieties, the explorative work of these counterhistorians deliberately cast in an affective as well as an intellectual mode. The comical syncopation of *Representations'* founders' disciplinary inquiries betrayed their concern with "sophistication," with losing a step or two in the race to be at the forefront of an emerging field.[4] In other words, the metaphor of cross-dressing frames disciplinary inquiry as a sequential enterprise in time.

The New Historicists' predicament was shared, perhaps unconsciously, by scholars of queer discourse and representation. In 1990 Sedgwick could "not know in advance" how the tensions within "antihomophobic" inquiry would play out. We *can know* now, since *Epistemology of the Closet* has become a historical document. Queer theory wanted to move ahead, and the way it did so was to remove the confining clothing of its feminist mothers and its gay fathers. Butler's *Gender Trouble* began by being troubled with feminism. Theorists reappropriated the old pejorative term *queer,* arguing, as David Macey writes, that "homosexuality is a category of knowledge rather than a tangible

---

4. And envy (resentment? regret?) too. "We experienced the odd sensation one might feel at seeing one's own discarded possessions sold at auction for a handsome profit" (4).

reality" (321).[5] Quite quickly, queer became a mark of futurity; gay was passé, an antiquating term, fixed in the particular temporal moment of modernism, sincere, self-chosen, anchored as a (seemingly) stable sexual identity. The term "queer," in contrast, began as an ironic appropriation of a pejorative slur. The queer encapsulated the process of reverse discourse, and gathered power as it distanced itself from the particular. The idea of the queer became more broadly synonymous with any nonnormative impulse.

Queer theory began, not just as a totalizing vision—but rather as a totally anti-essentialist one. The goal was to illustrate how *constructed*, how *unnatural* essentialist assumptions about identity were, not merely to observe how power worked on subjects. This may seem at first to be a question of scale, but actually it was a resistance to the perceived limitations of living in time. The concept of gay identity seemed too anchored in a particular historical moment, too determinative, too dependent on troublingly fixed conceptions of gender and difference.

This last point is most salient in comparing methodologies. The circumstances of lived gay lives, documented by scholars like George Chauncey, Ken Plummer, and Jeffrey Weeks, evinced a particularity of evidence in time and place that did not privilege the possibility of change. (For example, the men who identified as "queer," in Chauncey's study of a scandal at the Newport Naval Training Station in 1919, "reproduced many of the social forms of genderized heterosexuality, with some men playing 'the woman's part' in relationships with conventionally masculine 'husbands'" [193]. Is this queer or deeply normative? Or—queerly—beyond binary description?)

The queer resistance to the narrative of actual gay lives is not that they are too conventional, I think; nor that the evidence is archival and must be painstakingly gathered. Rather, the depressingly consistent evidence of homophobia reminds the theorist of the complex and often the limited agency of the queer subject. Rare is the evidence of unfettered freedom, of utopian escape from the narrative pull of pathos or tragedy. Queer heroes of the past *disappoint.*

The goal for theorists became instead to track and expose the operations of power—not to trace the narratives of individual lives. The fluidity of subject-formation invited a dispassionate separation from the "reality" of embodied selves. But this goal becomes, as Sedgwick points out in *Touching Feeling,*

---

5. For more detailed discussions of the reverse discourse of queer identity, see Jeffrey Weeks, *Coming Out: Homosexual Politics in Britain from the Nineteenth Century to the Present,* Steven Seidman, *Queer Theory/Sociology,* and Joseph Bristow, *Sexuality.*

its own kind of normative rule, when queer policing of anti-essentialism becomes a kind of purity test. She calls this moment "the strange metamorphosis from anti-essentialist to ontological private eye" (110).

Sedgwick's devotion to the full array of "narrative consequences" awakened this discovery, as did the strangeness of her bodily experience of dying over a prolonged span of time (124). Stepping back, thinking temporally, she repudiated a flattening impulse she found in some of her earlier work, and the work of other queer scholars. Tracing Paul Ricoeur's "hermeneutics of suspicion" to a pattern of exposing the falseness of dominant narratives that she called "paranoid reading," Sedgwick posited that a habit of mind in queer studies had hardened into a methodological doctrine. It was not that there was anything essentially *untrue* about paranoia. "In a world where no one need be delusional to find evidence of systematic oppression, to theorize out of anything but a paranoid critical stance has come to seem naïve, pious, or complacent" (126).

For Sedgwick, the important question for this method, or any method, was what does knowledge *do*? (124). She cannily saw that the temporal position encased in the paranoid critical approach required its practitioners to go backward, to fix the terms of the outcome so that it could be "exposed" in a revelatory flourish. She argued that the paranoid method was locked in a defensive posture whose first principle was "there must be no bad surprises" (130). In the paranoid stance, being "unanticipated"—being caught off guard—was "more dangerous . . . than to be unchallenged" (133). Here is where the desire to stay ahead in queer theory paradoxically becomes a bind. Specifically, she finds the narrative structure of paranoia monotonously "inescapable," "rigidly" tied to a temporal position both "*anticipatory and reactive*" (138, 130; emphasis mine). Sedgwick's principal critique of the paranoid strain in queer inquiry was that it limited the narrative range of the possible.

The narrator—the theorist—subsumed the story. In *Touching Feeling* Sedgwick called out Judith Butler for her "tacit or ostensibly marginal but *in hindsight* originary and authorizing relation to different strains of queer theory" (129). In invoking the damning word "authorizing," Sedgwick in effect charges Butler with hypocrisy. The "anticipatory and reactive" frame allows the queer theorist to appropriate an authorizing power at the moment she is celebrating creative misrule.

Catherine Gallagher and Stephen Greenblatt argued, "Bodies cannot be reduced to representation" (15). The countermove of "reparative reading" meant reopening questions of "the biological," and facing the final taboo of the anti-essentialist enterprise in the queer. The local individual body and its feelings came to the center of Sedgwick's last inquiry. She believed that we need to think through the effect of theory-stories on real bodies. She imagined that exploring affect and effect on real bodies was an imaginative act that could engender new narrative forms.

> For all its interest in performativity, the thrust of *Touching Feeling* is not to expose residual forms of essentialism lurking behind apparently nonessentialist forms of analysis. . . . I have tried . . . to explore some ways around the topos of depth or hiddenness. . . . *Beneath* and *behind* are hard enough to let go of; what has been even more difficult is to get a little distance from *beyond,* in particular the bossy gesture of "calling for" an imminently perfected critical or revolutionary practice that one can oneself only adumbrate. . . . The most salient preposition in *Touching Feeling* is probably *beside. Beside* permits a spacious agnosticism. (8)

At the end of her life Sedgwick was most interested in keeping the queerness of the story alive.

In *Touching Feeling,* Sedgwick rejected teleology (as she had years before in *Epistemology of the Closet*) in favor of an unfixed narrative. She did not forsake narrative for the promise of antinarrative. For her, rethinking narrative is better than forsaking it. Dying, she seemed positively relaxed about the prospect of the future. We don't know where the story will go. When we try to imagine the arc of queer theory in the future, we need to acknowledge the bind queer theory has written itself into: the almost ritualistic assertion of the unknowingness of inquiry, the predictable interpretive flourish in the *ta-dah* of unmasking (Sedgwick calls this "exposure"). We recognize it in the papers our students write, eagerly looking for our approval. The story of the history of sexuality has become formulaic because theory has become the story.

Asking "what does knowledge *do?*" (124) is an especially pointed question for teachers of the queer. In practice, in departments I have taught in and observed, the story of queerness is built foundationally on a handful of theoretical texts taught over and again in English and women's and gender studies classes. And in invoking this genealogy, we have ourselves created a normative epistemology and pedagogy. I add my voice to the chorus of voices in this book who are questioning the effects of insistent *retelling.* What are the effects of endlessly (for example) retelling the story of how a culture disciplines, and in doing so creates, its subjects? What is the purpose of this orthodoxy? What are we teaching? Can there never be a surprise, never a new story?

Narratives of the Miniature and the Gigantic, or: The Queer in the World[6]

What *size* is a queer story? Ever since Clifford Geertz showed us that we must "widen out" to see culture at work, scholars have been wrestling with the question of scale of the evidence (19). The turn to the small and the contingent was impelled by resistance to bad storytelling—what Catherine Gallagher and Stephen Greenblatt call "Big Stories" that explain everything (51). To resist reifying proportionality and other manifestations of normativity, scholars turned to creative, metonymic forms, something richer and looser than the *exemplum*. The narrative forms of this impulse were most often small: the anecdote and the case.

The anecdote came first, because in the hands of the New Historicists it was the perfect tool to "puncture the historical *grand recit* into which it was inserted" (Gallagher and Greenblatt 49). For Catherine Gallagher and Stephen Greenblatt, the tool of the anecdote

> offered access to the everyday, the place where things are actually done, the sphere of practice that even in its most awkward and inept articulations makes a claim on the truth that is denied to the most eloquent of literary texts. (48)

Though it seems like an affirmation of the value of cultural criticism, Gallagher and Greenblatt's turn to "the place where things are actually done" reflects an anxiety about the authenticity of hermeneutics itself. The reversal of figure and ground have been an inevitable consequence of theory's self-conscious attention to the affect of its practitioners; but the inquiry itself supplanted the object of study as the place to attend to.

That the anecdote in its handy shape seemed to offer a hold on "the real" was only one part of its appeal as a narrative tool. The selection of the anecdote, the decision of how to frame the example, felt like a creative act:

> Several of us particularly wanted to hold on to our aesthetic pleasures; our desire for critical innovation; our interest in contingency, spontaneity, improvisation; our urge to pick up a tangential fact and watch its circulation; our sense of history's unpredictable galvanic appearances and disappearances. (4)

---

6. I want to acknowledge the influence in this essay, and in my life, of Susan Stewart's *On Longing*.

The critical turn from the anecdote to the case was a movement toward still greater legitimacy and self-reflexivity. Scholars turned to "the case" as a more efficient unit of inquiry, because its framing encapsulates both story and the interpreter's insight, both an event and the power to illuminate its meaning. In the summer of 2007 *Critical Inquiry* devoted two special issues edited by the queer scholar Lauren Berlant to consideration of the critical genre of "the case."

There are several reasons that the case seemed to offer greater narrative possibility than the anecdote. Berlant argues that the authorizing function embedded in its structure, "the practice or expression of expertise" is the defining feature of the case ("What Does" 1). Framed as a problem that contains its own solution, the case is "animated by judgment ("Case" 663). Because it only awakens under a critical eye, the narrative form seems to encompass a wider temporal range than a mere anecdote or event: "One might say that the case *is what an event can become*" ("Case" 670). The case is flexible in its applications, and notably interdisciplinary—whether from history, literature, psychoanalysis. Best of all, the case—as Berlant humorously implied—seems to offer critical distance: "The case represents a problem—an event that has animated some kind of judgment. Any enigma could do . . . any irritating obstacle to clarity" (663).

Berlant is at once mocking and invoking the concept of narrative closure here. But since expertise is inscribed in its form, the case invites what Brian Carr calls "realtight" closure—the narrative position that "refuses" externality altogether (283). The narrative structure of the case is quite literally (to use Sedgwick's terms) "anticipatory and reactive." The case especially features a static mimetic structure. We must stop to look at the case, to watch it expertly be solved. It is designed to be solved.

Thus, in a *mise-en-abîme*, while the case promises to lay open the event and its terms of critical scrutiny, often embedded it becomes invoked tautologically in sweeping pseudonarratives in queer studies.[7] Two monitory occasions prove the case is an ill-fitting form for exploring real queer lives. Michel Foucault's late work is the apotheosis of this tendency. Toward the end of his life, Foucault imagined collecting "an anthology of existences," of what he called infamous men—"singular lives . . . those which have become . . . strange poems: that is what I wanted to gather in a sort of herbarium" (76). This is the life-as-case *par excellence*. Foucault's detachment is exquisite and revelatory. The scholar who unveiled the process by which the homosexual

---

7. For a thoughtful critique of the "moralistic tautology" in Foucault's *History of Sexuality, Vol. I*, see Sedgwick, *Touching Feeling* 9–13.

became marked culturally as a "species" has fashioned biography into *specimen* (43).

Theorizing real queer bodies into encoded metaphors can actually do harm. Jay Prosser argues that Judith Butler's celebration of the subversive power of "ambivalent significance in performative (transgender) crossings" rather misses the point. Butler celebrates the transgressive power of Venus Xtravaganza, a drag performer interviewed in Jennie Livingstone's 1990 documentary *Paris Is Burning*. But in the lived world, Venus Xtravaganza was often beaten and was subsequently murdered. Prosser writes drily, "Butler's essay ["Gender Is Burning"] locates transgressive value in that which makes the subject's real life most unsafe" (49). By awakening us to the lived experience of transgendered people, Prosser detaches us from detachment and calls us to empathy. Neither the anecdote nor the case preemptively solves the narrative problems of the inherent questions of scale and authenticity in queer narrative.

The Form of a Queer Past

> *Beside* is an interesting preposition because there's nothing very dualistic about it. . . . *Beside* permits a spacious agnosticism about several of the linear logics that enforce dualistic thinking: . . . cause versus effect, subject versus object.
>
> —Sedgwick, *Touching Feeling*

And what of the lived queer experience in time? Who are the bodies under these clothes?

In his narrative meditation *Who Was That Man? A Present for Mr. Oscar Wilde,* the queer playwright Neil Bartlett interrogates the example of Oscar Wilde. As one of a generation of gay men who came to London in the 1980s, Bartlett has imbued Wilde with mystical power. In a creative *tour de force,* Bartlett explores the complexities of queer identification with the figure of Wilde, whose life is a Möbius strip of paradox: he was not only a martyr, he was also a liar. The chapters are titled history, flowers, faces, words, evidence, forgery, possessions, pretexts, messages, history, notes. It's not really possible to describe or categorize this queer life narrative. More of a *beside* narrative function than a case, *Who Was That Man?* positions itself *beside* its subject, somewhere in the textural play of what a story—a historical story—*is* and *how* it means.

The first way it does so is to recalibrate the normative audience. Bartlett directs his observations toward an inclusive "us," himself and his queer audience. Alan Sinfield argues that Bartlett's assumption of the queer "we" is the first such usage, a seminal moment in the history of queer scholarship (4).

Bartlett demonstrates that the construction of a queer canon—what I would call a documentable queer textual past—is foundational to the construction of gay identity. For him queer inquiry and identity necessarily shape each other. In describing his own youthful attempt to recuperate the gay past, Bartlett writes:

> The place I started looking for my story was not the city, but the [British] library . . . I pursued texts with the dogged energy I usually reserve for cruising; I became excited by the smallest hints; I scrutinized every gesture for significance . . . I went to the most unlikely places. (26, 28)

Bartlett's desire for a transmittable past is linked wittily to more corporeal desires. Cruising and paying close attention to the hidden trail of gay literary legacy are metaphors for the same inquiry; indeed the methods sharpen and inform each other.

Bartlett's search for "his story" has two modes: looking (cruising) and sharing the vulnerability of being seen to be looking. Though Bartlett's metaphor is camp, it's not about voyeurism. It's about incompleteness. He understands that the social conditions of gay desire—whether for history or for love—mean that the act of discovery is always an act of risk-taking: in searching for the gay past "we are always held between ignorance and exposure" (99).

This suspended place in Bartlett corresponds to ways of reading and knowing. While the gaps of an incomplete reading offer a means of self-protection, they always isolate the person looking for his own identity. Incompleteness is a figure of a kind of safety: to "read" is to risk making connections. To be seen reading, or to share secret readings, courts the danger of being seen to be looking. This incompleteness is both singular and collective. Bartlett's "we" can't be "ourselves" without a queer culture, because we can't recognize "ourselves" without a communal sense of the signs of a queer self; and "we" are always suspended between being alone and finding a community. Bartlett's subject—the gay man trolling for a past—is a reader locked in a paradox of mixed over- and underdetermination.[8] The "safety" of underdeter-

---

8. *A Passage to India* prefigures Bartlett's configuration of the gay subject position. Forster's realization in *A Passage to India* that the negative space of the connection he sought was

mined or incomplete reading simultaneously erases the collective activity of gay culture, and people forget. That is why gay writers must keep discovering gay culture over and over again: Suspended between overdetermination and underdetermination, the gay past is always simultaneously being forgotten and recuperable.

Bartlett seeks a form of narrative that will be "true" to the problems of incompleteness without paralyzing the reader or erasing the possibility of building a queer culture. For him the interdependence of gay male subjectivity (who "we" are) and the power to interpret (to "fill in the gaps") reinforce each other. There is always a space for wanting in these constituent elements of constructing queer identity. This is why Bartlett believes that the only "true history" of queer culture must exist in a particularly fractured form. He argues that pastiche is the only possible genre for a gay canon since it "embodies [the] omissions" inherent in gay identity: "*The scrapbook is the true form of our history,* since it records what we remember, and embodies in its omissions both how we remember and how we forget our lives" (99).

In one sense, in my experience of the archives, Barlett's axiom has proved to be literally true. Over and again in the archives, I found shards of evidence pasted into books by queer men—the scrapbooks of George Platt Lynes, Carl Van Vechten, E. M. Forster. But as figure, this queer embodiment of history has particular power: how can we embody in omissions the possibilities of queer life? How can this *besideness,* this space, help those of us who look to the queer past dodge "a seemingly unavoidable repetition and reification" of what it means for lives to be queer (Sedgwick 9)?

The Promise of Queer Biography

At the Project Narrative conference in 2011, I heard a lot of yearning for the empirical, the inductive, the grounded. These are ways of acknowledging that

---

the gap of desire itself, engendered in him a much more frank and homoerotic reading of the world. The people in the novel are always wanting, in both senses of the word: lacking and desiring. In this gap he places Prof. Godbole's curious song of invitation, which simultaneously represents the desire to connect and the impossibility of connection:

> I say to Shri Krishna "Come! Come to me only." The god refuses to come. I grew humble and say: "Do not come to me only. Multiply yourself into a hundred Krishna's, and let each one go to each of my hundred companions, but one, . . . come to me." He refuses to come. This is repeated several times. . . .
> "But he comes in some other song, I hope?" said Mrs. Moore gently.
> "Oh no, he refuses to come," repeated Godbole. "I say to Him, Come come, come come, come come. He neglects to come." (85)

theory has occluded a part of the story. My part in the symposium, I believe, was to meditate on the practical relation between textured lives and the innovations of queer (and in my case, also feminist) theory in biography. After all, I had spent a decade writing a recuperative biography of the British novelist E. M. Forster, which is a pretty queer thing to do.

For me biography was not a *via media,* a synthetic exercise of finding a middle ground between the past and the present, but an *electrical ground* between theory and history. I spent more than a decade shuttling between the sliver of text, the piece of ephemera in the archive, and the larger cultural inquiry that would open us to a different biographical form.

On the face of it, we already know the story of Forster's life—or several stories, all of them quite conventional. Forster was an Edwardian writer, whose novels of manners like *A Room with a View* and *Howards End* inspired the Merchant Ivory costume dramas; a man who published *A Passage to India* in 1924 and then packed it in, living almost another fifty years. Or there's the posthumous story, a conventional story of a closeted man who lived with his doting mother until he was almost seventy. These stories are incompletely true. Over the course of the second half of his long life, E. M. Forster cultivated and collaborated in the persistent myth of his benign Edwardian presence. He understood how his sexuality necessitated the bifurcation of his public and private lives, how it shaped and distorted his writing. Forster demanded that his authorized biography—P. N. Furbank's 1978 *E. M. Forster*—should be candid and frank about his homosexuality. But he also understood that the redress of the posthumous life cannot possibly extinguish the foundational narrative that erased and ignored his queer existence.

Forster also shrewdly, painstaking preserved an archive of his private life. The scrapbook was the true form of my method as a biographer. Researching *A Great Unrecorded History: A New Life of E. M. Forster,* it was difficult to find the evidence—or sometimes to recognize it as evidentiary at all. (Once, during an interview with one of Forster's friends in a sitting room in Hampstead London, I saw a perfectly conventional black and white photograph of Forster as a grand man of letters on a bookshelf. It turned out to be the anomaly—the only "straight" portrait in a sequence taken of Forster and his partner, the policeman Bob Buckingham, by the noted queer photographer George Platt Lynes.)

It was difficult too to frame the meaning of Forster's life in terms legible both to my subject and to contemporary readers. Making the events of a singular subject's life legible to other humans at a later moment in time demands that we pull back into the past, to the now-lost frame of reference that the cultural art historian Michael Baxandall called "the period eye." This is particularly important when writing about a man like Forster, who understood his sexual identity to be central to his writing and his life, but did not describe himself in terms like gay or queer. He only knew he "did not resemble other people" and repudiated labels as part of a "herd instinct" to oppression.[9]

Inevitably my biography was deeply informed by queer theory, and by the innovations at the heart of both feminist and queer inquiry—Crenshaw's intersectionality, Butler's performativity, Scarry's embodiment. Forster's life is a story full of cross-dressing, canny appropriations of power/knowledge, and sad, funny, surprising occasions of intersectionality. I'll offer just one example. While serving as a Red Cross searcher during the First World War in Alexandria, Forster fell in love with a young Egyptian tram-driver named Mohammed el Adl. After meeting many times as Forster rode the tram, the two arranged their first private assignation.

> The encounter began like an O. Henry story. Forster brought another hapless gift, the kind of expensive sticky cakes he had heard were a particular delicacy for Egyptians. He did not know that el Adl's mother had warned him against taking sweets from strangers. Though we know Forster to be an unimposing and sincere personage, el Adl later told Forster he feared they might be drugged. For his part, el Adl stood beside Forster for some time, unrecognized. [Forster] didn't see him because he came in an unexpected disguise: in complete tennis whites, right down to the gutta-percha-soled shoes. For ten full minutes, the sensitive Red Cross searcher had been looking past him, unconsciously seeking the familiar uniform. But Mohammed came disguised as a British gentleman. (Moffat 156)

Quite soon the two men made canny use of public space, depending on the colonial misapprehension that men of their race and class must be master and servant. Disgusted by British imperialism, Forster used it to extend metaphorical cover to his lover. But even in private, they conducted a tongue-in-cheek riff on cross-dressing.

> [Ed Adl] took great pleasure in teasing [Forster] about his shabby clothing and great pride in the care of his own dress. "Taking me by the sleeve last

---

9. E. M. Forster describes the colonial attitude of the English in Chandrapore anthropologically, as the "herd-instinct" in chapter 7 of *A Passage to India*. His diary entry that "I do not resemble other people," dates to 13 December 1907. (The diary reposes in King's College Archive Centre in Cambridge.) For a reading of Forster's use of the "herd-instinct" as a metaphor for homophobia, see my *A Great Unrecorded History: A New Life of E. M. Forster* 36, 131, 245.

night he said gently, 'You know Forster, though I am poorer than you I would never been seen in such a coat. I am not blaming you—no, I praise—but I would never be seen, and your hat has a hole and your boots have a hole and your socks have a hole.'" "Good clothes are an infectious disease," Mohammed admitted. "I had much better not care and look like you, and so perhaps I will, but only in Alexandria." He wouldn't be seen like that at home. The young man who first appeared in blinding tennis whites knew how to distinguish himself and how to become inconspicuous. (167)

The men consciously and playfully appropriated costume as disguise and parodically subversive tokens of their queer status. When el Adl had to leave Forster to work in the Canal Zone in 1918, Forster arranged to have his photograph taken as a keepsake. The young man arrived for the session wearing his lover's shabby khaki military uniform. "In another queer cultural cross-dressing, that summer the men commissioned a single dress suit, too big for Mohammed, slightly too small for Morgan, for them to share" (167). Without a queer eye to the relations between texts and visual evidence, these subtle queer gestures can be flattened or occluded as they recede into the past. That photograph of Mohammed is now lost. Another, that survives, shows him "resplendent" in Egyptian dress—no doubt enacting an orientalist fantasy for the viewer. A recuperative reading reveals that despite his subaltern position, Mohammed had real agency.

Biography is a kinetic art. The archives revealed Forster as a figure very close to Lauren Berlant's concept of the queer subject. In a recent interview in *Biography*, she says:

> I have a really different view of the subject, and this is what I'm trying to write into being. I think it begins and proceeds as a porous and disorganized thing that is constantly impelled (compelled and desiring) to take up positions in relations to objects, worlds, and situations, but the available clarifying genres of personhood underdescribe the range of practices, knowledges, impulses, and orientations that people have when they're foregrounding being this or that kind of thing at a particular moment. (187)

And how could it not be so for a gay man who was a teenager when Wilde was sent to prison, and died a year after the Stonewall riots? It is impossible to untangle the public and the private in Forster's story. They are alloyed by his sexuality, and his cultural knowledge that "what the public really loathes in homosexuality is not the thing itself but having to think about it" ("Notes" 220). Think about it he did. Shot through Forster's life and work is a complex narrative interplay, a consciousness of this life and the life to come, an acknowledgment of multiple audiences.

Narrative biography is perhaps the most predictable of literary forms. (When I decided to begin my story at the birth of Forster's posthumous life; my British publisher, convinced the audience would be confounded by a nonchronological life story, suggested that I call that chapter a prologue, not chapter 1.) And yet Forster's life curled back on itself. So dependent on literary convention, so embedded in the circumstances of gay history, Forster's life was ineluctably queer, partly because so much of its textual evidence had been preserved, like a bee in amber, for a future life.

Christopher Isherwood's critical exhortation to his friend John Lehmann as they undertook the editing of *Maurice*, Forster's posthumously published queer novel, became my narrative touchstone: "Unless you start with the fact that he was homosexual, nothing's any good at all" (Lehmann 121). *Start* with the fact. Begin with the queer subject. It took me several years of thinking about this—and reading Neil Bartlett's work—to understand what Isherwood meant. For Isherwood, starting was not only a temporal but a subject position—a realignment with a queer "us." After my book was published, I noticed that some reviewers thought they knew what this statement meant and the story it implied: their emphasis was on the *homosexual*. But Isherwood meant to emphasize the word *start*. He wanted from here on in to set the frame of reference toward the queer.

Following Isherwood's instructions, I started with a very simple question that turned into very complicated research. I wondered: what did Forster think and feel about his desire? I tried as much as I could to find out how he would have understood his own experience, amply helped by the fact that he is a magnificent and sensitive observer of his own psyche and body. His bifurcation of the public and the private caused a temporal rupture—a posthumous overlay of counterinterpretation. But starting with the facts meant interpellation of the diaries and letters, the secret queer writing, the photograph and stories of his friends. Realignment of the newly discovered truth that was there from the start with the received knowledge of his public life and writing does not yield seamless integration. The simplest narrative questions—what was the tone of his story?—proved the most complicated to articulate.

Forster's story and the story of finding Forster's story in the archive, too, were interwoven in complex ways. Both had their own closetedness and queerness. The archive was an excellent place to observe the cultural operations of homophobia at work. Almost the first day of my reading in King's College archive, I came across an innocuous little unpublished essay entitled "My Books and I." What I supposed would be a reflection of his habit of acquiring a library over time was revealed to be a thoughtful, funny essay, read aloud to Virginia Woolf and Maynard Keynes among others, on his coming to consciousness as a gay writer. When I found this essay it had been sitting in plain sight for almost thirty years. Numberless scholars had been looking at—and looking through—this little memoir. Yet the essay "My Books and I" remains unpublished—except as an appendix to the British edition of his novel *The Longest Journey*. Even now, the normalized myth of Forster exerts considerable power. Philip Gardner's authorized edition of Forster's journals and diaries, published in 2011, omits almost all Forster's significant reflections on his sexual feelings. Isherwood, who thought that the whole of literary history would be upended by the publication of *Maurice* in 1970, saw to his chagrin how puny his efforts to reframe the Forster myth were. I'm sure I'll have to get in line behind him.

In the past few years, the fruit of careful work in the archives has brought new queer lives, and lives newly queered, into the mainstream of American publishing. Justin Spring's *Secret Historian: The Life and Times of Samuel Steward, Professor, Tattoo Artist, and Sexual Renegade*; Tripp Evans's *Grant Wood: A New Life*; and Lisa Cohen's *All We Know: Three Lives* (among others) show how the circumstances, the canon, and the evidence of queerness in the past is (to paraphrase Virginia Woolf) a little other than custom would have us believe.

We can't rush on to the future of queer studies because we don't know the story yet. I'm arguing that the future of queer theory is in the past. It will come in queer life work. Sexual biography is reparative work because it is so full of surprises. It consistently punctures our theoretical "understandings." We have so much work to do going backwards. I can tell you that we really are just beginning to know these stories. Then, once we have more real stories of sexuality, we can resume theorizing them.

Works Cited

Bartlett, Neil. *Who Was That Man? A Present for Mr. Oscar Wilde*. London: Serpent's Tail, 1988.

Baxandall, Michael. *Painting and Experience in 15th Century Italy*. Oxford: Oxford UP, 1972.

Berlant, Lauren. "On the Case." *Critical Inquiry* 33.4 (Summer 2007): 663–72.

———. "What Does It Matter Who One Is?" *Critical Inquiry* 34.1 (Autumn 2007): 1–4.

Berlant, Lauren, and Prosser, Jay. "Life Writing and Intimate Publics: A Conversation." *Biography* 34.1 (Winter 2011): 180–87.

Bristow, Joseph. *Sexuality*. London; New York: Routledge, 1997.

Butler, Judith. *Bodies That Matter: On the Discursive Limits of Sex*. London: Routledge, 1993.

———. "Gender Is Burning: Questions of Appropriation and Subversion." *Feminist Film Theory, a Reader.* Ed. Sue Thornham. Edinburgh: Edinburgh UP, 1999. 336–53.

———. *Gender Trouble: Feminism and the Subversion of Identity.* London: Routledge, 1989.

Carr, Brian. "Paranoid Interpretation, Desire's Nonobject, and Nella Larsen's *Passing.*" *PMLA* 119.2 (2010): 282–95.

Chauncey, George. "Christian Brotherhood or Sexual Perversion: Homosexual Identities and the Construction of Sexual Boundaries in the World War One Era." *Journal of Social History* 19.2 (1985): 189–211.

Cohen, Lisa. *All We Know: Three Lives.* New York: Farrar, Straus and Giroux, 2012.

Culler, Jonathan. *Literary Theory: A Very Short Introduction* 2nd ed. Oxford: Oxford UP, 2011.

Evans, R. Tripp. *Grant Wood: A Life.* New York: Knopf, 2010.

Forster, E. M. "Notes on Maurice." *Maurice.* Ed. Philip Gardner. London: Andre Deutsch, 1999. 215–24.

———. *A Passage to India.* Ed. Oliver Stallybrass. London: Edward Arnold, 1978.

Foucault, Michel. "The Lives of Infamous Men." *Power, Truth, Strategy.* Trans. and ed. Meaghan Morris and Paul Patton. Sydney: Feral, 1979. 76–91.

Furbank, P. N. *E. M. Forster: A Life.* New York: Harcourt Brace Jovanovich, 1978.

Gallagher, Catherine, and Stephen Greenblatt. *Practicing New Historicism.* Chicago: U of Chicago P, 2001.

Gardner, Philip, ed. *The Journals and Diaries of E. M. Forster.* London: Pickering & Chatto, 2011.

Geertz, Clifford. "Thick Description: Toward an Interpretive Theory of Culture." *The Interpretation of Cultures: Selected Essays.* New York: Basic Books, 1973.

Lehmann, John. *Christopher Isherwood: A Personal Memoir.* New York: Henry Holt, 1988.

Macey, David. *The Penguin Dictionary of Critical Theory.* London; New York: Penguin, 2001.

Moffat, Wendy. *A Great Unrecorded History: A New Life of E. M. Forster.* New York: Farrar, Straus and Giroux, 2010.

Plummer, Ken. *Modern Homosexualities.* London; New York: Routledge, 1992.

Porter, Kevin, and Jeffrey Weeks. *Between the Acts: Lives of Homosexual Men, 1885–1967.* London; New York: Routledge, 1991.

Prosser, Jay. *Second Skins: The Body Narratives of Transsexuality.* New York: Columbia UP, 1998.

Ricoeur, Paul. *Freud and Philosophy: An Essay on Interpretation.* New Haven: Yale UP, 1970.

Sedgwick, Eve Kosofsky. *Epistemology of the Closet.* Berkeley: U of California P, 1990.

———. *Touching Feeling: Affect, Pedagogy, Performativity.* Durham: Duke UP, 2003.

Seidman, Steven, ed. *Queer Theory/Sociology.* Oxford: Blackwell, 1996.

Sinfield, Alan. *Gay and After.* London: Serpent's Tail, 1999.

Spring, Justin. *Secret Historian: The Life and Times of Samuel Steward, Professor, Tattoo Artist, and Sexual Renegade.* New York: Farrar, Straus and Giroux, 2010.

Stewart, Susan. *On Longing: Narratives of the Miniature, the Gigantic, the Souvenir, the Collection.* Baltimore; London: Johns Hopkins UP, 1984.

Weeks, Jeffrey. *Coming Out: Homosexual Politics in Britain from the Nineteenth Century to the Present.* London: Quartet, 1977.

JESSE MATZ

"No Future" vs. "It Gets Better"
Queer Prospects for Narrative Temporality

> Our queerness has nothing to offer a Symbolic that lives by denying that nothingness except an insistence on the haunting excess that this nothingness entails, an insistence on the negativity that pierces the fantasy screen of futurity, shattering narrative temporality with irony's always explosive force. And so what is queerest about us, queerest within us, and queerest despite us is this willingness to insist intransitively—to insist that the future stop here.
>
> —Lee Edelman, *No Future: Queer Theory and the Death Drive*

> Many LGBT youth can't picture what their lives might be like as openly gay adults. They can't imagine a future for themselves. So let's show them what our lives are like, let's show them what the future may hold in store for them.
>
> —*It Gets Better Project*

> There's joy coming for you.
>
> —Jules Skloot, "Stay With Us," *It Gets Better: Coming Out, Overcoming Bullying, and Creating a Life Worth Living*

No Future is Lee Edelman's imperative against the specious futurity of normative politics. *It Gets Better* is Dan Savage's message of hope to LGBTQ kids at risk of suicide. *No Future* insists against the image of the Child, defining queerness as a refusal to reproduce the futurity that image represents. *It Gets Better* broadcasts futures for real kids who otherwise might not have them, let alone represent them. *No Future* might seem to disallow

Savage's optimism, and *It Gets Better* sounds likely to reject Edelman's theoretical intransigence. But these two versions of futurity offer complementary ways to think about queer time. If *It Gets Better* is optimistic, its optimism is mitigated by something very much like Edelman's negativity, which reconfigures its futurity. If Edelman seems to promote an impracticable negation of time itself, Savage's project indicates how that negation might usefully inflect even our most practical utterances. This complementarity invites a better appreciation of *It Gets Better* even as it proves that Edelman's theory, despite its intransigence, has positive real-world applications. And positive implications for narrative theory: despite Edelman's interest in "shattering narrative temporality," *No Future* lends itself to ways to rethink narrative temporality as a pattern for queer practice. If *It Gets Better* does respond to Edelman's imperative, it does so through pedagogies at work in narrative temporality itself. To set these two imperatives against each other is to discover a shared form of queer dissent in the very time it takes to tell a story of what's to come. It is to learn what narrative temporality means for queer possibility.

Edelman attacks "reproductive futurism" for its heteronormative compulsion. Making the image of the Child the "perpetual horizon of every acknowledged politics," this futurism makes social reality a compulsory fantasy and a perpetual deferral of anything we might really want (3). The politics of futurity abject queer possibility. Queer resistance must therefore be something other than a politics. It must oppose itself to futurity as such, aligning itself with the death drive: "The death drive names what the queer, in the order of the social, is called forth to figure: the negativity opposed to every form of social viability" (9). Precisely because the queer is called forth to figure the death drive, it must do so, for only then can it "[imagine] an oppositional political stance exempt from the imperative to reproduce the politics of signification" (27). Only then, in other words, can it do what it must: offer access to *jouissance,* alert us to the fantasies that structure sociality, refuse identities, and disrupt norms. These fundamentals of queerness depend on a refusal to fantasize about the future of children.

Dan Savage, by contrast, has encouraged a widespread phantasmatic culture of futurity, in which thousands of videos claim that time will naturally bring about a queer future. Savage launched *It Gets Better* in response to the deaths of Justin Aaberg and Billy Lucas in 2010. Aaberg killed himself at fifteen after years of bullying at his suburban Minnesota high school. Lucas hanged himself in a barn on his grandmother's farm in Greensburg, Indiana— also at fifteen, also due to homophobic bullying. Savage says these two deaths prompted him to think about the problem of antigay bullying—to recall how it had destroyed his own life at that age, and to contrast those awful years with the happiness of his life today. If only those boys could have known how things would change; if only there were some way to tell them, in spite of the fact that "schools would never invite gay adults to talk to kids; we would never get permission" (Introduction 4). Savage recalls the day he thought of a way:

> I was riding a train to JFK Airport when it occurred to me that I was waiting for permission that I no longer needed. In the era of social media—in a world with YouTube and Twitter and Facebook—I could speak directly to LGBT kids right now. I didn't need permission from parents or an invitation from a school. I could look into a camera, share my story, and let LGBT kids know that it got better for me and it would get better for them too. I could give 'em hope. (4)

Together with his husband, Terry Miller, Savage made the project's inaugural video, in which the two men say that all the bullying they suffered in school, all the family rejection and self-hatred, did not last. Enthusing about their sixteen-year relationship as well as their adopted son, D. J., they promise young viewers that "however bad it is now, it gets better, and it can get great, and it can get awesome." Four weeks after the video made its debut—as Savage notes in his dramatic account of the project's runaway success—he got a call from the White House: "They wanted me to know that the president's It Gets Better video had just been uploaded to YouTube" (5). Savage heard from young people, too, and from parents, who confirmed that the project's increasing number of videos—more than ten thousand, at this point—were indeed giving them hope. A vast host of major public figures and first-time videographers have contributed to this celebration of LGBTQ futurity. Untold millions of viewings have transformed public discourse as well as private lives, supporters will argue, so that kids who once might have been unable to think past the bully around the corner now can imagine how easily he will become a thing of the past.

Edelman might note that the future Savage would gain for our queer children actually has no place for them. Moreover, he might note that young people hopeful about the future will fail to redefine the social order in the way queerness should—in the only way queerness can and must do so. They achieve happiness only by "shifting the figural burden of queerness to someone else," to quote Edelman's account of what happens when queer people fail to identify with the negativity of the death drive (27). This is not to say that Edelman's theory demands any rejection of Savage's project—indeed, the two obtain at very different levels of engagement, and Edelman makes clear that he is not talking about "the lived experiences of any historical children"—but rather to say that Edelman's theory should make us question the temporality through which *It Gets Better* hopes to make a difference in the lives of LGBTQ youth (11). This questioning has already begun, in terms that amount to an applied version of *No Future*. Activists, for example, have noted that promising LGBTQ kids a better future may make them unlikely to seek betterment in the present. Rather than agitate for high school reforms, these kids might just decide to wait it out, producing a situation similar in everyday terms to the burden-shifting and political deferrals Edelman warns against. Other responses to *It Gets Better* would seem to confirm Edelman's sense that futurity really only reproduces ideological norms. Jack Halberstam has noted not only that "the representation of adolescence as a treacherous territory that one must pass through before reaching the safe harbor of adulthood" is "a sad lie about what it means to be an adult," but that "only a very small and privileged sector of the US population can say with any kind of confidence: 'It gets better!'" Even if "silver spoon in the mouth gays" are now happy enough, the idea that "teens can be pulled back from the brink of self-destruction by taped messages made by impossibly good looking and successful people smugly recounting the highlights of their fabulous lives is just PR for the status quo." Halberstam's rejection of *It Gets Better* shares Edelman's intransigent refusal of the promise of a false future, one invalidated by cryptonormativity and false optimism—futurity as status quo. Other responses stress the fact that the occasion for the project has been a dubious sentimentality that singles out recent teen suicides for special, tokenizing compassion, further confirming that deep suspicion of *It Gets Better* gets theoretical support from *No Future*.

Moreover, Edelman's critique of the futurity embraced by *It Gets Better* corresponds more generally to queer critiques of temporality—critiques that also cast doubt upon any hopeful sense that time naturally unfolds toward queer outcomes. Elizabeth Freeman, Judith Roof, Judith Halberstam, and others have argued that "chrononormativity" and "reprofuturity" demand that we define queerness against time. Indeed, the queer critique of time generalizes Edelman's sense that queerness itself has an antitemporal basis or posture and that it depends upon its chances of queering the normative patterns time enforces. For Freeman and Halberstam, queer temporalities subtend any truly queer possibilities, supplying the basis for sustaining historiographies and subcultural survival. Freeman defines "chrononormativity" as "the use of time to organize individual human bodies toward maximum productivity," and she explores those queer forms of representation that are queer for their resistance to normative temporal practice (3). In that exploration, and in her account of "reprofuturity" and what it takes to refuse it, Freeman links "temporal dissonance" to "sexual dissidence" (21, 1). Halberstam "[tries] to think about queerness as an outcome of strange temporalities," and notes that this estrangement can enable us to "detach queerness from sexual identity" and understand it more fully as a Foucauldian "way of life" (1). For Roof, time asserts its normative effects in the linear, teleological narratives that structure human possibility, through "narrative's heteroideology" so that the viability of any queer possibility demands resistance to just the kind of normative implications asserted by the presumptive futurity of *It Gets Better* (xxvii).

But if this mode of critique of temporality sets Queer Theory against the optimistic possibility promoted by *It Gets Better*, it also indicates how and where we might locate a reconciliation, one that would not only reframe *It Gets Better*, and not only demonstrate compatibility between Queer Theory and LGBTQ practice in this instance, but enable us to rethink the long-standing conflict between queerness and narrativity. Roof, Edelman, and others assert that narrative temporality is the very essence of normativity, and this assertion has often led us to believe that true queerness only exists to the extent that it can defy narrative temporality. And yet these theorists themselves read narrative in such a way as to suggest that narrative temporality need not be queered in order to serve queer interests—that it is itself a mode of queer pedagogy. Seen this way, narrative temporality switches sides: it becomes what enables projects like *It Gets Better* to realize queer possibilities in the face of normative compulsions, and it becomes what enables *No Future* to extend into practical, real-world resistance to the sort of futurity that would only replicate the past. The point, then, is not to defend *It Gets Better* from valid and serious criticism of its motives and implications, but rather to argue that its temporality has more in common with *No Future* than we might expect. It can therefore teach us something about narrative temporality and its relationship to queer possibility.

Edelman claims that queer negativity demands a refusal of "history as linear narrative (the poor man's teleology) in which meaning succeeds in revealing itself—*as itself*—through time" (4). Queerness cannot permit this "narrative movement," this "fantasy of meaning's eventual realization"; instead, it blocks "every social structure or form" (4). In this linkage of normative structure and narrative movement, Edelman develops a theory that is at once formal and political, a theory that makes narrative temporality largely responsible for the political futurity he would oppose. He equates "translation into a narrative" with "teleological determination," and, in turn, with heteronormativity (9). And certainly the point is well taken by any narrative theorist who knows that narrative itself is defined in terms of its sequential logics, its drive toward closure, and its implication that meaning develops over time.

Further to justify blaming narrative temporality for the specious futurity in question here, Edelman cites Paul de Man—specifically, de Man's theory of the relationship between narrative and irony, relevant here because Edelman claims irony, as de Man defines it, for the queer refusal to participate in certain rhetorics of temporality. Irony and queerness are alike in their "constant disruption of narrative signification" (24); both refuse narrative *allegorization* of irony, which would make it conform to a rhetoric of temporality that "always serves to 'straighten' it out" (26).

This relationship between narrative, allegory, and irony omits something important to de Man's account, something that might give narrative a different role to play in queer figuration. For de Man, allegory is by no means simply a narrativization of what irony would more authentically disrupt, but a valid form of temporal rhetoric. If allegory does pattern itself out in time, it does so in contrast to the mystifying synchrony of the symbol. In the world of the symbol, image and substance coincide simultaneously. In the world of allegory, "time is the originary constitutive category"; allegory "establishes its language" in the void of "temporal difference," and this difference is no "straightening" of time but rather exactly what is needed to disabuse any fantasy of self-identity (207). Symbolism is a mode of "tenacious self-mystification"; allegory undoes it, and even if it does so less explosively than irony, de Man stresses that "allegory and irony are . . . linked in their common discovery of a truly temporal predicament" (208, 222). Irony is certainly what Edelman claims, in itself and in its work against futurity, since it "divides the flow of temporal experience into a past that is pure mystification and a future that remains harassed forever by a relapse within the inauthentic" (222). But irony is not alone in this enforcement of temporal authenticity. De Man notes that "the knowledge derived from both modes is essentially the same," and he does not suggest that it is essentially an antinarrative property (226). Indeed, even if irony has the more "explosive" negative force toward which queerness might aspire, de Man suggests that allegorical texts might surpass it by becoming "meta-ironical" and "[transcending] irony without falling into the myth of an organic totality or bypassing the temporality of all language" (223). This possibility encourages us not only to rethink allegory as a mode in which narrative achieves authentically temporal demystification of symbolic figurations, but to ask if *It Gets Better* has something like "meta-ironical" status—encompassing what irony knows but sustaining its power.[1]

---

1. When Edelman elaborates upon his use for de Man's theory of irony, he does of course recognize de Man's explanation of the potential collusions of irony and allegory. In his critique of "compassionate love," Edelman asks if we might "think of compassion in terms of allegory's logic of narrative sequence, which resists, while carrying forward—through and as the dilation

Allegory's intermediary position (between symbolism and irony) may actually correspond to something very much like the place to which Edelman assigns queerness. Edelman does not claim that queerness can or should amount to any absolute refusal of the politics of signification. Rather, he argues that queerness must embody the figuration to which heteronormativity assigns it, the better to assert resistance to the social from within. Its relationship to narrative is therefore one of "perverse refusal" (4), locating queerness at the place where "narrative realization and derealization overlap" (7). Queerness is a "particular story . . . of why storytelling fails," and, as such, it has an antinarrative force peculiarly amenable to narrative form (7). In de Man's terms, it is allegorical, not because it would "straighten out" ironical queerness but because it is the place where ironic disruption and allegorical time overlap. In other words, that "paradoxical formulation" through which Edelman defines "queer oppositionality" at once as accession and resistance to the politics of figuration actually lines up well with narrativity and, by extension, narrative temporality. In other words, the queerness Edelman associates with de Manian irony might actually be a property of de Manian allegory, which is not the form of teleological futurity Edelman makes it out to be. If we uncouple narrative temporality and teleological futurity, we may discover that the former can subvert the latter in the spirit of queer oppositionality itself—that the allegorical act opens futurity to antinormative alternatives.

Responses to Edelman's argument have stressed the need to mitigate his negativity. John Brenkman suggests rethinking queerness as an "innovation in sociality," not apart from it, to recognize more fully the power Edelman himself assigns to queer subversion, which otherwise lacks purchase upon normativity (180). José Esteban Muñoz has asked if queer theory's antifutural doctrine might not align it with social realities threatening to the lives of young queer people of color. For very good reasons, Muñoz opts against "no future" in favor of a "'not yet'" where queer youths of color actually get to grow up" (96). Muñoz takes a different view of the future as the site of yet to be realized queerness. Inverting Edelman's argument, forestalling absolute negativity, he prepares the way toward the reconciliation that matches Edelman's paradoxical formulations to the mixed needs of real queer people—of young queer

---

of time—the negativity condensed in irony's instantaneous big bang" (92). To do so, he says, would be to "allegorize, to the profit of dialectic, the expense of the unrecuperable irony that compassion necessarily abjects in whomever it reads as *sinthom*osexual, whomever it sees as a threat to the law (understood as the law of desire) by figuring an access to jouissance that gives them more bang for their buck" (92). Here Edelman describes allegorization as a loss to irony, whereas de Man might be read to allow for a less agonistic effect, or a rhetorical situation in which allegory does not necessarily contain irony by narrativizing it.

people, not coincidentally. "Not yet" stresses the need for futurity, however threatening, and elaborates the means by which queerness might appropriate it. In doing so, it leads the way toward recognition of similar rhetorical compromises struck by *It Gets Better*. Muñoz speaks a narrative language, but one that develops paradoxical formulations able to hold off the future, to allow for a certain provisional need of it. *It Gets Better* does the same, developing a whole rhetoric of such formulations, supplying the critical language whereby Edelman's "perverse refusal" might make its way into the public discourse.

It Gets Better demonstrates that narrative temporality works toward the practical goals of *No Future*. Its stories do not pattern themselves straight toward a future always yet to come. They do not simply take part in ideological deferral in the name of the Child, but rather speak to the queer child in narrative languages that transform futurity. And they do so not because they shatter narrative time but through narrative forms well suited to a pedagogical practice of temporal dissent. What reconciles *It Gets Better* to *No Future* is narrative temporality itself. Its temporal dynamics are at once optimistic and negative, practically positive but aligned with negative critique. Understood as a force against merely teleological futurity, narrative temporality helps say "no future," mitigating the optimism that might otherwise make "it gets better" a false promise. And it does so not in spite of narrativity, but because narrative discourse itself generates just these possibilities. What follows here is a reading of the rhetoric whereby narrative temporality makes *It Gets Better* a practice of queer negativity as well as normal optimism, a practice through which LGBTQ people teach the temporalities necessary to have no future while yet living for a queer one.

What are the temporalities of *It Gets Better*? The title and the purpose of the project would seem to indicate just the kind of ideologically teleological optimism Edelman exposes, leading us perhaps to expect each of the project's narratives to have a conformist temporal procedure. We might expect each story to begin with an account of how it got better for the narrator, with a strong teleological drive toward final happiness, with all the dynamics of a classic narrative fraught with conflict but neatly resolved. And we might then expect each story to say how it will likewise get better for the troubled teen, repeating the teleological desire for a positive future finish. Such a procedure would indeed prompt us to want to insist against futurity insofar as it would capitulate to straight frameworks (in the first moment) and ideologically impose them (in the second). But *It Gets Better* tends not in fact to meet these expectations—most notably, by avoiding the future tense. We might expect the future tense to dominate here as adults tell teens what they *will* find, what *will* occur, how happy they *will* be. But instead these narratives tend toward the present tense and stress the present existence of the future state to come: "You've got to hold your head up and you've got to look for the light at the end of your tunnel. Because it's there, even if you don't always recognize it or you can't find it, it's there all the same, and always has been" (Daring 65).[2] This chronotope "detenses" the future; spatial form here collapses the future into the present, and even the past.[3] Consider the difference between saying "you will have a better life" and this typical statement: "a better life is in your future and you can make it there" (Gaudet 29): here again tense gives way to location, in such a way as to bring the future into view. There are at least two interesting variants of this present future place. One involves the present existence of communities waiting to be discovered. "It is important to remember that there are others everywhere who are like us and will love us for who we are" (Feinstein 91): in this case, you *will* be loved by others who are already like you, and the current existence of social alternatives is really a nonfutural basis for what is to come. This nonfuturity is perhaps more explicit in phrases such as "there's a whole other world out there of people who can support you" and "we're waiting for you with open arms" (Mandelin 156; Breedlove 231). The temporality of the waiting future is particularly significant to the project's location of hope: "The good parts—they're totally out there waiting for you"; "Just keep in mind there is a big, beautiful world out there waiting for *you*" (Holmes 191). The future becomes an alternative present, rewriting the present as a place for friendly attention very different from the one where bullies await you around every corner.

The presence of the future in these cases is actually implicit in the phrase "it gets better," which, different from "it will get better," makes the future now. It connotes a certain iterative permanence, a certain timelessness, which has unexpected affinities with Edelman's negativity. Edelman rejects futurism's tendency to defer the good into deceptive betterment; his stress on *jouissance*

---

2. Citations of *It Gets Better* narratives will refer to the edited collection of them published by Savage and Miller as *It Gets Better: Coming Out, Overcoming Bullying, and Creating a Life Worth Having*. This choice of archive has a number of significant and perhaps questionable implications. Rather than try to reckon systematically with the thousands of video narratives posted on www.itgetsbetter.org, I have decided to recognize the published print collection as a representative sample. To do so is to disregard those videos not taken to be representative by Savage and Miller—many that might depart from or question the project's conventional expectations and presumptions. Moreover, it focuses attention on videos made by "important" people Savage and Miller questionably consider to be the best evidence that it gets better. To my mind, however, those implications make the text collection appropriate to the purposes of my argument: for better and for worse, it emphasizes the project's priorities as well as its problems, and is actually therefore representative in a valid sense.

3. For an account of the tenseless theory of time and what it might mean to engage in "detensing," see Oaklander and Smith as well as my own "*Maurice* in Time."

favors more immediate gratification. "It Gets Better" likewise refuses to defer the future; it does not concede the good to what will come of the false innocence of the Child, but gives it real existence among queer people today. This futurity does not involve hope for the child's future; it reverses that hope, implying that betterment comes when the uncertain future defers to the real present. The peculiar progressive present of the phrase "it gets better" makes development into the future an ongoing project based in the current moment.

Normative futurity collapses in another way as well: these narratives have a penchant for unlikely sequences or juxtapositions—sudden turning points that bind different states or events. We might expect gradual change as unhappiness yields to contentment and stories slowly build pride, confidence, and opportunity. But change happens suddenly, in narratives that dramatize an inspiring difference between life's moments by putting them together. For example: "If you had told me when I was in high school that one day I'd be the commissioner of a gay sports league, I wouldn't have believed you" (Knaub 246). Such a statement explicitly makes the remote future available; the leap from school-sports abjection to sports-league leadership reverses futurity's withdrawal. The most common version of the unlikely sequence is that which tells of a transformative transition from high school to college:

> I wanted to die. Everything was so sad and so horrendous. Before this all exploded, I was trying to get into college; now, on top of that, I was supposed to figure out how to be gay, too. I felt overwhelmed and hopeless. . . . Yet the moment I walked through those high school doors for the last time, diploma in hand, it instantly, *instantly* got better. In fact, it got wonderful. I immediately fit in at college. (Ridgway 280)

Instant gratification is again at work here. And a related kind of suddenness hurries a host of other truncated narratives: "After college, and a short-lived job in Los Angeles, I tried to kill myself. I was in intensive care for three days. I was twenty-two years old. But here's the thing: just six months later, things started to get better. I met someone. I got a job" (Gaines 60). Or more dramatically, this summary narrative in which teen misery simply becomes grownup success: "I've made a career out of my rage. I've turned it into a job" (Shears 126). Rage itself becoming success is a queer futurity indeed; this short narrative could even appear on a résumé for queer theory. To say my rage became my job is to allow negativity to commandeer sequence. Sometimes the truncated unlikely sequence becomes a frame for a more leisurely subsequent narrative: "And so, I'd like to tell you how I got from that world of impossibility to the dinner I cooked one recent Friday night," the dinner in question being one this narrator cooked for his partner's parents (Roberts 82). The long temporal distance between that world of impossibility to Friday's recent possibility is minimized, and the minimization is what gives hope. To confront an unhappy teenager with a long wait for a better life is probably to make her feel like it will never get better; to put the goal right here is to get the feeling of the future now, its charge of insouciant joy without the distance entailed in more normative forbearance.

But this insouciance can be shocking, especially to those of us who expect testimony about traumatic pasts to deny possibilities for easy recovery or even to stress that violence—implicit in homophobia even when not explicitly at work in these stories—does damage that never gets better. Testimonials confident about recovery and, what's more, willing to promise it to an unspecified audience would seem to reflect a troublingly heedless faith in what time can do. By contrast, theories of trauma, testimony, and recovery work with a very different sense of time, one much more compatible with Edelman's skepticism about the relationship between past, present, and future. If Edelman warns that our futures are really versions of the past that void the present, theorists of trauma and recovery likewise question any progressive movement away from a traumatic past through a therapeutic present to a better future. The future promises only the past's return, unless a broader transformation—"recovery" well beyond the subject—changes cultures of violence rather than just their subjective effects. Edelman also calls for attention to subjective particularities that would rupture any general fantasies of futurity, and theories of testimony share his sense that recovery depends, perhaps hopelessly, on remediation of implacably singular symptoms. But if the insouciance of It Gets Better contrasts shockingly with this rigorous refusal of what recovery might fake, the project also entails tactics better geared toward scrupulous response. Our skepticism about the project's underestimation of trauma might highlight contributions that likewise stop short of any confidence that psychic wounds heal. Some contributions, for example, say something more like "give it time," stressing not that trauma will certainly give way to recovery but rather that futurity itself is a form of caring ministration focused on modest gains. In these cases, yet another alternative future comes into play: a temporality of suspension, connoted by phrases like "hang in there" and "you just need to hang around and wait" (Bono 145). More generally, contributors do not so much promise recovery as model the sort of self-authorship that can be a vital first step toward reclaiming selfhood lost to traumatic experience.[4] As

---

4. Recognizing this need has been foundational to theories of trauma testimony, including Dori Laub's recognition that "survivors did not only need to survive so that they could tell their stories; they also needed to tell their stories in order to survive" (63).

we will see, the time scheme implied in the title of the project is less a promise of recovery and more a performance of a practice whereby LGBTQ teens might learn to intervene in the temporal dynamics that structure the stories they live by. And short of that, there is the meaning of the project's title itself: in the context of skepticism about its underestimation of trauma, "it gets better" sounds less promising and more ironic—less like a claim that suffering will come to an end, and more like the kind of grudging, knowing concession gay people have always made to each other when trying to face the future together.[5]

These subversions of normative futurity are peculiarly conventional. The point here is not that *It Gets Better* innovates queer languages unavailable to other modes of engagement, or that its narratives develop means of disruption notable for their categorically special temporality. Sociolinguistic analysis and forms of inquiry available also in narrative linguistics routinely discover these rhetorical temporal practices, and indeed the temporalities performed in *It Gets Better* correspond to many of those which sociolinguists have found active in "folk narrative," what William Labov and Joshua Waletzky long ago called "oral versions of personal experience." Labov and Waletzky helped found an approach to understanding narrative forms in terms of their natural originating functions. Noting that "it will not be possible to make very much progress in the analysis and understanding of . . . complex narratives until the simplest and most fundamental narrative structures are understood in direct connection with their originating functions," Labov and Waletsky analyzed a set of tape-recorded, face-to-face narratives not unlike those included in *It Gets Better* (12). Their "functional" analysis enabled them to characterize narrative as a technique for recapitulating experience by making it conform to the terms of temporal sequence. But that matching process entails activity beyond sequential development. In their account, Labov and Waletsky attribute definitive significance to those features of narrative clauses and their contexts that complicate simple sequence, often in order to provide the "overall structure" upon which any narrative depends for its significance. The "overall structure of narrative" depends upon functions of "orientation," "complication," "evaluation," "resolution," and "coda," all of which appear as conventional features of any oral version of personal experience, and all of which might well open narrative sequence to the sort of complicating (and even queer) effects at work in *It Gets Better* (32–41).

---

5. It might also be possible to argue that the forms of trauma glossed over by *It Gets Better* might be the "ordinary" kind potentially appropriate to more routine forms of representation, transmission, and archivization. For discussions of trauma of this kind, see Cvetkovich (10) and Berlant (81–82).

To analyze the narrative-linguistic features of *It Gets Better* and to discover in them folk-statements that disallow straightforward futurity is simply to discover the narrative resourcefulness available whenever people attempt to explain their experiences to each other. Which is not to say that oral versions of personal experience are always queer, but rather that narrative temporality offers resources for representing what is queer in personal experience. What makes the difference is what Labov and Waletsky call the "originating function"—not the purpose of the utterance itself (which could only have little power against heteronormative prohibitions) but the larger pragmatic orientation of the performance meant (in this case) to queer time itself. Recent contributions to narrative linguistics by scholars including Wallace Chafe, Elliot Mishler, and Deborah Schiffrin provide further context for sociolinguistic analysis that would link narrative action, temporal innovation, and dynamic identities.[6]

Often, *It Gets Better* appropriates highly formulaic narratives in order to innovate queer forms of futurity. For example, two micronarratives we might name "If you die, they win" and "I promise it gets better." Nothing could be more conventional than the strong plot at work in narratives that encourage kids not to let the bullies win: "But if you are feeling hopeless and you are thinking about doing something drastic, maybe hurting yourself or even suicide, don't, because they win" (Members 69); "The best revenge against all of those people who insulted you and made you feel bad is to live well" (Orue 36); "Please, please, please do not let the bullies win" (Steward 265). Sounds like the specious comfort people too often give to victims of violence; sounds like proof, perhaps, that narratives tend too much toward stock futures—normative ones, even despite their affirmative content. But the lack of true prospects in these cases—the normalized future—also sounds a lot like the kind of figuration Edelman wants, that which would dramatize the artificiality of social reality. Performativity asserts itself, stylizing futurity. Precisely because this micronarrative conforms to what people expect to hear, it makes a queer difference, harnessing the power of antiterrorist sentiment (one recent source for this narrative) and even the charisma of athletics (presumed to be an anti-queer endeavor) for sequences that would reverse their sociopolitical ends. Rather than capitulating to some normative futural framework, the queer kid inspired by "if you die, they win" actually finds a way to recognize the figural oneness of queerness and the death drive without having to become a martyr to it.

---

6. See Schiffrin's "Crossing Boundaries: The Nexus of Time, Space, Person, and Place in Narrative" for revisions to Labov and Waletsky through which to read narrative performances as chronotopic constructions of diverse self–other relationships.

Something similar happens when *It Gets Better* makes promises. "I promise you that if you stick it out, it gets better": here the commonplace performative of the promise adds a peculiar temporality to the simple futurity of the phrase it frames (Tannen et al. 49). It reminds us, first of all, that any account of narrative temporality must consider the difference made by the intervention of a narratorial presence: when a narrator testifies to the sequence entailed in a narration, the relationship between that sequence and the narrator's temporal position undoes any simply linear procedure, undermining logics of sequence even as it would seem to confirm them. More simply, narrator and narration have different temporalities, disallowing any singular timeline. Even apart from that complexity, however, the promise in question testifies to powers LGBTQ people would be presumed not to have: power over the future, as well as the credibility that promises presuppose. The promise takes part in queer performativity as Eve Sedgwick defines it, counteracting the shame that might lead to suicide by inverting its temporality: to promise that things get better is to perform optimism rather than to feel it, with all the difference that distinction entails for what Sedgwick redefined as "transformational grammar" ("Queer Performativity" 609). Even if Edelman might have reason to question the futurism of the "promissory," which would make our alienation "vanish into the seamlessness of identity at the endpoint of the endless chain of signifiers" (8), this particular promise really resolves alienation at the start, less a promise for the future than a performance of present authority.

We might also describe this effect in terms of the way the rhetorical relationship in play here makes presence possible, its address to its prospective audience actually bringing that audience into being. Barbara Johnson has explained how this sort of direct address, epitomized in *apostrophe*, makes its addressee "present, animate, and anthropomorphic" (185). Building upon Jonathan Culler's foundational discussion of apostrophe's way of "peopling the world with fragments of the self" within a "timeless present" (66), Johnson defines apostrophe as "a form of ventriloquism through which the speaker throws voice, life, and human form into the addressee" (185). This effect is vital to both the goals and the questionable implications of *It Gets Better*. Insofar as *It Gets Better* exists to throw life to LGBTQ youth by making them the subject of a personifying address, it works less through any message it sends than through the simple dynamics of a rhetorical relationship.[7] Irene Kacandes

---

7. Johnson's argument has further relevance here, since she focuses on the problem of animating the unborn child—an activity not unlike that undertaken by *It Gets Better*, which also shares the self-actualizing results of anti-abortion rhetoric. In both cases, "life-and-death dependency" raises questions about the directionality of apostrophe and its effects (198).

has explained a similar result in terms of the ways apostrophic "talk fictions" aim to "fulfill a need for connection," and do so by engineering dynamics of identification that shore up fragile identities (145). Talk fictions are indeed fictions—they should not be presumed to achieve what they promise—but they entail a temporality that makes the futurity of *It Gets Better* a matter of rhetorical presence. Once again, futurity gives way to the present, because to say "it gets better" is less to speak to the future and more to invoke the present vitality of the addressee. Put more simply, Culler, Johnson, and Kacandes help prove that talk of the future enlivens present identity precisely because it is not really talk of the future at all. But this deception is not the ideological one Edelman describes. These queer apostrophic performances focus on the future mainly because exaggerated futurity strengthens the affective power theorists attribute to apostrophe, trading futurity for current gratification in the manner of what Edelman expects from queer figuration.[8]

In other significant ways, too, the future as such is not really at issue here. Often contributors to *It Gets Better* deliberately conflate their narratees with their own past selves. They say to kids today what they wish they could have said to themselves at that age: "If I could now, at twenty-six, speak to my fourteen-year-old self . . . I would say don't worry about being gay. That's who you are" (Tannen et al. 51–52); "It is too late for me to speak to my own sixteen-year-old self, so instead I want all of the misfits and weirdos and artists and queer kids to know a couple of things I wish someone had told me back then" (Coyote 88). Not really about the future, this is a reparative effort, fairly self-involved, and perhaps evidence of what Edelman describes when he says the alleged future is all too often really a fantasy of a more perfect past. And yet we might again reconcile Edelman to *It Gets Better* by noting that this conflation of narratee and past narratorial self—this strange version of dissonant self-narration—transforms the image of the Child. For Edelman the Child is a deferred ideal—a deferral of our own freedom to some prospective better recipient of it. That relationship is put right when "It Gets Better" speaks to past selves: the child becomes but father to the man. In other words, it does not get better because we give way abjectly to children and to some sense of what they will become. It gets better because *we know better*: the time scheme of experience supersedes that of innocence to get time really moving again.

---

8. Culler defines apostrophe against narrative time: "Apostrophe resists narrative because its *now* is not a moment in temporal sequence but a *now* of discourse, of writing" (68). Nevertheless it is fair to argue, despite Culler's association of narrative form and temporal sequence, that there is apostrophic narrative, and that it demonstrates the extent to which narrative temporality might accommodate the sort of tactics that "neutralize" time in lyric poetry.

The difference is crucial. It gives us the opportunity to reconcile these two versions of queer futurity, because it changes the role played by narrative temporality. What may seem to be a linear imposition—the innocent child will become the experienced adult—is in fact a pedagogical proposition: learn how to think futurity as yourself-to-come speaking to yourself-today. Because this pedagogical proposition not only sidesteps linearity but reorients futurity as Edelman defines it, it functions also as a queer form of tutelage. Perhaps the best example of this queer temporal pedagogy at work is what happens in a certain counterfactuality that many "It Gets Better" narratives cultivate. Sometimes these narratives stress not just what did happen but what might have happened had they not found hope for the future: "If I had done something drastic then, I would have missed out on the best times of my life" (Bono 146); had I committed suicide, "I never would have gotten a chance to experience love" (Legacy 262). Such statements may seem to be teleological for the way they affirm a right choice at a critical moment. But they actually confirm only a conditional teleology, laying bare the fragile contingency of life's "best times." They adumbrate the sideshadows of time, its forking pathways, and they would prompt young people to practice queer forms of hope embedded most usefully in narrative forms.

"Sideshadowing" is Gary Saul Morson's term for the narrative development of nonlinear plurality, the "open sense of temporality" generated when narrative represents the variety of possibilities that actually condition the present moment and its futures (*Narrative and Freedom* 6; 118). Morson is relevant here for the way he has helped narrative theory rethink narrative time: in *Narrative and Freedom* and also in his theory of "tempics," Morson urges us to understand narrative time as a practice of freedom and plural forms of engagement, not if and when it ruptures chronological linearity, but even in its conventional instances ("Essential Narrative" 279). Morson is one of many theorists who, extending upon classical theories of narrative's temporal complexity, shift our attention from the linear structure of narrative time to the diversity of temporalities enacted in the practice of it. A main source of this approach to narrative temporality is, of course, Paul Ricoeur, for whom the relationship between time and narrative is one in which any effort to pattern time into linearity runs afoul of time's prodigious aporias and, as a result, ends in implicit metanarrative speculation about the problem of time itself. Important also to the foundational theories of Bakhtin, Lukács, and Genette as well as recent work by Hilary Dannenberg, Mark Currie, David Herman, Wai Chee Dimock, and others, this more pluralistic approach to narrative temporality lays stress upon the ways narrative form inculcates temporal complexity. It departs from skepticism about the ideological effects of narrative linearity to understand those effects as part only of a larger scheme of practical engagement in which narrative pragmatically enables diverse forms of temporal recognition. This theoretical context helps explain why we might regard the practice of narrative engagement promoted in *It Gets Better* as something closer to *No Future* than its title might suggest. Just as *It Gets Better* promotes the sort of counterfactual sideshadowing Morson theorizes, it also promotes the inventive temporalities recognized by theorists for whom narrative engagement is all about temporal diversity—for whom narrative temporality amounts to a queering practice. It is no coincidence, as Susan Lanser has noted, that Genette develops his classic account of the temporal dynamics of narrative discourse in response to Proust's violation of its categories (250–51). Those queer violations are themselves classic—conventional forms of narrative instruction. Indeed, we might liken Genette's project to that of *It Gets Better*. Both engage conventional narrative forms only to find that their performance readily teaches narrative insurrection.

This reversal—this way to relocate conventional narrativity to queer theory—has been of interest to queer theorists eager to rethink queer time. Annamarie Jagose has noted that "it's important to question the reification of queer temporality, the credentialing of asynchrony, multitemporality, and nonlinearity as if they were automatically in the service of queer political projects and aspirations" (Dinshaw et al. 191). They are not—and nor are their opposites automatically or simply straight. Jagose goes on to ask, "Rather than invoke as our straight-guy a version of time that is always linear, teleological, reproductive, future-oriented, what difference might it make to acknowledge the intellectual traditions in which time has also been influentially thought and experienced as cyclical, interrupted, multilayered, reversible, stalled—and not always in contexts easily recuperated as queer?" (186–87). One such intellectual tradition is narrative theory itself, for which normative teleological linearity has only been one aspect of a temporal complexity able at once to determine conventional traditions and to enable the projects and aspirations we now call queer. Now that queer theory recognizes reasons to turn from the straight-guy version of time to one that draws on the fuller range of temporal possibilities, it might turn to narrative theory, where study of ways narrative invents temporal possibility out of time's aporetics could enrich efforts to say how best to forward a queer agenda. What this turn means for futurity specifically is a minor but significant change to the relationship between *No Future* and narrative temporality: if Edelman were to accept Jagose's suggestion, he might include narrative temporality within the practice of queer figuration, as he does, in his own fashion, in his reading of *sinthom*osexuality in Hitchcock's *North by Northwest* and other texts (109). That revised version of his theory might then apply well to what *It Gets Better* does with narrative, not simply so that we might redeem narrative temporality specifically or defend it from skepticism, but so that we might attend to the ways a queer practice of time specifically operates in and through narrative forms.

Jagose might also be open to another intellectual tradition in which time has been thought of as something differently compatible with queer prospects: cognitive psychology. Here again is a field of inquiry in which narrative temporality has been emerging as a practical endeavor not incompatible with the demands of queer figuration. Whereas cognitive psychology might seem to entail the sort of naturalizing, essentialist, normative principles antagonistic to queer possibility, it also recognizes cognitive problems that match up with those dynamics of rupture and revision essential to antinormative practices. Daniel Gilbert, for example, has found that human cognition has problems distinguishing the future from the present. In general, Gilbert shows, "we find it permanently difficult to imagine that we will ever think, want, or feel differently than we do now" (114). When people think about the future, most often they are really projecting present feelings into some empty space of time—often with bad results, because the projection and the emptiness can be a double threat against happiness. Worried about the future, people are likely just to project that worry into an imagined situation devoid of the vivacity necessary to make the future seem like an inviting reality. As a result of this cognitive failing, the future is often just what Edelman says: a specious projection of present anxieties (albeit one unembellished by the ideological fantasies Edelman rejects). What enables us to compensate for this failure and truly to reckon with futurity, in Gilbert's account—what enables us to get beyond the present and conceive of a future that is actually a full moment rather than an empty space—is information provided by other people. Other people with experience in what we are likely to encounter can teach us futurity even though they tell us about their past experiences in the present: "Instead of remembering our past experience in order to simulate our future experience, perhaps we should simply ask other people to introspect their inner states. Perhaps we should give up on remembering and imagining entirely and use other people as *surrogates* for our future selves" (224). In this surprising surrogacy, Gilbert actually gives us a good characterization of narrative temporality in practice: people recounting experiences that may lie in our future and thereby enriching futurity itself might be what occurs in cultures of narrative engagement like *It Gets Better,* in which people enact the process through which empty futures fill with true prospects.

On one hand, then, there is the approach to queer temporality that presumes a need for absolute rupture, as if queering temporality must mean total refusal of forms of linearity presumed to be essentially heteronormative. On the other hand, there is what *It Gets Better* and *No Future* together suggest: that queer temporality obtains in forms we take to be conventional—forms of narrative engagement, which respond to temporal aporetics in such a way as to innovate queer time-schemes. But *It Gets Better* further suggests that the queer temporalities enabled by narrative forms become real possibilities through their social practice. Its narratives perform queer futurity, teaching it to future generations, suggesting that narrative itself functions as a form of temporal pedagogy. *It Gets Better* and *No Future* help us understand the pragmatic bearing essential to narrative temporality, building upon classical narrative theory to extend its long-standing view of temporal pragmatics into new territory, so that narrative temporality emerges as a queer practice at once able to make a difference in the lives of LGBTQ young people and to transform the theory of narrative. The relationship between time and narrative now coincides with a relationship between narratological analysis and queer activism, insofar as narrative temporality is at once what develops when "storytelling fails" and when people succeed in teaching each other how to think around conventional futurity.

To characterize narrative temporality as queer pedagogy is to include it among pedagogical practices through which queer people create or restore queer possibilities. Eve Sedgwick's account of the "queer tutelage" at work in *The Importance of Being Earnest* trades enthusiasm for Wilde's all-out deconstruction of normative sexuality for a more pragmatic interest in the way Wilde models intergenerational "avuncular" instruction (*Tendencies* 55–59). Recent contributions to queer historiography explain how archives constructed by queer people have circumvented prohibitions against homosexual historicity, preserving for future generations the structures of feeling through which homosexuality might express itself despite compulsory heterosexuality. Work by Chris Nealon, Ann Cvetkovich, Heather Love, and others has taught us how to endow queer people with temporality despite their exclusion from historical time. And some responses to *It Gets Better* itself have discovered that problems with the project—its insouciant optimism, its potential quietism—become less troubling when the project is subsumed within a pedagogical mission. Ann Pellegrini reports that she has made the project the object of valuable pedagogical work by inviting students to produce their own contributions to *It Gets Better* within the framework of a course dedicated to the forms of critique Edelman and Halberstam promote. Similarly, Gail Cohee notes that teen suicide is the kind of crisis that should compel us to "normalize queerness as a topic" and to allow for compromises between the theoretical rigor that would refuse any normativity and a strategic, practical co-optation of it. The pedagogical framework has focused attention on the way practical need transforms theory's ideals; doing so in response to *It Gets Better* specifically encourages us to understand the project's time schemes similarly as pedagogical endeavors. As forms of tutelage, these time schemes have a status different from what we might impute to them in the abstract. Moreover, their urgent practicality has an ally in the pragmatics of narrative temporality itself, the storied habit of construction recognized by Ricoeur and like-minded theorists for whom human time is developed in and through narrative engagement. Temporal tutelage is something important both to queerness and to narrativity, a peculiar but significant crux of compatibility between them.

If this discovery of essential compatibility between queerness and narrativity sounds too optimistic, it is worth noting that this sort of temporally reformed optimism has lately been important to queer theorists eager to modify without rejecting the critical pessimism that was necessarily its founding disposition. Muñoz, who hedges against antifuturism, also defines queerness in terms of future-focused temporal instruction, as "a structuring and educated mode of desiring that allows us to see and feel beyond the quagmires of the present" (1). Muñoz joins other optimists—Eve Sedgwick, Michael Snediker—in allowing for practices through which queer people make a difference not just to their future but to time itself. When these theorists look on the bright side, they work with a rigorous intent to change fundamental patterns of recognition, aware that shame and paranoia have temporalities as problematic as normative linearity. They call for change to time itself, much the way *It Gets Better* understood in terms of *No Future* bespeaks its optimism only while transforming what it would mean to think about the future as such. That transformation corresponds to Snediker's redefinition of optimism, which in his account becomes a way of taking an interest in the present rather than an expectation of a better time to come (30).[9] Optimism has been co-opted by a queerness that understands the risks of futurity and nevertheless finds encouragement by making forward-looking demands upon the present. Even if these demands themselves capitulate to the status quo, they also redescribe it, and this dynamic makes plausible

---

9. Snediker claims that "optimism's limited cultural and theoretical intelligibility calls not for its grandiose excoriation, but for its (no less grandiosely) being rethought along non-futural lines" (23).

the compatibility between queerness and narrativity. Narrative temporality understood as a form of pedagogical engagement through which transformative time-schemes become available justifies this reconciliation, developing new prospects not just for narrative temporality but for real queer people who have present need for its tutelage.

Even so, these prospects might amount to what Lauren Berlant has recently called *cruel* optimism. Even if (or especially because) narrative temporality as performed by *It Gets Better* and understood to have the subversive potential of *No Future* teaches LGBTQ kids how to imagine a queer future, those kids might come to believe promises that do them no real good. This is the simple way to sum up the reaction against *It Gets Better*—the various reasons to think it might actually do more harm than good—and it corresponds to what Berlant has in mind when she says "a relation of cruel optimism exists when something you desire is actually an obstacle to your flourishing" (1). When crises produce hopes for a better future that actually encourage "maintaining an attachment to a significantly problematic object" (24), optimism determines forms of present commitment that might be just the reverse of the culture of queer tutelage through which *It Gets Better* teaches futurity: a culture of denial, in which charismatic performances of privilege seduce young people away from demanding what might actually allow them to flourish. But Berlant takes no such entirely negative view of the attachments that cruel optimism entails, and her more mixed sense of its implications can offer one final reason to pursue reconciliations of what *It Gets Better* and *No Future* imply. Berlant speaks of scenes of "negotiated sustenance"—what "makes life bearable as it presents itself ambivalently, unevenly, incoherently" (14). Optimism may help this forbearance cruelly, since it reconciles us to crisis, but it also does get us through, and that merely sustaining negotiation is itself a compelling rhetoric of temporality. Perhaps what is at issue here is less futurity itself than an alternative way to refuse our present circumstances, one neither as intransigent as *No Future* nor as blithely hopeful as *It Gets Better* but determined by a more truly innovative temporality. Stressing its pedagogical character, I have hoped to shift attention from time schemes that shape our lives to those that are shaped by our practices and rhetorics. Neither *No Future* nor *It Gets Better* recognizes the possibility that time itself (rather than our hopes within it) might be open to change, but together they amount to a critical temporal pedagogy that promises transformations at that level. Together, that is, they envision truly queer prospects, forms of futurity not yet determined by norms we know but subject to chance desires and practiced upon by narrative engagements.

Works Cited

Bakhtin, Mikhail. "Forms of Time and of the Chronotope in the Novel." *The Dialogic Imagination: Four Essays.* Ed. Caryl Emerson and Michael Holquist. Austin: U of Texas P, 1981. 84–258.

Berlant, Lauren. *Cruel Optimism.* Durham: Duke UP, 2011.

Bono, Chaz. "Community." *It Gets Better.* 145–46.

Breedlove, Lynn. "Haters Can't Hate Someone Who Loves Themselves, and If They Do, Who Cares." *It Gets Better.* 228–31.

Brenkman, John. "Queer Post-Politics." *Narrative* 10.2 (May 2002): 174–80.

Chafe, Wallace. *Discourse, Consciousness, and Time.* Chicago: U of Chicago P, 1994.

Cohee, Gail. "Bridging Queer/Feminist Theory and Practice." 18 Nov. 2010. *Queer Suicide: A Teach-In.* Accessed 18 Dec. 2011.

Coyote, Ivan. "What I Wish I Knew." *It Gets Better.* 87–90.

Culler, Jonathan. "Apostrophe." *Diacritics* 7.4 (Winter 1977): 59–69.

Currie, Mark. *About Time: Narrative, Fiction, and the Philosophy of Time.* Edinburgh: U of Edinburgh P, 2007.

Cvetkovich, Ann. *An Archive of Feelings: Trauma, Sexuality, and Lesbian Public Cultures.* Durham: Duke UP, 2003.

Dannenberg, Hilary. *Coincidence and Counterfactuality: Plotting Time and Space in Narrative Fiction.* Lincoln: U of Nebraska P, 2008.

Daring, A. Y. "This I Know for Sure." *It Gets Better.* 64–66.

de Man, Paul. "The Rhetoric of Temporality." *Blindness and Insight: Essays in the Rhetoric of Contemporary Criticism.* 2nd ed. Minneapolis: U of Minnesota P, 1983. 187–228.

Dimock, Wai Chee. *Through Other Continents: American Literature across Deep Time.* Princeton: Princeton UP, 2006.

Dinshaw, Carolyn et al. "Theorizing Queer Temporalities: A Roundtable Discussion." *GLQ* 13.2–3 (2007): 177–96.

Edelman, Lee. *No Future: Queer Theory and the Death Drive.* Durham: Duke UP, 2004.

Feinstein, Michael. "Freedom from Fear." *It Gets Better.* 91–93.

Freeman, Elizabeth. *Queer Temporalities, Queer Histories.* Durham: Duke UP, 2010.

Gaines, Barbara. "And the Emmy Goes to . . ." *It Gets Better,* 59–61.

Gaudet, Brinae Lois. "You Are a Rubber Band, My Friend." *It Gets Better.* 27–29.

Genette, Gérard. *Narrative Discourse: An Essay in Method.* Ithaca: Cornell UP, 1980.

Gilbert, Daniel. *Stumbling on Happiness.* New York: Knopf, 2006.

Halberstam, Jack. "It Gets Worse." November 20, 2010. *Queer Suicide: A Teach-In.* Accessed 18 Dec. 2011.

Halberstam, Judith. *In a Queer Time and Place: Transgender Bodies, Subcultural Lives.* New York: NYU P, 2005.

Herman, David. *Story Logic: Problems and Possibilities of Narrative.* Lincoln: U of Nebraska P, 2006.

Holmes, Dave. "It Gets Better *Because* You're a Little Different." *It Gets Better.* 189–91.

It Gets Better Project. <http://www.itgetsbetter.org>.

Johnson, Barbara. "Apostrophe, Animation, and Abortion." *A World of Difference.* Baltimore: Johns Hopkins UP, 1987. 184–99.

Kacandes, Irene. *Talk Fiction: Literature and the Talk Explosion.* Lincoln: U of Nebraska P, 2001.

Knaub, Wayne. "Stepping Off the Sidelines." *It Gets Better.* 245–47.

Labov, William, and Joshua Waletzky. "Narrative Analysis: Oral Versions of Personal Experience." *Essays on the Verbal and Visual Arts: Proceedings of the 1966 Annual Spring Meeting of the American Ethnological Society.* Ed. June Helm. Seattle: American Ethnological Society, U of Washington P, 1967. 12–44.

Lanser, Susan. "Queering Narratology." *Ambiguous Discourse: Feminist Narratology and British Women Writers.* Ed. Kathy Mezei. Chapel Hill: U of North Carolina P, 1996. 250–61.

Laub, Dori. "Truth and Testimony: The Process and the Struggle." *Trauma: Explorations in Memory.* Ed. Cathy Caruth. Baltimore: Johns Hopkins UP, 1995. 61–75.

Legacy, Luan. "The Power of 'You.'" *It Gets Better.* 261–63.

Love, Heather. *Feeling Backward: Loss and the Politics of Queer History.* Cambridge: Harvard UP, 2007.

Lukács, Georg. *Theory of the Novel.* Trans. Anna Bostock. Cambridge: MIT P, 1971.

Mandelin, Natalie Sperry. "Where Happiness Is." *It Gets Better.* 153–57.

Matz, Jesse. "*Maurice* in Time." *Style* 34.2 (Summer 2000): 188–211.

Members of the Broadway and New York Theater Community. "It Gets Better Broadway." *It Gets Better.* 67–70.

Mishler, Elliott. "Narrative and Identity: The Double Arrow of Time." Ed. Anna De Fina et al. *Discourse and Identity.* Cambridge: Cambridge UP, 2006. 30–47.

Morson, Gary Saul. "Essential Narrative: Tempics and the Return of Process." *Narratologies: New Perspectives on Narrative Analysis.* Ed. David Herman. Columbus: The Ohio State UP, 1999. 277–314.

——. *Narrative and Freedom: The Shadows of Time.* New Haven: Yale UP, 1994.

Muñoz, José Esteban. *Cruising Utopia: The Then and There of Queer Futurity.* New York: NYU P, 2009.

Nealon, Christopher. *Foundlings: Gay and Lesbian Historical Emotion before Stonewall.* Durham: Duke UP, 2001.

Oaklander, L. Nathan, and Quentin Smith. *The New Theory of Time.* New Haven: Yale UP, 1993.

Orue, Alex R. "The Person Worth Fighting For Is You." *It Gets Better.* 35–37.

Pellegrini, Ann. "Making It Better in the Classroom: Pedagogical Reflections." 21 Nov. 2010. *Queer Suicide: A Teach-In.* Accessed 18 Dec. 2011.

Queer Suicide: A Teach-In. Social Text: Periscope. <http://socialtextjournal.org/periscope_topic/queer_suicide_a_teach-in/>.

Ricoeur, Paul. *Time and Narrative.* 3 vols. Trans. Kathleen McLaughlin and David Pellauer. Chicago: U of Chicago P, 1983–85.

Ridgway, Shaun. "The Doors of Acceptance." *It Gets Better.* 279–81.

Roberts, Adam. "The Dinner Party." *It Gets Better.* 82–86.

Roof, Judith. *Come as You Are: Sexuality and Narrative.* New York: Columbia UP, 1996.

Savage, Dan. *Introduction. It Gets Better.* 1–8.

Savage, Dan, and Terry Miller. *It Gets Better: Coming Out, Overcoming Bullying, and Creating a Life Worth Having.* New York: Dutton, 2011.

———. *It Gets Better: Dan and Terry.* <http://www.itgetsbetter.org/video/entry/1238/>. Accessed 28 Apr. 2011.

Schiffrin, Deborah. "Crossing Boundaries: The Nexus of Time, Space, Person, and Place in Narrative." *Language in Society* 38 (2009): 421–45.

Sedgwick, Eve Kosofsky. "Queer Performativity: Henry James's *The Art of the Novel.*" *The Novel: An Anthology of Criticism and Theory 1900–2000.* Ed. Dorothy Hale. Oxford: Blackwell, 2006. 605–20.

———. *Tendencies.* Durham: Duke UP, 1994.

Shears, Jake. "Art from Rage." *It Gets Better.* 125–26.

Skloot, Jules. "Stay With Us." *It Gets Better Project.* 23 Sept. 2010. <https://www.youtube.com/watch?v=Linh8AQovWk>. Accessed 28 Apr. 2011.

Slongwhite, Laurel. "You Will Find Your People." *It Gets Better.* 11–14.

Snediker, Michael. *Queer Optimism: Lyric Personhood and Other Felicitous Persuasions.* Minneapolis: U of Minnesota P, 2009.

Steward, Dwayne. "It Gets Better for Small Towners, Too." *It Gets Better.* 264–66.

Tannen, Mark et al. "Coming Out of the Shtetl: Gay Orthodox Jews." *It Gets Better.* 48–53.

PART IV

Emplotment, or the Shapes of Stories

PAUL MORRISON

Maurice, or Coming Out Straight

*T*wo propositions, the one as seemingly outrageous as the other:

(i) There are no bad heterosexuals;
(ii) There are no conservative homosexuals.

Both statements are demonstrably untrue—the first, I would say, even more so than the second—yet both enjoy considerable, if largely unacknowledged, literary, cultural, and political currency. No less an authority than Freud, for instance, implicitly argues the validity of my first proposition:

> In my experience anyone who is in any way, whether socially or ethically, abnormal mentally is invariably abnormal also in his sexual life. But many people are abnormal in their sexual life who in every other respect approximate to the average, and have, along with the rest, passed through the process of human cultural development, in which sexuality remains the weak spot. (*Three Essays* 149)

There are, to be sure, some good homosexuals, although the best among them—Freud's primary example is Leonardo—effectively sublimate their sexuality out of existence. But there are, by Freudian definition, no bad heterosexuals: examine the latent proclivities of the socially or ethically abnormal and you invariably find a practicing or a repressed pervert. The connection between social and sexual aberrance is causal, not casual, and it is homosexuality, not sexuality as such, that remains the weak spot in the process of human cultural development. Small wonder, then, that Freudianism proved an unprecedented historical success. The new science of the soul guarantees the ideological innocence of the regime of the norm.[1]

E. M. Forster concurs with the etiology: sex is the prime mover, at least in *Maurice*, the most explicitly homosexual of his novels. But therein lies the extent of the similarity. What Freud construes as "the process of human cultural development" Forster exposes as the work of normalization; what Freud identifies as "the weak spot" in that process Forster celebrates as a happy redemption from it. Were it not for the seemingly trivial matter of the gender of his object choices, for instance, Maurice would have stepped smartly, as the novel puts it, "into the niche that England had prepared for him" (55). England proves accommodating, however, only to the marrying kind, and Maurice and Alec famously retreat into a "greenwood" that is literally utopian, socially no-place. Forster's conclusion was much revised; it is still much reviled; yet it is in perfect keeping (or so I want to argue) with the broader sexual politics of a novel that utterly rejects the assimilationist fantasy that the perverse should approximate to the norm. Maurice is aggressively ordinary, yet he cannot be positioned within our dominant narratives of (homo)sexual self-fashioning and self-knowledge, cannot, in fact, be positioned within the conventions of narrative itself. Bakhtin holds that the novel is infinitely capacious, endlessly accommodating: there is no experience, meaning, or value that cannot be embraced in its heteroglossia.[2] Forster suggests otherwise. The traditional novel accommodates only the traditional couple (or ersatz variations thereof), and *Maurice* insists that its normalizing proclivities acknowledge themselves as such. Etymology mystifies. It is actually the "hetero," the self-proclaimed dispensation of difference, that is given to the social reproduction of the same, the narrative return of the same. It is the "homo" that makes a difference.

There may be no conservative homosexuals in Forster's novel, to return to the second of my two propositions, but it isn't for want of trying. The young Maurice labors manfully to step into the niche that England has prepared for him, and if the early indications are to be trusted, he is well on his way to becoming a poster boy for heteronormativity. As luck would have it, however,

---

1. On this theme, see Morrison.
2. See Bakhtin.

homosexuality intervenes, and homosexuality, as Forster insists in his "Terminal Note," transforms everything:

> In Maurice I tried to create a character who was unlike myself or what I supposed myself to be: someone handsome, healthy, bodily attractive, mentally torpid, not a bad business man and rather a snob. Into this mixture I dropped an ingredient that puzzles him, wakes him up, torments him and finally saves him. (250–51)[3]

Normalness is not, as it is in Freud, something that the best of homosexuals should approximate to; on the contrary, it is everything that Maurice, the most sublimely ordinary of men, is spared. Lukács faults the modern novel for failing to negotiate a proper relation between "the eccentric and the socially average"; in privileging the former, it renders "sexual perversity" a type of "the condition humaine" (*Realism* 31). Forster's novel explicitly thematizes the relation between the socially average and the sexually aberrant, but only to insist on their absolute incompatibility: "He [Maurice] had acted wrongly, and was still being punished—but wrongly because he had tried to get the best of both worlds" (215). Try as he might, Maurice cannot forge a working compromise between "both worlds," cannot be both socially normative and sexually deviant. To mar Elvis Costello: homosexuality does something special to Mr. Average.

Or to quote Forster himself: "By pleasuring the body Maurice had confirmed—the very word was used in the final verdict—he had confirmed his spirit in its perversion, and cut himself off from the congregation of normal men" (214). Deed and identity. The passage inevitably suggests Foucault's distinction between the sodomite, the perpetrator of perverse acts, and the nineteenth-century homosexual, the perverse individual. But where Foucault constructs a narrative of historical supersession—"the Great Paradigm Shift," as Eve Sedgwick terms it—Victorian sexology acknowledges the definitional pull of both deed and identity.[4] Krafft-Ebing, for instance, cautions that "*perversion* of the sexual instinct"

---

3. The posthumous publication of *Maurice*—which is to say, the transformative power of the belated revelation of homosexuality—structures the critical reception of the entirety of Forster's oeuvre. The prologue to Wendy Moffat's engaging biography of the novelist, for instance, takes its title from a remark by Christopher Isherwood: "Start with the Fact That He Was Homosexual." Turnabout would not, however, be considered fair play, and it is difficult to imagine a biography of a straight novelist beginning with a prologue that posits heterosexuality as its explanatory key. See Moffat 1–21.

4. Foucault, *History of Sexuality* 43; Sedgwick 44–48. Forster himself distinguishes between deed and identity: "Thoughts: he [Maurice] had a dirty little collection. Acts: he desisted from these after the novelty was over, finding they brought him more fatigue than pleasure" (23).

is not to be confused with *perversity* in the sexual act, since the latter may be induced by conditions other than the psychopathological. The concrete perverse act, monstrous as it may be, is clinically not decisive. In order to differentiate between disease (perversion) and vice (perversity), one must investigate the whole personality of the individual and the original motive leading to the perverse act. Therein will be found the key to the diagnosis.[5]

If "*perversity* in the sexual act" suggests the Victorian afterlife of sodomitical practices, "*perversion* of the sexual instinct" anticipates modern homosexual identity. And the one, Krafft-Ebing insists, cannot be confused with the other. For the former to issue in the latter, for vice to be indicative of a psychosexual disturbance, "the whole personality" must come into play. "Contrary sexual feelings," a gender-inappropriate identity, is the "key." Maurice, however, is clearly butcher than his soon-to-be-heterosexualized friend, yet it is Maurice, not Clive, who finally attains to full-fledged "perversion of the sexual instinct." In Forster, the "concrete perverse act" confirms the otherwise normative in the spirit of his perversion.

Freud is our great theoretician of the homosexual as Mr. Average, for Freud, unlike Krafft-Ebing, acknowledges the oxymoronic possibility (or is it?) that so dominates (or is it deforms?) gay personal ads: the "straight acting," "straight appearing," homosexual man. It in no way follows, however, that Freud holds the "key." Like Krafft-Ebing, Freud maintains that the concrete perverse act, however monstrous, does not a pervert make; indeed, no sexual act is decisive. As Deleuze and Guattari note: "Freud's greatness lies in having determined the essence or nature of desire, no longer in terms of objects, aims, or even sources (territories), but as an abstract subjective essence—libido or sexuality" (270). But again, therein lies the extent of the similarity. Krafft-Ebing maintains that perversity proper—perversions of the sexual instinct as opposed to perversity in the sexual act—is always attended by gender confusion or inversion. Freud argues that "the most complete mental masculinity can be combined with inversion" (*Three Essays* 142). For Krafft-Ebing, a gay man who is functionally indistinguishable from all other men in every respect save that of his sexuality is a contradiction in terms. For Freud, he is the perverse norm. Hence, the monumental 1915 footnote—but only a footnote—to *Three Essays on the Theory of Sexuality*: "Psycho-analytic research is most decidedly opposed to any attempt at separating off homosexuals from the rest of mankind as a group of a special character" (145n1).

Like Freud, Forster gives us a straight-acting, straight-appearing gay man who is functionally indistinguishable from all other men in every aspect save

---

5. As quoted in Davidson 80. See also Halperin's reading of this passage (113–15).

that of his sexuality—the singularly unremarkable Maurice Hall. Unlike Freud, however, Forster radically separates off Maurice from the rest of humankind as an individual of a special character. In pleasuring the body, Mr. Average both confirms himself in his "spirit of perversion" and divorces himself "from the congregation of normal men." Why the difference? Freud is only too eager to welcome sexual deviants into the psychoanalytic "congregation." Why does Forster decline the invitation?

To argue Forster's distance from Freud—his distance, that is, from the normative construction of the aberrant—is not to argue for any explicit dialogue between the two. When Maurice seeks medical advice, he is informed by Dr. Barry that his sexual proclivities are a "temptation from the devil" (159). The judgment is termed "theological," which is to say, pre-Freudian. Dr. Barry regards anything written in German with suspicion, but were the doctor less phobic about continental developments, his judgment might have been more of the moment. (Freud was, of course, largely instrumental in the still ongoing project of repositioning sexuality beyond good and evil. But not, alas, beyond a more insidious binary of the normal and the aberrant, the healthy and the sick.) Maurice next visits Mr. Lasker Jones, a hypnotherapist, who diagnoses "congenital homosexuality" (180). Where Barry is disgusted, Lasker Jones is dispassionate, but the latter is no more efficacious than the former, and he too is, or soon will be, anachronistic: psychoanalysis becomes fully itself only when it breaks with the techniques of hypnosis pioneered by Charcot. True, the line "Maurice had two dreams; they will interpret him" (22) might have been lifted from a Freudian case study, and *Maurice* clearly participates in the lowering of the threshold of representation, the negotiation of interior spaces, that is now associated with all things Freudian. In the language of Forster's own *Aspects of the Novel*:

> "Character," says Aristotle, "gives us qualities, but it is in actions—what we do—that we are happy or the reverse." We have already decided that Aristotle is wrong and now we must face the consequences of disagreeing with him. "All human happiness and misery," says Aristotle, "take the form of action." We know better. We believe that happiness and misery exist in the secret life, which each of us lives privately, and to which (in his characters) the novelist has access. And by the secret life we mean the life for which there is no external evidence. (113)

The Aristotelian insistence on the priority of praxis over ethos, doing over being, logically subtends the category of the sodomite. Freud's and Forster's emphasis on "the secret life" heralds both the emergence of a new category of person, the modern "homosexual," and a new modality of literature, the novel of psychological depth.[6] Forster, however, makes explicit what is implicit in psychoanalysis. The negotiation of the secret life is no less a theory of the social for its strategic insistence on the priority of the individual.

Certainly Mr. Ducie's lecture to the young Maurice on the mysteries of reproductive sex—apparently little boys need to be schooled into heterosexuality no less than Greek grammar—argues the imbrication of the psychosexual and the social. "You don't understand now, you will some day," Ducie assures Maurice, "and when you do understand it, remember the poor old pedagogue who put you on the track. It all hangs together—all—and God's in his heaven, All's right with the world. Male and female! Ah wonderful" (15). It does indeed all hang together, the cosmic and the social, and cross-gender desire is the linchpin. God made Adam and Eve, not Adam and Steve—the religious right is witless but not less right for that—and heteronormativity subtends the whole rotten system. Maurice loses his religion before his virginity; at Cambridge, he first succumbs to Clive's atheism:

> "Well, the whole show all hangs together."
>> "So that if the Trinity went wrong it would invalidate the whole show?"
>> "I don't see that. Not at all." (48)

But as Mr. Ducie predicts, Maurice eventually does see that it all hangs together, and his first act of rebellion is to follow Clive in rejecting Holy Mother Church. It is finally sexual deviance, however, not theological apostasy, that invalidates "the whole show." Borenius, the minister at Penge, Clive's family home, is appropriately apocalyptic on the subject of sexual irregularity: "when the nations went a whoring they invariably ended by denying God, I think, and until all sexual irregularities and not some of them are penal the Church will never reconquer England" (237). This might seem, of course, only an added incentive to go a-whoring—as if there were not rewards enough— but Maurice comes to see in Rev. Borenius's words the presence of a seriously skewed, but nevertheless legitimate, insight: "he knew now that there is no secret of humanity which, from a wrong angle, orthodoxy has not viewed, that religion is far more acute than science, and if it only added judgement to insight would be the greatest thing in the world" (237). The orthodox can imagine, if not appreciate, the possibility of a catastrophic rupture in the social order, and the orthodox, to their credit, know their enemies. "Unspeakables of

---

6. When in need of nomenclature, Freud tended to raid classical literature, particularly Greek drama. Freud is, however, less Greek than he believed: the psychoanalytic construction of homosexuality finds its logical corollary in the priority of ethos over praxis. The significant precursor is the novel of psychological depth.

the Oscar Wilde sort" (156) are now everywhere—no fashionable dinner party or academic conference is without at least one—but Forster reminds us not to get too comfortable at the table. Despite what the song claims, there is no place for us, at least as the social order is currently construed.

There is no place for us because homosexuality threatens the heterosexual reproduction of the same with difference, and heterosexuality is the dispensation of difference in name only. Forster is sufficiently Freudian (we all are) to register the significance of a slip of the tongue:

> "He is a most clever man," said Mrs Hall with finality, "and Mrs Barry's the same."
>
> This slip of their mother's tongue convulsed Ada and Kitty. They would not stop laughing at the idea of Mrs Barry's being a man. (53)

The possibility that so amuses Ada and Kitty *Maurice* entertains in earnest: heterosexuality is predicated on the desire for "the same," the return of "the same." Maurice, like his father before him, is sent to Mr. Abraham's school: "There is much to be said for apathy in education, and Mr Abraham's pupils did not do so badly in the long run, became parents in their turn, and in some cases sent him their sons" (9). For Freud, the process by which children become parents who (re)produce children who becomes parents—the process, that is, by which the social order achieves stasis through the illusion of generational opposition and change—is nothing less than the master narrative of civilization itself:

> At the same time as these plainly incestuous phantasies [the son's desire for the mother, the daughter's desire for the father] are overcome and repudiated, one of the most significant, but also one of the most painful, psychical achievements of the pubertal period is completed: detachment from parental authority, a process that alone makes possible the opposition, which is so important for the progress of civilization, between the new generation and the old. At every stage in the course of development which all human beings ought by rights to pass, a certain number are held back. (*Three Essays* 227)

"The reward for filial disobedience," as Jane Austen terms it, is the reproduction of parental, heterosexual privilege, and only those of us incapable of detaching ourselves from parental authority fail to attain to it. (For example: boys who don't turn out to be the marrying kind or girls who do but thereafter refuse "to give their husbands" their "due" [*Three Essays* 227].) The "course of development which all human beings ought by rights to pass" thus pays a double dividend. Opposition to compulsory heterosexuality is evacuated of all efficacy, even as the heterosexual reproduction of the same is preserved as hetero. The Maurice who is told "to copy" his father in every way (11), who is enjoined to "present the expectant world with a Maurice the third" (27), is a revolutionary in training. By the same (il)logic, the Maurice who breaks with his class and upbringing to abscond with Alec remains pathologically bound to his mother's apron strings. Or so, in any case, psychoanalysis would have us believe. Foucault is routinely dismissed as a fetishist of power. Nothing in his work, however, rivals the dexterity with which Freud recuperates "disobedience" for the status quo.

Freud insists that etymology gets it right, that heterosexuality is in fact hetero in all things. In *Group Psychology and the Analysis of the Ego,* for instance, he argues that cross-gender desire "breaks through the group ties of race, national divisions, and the social class system"; like the Lawrence of *Lady Chatterley's Lover,* he celebrates heterosexuality as the great solvent of class barriers (141).[7] Yet the psychoanalytic guarantee that the parent–child relationship is at the root of everyone's sexuality, that the nuclear family is the alpha and omega of all psychosexual development, suggests otherwise. In a premodern, predisciplinary "system of alliances," children—specifically girls—are given in marriage as sacrifices to class solidarity or ambition. In the kinder, gentler world of bourgeois familialism, however, children give themselves, for better or worse, in love. Parents are denied sovereign authority over their children's bodies, but only to be granted a compensatory, if less immediately discernible, privilege: the overt coercion of an older familialism is simply translated into an ideology of desire itself. (Again, psychoanalysis is no less a theory of the social for its strategic insistence on the priority of "the secret life.") As Foucault puts it: psychoanalysis "made it possible—even when everything seemed to point to the reverse process—to keep the deployment of sexuality coupled to the system of alliance" (*History of Sexuality* 113). Or, as the songwriter puts it: psychoanalysis insists that I should want to marry a girl—were I the marrying kind—just like the kind of girl who married dear old dad. Maurice's sense of solidarity with his class survives his first night of sex-making with Alec. "But I must belong to my class, that's fixed," he tells himself, "Anyhow, I must stick to my class" (215). It does not, however, survive the novel to which he lends his name.

The association of same-sex desire with cross-class alliances is not, of course, the newest news in town. Spectators at the trial of Oscar Wilde, for example, or at least those unfamiliar with the term "gross indecency,"

---

7. "If the lady marries the gamekeeper," Lawrence says of Connie and Mellors in "A Propos of *Lady Chatterley's Lover*," "it is not class spite, but in spite of class" (334).

might reasonably have taken it to mean an eroticism unconstrained by the demands of class solidarity. Certainly Maurice initially understands homosexuality exclusively in class terms: "The feeling that can impel a gentleman towards a person of lower class stands self-condemned" (151). (*Mutatis mutandis*: the feeling that can impel a gentleman towards a person of the same class stands as the self-evident good that is heterosexuality.) Nothing in the novel challenges Maurice's sense of homosexuality as a threat to class solidarity. Everything, however, conspires to challenge his evaluation of same-sex, cross-class liaisons. Mr. Cornwallis, the Don who sends Maurice down from Cambridge, thinks that class opposites should not attract: "It was not natural that men of different characters and tastes should be intimate, and although undergraduates, unlike schoolboys, were officially normal, the dons exercised a certain amount of watchfulness" (79–80). Were Maurice, like Clive, a member of a decaying gentry, rather than a solid bourgeois, apparently the same surveillance would not be necessary. Dr. Barry thinks it well and good that Maurice is sent down. "You got yourself into an atmosphere for which you are not suited," he informs the disgraced undergraduate, "and you've very properly taken the first opportunity to get out of it" (84). Although Cambridge affords limited opportunities for class mobility, Maurice's proper place, according to the doctor, is taking up the position in the firm of Hill and Hall previously occupied by Mr. Hall senior—henceforth, presumably, Hill, Hall, and Homosexual. For his part, Clive considers "intimacy with a social inferior . . . unthinkable" (242), which may well be what saves him for the regime of compulsory heterosexuality. Once he snaps straight, he returns to Penge and its leaky roof, marries a woman of his own class, and pursues his father's "seat"—the locution really deserves to be read—in Parliament. The heterosexual Clive seems a changed man, yet the change merely guarantees that nothing does change, nothing can change.

Edward Carpenter, whom Forster knew and admired, considered homosexuality the antidote to all this hetero cloning of the same:

> It is noticeable how often Uranians of good position and breeding are drawn to rougher types . . . and frequently very permanent alliances grow up this way, which although publically not acknowledged have a decided influence on social institutions, customs and political tendencies—and which could have a good deal more influence if they could be given a little more scope and recognition. (237)

Forster concurs, but without the liberal faith. Homosexuality does not require just a little more scope and recognition in order to work its special magic; rather, social institutions are constitutively heterosexual and heterosexualizing. In his "Terminal Note," Forster recalls that Carpenter "had hoped for the generous recognition of an emotion and for the reintegration of something primitive"—that is, something gay—"into the common stock." Forster characterizes himself as "less optimistic," although nevertheless given, at least at one time, to the traditional humanist faith "that knowledge would bring understanding" (255). Sadly, however, the only shift Forster can discern in the fifty-odd years between the writing of *Maurice* and the "Terminal Note" is "the change from ignorance and terror to familiarity and contempt" (255). "I belong," Forster remarked in a 1946 broadcast, "to the fag end of Victorian liberalism" (qtd. in Smith 106)—again, the locution really deserves to be read— and it is precisely Forster's commitment to traditional liberal values that is characteristically said to mark his distance from the poetics and politics of High Modernism. *Maurice* is an exception. Unlike the conservative or the radical, the liberal is constitutively incapable of imagining a catastrophic rupture in the social order. Forster, however, can and does: the rupture went by the name of that which cannot be named among Christians. Organizational meetings for gay pride parades and the like invariably devolve into debates about what the public face of homosexuality should be. Nice little, white little, polite little boys and girls—nothing special, nothing threatening, about us— or dykes on bikes. Consistency would demand that the author of *Maurice,* the man once dubbed "The Closet Queen of the Century," would recommend the dykes. Forster's representation of "the homosexual" was already considered anachronistic in 1971, and today it is frequently dismissed as little more than quaint, a remnant of the bad-old-days before the Liberation. Yet at a time when the sexually perverse can imagine no greater good than the attainment of the legal right to have and to hold, a sense of the homosexual as social catastrophe is needful. E. M. Forster, seemingly the most anodyne of liberal apologists, does precisely that.

In his "Terminal Note," Forster concedes that both Clive and his treatment of him deteriorate once he snaps straight (251), but the conversion to heteronormativity is no less instructive for that. After suddenly abandoning his same-sex, cross-class object (Maurice) and before settling on his cross-sex, same-class object (Anne Woods), Clive flirts with Ada, Maurice's sister, a cross-sex, cross-class object. In a line that anticipates the opening moments of *The Waste Land,* which is itself a monument to the eternal return of the same, Ada is characterized as a "compromise between memory and desire" (124). She is, however, the wrong compromise—Clive's one anxiety while flirting with her is that Maurice will show up, "for a memory should remain a memory" (125). Clive imposes a strategic ban on any mention of his Cambridge indiscretions in the belief that homosexual memories should be relegated to the safety of the past. Once he snaps straight, however, desire more than "compromises" with memory; it is absolutely coincident with it. In *Three Essays,* Freud insists that the heterosexual "finding of an object is in fact a refinding of it" (222), which is thus anything but "hetero" in relation to its origins. Forster concurs. Although her husband's will specifies that Mrs. Durham occupy the Dowager House once her son marries, she never quite manages to move out. As in *Oedipus,* the prototype of all psychosexual development in Freud, the seriatim order of one after the other (mother then wife) collapses back on itself (wife as rediscovered, reconstituted mother). For Freud, the ostensible opposition between the generations is precisely what allows the younger generation to replicate the older. Forster, however, refuses to mystify the return of the same as the developmental: "Both houses and estate [Penge] were marked, not indeed with decay, but with the immobility that precedes it" (86). Penge is the privileged site of heterosexuality, and its genteel immobility bespeaks an exhausted social order.

In *Beyond the Pleasure Principle*—a late work that makes explicit the recursive logic already operable in *Three Essays on the Theory of Sexuality*—Freud defines the instinctual "*as the urge inherent in all organic life to restore an earlier state of things.*" Far from "impelling us toward change and development," as common sense or convention would have it, "the instincts are the expression of the *conservative* nature of living substance" (36). This may or may not be true of all "organic life"; it is certainly true, however, of all narrative life, which is structurally incapable of imagining an ending that is not determined by a "prior state of affairs." Peter Brooks argues that narrative "operates as metaphor in its affirmation of resemblance"; it brings into relation different actions, combines them through perceived similarities, and appropriates them to a "common plot," which requires "the rejection of all merely contingent (or unassimilatable) incident or action" (91). The "affirmation of resemblance" is the reproduction of the same but once removed, which suggests that narrative is also an expression of the "*conservative*"—small "c"—nature of all things. (Or, better, narrative is a conservative structuring of what is thus mystified as the conservative nature of all things.) The eponymous hero of John Weir's *The Irreversible Decline of Eddie Socket* comes to regret "his failure to imagine a world in which there were any options other than the ones his parents presented" (166).[8] The novel expresses the failure in psycho-

---

8. In *Maurice,* the options presented by the father include the familiar reduction of homosexuality to "just a phase": "The ethereal past had blinded him [Maurice], and the highest happiness he could dream was a return to it. As he sat in his office working, he could not see the vast curve of his life, still less the ghost of his father sitting opposite. Mr Hall senior had neither fought nor thought; there had never been any occasion; he had supported society and moved

logical terms, but responsibility may well reside with Eddie's generic dispensation. As early as June 1911, Forster wrote in his diary of his "weariness of the only subject I can and may treat—the love of men for women & vice versa" (qtd. in Moffat 6). The weariness is easily explained, then as now. It's still the same old story—every Jack shall have his Jill—which is itself the story of the return of the same.

The married Clive literally returns to his family home at the novel's end, the better to reproduce the same: the aptly named family "cell" remains the alpha and omega of all normative psychosexual development. "Beautiful conventions"—at once social and narrative—await the conjugal couple:

> His [Clive's] ideal of marriage was temperate and graceful, like all of his ideals, and he found a fit helpmate in Anne, who had refinement herself, and admired it in others. They loved each other tenderly. Beautiful conventions received them. (165)

To love tenderly is not, however, to love passionately:

> When he [Clive] arrived in her [Anne's] room after marriage, she did not know what he wanted. Clive was as considerate as possible, but he scared her terribly, and he left feeling she hated him. She did not. She welcomed him on future nights. But it was always without a word. They united in a world that bore no reference to the daily. . . . They ignored the reproductive and the digestive functions. (164)

So temperate an ideal might seem anathema to the poetics of High Heterosexual Romance, but then so temperate an ideal need not be admitted as authentically heterosexual at all. Debrah Raschke, for instance, suggests that "rather than a confirmation of his heterosexuality," Clive's marriage "seems more an extension of his Platonism" (160). Curiously, however, Raschke does not extend the same hermeneutic principle to the sexually perverse. Forster's novel explicitly associates the reading of Plato with an inducement to same-sex desire, yet no one construes Maurice's homosexuality as the logical extension of his undergraduate education. When homophobic convenience dictates, heterosexuality can always be made to mean its demonized "other." Homosexuality "proper," however, is always and only itself.

---

without a crisis from illicit to licit love" (151). Maurice ultimately pursues a different, a better, happiness.

In "Über die allgemeinste Erniedrigung des Liebeslebens"—alternately translated as "On the Universal Tendency to Debasement in the Sphere of Love" or "The Most Prevalent Form of Degradation in Erotic Life"—Freud argues that civilized man cannot reconcile "affectionate and sensual impulses" (187). Because the heterosexual finding of a love object is always a re-finding, because the child's experience at the mother's breast is the "prototype of every relation of love" (*Three Essays* 222), normative desire is constitutively incestuous. Yet the family that is a structural incitement to incest also guards against it, which prevents any happy coupling of the "affectional and sensual impulses." The "refinding" cannot be literal; erotic desire must be directed away from the prohibited object (and/or surrogates that too obviously or palpably invoke it) toward women of an inferior class or ethical status, for whom normative man need not feel any affection. Hence, the schizophrenia: "Where they love they do not desire and where they desire they cannot love" (*Universal Tendency* 183). And it is schizophrenia till death do they part: "The damage caused by the initial frustration of sexual pleasure is seen in the fact that the freedom later given to that pleasure in marriage does not bring full satisfaction" (187). The incest taboo guarantees exogamy:

> Respect for this barrier is essentially a cultural demand made by society. Society must defend against the danger that the interests which it needs for the establishment of higher social units may be swallowed up by the family; and for this reason, in the case of every individual, but in particular of ado-lescent boys, it seeks by all possible means to loosen their connection with the family. (*Three Essays* 225)

But it is a minimal exogamy, for by systematically inciting the incestuous desires it nevertheless guards against, the family also guarantees endogamy. Class solidarity is preserved, but at the cost of a massive erotic impoverish-ment. The most prevalent form of degradation in erotic life is more than just "prevalent," more than even "universal." It is, rather, constitutive, to a greater or lesser degree, of "the love of civilized man" as such (*Universal Tendency* 184). The married Clive is not the exception that proves the rule of hetero-sexual passion. On the contrary. He becomes what Maurice once was: Mr. Average.

There is no place for Maurice—not even Greece, the classical home of homosexuality, but in *Maurice,* the paradoxical site of Clive's conversion to heterosexuality. "Omit: a reference to the unspeakable vice of the Greeks" (51), Mr. Cornwallis famously remarks, but Clive will have none of it: "I regard it as a point of pure scholarship. The Greeks, or most of them, were that way inclined, and to omit it is to omit the mainstay of Athenian society" (51). Clive is exactly right. The structured, formalized inequalities of classical pederasty sustained the social order, and Maurice is in search of an alternate tradition. There is, then, nothing innately subversive about same-sex desire. As Foucault insists: to say yes to sex—any form of sex, including sex with your gardener or gamekeeper—is not necessarily to say no to power. But if *Maurice* is thus at an extreme remove from the sublime sexual idiocy of, say, *Lady Chatterley's Lover,* it is hardly an apology for erotic pessimism or the de-politicization of sensuous enjoyment. True, the repercussions of Clive's and Maurice's sexless dalliance do not extend beyond a more or less socially irrelevant rejection of the Trinity and Holy Mother Church. Maurice's night of sex-making with Alec, however, initiates a process that irrevocably exiles the two from the congregation of normal men. The newly heterosexualized Clive returns to the eternal sameness of Penge. The homosexualized Maurice inhabits a greenwood in which he is free to forge relations that do not answer to the kinship or class demands of larger social institutions and agendas. "I have my own notion," Maurice tells Lasker Jones. "It strikes me there may have been more about the Greeks—Theban Band—and the rest of it. Well, this wasn't unlike. I don't see how they could have kept together otherwise— especially when they came from such different classes" (212). Maurice devises an indigenous version of the myth of the Theban Band in the story of Robin Hood and the greenwood, which is also the socially unauthorized work of gay community building. Relations of structured inequality continue to sustain the social order. They are what we call "heterosexual," the happy coupling of gender inequality and class solidarity that underwrites the social reproduction of the same.

Lukács argues that the historical novel privileges "middle-of-the-road" protagonists: "The relative lack of contour to their personalities, the absence of passions which would cause them to take up major, decisive, one-sided positions, their contact with each of the contending hostile camps, etc., make them specially suited to express adequately, in their own destinies, the complex ramifications of events in a novel" (*Historical Novel* 149). *Maurice* is manifestly not a historical novel in Lukács's (or, for that matter, anybody's) sense of the term, yet it registers its historical insights in precisely the manner suggested above. Forster's protagonist is aggressively middle-of-the-road, and it is the lack of contour to Maurice's personality, his want of passionately or consciously held ideological beliefs, that allows the novelist to express the complex ramifications of sexuality, which extend well beyond sexuality proper, in a world grown increasingly Freudian. The premodern world characteristically conducts its political struggles in and through the theological. (Recall Dr. Barry's judgment on Maurice's "condition.") The modern world privileges the sexual. Barry's theological judgment gives way to Lasker Jones's quasi-medical advice, and it is finally sexual deviance, not theological apostasy, that severs Maurice from the "congregation" of normal men. (Forster's diction seems intent on registering the historical transition.) Lytton Strachey, the original of the character of Risley, considered "the Class question . . . rather a red herring," but he could hardly have been more wrong.[9] In *Maurice* as in the modern world in general, the Class question is the Sex question, the Sex question is the Class question:

> All that night his [Maurice's] body yearned for Alec's, despite him. He called it lustful, a word easily uttered, and he opposed it to his work, his family, his friends, his position in society. In that coalition must be included his will. For if the will can overleap class, civilization as we have made it will go to pieces. (207)

Maurice chooses Alec, civilization be damned. Homosexuality heroicizes Mr. Average.

Consider, in this context, Forster's relation to Austen, an author he is frequently said to resemble. In *Pride and Prejudice*, the vivacious Elizabeth Bennet nets the sexually and socially desirable Darcy, and their union validates the status quo by promoting the illusion of unlimited mobility within it. In *Maurice*, however, mobility is downward, and it is bound exclusively to the gender of one's object choice. The aggressively average Maurice Hall nets the hot, but socially undesirable, Alec, and their relationship costs a moribund social order a citizen who would otherwise have been an efficient cog in it. Forster considered a "happy ending" to be "imperative" (250), but to the extent that the traditional novel admits of homosexuality, it insists on the tragic. (Heterosexual happiness makes for the marriage plot, the novel-as-usual. Homosexual happiness, to judge from the critical reception of *Maurice*, produces the ideological deformations of "the thesis novel.") True, both *Pride and Prejudice* and *Maurice* are novels of realized desire, and thus eccentric in relation to "the great tradition." Compromised desire is the order of the day.[10] Why risk all on the remote prospect of a Darcy or the dangerous

---

9. From a letter to Forster, 12 Mar. 1915; Forster quotes from the letter in his "Terminal Note" (252).

10. Lukács terms this, interestingly enough, "virile maturity," by which he means "self-imposed limitation." The hero abandons his quest for authentic values in a degraded world, but without fully capitulating to things-as-they-are. Lukács has nothing to say about women who

allure of an Alec—or so the traditional novel would have us believe—when, finally, something on the order of a Mr. Collins will do? (Charlotte's husband is, of course, more than usually repulsive, but then Austen is more than usually uncompromising in her critique of the sexual politics of the plot of compromised desire.) Yet if *both Pride and Prejudice* and *Maurice* refuse to celebrate the compromised as the "mature," desire nevertheless functions differently in each. *Pride and Prejudice* might have taken as its subtitle "Vivacity Rewarded," and its Cinderella-like marriage finally mystifies, rather than threatens, the social order it thus serves to perpetuate.[11] Maurice and Alec cast their lot with Robin Hood and his men, the agents of the forced redistribution of wealth.

Or consider Forster's relation to D. H. Lawrence, a novelist he is said to resemble not at all. In *Lady Chatterley's Lover*, Mellors's politics and Connie's income (she has an annuity from her mother) make for strange bedfellows, yet wealth proves to be an eminently surmountable barrier (or, perhaps, a remarkably powerful aphrodisiac). The future is uncertain—Clifford has yet to consent to a divorce at the novel's end—but the lovers remain the beneficiaries of an economic order that the novel purports to condemn. For Mellors and Connie, cross-class desire is without significant economic consequences. Maurice and Alec, however, face a future of economic uncertainty. (Homosexuality is traditionally construed as a vice endemic to the upper classes or culture elites, and even today, white gay men are reputed to participate fully in the economic privileges of their gender and race. No matter that they earn, on the whole, 17 percent less than their straight counterparts. The myth of gay male economic privilege neither requires empirical verification nor brooks empirical correction, my own included.)[12] Criticism characteristi-

---

settle for the likes of Mr. Collins. See Lukács, *The Theory of the Novel*.

11. Elizabeth reminds Lady Catherine that she is a gentleman's daughter, and thus Darcy's equal, but by any standards, her husband is a catch. To be mistress of Pemberley is indeed "something."

12. The myth of gay male economic privilege is a perfect example of the workings of ideology as defined by Žižek: "An ideology is really 'holding us' only when do not feel any opposition between it and the reality—that is, when the ideology succeeds in determining the mode of our everyday experience of reality itself." See Žižek 49. But if this endnote is thus an exercise in futility—assuming, of course, that I am not simply preaching to the choir—I nevertheless feel compelled to provide it. Gay men earn on the average 17 percent less than their straight counterparts of the same age, race, location, occupation, and educational level; see Badgett 3–4. To the extent that the myth of gay male economic privilege does condescend to justify itself, it tends to make use of surveys designed to produce the expected results. The widely influential Simmons Market Research Bureau Survey, which the *Wall Street Journal* published in 1991, is perhaps the most conspicuous case in point. Gay men were indeed shown to be wealthier than their straight counterparts, but as the survey restricted itself to the readership of a number of "elite" gay magazines and newspapers, the results should not have come as a

cally reduces Forster's investment in "the Class question" to the biographical, which is to say, the homosexual. (And when the threat to the "social class system" is gay, it goes by the name of "sexual slumming.") Yet if criticism privileges the homobiographical, *Maurice* insists on the structural. Heterosexuality in its modern form is systematically bound to the reproduction of class hierarchy. Homosexuality, the "weak spot" in the process of human cultural development, is not.

Strachey didn't have high hopes for Maurice and Alec. He thought their relationship based on "lust and sentiment," and he predicted "a rupture within six months—chiefly as a lack of common interests owing to class differences" (qtd. in Martland 155). Here he may be right. When there are no external compulsions keeping the lovers tied and true, the future is always in doubt. But so what? Neither Maurice nor Alec ever utters the words "till death do us part," and the novel ends, it bears emphasizing, not in the greenwood, but with Clive returning to Anne, preparing to conceal the truth from her. Forster positions Maurice within an England "where it was still possible to get lost," to elude scrutiny (254). Appropriately, the lovers ultimately elude novelistic representation as well. In one sense, *Maurice*—posthumously published, dedicated "to a happier time"—is a novel in search of an audience, the homosexual evermore-about-to-be. (*The Life to Come* is the title of a posthumously published collection of Forster's stories.) In another sense, however, *Maurice* is a cautionary tale, a remarkably prescient exploration of the conditions under which the modern homosexual did in fact gain access to representation. It is, after all, Lasker Jones who encourages Maurice to commit his "secret life" to paper—he insists that the "confession" be "exhaustive" (213)—and it is Lasker Jones who means to "cure" Maurice of his condition:

> Then he wrote his statement. It took some time, and, though far from imaginative, he went to bed with the jumps. He was convinced that someone had looked over his shoulder while he wrote. He wasn't alone. Or again, that he hadn't personally written. Since coming to Penge, he seemed a bundle of voices, not Maurice, and now he could almost hear them quarrelling inside him. (176)

---

surprise to anyone. As Badgett notes, it is rather like surveying straight America on the basis of the readership of the *New York Times* (3). The myth of gay male affluence has, I suspect, a great deal to do with straight resentment of the *disposable* income gay men are alleged to command, money not mortgaged, as it were, to futurity. But the issue of benefits is, if anything, of greater significance than salary, and many benefits continue to be bound to one's marital status: "Over a ten-year period, an [unmarried and partnered] worker earning $40,000 a year may earn as much as $55,800 less in benefits than a married co-worker." A marriage penalty indeed. See Ingraham 69.

Foucault argues that "the obligation to confess is now relayed through so many different points, is now so deeply ingrained in us, that we no longer perceive it as the effect of a power that constrains us; on the contrary, it seems to us that truth, lodged in our most secret nature, 'demands' only to surface" (*History of Sexuality* 60). Confession may be good for the soul, as proverbial wisdom has it, but Maurice experiences the obligation to confess very much as an obligation. "He wasn't alone" and "he hadn't personally written": what "demands only to surface," what seems to emerge spontaneously from within, is first imposed from without. The so-called right to representation is not an unproblematic good, and it is not easily distinguished from the normalizing project of surveillance.

Foucault argues that our modernity, both literary and political, is constituted by a lowering of the threshold of representation: "And if from the early Middle Ages to the present day the 'adventure' is an account of individuality, the passage from the epic to the novel, from the noble deed to the secret singularity, from long exiles to the internal search for childhood, from combats to phantasies, it is also inscribed in the formation of a disciplinary society" (*Discipline* 155). A secret life "for which there is no external evidence," to return to the language of *Aspects of the Novel*, is necessarily violated by its novelization, which renders Forster's own project, no less than the confession solicited by Lasker Jones, complicit in "the formation of a disciplinary society." Certainly both are invested in ferreting out *the* secret, which, in the modern world, is invariably homosexuality. Lasker Jones's "writing cure," for instance, is a precursor of the "talking cure," and the talking cure places sexual deviance in an explanatory relation to everything in need of explanation. (Again, there are no bad heterosexuals. "Anyone who is in any way . . . abnormal mentally is invariably abnormal also in his sexual life.") Mr. Average, however, reverses the trajectory adumbrated by Foucault. Maurice actively seeks to elude representation; he cannot rely on exclusion from it. Like Freud's Dora, his "noble deed," his modest heroism, is to refuse the discourse of "the secret singularity," which includes the novel that bears his name.

Like Dora and, in a way, like Forster himself. After *Passage to India* (1924), Forster simply stopped writing novels, for reasons that he was to explain some three decades later: "sex," he claimed, had prevented him from becoming a more prolific and "famous writer" (qtd. in Kermode 125). This might seem yet another incentive to go a-whoring—would that more novelists had more sex—but Forster cannot be taken straight. The translation of (deviant) sex into discourse is a distinctly modern compulsion, and it would have made Forster (as well he knew) an even more famous author: "Since the eighteenth century, sex has not ceased to produce a kind of generalized discursive erethism. And these discourses on sex did not multiply apart from or against power, but in the very space and the means of its exercise. Incitements to speak were orchestrated from all quarters . . ." (*History of Sexuality* 32). A disciplinary society construes homosexuality as an "incitement to discourse;" Forster renders it a discursive prophylactic. Like his protagonist, the author of *Maurice* evidently thought it possible, at least in his own lifetime, to elude psychosexual scrutiny, to get lost.

Clive and Anne are not so fortunate. Although the novel originally ended with a chance meeting between one of Maurice's sisters and the two "outlaws," Forster decided—wisely, in my opinion—to conclude with the couple legally conjoined. The so-called marriage plot of nineteenth-century novelistic fame really isn't: betrothal, not the eternity of having and holding, is the conventional fulfillment. Like the vision granted Adam and Eve at the end of *Paradise Lost,* a seminal moment for nineteenth-century novelistic closure, the prospects seem so vast and various only because they are strategically unspecified. *Maurice,* however, subjects marriage to the indignity of representation—for indignity it is—and the future, which stands in an essentially recuperative or regressive relation to the past, is simply more of the same. Clive and Anne's relation is manifestly innocent of lust, and it will doubtless be till death do they part, chiefly as a result of lack of different interests owing to class similarity. More's the pity.

But all this is predicated, of course, on Clive's snapping straight, and in our culture, snapping straight is an unintelligible concept. Clearly the 1987 James Ivory film considers it as such. Clive suddenly becomes the marrying kind only after his queeny friend Risley is tried, in the expected Oscar Wilde–like fashion, for same-sex, cross-class dalliances. Willed or socially motivated conversions to heteronormativity are a dime a dozen, but in Forster's novel, Clive's about-face is apparently reluctant, nonvolitional: "Against my will I have become normal. I cannot help it" (116). The declaration seems unequivocal, but can it be believed? Should it be believed? Do we have in *Maurice* that rarest of all literary and cultural phenomena, the straight coming-out narrative?

Three Essays begins by positing the category of the "absolute invert": "Persons of the opposite sex are never the object of their sexual desire, but leave them cold, or even arouse sexual aversion in them" (136). Freud admits, however, of no absolute successes, no unimpeachable heterosexuals: "By studying sexual excitations other than those that are manifestly displayed, it [psychoanalysis] has found that all living beings are capable of making a homosexual object-choice, and have in fact made one in their unconscious" (145n1). Why the asymmetry? Why do some of us fail so spectacularly while others succeed only equivocally? And again, what of Clive? Is he a latent heterosexual during his sexless dalliance with Maurice? Or a repressed homosexual during his passionless marriage to Anne?

That only Clive's sexuality is subject to speculation is telling. Maurice's homosexual credentials, even before he has sex with a man, are unimpeachable. Clive's heterosexual credentials, even after he marries a woman, are dubious. In theory, psychoanalysis holds that all sexual identities ("absolute inverts" excepted) are porous and mutable. In practice, however, certain sexualities prove more mutable than others, and mutability does not, in any case, threaten the regime of compulsory heterosexuality. Alec, to cite the obvious example, is bisexual, but no one, Strachey included, predicts a rupture with Maurice within six months because of a woman. Assertions of heterosexual credentials tend to be received with a fair degree of skepticism; confessions of deviant desire, by contrast, immediately command conviction (or they are met with the smug rejoinder: "I always knew"). Forster, however, orders these things differently. Maurice eventually comes to accept Clive's sudden conversion to heteronormativity as the truth of his erstwhile friend, and Clive initially receives Maurice's confession that he too is "that way" as an expression of mere decency or politeness. Even the emotions that attend the subject's recognition or acknowledgment of its own sexuality seem curiously inverted. Clive cozies up to his newfound heterosexuality only reluctantly; given the apparent anguish that he experiences, one might well think he was coming out queer:

> Clive did not give in to the life spirit without a struggle. He believed in the intellect and tried to think himself back to his old state. He averted his eyes from women, and when that failed adopted childish and violent expedients. (120)

Any number of perks and privileges await the newly heterosexualized Clive, but they in no way motivate his emergence into normative desire. Maurice henceforth inspires in him a "physical dislike" (120), and there is apparently no erotic commerce between his pre- and post-conversion selves. Clive's sense of the absolute division between his homo past and his hetero future is not now the fashion, and the psychoanalytically inclined might well accuse him of protesting too much. Certainly "physical dislike" is easily construed as evidence of an abiding, if now violently repressed, homosexuality. There is a sense, however, in which the sexual politics of Forster's novel requires us to take Clive at his word. The logical corollary to the contention that same-sex desire casts the pervert out from the congregation of normal men is that the congregation of normal men is cut off from the band of perverts. All this might seem, of course, tautological, if not downright reactionary. It is Freud's refusal to "separate off" homosexuals as "a group of a special kind," as opposed to Forster's "minoritizing" stance, that is generally considered the progressive position. Yet if one admits of what psychoanalysis does not—there are in fact heterosexuals, pure and simple—the charge of latent or repressed homosexuality can no longer underwrite the ideological innocence of the regime of the norm. Freud makes possible the situation in which homosexuality can mean either nothing or everything, as homophobic convenience dictates. Nothing, when the pervert steps smartly into the niche that the social order has prepared for him or her, and by all accounts, we are headed for the chapel. Adam and Eve, Adam and Steve. So long as gay relations remain ersatz imitations of the norm, the gender of one's object choices is strictly irrelevant. But when the hetero reproduction of the same is threatened with difference, or when the hetero reproduction of the same is exposed for what is, homosexuality magically acquires unlimited explanatory power. A strictly Freudian reading of Clive—which is to say, every reading of Clive that questions the legitimacy of his conversion—diagnoses repressed homosexuality, and homosexuality explains everything from the leaking roof at Penge to the passionless marriage to Anne. (Not to mention, on a different level, the apparent inadequacies of Forster's prose and the didacticism of his novel. Either Forster is not homosexual enough or he is too much given to homosexual special pleading. Damned if you aren't, damned if you are.)[13] Take Clive at his word, however, and heterosexuality means precisely and only itself. The immobility of Penge, the temperate zone that is Penge, is the authentic site of normativity. The Closet Queen of the Century outs heterosexuality.

Works Cited

Badgett, N. V. Lee. *Money, Myths, and Change: The Economic Lives of Lesbians and Gay Men.* Chicago: U of Chicago P, 2001.

Bakhtin, M. M. *The Dialogic Imagination: Four Essays.* Trans. Caryl Emerson and Michael Holquist. Austin: U of Texas P, 1981.

Brooks, Peter. *Reading for the Plot: Design and Intention in Narrative.* New York: Knopf, 1984.

Carpenter, Edward. *Selected Writings.* Vol. 1. London: Gay Men's Press, 1984.

Davidson, Arnold I. "Closing Up the Corpses: Diseases of Sexuality and the Emergence of the Psychiatric Style of Reasoning." *Homosexuality & Psychoanalysis.* Ed. Tim Dean and Christopher Lane. Chicago: U of Chicago P, 2001. 59–90.

---

13. In one sense, the homosexual of the future to which the novel is dedicated is Forster himself: he had not yet had sex with a man when he began writing it. Hence, the charge that he is not homosexual enough.

Deleuze, Giles, and Félix Guattari. *Anti-Oedipus: Capitalism and Schizophrenia.* Trans. Robert Hurley, Mark Seem, and Helen R. Lane. Minneapolis: U of Minnesota P, 1983.

Forster, E. M. *Aspects of the Novel.* London: Edward Arnold, 1927.

———. *Maurice.* New York: Norton, 1971.

Foucault, Michel. *Discipline and Punish: The Birth of the Prison.* Trans. Alan Sheridan. New York: Vintage, 1979.

———. *The History of Sexuality.* Vol. 1. Trans. Robert Hurley. New York. Vintage, 1978.

Freud, Sigmund. *Beyond the Pleasure Principle.* Vol. 18 of *The Standard Edition of the Complete Psychological Works of Sigmund Freud.* Trans. James Strachey. 24 vols. London: Hogarth, 1953–74.

———. *Group Psychology and the Analysis of the Ego.* Vol. 18 of *The Standard Edition.*

———. *On the Universal Tendency to Debasement in the Sphere of Love.* Vol. 11 of *The Standard Edition.*

———. *Three Essays on the Theory of Sexuality.* Vol. 7 of *The Standard Edition.*

Halperin, David M. *How to Do the History of Sexuality.* Chicago: U of Chicago P, 2002.

Ingraham, Chrys. *White Wedding: Romancing Heterosexuality in Popular Culture.* New York: Routledge, 1999.

Kermode, Frank. *Concerning E. M. Forster.* New York: Farrar, Straus and Giroux, 2009.

Lawrence, D. H. "A Propos of *Lady Chatterley's Lover.*" *Lady Chatterley's Lover.* Ed. Michael Squires. Cambridge: Cambridge UP, 1993. 303–35.

Lukács, Georg. *The Historical Novel.* Trans. Hannah and Stanley Mitchell. Harmondsworth: Penguin, 1962.

———. *Realism in Our Time: Literature and the Cass Struggle.* Trans. John and Necks Mander. New York: Harper & Row, 1964.

———. *The Theory of the Novel.* Trans. Anna Bostock. Cambridge: MIT P, 1974.

Martland, Arthur. *E. M. Forster: Passion and Prose.* London: Gay Men's Press, 1999.

Moffat, Wendy. *A Great Unrecorded History: A New Life of E. M. Forster.* New York: Picador, 2010.

Morrison, Paul. *The Explanation for Everything: Essays on Sexual Subjectivity.* New York: NYU P, 2001.

Raschke, Debrah. "Breaking the Engagement with Philosophy: Re-envisioning Hetero/Homo Relations in *Maurice.*" *Queer Forster.* Ed. Robert K. Martin and George Piggford. Chicago: U of Chicago P, 1977. 151–65.

Sedgwick, Eve Kosofsky. *Epistemology of the Closet.* Berkeley: U of California P, 1980.

Smith, H. A. "Forster's Humanism and the Nineteenth Century." *Forster: A Collection of Critical Essays.* Ed. Malcolm Bradbury. Englewood Cliffs, NJ: Prentice-Hall, 1966. 106–16.

Weir, John. *The Irreversible Decline of Eddie Socket.* New York: Harper, 1991.

Žižek, Slavoj. *The Sublime Object of Ideology.* London: Verso, 1989.

VALERIE ROHY

Strange Influence

Queer Etiology in *The Picture of Dorian Gray*

> It is not made sufficiently clear that the writer does not prefer
> a course of unnatural iniquity to a life of cleanliness, health,
> and sanity.
>
> —Review of *Dorian Gray* in *The Scots Observer,* July 5, 1890

*I*n the 1928 trial of *The Well of Loneliness,* when the novel's British publisher was charged with violating the Obscene Publications Act of 1857,
the chief magistrate's argument rested not on the book's content, but rather
on its probable effect on its readers; it cited the legal definition of obscen-
ity as any material that tended to "deprave and corrupt those whose minds
are open to such immoral influences, and into whose hands a publication
of this sort may fall" (Biron 41). That premise lies at the heart of a paranoid
mythology about the causation of same-sex desire that continues to this day.
Straight culture's fear of queer increase—what I will call *homosexual reproduction*—impels the question of what causes homosexuality. Antigay voices assert
that it results from seduction, recruitment, contagion, or bad influence. In
their response, queer communities have increasingly claimed homosexuality
as immutable and essential, citing theories of biological determinism based
on studies of genetics or prenatal hormones, or more colloquially, maintaining that we are "born gay."[1] But why should etiology—the science of causes—
dominate arguments about gay and lesbian equity?

---

1. See, for example, Wilson and Rahman.

The problem is not how we answer the etiological question but the fact that we continue to ask it. Etiology is burdened by literary and scientific conventions: chronological sequence, the implication of pathology, focus on the deviant individual, presupposition of scientific rationality, and the putative closure of meaning. Only by seeing the etiology of homosexuality as a narrative form—as in the origin myth, the case study, the detective plot—can we denaturalize it and think causality differently. Take, for example, *The Picture of Dorian Gray*, an early narrative of queer etiology in which something called "influence" causes something not called, but fully legible as, homosexuality. Published in *Lippincott's Magazine* in 1890 and as a book in 1891, the novel foregrounds metonymic effects of proximity, persuasion, example, and imitation as the probable causes of Dorian's corruption. As Lord Henry explains, "to influence a person is to give him one's own soul. He does not think his natural thoughts, or burn with his natural passions" (40). Influence implies intimacy: as Stephen Guy-Bray notes, the term, "in Latin, literally, 'flowing in(to)'—could have literal and sexual connotations as well as metaphorical and mental ones" (xi).[2] Influence informs one of two divergent theories in *Dorian Gray*: one, a notion of innately homosexual persons consonant with the sexological notion of "congenital inversion," and two, a vocabulary of acquired perversion.[3] Both were available to Wilde. The concept of homosexuality predated *Dorian Gray* by two decades; coined in 1869 by Karl-Maria Benkert, it informed Victorian sexologists such as Karl Ulrichs. Noting the deployment of sexological theories of innate homosexuality in *Teleny*, written concurrently with *Dorian Gray*, Ed Cohen argues that Wilde would have been familiar with such models by 1890 ("Writing" 805).

Yet Wilde would also have known a quite different etiology, in which homosexual tendencies were suspected to be both acquired and acquisitive. Shortly before *Dorian Gray*, the notion of queer influence was prefigured in Henry James's *The Bostonians*, whose Verena Tarrant responds to the persuasion of Olive Chancellor: "The girl was now completely under her influence . . . the touch of Olive's tone worked a spell" (120).[4] Remaking Verena as a feminist, Olive makes them both embodiments of a particular, recognizable pathology, whose morbidity, Basil reflects, defines "such a type as that." The homosexual legibility of such relationships in the 1890s was evident at Wilde's first trial: prosecuting Counsel Charles Gill wrote that Lord Alfred Douglas should not be tried because Wilde's "strong influence" had made Douglas one of his "victims," and Director of Public Prosecution Hamilton

---

2. On seduction as influence, see also Hanson 268.

3. See Terry 44.

4. While James attributes strenuous persuasion to Basil Ransom as well, the notion of influence is primarily feminine in *The Bostonians*.

Cuffe asserted that Wilde's "great influence" over Douglas had "induced him to enter on these evil practices" (Holland 294, 296). Queensberry's attorney Edward Carson explained that his client "was trying to free his son from the influence of this man," an influence that amounted to "the domination by Mr Wilde of this unfortunate Lord Alfred Douglas" (Holland 262). Readily available for paranoid reading, influence is, according to the *OED*, "the exertion of action of which the operation is unseen or insensible (or perceptible only in its effects), by one person or thing upon another." But the juxtaposition of visible effects with invisible causes is precisely what Wilde's notion of influence does *not* entail; on the contrary, *Dorian Gray* gives us visible causes and invisible effects. While its rhetoric of influence recalls anxieties about homosexual reproduction, the text's reticence around the meaning of Dorian's deviance makes it impossible to specify—though speculation is rife—the effect of which Lord Henry, Basil Hallward, or the yellow book is the cause.

The peculiar status of queer desire in the novel has everything to do with the etiological questions set in motion by Wilde's extended meditation on influence and the eventual collapse of its narrative logic. Homosexuality first appears in the text as the missing second term of a causal sequence, the presumed but unproven effect of so much bad influence, but it also functions as the absent cause of the novel, its invisible motive. In *Dorian Gray*, that is, homosexuality operates much like Lacan's unconventional forms of causality, the absent and retroactive causes capable of impossible effects. For Lacan, the Real is both a byproduct of the Symbolic order and its retroactive cause, much as queerness is the constitutive outside and the internal resistance of the heteronormative Symbolic order, the externalized fantasy of what is in fact an internal failure. As a positive term, homosexuality could not normally be compared to the Real, whose essential impossibility aligns it with the negativity of queerness; yet in *Dorian Gray* it is the paradoxical absent presence of gay desire that allows it to constitute, like the Real, a retroactive or "lost" cause. As such, the text's causality is profoundly recursive, lacking a point of origin and vacating sequential temporality. Indeed, the novel's homosexuality "returns from the future" when *Dorian Gray* is read through the lens of Wilde's fate and subsequent forms of gay identity (Žižek, *Sublime* 57); the text determines the future that only later will make it decidedly queer.

"Strange Rumours"

While *Dorian Gray* alludes to homosexual reproduction, that is only one of the many causal narratives that Wilde sets in motion. From one perspective, it is unclear whether Dorian changes at all. True, at their first meeting Lord

Henry sees him as immaculate—"All the candour of youth was there, as well as all youth's passionate purity. One felt that he had kept himself unspotted from the world" (39). Accordingly, the novel's first chapter sets the scene for a fall from Eden, its garden rich with "tremulous branches" of laburnum (23), but tautologically, to inhabit this scene one must already have fallen from grace. The garden always contains the cause of its own annihilation, much as Dorian already manifests the weakness that will motivate his terrible wish. At the same time, the text insists that Dorian responds to some obscure external force. Awash in superfluous causes, Dorian is doomed by his family legacy, trapped by a Faustian wish, tempted by Lord Henry's bad influence, and lured by reckless reading. Dorian, we are told, "loved to stroll through the gaunt cold picture-gallery of his country house and look at the various portraits of those whose blood flowed in his veins" (175). Acknowledging the possibility of "strange legacies of thought and passion," Dorian wonders whether a "strange poisonous germ" in his family line has made him "so suddenly, and almost without cause" utter "the mad prayer that had so changed his life" (175).

Yet having entertained that idea, Wilde is quick to turn away, evoking a queerer form of inheritance: "one had ancestors in literature, as well as in one's own race, nearer perhaps in type and temperament, many of them, and certainly with an influence of which one was more absolutely conscious" (176).[5] After the drama of Sibyl Vane's death and his banishment of the portrait to the schoolroom, Dorian idly picks up a "yellow book" that Lord Henry has given him, "a novel without a plot" whose fascination lies instead in its "curious jewelled style" and its character study of a man very like Dorian. The book seems capable of a mesmeric influence on its reader, for the "reverie" and "malady of dreaming" it inspires in Dorian last far beyond its final pages (156). What does it mean to say that "Dorian Gray had been poisoned by a book" (179) in a book about perilous exposures, a book that returns obsessively to questions of influence? What we might call an epidemiological theory of reading posits immoral suasion as endlessly contagious, replicating its effects on characters, the text itself, and finally Wilde's own readers. When Lord Henry recalls "a book that he had read when he was sixteen, a book which had revealed to him much that he had not known before" (43), he evokes a textual genealogy that extends from his own reading to Dorian's reading, and in turn to our reading

---

5. Stephen Kern initially criticizes Wilde's "heavy-handed ancestral explanations for his murderer," but goes on to acknowledge a more complex causality at work in the novel (39, 317–18). Kern's conclusions follow from his choice to read the novel as a murder plot; a rather different causal system would emerge from *Dorian Gray* as a narrative of secret sexual identity.

of Wilde. Wilde himself seems caught in the chain of abyssal reading: when six years later, in *De Profundis,* he calls Pater's *Studies in the History of the Renaissance* the "book which has had such a strange influence over my life," we cannot say whether he recognizes himself in the book or remakes himself in its image (Novak 72). Similarly, the yellow book fails to explain Dorian's fall. We are told that "for years, Dorian Gray could not free himself from the influence of this book. Or perhaps it would be more accurate to say that he never sought to free himself from it" (158). Upon that "or" turns the problem of causality. After all, the influence one seeks out and embraces is not an influence at all, but a reflection of one's extant leanings. As the portrait's degeneration confirms, Dorian is already corrupt before he opens the yellow book, well toward the end of the novel. Perhaps, as Wilde suggests, it is not that the book makes Dorian like its protagonist, but that Dorian's likeness to its protagonist makes him love the book, taking its hero as "a kind of prefiguring type of himself," so much so that "the whole book seemed to him to contain the story of his own life, written before he had lived it" (158).

However, the influence with which the novel is most concerned is not literary but personal. Basil Hallward credits Dorian with changing his aesthetic perception when "some subtle influence passed from him to me" (33) but warns Lord Henry: "Don't try to influence him" (36). His interest piqued, Dorian asks Lord Henry "Have you really a very bad influence?" and is told "There is no such things as a good influence, Mr Gray . . . all influence is immoral" (40). Moments later, Dorian "was dimly conscious that entirely fresh influences were at work within him. Yet they seemed to him to have come really from himself" (42)—a paradox that will echo in Dorian's assessment of the yellow book. Later in their acquaintance, Henry reflects that "there was something terribly enthralling in the exercise of influence" (60), planning to extend his reach: "He would seek to dominate him—had already, indeed half done so" (61). Dorian freely confirms that power, telling Henry "You have a curious influence over me" (77). While this rhetoric opens *Dorian Gray* to a familiar anxiety about homosexual reproduction—the supposed ability of queers to make more queers—the text cannot name the effect of which bad influence is the cause. Wilde takes Lord Henry's seduction of Dorian to the utmost verge of plausible deniability: Dorian feels that Henry's words "had touched some secret chord that had never been touched before, but that he felt was now vibrating and throbbing to curious pulses" (42). The altered portrait attests to his "cruelty" (119), "sin," "ruin" (125), "evil" (159), and "foulness" (173), and he is the subject of "strange rumours" hinting of "dishonour" (159), which cause men to "whisper to each other in corners, or pass him with a sneer" (173). Basil and Dorian both acknowledge that they have secrets;

Dorian knows "the terrible pleasure of a double life" (210). And the designation of Basil's love for Dorian—the source of his own "double life"—as "such love as Michael Angelo had known, and Montaigne, and Winckelmann, and Shakespeare himself" (149) shows an effort to imagine a male homosexual tradition. It is Basil, appropriately, who calls Dorian "fatal to young men," reminding him of "that wretched boy in the Guards who committed suicide," another man "who had to leave England, with a tarnished name," and yet another who met a "dreadful end" (183), suggesting Dorian's ability to communicate to others the influences that have worked on him.

From the novel's first publication to the present day, readers have seen in it the possibility of a homosexuality that remains ineffable, at once present and absent, not only as a function of semantic delicacy but, as we shall see, through the very structure of the novel's causality. As Paul Morrison writes, "Homosexuality is presumed to be at the root of all Dorian's actions, but how do we know what we all think we know, even if that knowledge characteristically goes under the gentlemanly decorum of 'it goes without saying?'" (18). Joseph Bristow notes "the notorious invisibility—and yet unwavering implication" of homosexuality in *Dorian Gray* ("Complex" 204); and Ellis Hanson finds that Dorian's misdeeds "are apparent without being certain" (210). Wilde's contemporaries felt much the same, to judge by a series of hostile reviews, one of which prompted retailer W. H. Smith to withdraw its copies of the book. Samuel Jeyes's 1890 review in the *St James's Gazette,* as well as his later published dialogue with Wilde, identified the text and its topic as perverse; noting its "esoteric prurience," Jeyes observed that *Dorian Gray* "constantly hints, not obscurely, at disgusting sins and abominable crimes" (Beckson 68).[6] A review in the *Daily Chronicle* charged that the novel indulges in "every form of secret and unspeakable vice," and should we wonder how many forms of vice were deemed unspeakable, *Punch* identifies Dorian as a "Ganymede-like" figure (Beckson 73, 75). On the text's 1891 publication as a book, a review in the *Athenaeum* called it "unmanly, sickening, vicious (though not exactly what is called 'improper'), and tedious" (Beckson 82). Each reader attempts to register his recognition of sexual impropriety while unable to declare, and thus decisively to condemn, the nature of that transgression. In 1964, U.S. Supreme Court Justice Potter Stewart famously asserted that even if he could not define "hard-core" pornography, "I know it when I see it," and much the same logic is at work in readers' responses to *Dorian Gray,* whether past or present, appalled or approving.[7]

---

6. Jeyes refers to the *Lippincott's Magazine* version of the novel.

7. Jacobellis v. Ohio, 378 U.S. 184 (1964).

In Wilde's case, however, we know homosexuality when we *do not* see it; the very occlusion of Dorian's actions in the novel opens them to modern sexual epistemologies. Hanson suggests that during the trials, "despite Wilde's vagueness, his circumlocution, his intentional obscurity, the novel was thought to be . . . sufficient evidence of very specific sexual crimes" (290). Regarding this collocation of secrecy and specificity, Eve Kosofsky Sedgwick argues that by the close of the nineteenth century, when "knowledge meant sexual knowledge, and secrets sexual secrets, there had in fact developed one particular sexuality that was distinctively constituted *as* secrecy" (*Epistemology* 73).[8] Striving to articulate the structure of this open secret, other readers invoke absence and lack. In Jeffrey Nunokawa's words, homosexuality constitutes a "desire whose subject is finally nowhere and thus everywhere at once" ("Disappearance" 189). Bristow concurs: due to "the notorious invisibility—and yet unwavering implication" of homosexuality in *Dorian Gray,* "the modern notion of 'homosexuality is nowhere proved and yet everywhere suspected" ("A Complex" 204, 210). Similarly, Richard Ellman writes, it is "not that all Wilde's principals are homosexuals, but they are scarcely anything else" (319).

Because the text cannot specify what effects follow from Dorian's many influences, that elision becomes a site of readerly projection. In a published reply to the negative review in the *Scots Observer,* a document later cited at his trial, Wilde described his attempt "to surround Dorian Gray with an atmosphere of moral corruption . . . . To keep this atmosphere vague and indeterminate and wonderful was the aim" (Sinfield 101). So strongly does this strategy resemble James's account of the indeterminacy in his 1898 novella *The Turn of the Screw* that one may suspect an influence of another kind. In his preface to the New York edition of *Turn,* James writes:

> Only make the reader's general vision of evil intense enough, I said to myself—and that is already a charming job—and his own experience, his own imagination, his own sympathy . . . will supply him quite sufficiently with all the particulars. Make him think the evil, make him think it for himself, and you are released from weak specifications. (128)

There is no evil in the text, James implies, except what the reader brings with him, the projected stuff of his and his culture's particular terrors. As a result, Shoshana Felman observes, "*we are forced to participate in the scandal . . .* the

---

8. Sedgwick calls *Dorian Gray* "the perfect rhetorical distillation of the open secret, the glass closet, shaped by the conjunction of an extravagance of deniability and an extravagance of flamboyant display" (*Epistemology* 165).

scandal is not simply *in* the text, it resides in our *relation to* the text" (97). I will return to the reader's part shortly, but first it is worth noting Wilde's articulation of this idea. Recalling an axiom spoken by Lord Henry, "The books that the world calls immoral are books that show the world its own shame" (257), in his reply to the *Scots Observer,* Wilde insists that "each man sees his own sin in *Dorian Gray.* What Dorian Gray's sins are no one knows. He who finds them has brought them" (Bristow, "Wilde" 53). He reiterated this point in the courtroom: asked whether Dorian Gray's sins may include sodomy, Wilde responded: "That is according to the temper of each one who reads the book; he who has found the sin has brought it" (Holland 78).[9] Though James was not known for his support of Wilde, he grasped Wilde's narrative strategy only too well. In an 1892 letter to a friend, he discusses *Lady Winder-mere's Fan* in terms that might well describe *Dorian Gray:* "Everything Oscar does," he writes, "is a deliberate trap for the literalist, and to see the literalist walk straight up to it, look straight at it, and step straight into it makes one freshly avert a discouraged gaze from this unspeakable animal" (Donoghue 235). When in *The Turn of the Screw* James echoes his remark on Wilde, insisting that "The story *won't* tell . . . not in any literal, vulgar way," he has truly inherited the position of his rival (3).

Just Cause

Lingering in the mode of perpetual beginning and concluding only with arbitrary violence, *Dorian Gray* charges its reader with the impossible task of deriving effect from cause, contrary to the normal sequence. As we know, the narrative form of a conventional etiological study resembles that of a mystery novel with the doctor in the role of detective; Philip Rieff compares Freud, the "master of detection," to Sherlock Holmes (viii, xii). Whether scientific, psychoanalytic, or literary, such investigations are fundamentally linear: given a phenomenon—say, the hysteria of Freud's Dora or the plumage of Darwin's male bird of paradise—they work backward to determine the cause. In such origin narratives, Freud will identify sexual dysfunction at the root of hysteria and Darwin will name sexual selection as the reason for the bird's display. But as Freud explains in an 1896 essay,

> The area of occurrence of an aetiological factor may be freely allowed to
> be wider than of its effect, but it must not be narrower. Not everyone who

---

9. Wilde admits that for the book publication he altered a passage that "would convey the impression that the sin of Dorian Gray was sodomy" (Holland 78–79).

touches or comes near a smallpox patient develops smallpox; nevertheless infection from a smallpox patient is almost the only known aetiology of the disease. (3:192)

Etiological narrative can find the earlier cause of a given effect, but it cannot know the eventual effects of a specific cause; it can explain the present by looking to the past, but it cannot predict what is to come.

Reflecting this failed etiology, *Dorian Gray* withholds, in several senses, the satisfaction of narrative closure. Unable to name the nature of Dorian's change, the broken narrative offers cause after unending cause. Most of the 1891 text's twenty chapters detail the formation or deformation of his character, offering a protracted prologue for a plot that effectively begins with Dorian's murder of Basil in chapter 13. Between two unrelated acts of arbitrary violence, Basil's murder and Dorian's suicide, the last portion of the narrative provides a generous wadding of irrelevant scenes. Surely the refusal of narrative progress has its own meaning, but no reader, I wager, savors Lady Narborough's "tedious party" or tea-time with the Duchess of Monmouth (211). Nor is there much reason for James Vane's sudden return, or much satisfaction in his accidental death, a third act of arbitrary violence. Appropriately, a narrative set in motion by Dorian's wish to avoid his own end finds itself equally averse to conclusion. Narrative conventions, of course, align closely with sexual conventions, in the marriage plot and beyond. As Judith Roof explains, "while healthy heterosexuality produces the proper reproductive narrative—like reproducing like and increasing (similar to well-invested capital)—perversions produce the wrong story: decrease, degenerescence, death" (35). No wonder, then, that readers have found in *Dorian Gray* a maddening perversion of novelistic form. John Paul Riquelme observes that "in this narrative garden of forking paths, there appears to be a virus that replicates itself in double, antithetical forms within a maze that leads us not to an exit but to an impasse" (616). Kevin Ohi notes that "while not, perhaps, 'a novel without a plot,' it does move in circles, rushing toward where it has already preemptively been" (81). Nunokawa is more blunt, declaring: "the book is boring . . . long stretches of the story are almost unbearably uninteresting" ("Importance" 151).[10] And if it is dull or circular, *Dorian Gray* owes that narrative dysfunction to its reversal of etiological conventions.

If homosexuality is an absent effect in *Dorian Gray,* it is also an absent cause. Presenting an absence that *is* homosexuality, rather than a mere absence *of* homosexuality, the novel evokes Lacan's impossible causality: a

---

10. For his part, Ellman calls portions of the novel "wooden, padded, self-indulgent" (314).

cause that both does and does not exist, with a capacity for retroactive effects. If in scientific etiology events are "understood as leading smoothly, in accordance with well-known 'laws,' to other events," Bruce Fink writes, "Lacan understands cause in a more radical sense, as that which disrupts the smooth functioning of lawlike interactions" (31). Refusing teleology and closure, he divorces causality from scientific logic and evacuates its accustomed clinical function. Unlike Freud, who sees symptoms as effects of unconscious repression, Lacan argues that "the cause of the unconscious . . . must be conceived as, fundamentally, a lost cause" (128). Something in the unconscious produces symptoms, but that cause remains opaque and inaccessible. What Lacan calls the Real is a stubborn node of unsymbolizable matter in the Symbolic order—in Slavoj Žižek's words, "a cause which in itself does not exist—which is present only in a series of effects, but always in a distorted, displaced way" (*Sublime* 163). As such, "the Real is the absent cause of the Symbolic" because it determines by opposition what the Symbolic order will privilege as presence, meaning, and the Law (*Metastases* 30).[11] The Real perversely defines the Symbolic order within which it appears absent. Žižek explains: "Although it does not exist (in the sense of 'really existing,' taking place in reality), [the Real] has a series of properties—it exercises a certain structural causality, it can produce a series of effects in the symbolic reality of subjects" (*Sublime* 163). That is precisely the ontological status of homosexuality in *Dorian Gray*: it cannot be proven to exist and yet it produces effects. Morrison offers a similar reading of that paradox, calling the place of homosexuality in *Dorian Gray* "an impossible epistemological quandary" that is "meant to underwrite the ontological incoherence, the essential nonbeing, of its object" (44).

When traditional etiology puts effects before causes, it fails to describe the backward narrative of *Dorian Gray*, to which homosexuality arrives belatedly as a retroactive cause. Renata Salecl argues that in Seminars XI and XX, Lacanian causality entails a temporal reversal: "the 'primary' element becomes delineated retroactively through the operation of the 'secondary' element, in which the primary is included, albeit as a foreign body" (133). As a retroactive cause, the Real is both the prerequisite for and the result of the Symbolic, and homosexuality is the retroactive cause of *Dorian Gray*. Here time runs backward, and not only because the portrait, as if to literalize Freud's theory of deferred action, suspends the effects of time on its subject.

---

11. Žižek's language differs from Lacan's: while Žižek repeatedly refers to the "absent cause" of the unconscious, for Lacan causality occupies an impossible position between existence and nonexistence (*Four* 128). Nonetheless, Lacan's terms for unconscious causality consistently involve negativity and lack: "hole," "split," and "gap" (*Four* 22).

Where sexuality is concerned the novel's causality becomes tautological, as Wilde himself becomes an effect of the text. Having read *Dorian Gray*, Alfred Douglas was eager to meet its author in July 1891, and at their next visit Wilde gave Douglas a special copy (Holland xvi). As a token of erotic exchange, the book became a cause or impetus for Wilde's eventual fate, which would in turn alter the text itself. When in the courtroom Carson asked whether the passage describing Dorian Gray as "fatal to young men" referred to sodomy, Wilde replied, "The passage you have read describes Dorian Gray as a man of very corrupt influence. There is no statement about what the nature of his bad influence was, nor do I think there is such a thing as bad influence in the world"—presumably as opposed to its role in fiction (Holland 102).[12] That evasion notwithstanding, the trial was all about influence and its relation to sodomy, if in a circular fashion: *Dorian Gray* showed Wilde to be a sodomite, whereas Wilde's crime remade Dorian in its own image. Bad influence, it seems, proliferates: a novel whose protagonist is famously malleable is itself blamed for ruining Douglas and other readers, betraying its author's power within and beyond the text. Historical exigencies have made *Dorian Gray* both a product and a precursor of Wilde's downfall. Sedgwick is right to note Wilde's "hyper-indicativeness as a figure of his age," but that representative function in no way obviates his role as a figure of ages to come (*Tendencies* 151). For modern readers, the cause of Dorian's desire has come not from the text but from its future, reflecting Wilde's 1895 trials and twentieth-century models of gay male identity.

To say, as Wilde did, that "each man sees his own sin in *Dorian Gray*" is to say that each man sees his own desire, and a century of readers have done just that. The text's backward causality includes both the ways in which later readers' identificatory energies become the belated cause of Dorian's homosexuality and the role of the Wilde trials in producing a public discourse of gay identity through which *Dorian Gray* would then be read. The most careful reader of *Dorian Gray* cannot help but bring to the novel her knowledge of what will follow, what has already followed. Christopher Craft suggests that the narcissistic doubling of Dorian and his portrait is reflected once again in readers' relation to "the uncanny looking glass we call *The Picture of Dorian Gray*" (132). Audrey Jaffe argues that readings of *Dorian Gray* which link the text to modern gay identity make Dorian's beauty "a kind of projection into the future" (301). But to see any part of the novel as a "projection into the future" requires a projection into the past: the novel has been subject, in Nunokawa's words, to an "*après coup* canonization as an Old Testament version

---

12. See also Bristow, "Wilde" 52.

of the exodus from the closet" ("Disappearance" 185). Alan Sinfield too associates *Dorian Gray* with anachronistic reading effects, noting that Wilde's "typicality is after the fact" (103, 3). In this circular causality, Wilde's life and works cause—that is, enable a way to articulate—the modern notions of gay identity that cause his life and works to "be" homosexual in the first place. By 1913 the eponymous hero of E. M. Forster's *Maurice* could confess that he is "an unspeakable of the Oscar Wilde sort," speaking his unspeakability in a language Wilde had authorized (Sinfield 3). Such temporally distorted reading-effects do not merely reflect the inevitable retrospection of a later reader's relation to a historically distant text, nor are they wholly driven by the desire of twentieth- and twenty-first-century readers for figures of gay experience. Instead, the strange narrative causality of *Dorian Gray* conscripts the reader to the impossible task of a backward etiology and informs twentieth-century projections of modern gay identity into a text that precedes them. Wilde's homosexuality both causes the gay male identity of the future and is caused by it; *Dorian Gray* both presages that role and is transformed by it.

Postscript

> If the post card is a kind of open letter (like all letters), one can always, in a time of peace and under certain regimes, attempt to make it indecipherable without compromising its making its way.
> —Jacques Derrida, *The Post Card*

Wilde's libel trial not only adduced *Dorian Gray* as evidence but also introduced a second queer inscription, the brief text that precipitated Wilde's suit against Alfred Douglas's irascible father and began the series of events leading to his destruction. On February 18, 1895, the Marquis of Queensberry came to the Albemarle Club in London, of which Wilde was a member. When he was refused entry, he wrote a message to Wilde on one of his calling cards and gave it to the hall porter.[13] The porter noted the time and date of its arrival on its back and put it in an envelope for Wilde, who received it on his visit to the club ten days later (Holland 4). The substance of that all but illegible text has been the subject of some debate. Queensberry may have written "For Oscar Wilde, posing as a somdomite," or perhaps "Poseur and Somdomite," or as the porter believed, "ponce and Somdomite." So contested is this question

---

13. For accounts of this incident, see Ellman 438; Bristow, "Complex" 200; and Donoghue 229, 241–42.

that not all scholars accept Queensberry's interpretation, during the first trial, of *his own note* as reading "posing as sodomite" (Holland 4).[14] The card is an "ambiguous" document in Queensberry's "scribbled," "scrawled," "none-too-legible hand" (Donoghue 241; Bronski 62; Cohen, "Wilde" 35). A perfunctory survey of Wilde scholarship turns up ten variant readings, distinguished by their form of address (For? To?), diction (Ponce? Posing? Poseur?), punctuation, capitalization, even the location of the message. During the trial Willie Mathews, an attorney for the prosecution, mistakenly described the card as reading on one side "'For Oscar Wilde, posing as sodomite,' whilst upon the other side of the card is either printed or lithographed the name and title of the Marquess of Queensberry." In fact, as the clerk of the court reminded him, the message to Wilde appears above Queensberry's name on the front of the card. Several scholars repeat the error, as if to restage the sodomite's supposed confusion of *recto* and *verso* (Holland 43).

Even considering its fateful role, the hermeneutic effort expended on this text is extraordinary: everyone agrees that the note is unreadable, everyone tries to read it, and everyone already knows what it means. But despite so many readings of Queensberry's unreadable message, in fact it has not been read closely enough. Consider the word "somdomite," which some critics regard as an "aristocratic misspelling" and others call "a moment of notorious illiteracy" (Ellman 438; Bristow, "Complex" 200). In court, Wilde's arch understatement—"The Marquess's spelling is somewhat unusual"—anticipated generations of queer scholars by whom superior literacy, not to say attitude, would be claimed as the privilege of the dispossessed. A century later, readers agree only that "somdomite" signifies "sodomite" (Kaufman 23). One effect of the calling card, then, is a disjunction between signifier and signified. Everyone knows, or thinks they know, *what* this text means, but they cannot tell *how* it means. Ellman anticipates a century of subsequent readers when he describes the porter at the Albemarle Club, who "had not deciphered the words—no one was to do so accurately—but he understood that an insult was intended" (438). How does one understand the indecipherable? What does illegibility itself mean? In an insightful reading, David Jays links the scribbled note to the historical questions haunting *Dorian Gray*: "Queensberry's blunder usefully reminds us that Wilde cannot easily be considered a modern homosexual. He is less a sod than a 'somd,' his own category of unique slippage that straddles the borders between Victorian *paterfamilias* and contemporary queer" (n.p.). Though Wilde's difference

---

14. This is the statement recorded in the transcript of the trial, although Ellman says Queensberry read the written message as "posing as a Somdomite" (438).

from the modern gay man recalls the commonplace understanding of the alterity of the past, Jays avoids the repressive hypothesis; instead of a Victorian silence, Queensberry's "somd" signals a surplus of meaning, a site of productive incoherence. For the card's brief message, ambiguity and error are significant in their own right.

The same vexed interpretation and radical undecidability describe the place of homosexuality in *The Picture of Dorian Gray*. Everyone says that it cannot be specified, and everyone attempts to read it nonetheless, confident that they know *what* the novel means even when they cannot say *how* it means. As texts whose meaning is, in Derrida's words for the postcard, both "open" and "indecipherable" at once, *The Picture of Dorian Gray* and Queensberry's calling card also share the dubious honor of their evidentiary appearance in Wilde's trial, where court proceedings extensively considered the relation between sodomy and interpretation (35). Defending Queensberry, Carson's opening speech assumed both the transparent legibility of homosexuality and the legitimacy of fiction as evidence: *Dorian Gray*, he said, "was designed and intended by Mr Wilde, and was understood by the readers thereof, to describe the relations, intimacies, and passions of certain persons of sodomitical and unnatural habits, tastes and practices" (Holland 39). In contrast, Wilde's attorney, Sir Edward Clarke, treated homosexuality as an open secret: *Dorian Gray*, he said, "describes—I will not say describes—it hints at and suggests, for it does not describe, vices and weaknesses of which Dorian Gray is guilty" (Holland 42). The difference between describing and hinting is the difference between certainty and doubt, clarity and ambiguity, the literal and the figural. Clarke's statement performs the same evasion it attributes to the novel, hinting at "sodomitical . . . habits" with "vices and weaknesses."

In Carson's view, interpretation is easy—the author's intent coincides exactly with the reader's understanding—but for Clarke the text forever evades the closure of meaning. Later in the proceedings, the issue returns:

CARSON: I will suggest to you *Dorian Gray*. Is that open to the interpretation of being a sodomitical book?

WILDE: Only to brutes—only to the illiterate.

CARSON: An illiterate person reading *Dorian Gray* might consider it a sodomitical book? (Holland 81)

Aligning sodomy with misinterpretation, Wilde disavows responsibility for what others may find in *Dorian Gray*, echoing his reply to the *Scots Observer*: "each man sees his own sin." But "an illiterate person reading" is at best paradoxical: the notion of illiterate reading as a figure for misinterpretation implies that some people read so badly that they are essentially not reading at all. This odd locution recalls the problem of Queensberry's calling card: here the illiterate and the illegible join in an unlikely hermeneutic project. It is not that the calling card's inscription is simply illegible; rather, like homosexuality in *Dorian Gray* it is both legible and illegible at once, easy enough to grasp but fundamentally resistant to meaning. Both are ambiguous, but the nature of their ambiguity is different: *Dorian Gray* does everything *but* name homosexuality, while Queensberry's message is all too easily reduced to "Wilde . . . sodomite." The calling card, accordingly, functions as a supplement, providing the signifier of homosexuality that the novel lacks; it is a postscript to *Dorian Gray,* a final chapter, which, though inscribed by another hand, works to rewrite the meaning of the text.

If the plot of the novel centers on the deferred action of Dorian's aging, this narrative device is repeated by temporal disturbances around the novel. Queensberry's calling card takes its place alongside the trials themselves and twentieth-century gay male identity as a site from which homosexuality "returns from the future" to *Dorian Gray.* The meaning of the 1890 novel comes to include, indeed *cannot exclude,* the narrative of Wilde's 1895 trials, and with it Queensberry's brief text. In the latter, the word "somdomite" purports to describe an existing person, but in fact it creates Wilde as that person, and it is Wilde's failed refusal of that interpellation that ensures its historical durability. Perversely, the card is also what causes Dorian Gray to "be" homosexual, for its insulting charge is the lens through which Wilde's previous writings will be read: some five years after the fact, it makes *Dorian Gray* and its eponymous protagonist the queer figures they will then have been all along. The chain of events set in motion by Queensberry's message causes the trials, which cause the exposure of Wilde's homosexuality, which belatedly causes the confirmation of the homosexuality of Dorian Gray, which is then returned as evidence against Wilde.

How then might this "lost," retroactive causality speak to more recent questions of queer etiology? If conventional etiology takes causality as its end, both antigay and "born gay" theories make causality *a means to an end,* a way to promote an ideological cause. But the fixation on the lost biological cause of homosexuality—"gay genes," "born gay"—is itself a lost cause, useless to advance queer equity. *Dorian Gray* invites us to imagine the relation between queerness and etiology differently, replacing the question of *what causes homosexuality* with that of *what homosexuality causes.* What then does homosexuality cause? Wilde offers two answers. *Dorian Gray* suggests that homosexuality *causes itself,* as if to elaborate, without apology, the myth of queer parthenogenesis. Perversion causes more perversion, recursively and perpetually circling back on itself, spreading its bad influence among characters, readers, the courtroom, Wilde himself, and later gay culture. Beyond Wilde's text as well, homosexuality perpetuates itself asexually, horizontally, promiscuously, in gay and lesbian cultures and identities. Yet Dorian Gray also insists that something more accurately called queerness proliferates in all its negativity, absence, impossibility. In heteronormative culture homosexuality may be "unspeakable," as Forster put it, but it also functions to stabilize a network of intelligible sexual identities, not least its own, whereas queerness is called to account for the inadequacy of the order within which it remains a "foreign body." This "lost cause," then, exerts its own—as Wilde might say—strange influence, pitting the closure of etiological narratives against the queerness of sexuality as such.

Works Cited

Beckson, Karl. *Oscar Wilde: The Critical Heritage.* New York: Routledge, 1997.

Biron, Charles. "Judgment." *Palatable Poison: Critical Perspectives on* The Well of Loneliness. Ed. Laura Doan and Jay Prosser. New York: Columbia UP, 2001. 39–49.

Bowie, Malcolm. *Lacan.* Cambridge: Harvard UP, 1991.

Bristow, Joseph. "'A Complex Multiform Creature': Wilde's Sexual Identities." *The Cambridge Companion to Oscar Wilde.* Ed. Peter Raby. Cambridge: Cambridge UP, 1997. 195–218.

———. "Wilde, *Dorian Gray,* and Gross Indecency." *Sexual Sameness: Textual Differences in Lesbian and Gay Writing.* Ed. Bristow. New York: Routledge, 1992. 44–63.

Bronski, Michael. *Culture Clash: The Making of Gay Sensibility.* Boston: South End Press, 1984.

Cohen, Ed. "Wilde, Wit, and the Ways of Man." *Performance and Cultural Politics.* Ed. Elin Diamond. New York: Routledge, 1996. 35–47.

———. "Writing Gone Wilde: Homoerotic Desire in the Closet of Representation." *PMLA* 102: 5 (1987): 801–13.

Craft, Christopher. "Come See About Me: Enchantment of the Double in *The Picture of Dorian Gray.*" *Representations* 91 (2005): 109–36.

Derrida, Jacques. *The Post Card: From Socrates to Freud and Beyond.* Trans. Alan Bass. Chicago: U of Chicago P, 1987.

Donoghue, Denis. *England, Their England: Commentaries on English Language and Literature.* New York: Knopf, 1988.

Ellman, Richard. *Oscar Wilde.* New York: Knopf, 1987.

Felman, Shoshana. "Turning the Screw of Interpretation." *Literature and Psychoanalysis: The Question of Reading: Otherwise.* Ed. Felman. Baltimore: Johns Hopkins UP, 1977. 94–207.

Fink, Bruce. *The Lacanian Subject.* Princeton: Princeton UP, 1995.

Freud, Sigmund. "The Aetiology of Hysteria" (1896). *The Standard Edition of the Complete Psychological Works of Sigmund Freud.* Trans. and ed. James Strachey. 24 vols. London: Hogarth, 1953–74. Vol. 3. 189–221.

Guy-Bray, Stephen. *Loving in Verse: Poetic Influence as Erotic.* Toronto: U of Toronto P, 2006.

Hanson, Ellis. *Decadence and Catholicism.* Cambridge: Harvard UP, 1997.

Holland, Merlin. *The Real Trial of Oscar Wilde.* New York: Harper Perennial, 2004.

Jaffe, Audrey. "Embodying Culture: Dorian's Wish." *Aesthetic Subjects.* Ed. Pamela Matthews and David McWhirter. Minneapolis: U of Minnesota P, 2003. 295–312.

James, Henry. *The Bostonians.* New York: Bantam, 1984.

———. "Preface to the New York Edition." *The Turn of the Screw: A Norton Critical Edition.* 2nd ed. Ed. Deborah Esch and Jonathan Warren. New York: Norton, 1999. 123–29.

Jays, David. "Wilde Disappointment." *New Statesman.com.* 25 Sept. 2000. http://www.newstatesman.com/node/138631. Accessed 19 Sept. 2013.

Kaufman, Moisés. *Gross Indecency: The Three Trials of Oscar Wilde.* New York: Vintage, 1998.

Kern, Stephen. *A Cultural History of Causality: Science, Murder Novels, and Systems of Thought.* Princeton: Princeton UP, 2004.

Lacan, Jacques. *The Four Fundamental Concepts of Psycho-Analysis.* Ed. Jacques-Alain Miller. Trans. Alan Sheridan. New York: Norton, 1981.

Morrison, Paul. *The Explanation for Everything: Essays on Sexual Subjectivity.* New York: NYU P, 2001.

Novak, Daniel. "Sexuality in the Age of Technological Reproducibility: Oscar Wilde, Photography, and Identity." *Oscar Wilde and Modern Culture: The Making of a Legend.* Ed. Joseph Bristow. Athens: Ohio UP, 2008. 63–95.

Nunokawa, Jeffrey. "The Disappearance of the Homosexual in *The Picture of Dorian Gray.*" *Professions of Desire: Lesbian and Gay Studies in Literature.* Ed. George Haggerty and Bonnie Zimmerman. New York: Modern Language Association of America, 1995. 183–90.

———. "The Importance of Being Bored: The Dividends of Ennui in *The Picture of Dorian Gray.*" *Novel Gazing: Queer Readings in Fiction.* Ed. Eve Kosofsky Sedgwick. Durham: Duke UP, 1997. 151–66.

Ohi, Kevin. *Innocence and Rapture: The Erotic Child in Pater, Wilde, James, and Nabokov.* New York: Palgrave Macmillan, 2005.

Rieff, Philip. "Introduction." *Dora: An Analysis of a Case of Hysteria.* Ed. Rieff. New York: Touchstone, 1997. vii–xix.

Riquelme, John Paul. "Oscar Wilde's Aesthetic Gothic: Walter Pater, Dark Enlightenment, and *The Picture of Dorian Gray.*" *Modern Fiction Studies* 46.3 (2000): 609–31.

Roof, Judith. *Come As You Are: Sexuality and Narrative.* New York: Columbia UP, 1996.

Salecl, Renata. "Love Anxieties." *Reading Seminar XX: Lacan's Major Work on Love, Knowledge, and Feminine Sexuality.* Ed. Suzanne Barnard and Bruce Fink. Albany: State U of New York P, 2002. 93–98.

Sedgwick, Eve Kosofsky. *Epistemology of the Closet.* Berkeley: U of California P, 1990.

———. *Tendencies.* Durham: Duke UP, 1993.

Sinfield, Alan. *The Wilde Century: Effeminacy, Oscar Wilde, and the Queer Movement.* New York: Columbia UP, 1994.

Terry, Jennifer. *An American Obsession: Science, Medicine, and Homosexuality in Modern Society.* Chicago: U of Chicago P, 1999.

Wilde, Oscar. *The Picture of Dorian Gray.* New York: Penguin, 1985.

Wilson, Glenn, and Qazi Rahman. *Born Gay: The Science of Sex Orientation.* London: Peter Owen, 2004.

Žižek, Slavoj. *The Metastases of Enjoyment: Six Essays on Woman and Causality.* New York: Verso, 1994.

———. *The Sublime Object of Ideology.* New York: Verso, 1989.

SUSAN FRAIMAN

Gendered Narratives in Animal Studies

This essay brings together four extremely short stories—anecdotes, really—about animals and animality. The creatures we will meet include a cat, a baboon, a pony, and an assortment of scholars. Settings range from a bathroom to a barbecue, from the plains of Kenya to small-town New York. In their original contexts, my tales are all first-person, autobiographical fragments located within larger critical or theoretical arguments, where they serve variously as introduction, conclusion, digression, or illustration. Extricated and assembled here, I call upon them as allegories of sorts, but not the kind in which animals stand in for people. They are scenes, rather, of animals *in relation* to people. I offer them as figures for different ways of imagining this relationship, a topic currently preoccupying scholars across the disciplines in the burgeoning area of "animal studies."[1] I also examine them as specifically gendered narratives—gendered in a way related but not reducible to the gender of their actual author. Other narrative features at work in their coding as "masculine" or "feminine" include the gender of the narrator, the gender of the principals, the affective tenor of the episode, and what we might

---

1. My reference is to "animal studies" in its broadest, contemporary sense to mean the sprawling, multidisciplinary field known by some as "animality studies" or "human-animal studies," and not to be confused with the scientific usage meaning lab studies involving animals. For simplicity's sake, I will generally be using "animal" to mean "nonhuman animal."

see as the "comic" or "tragic" arc of their miniature plots. I am interested, too, in the way their short, personal, specific, and quotidian nature lends all of them a "feminine" cast, especially given their interpolation within contrasting scholarly narratives generally assumed, by definition, to be sustained, objective, abstract, and thereby "masculine."

In addition to considering my stories as gendered narratives, several other aspects of my project resonate with feminist procedures and aims more broadly speaking. My ultimate goal is a feminist critique of the way gender operates to value some paradigms in animal studies over others—according less prestige to those marked as "feminine."[2] As a counter to this biased pattern of academic reception, I also model the feminist strategy of recuperation: recovering the contributions of a particular woman as well as, in this case, the larger feminist context for her work on animals. Finally, it is typically feminist to demonstrate not only the stubborn salience of gender categories but also, within and across texts, their complexity and instability: that "women" refers to a highly differentiated group; that "masculine" and "feminine" do not always adhere to male and female bodies. We will circle back later to these general, theoretical issues, but first I want to explore them by means of particular readings, tracking the effects of gender in animal anecdotes by four scholars: Continental philosopher Jacques Derrida, primatologist Barbara Smuts, feminist-vegetarian theorist and activist Carol Adams, and feminist philosopher of science Donna Haraway.

Story #1: Derrida's Cat

I begin with Jacques Derrida's memorable anecdote in "L'Animal que donc je suis (à suivre)." Originally given as a talk in 1997, "L'Animal" was published five years later in English as "The Animal That Therefore I Am (More to Follow)."[3] Derrida does not, of course, proceed in linear fashion from begin-

---

2. This critique is more fully elaborated in a longer version of this essay, "Pussy Panic versus Liking Animals: Tracking Gender in Animal Studies," *Critical Inquiry* (2012). There, my four stories frame an extended reading of work by animal studies scholar Cary Wolfe, whose prominence in both the 2009 animal issue of *PMLA* and a subsequent piece in *The Chronicle of Higher Education* suggest his role as leading spokesperson for the field. Noting that Wolfe has been nominated to define what *counts* as the new animal studies, I take him to task for two things: suppressing important ecofeminist precursors in favor of Jacques Derrida, whom Wolfe names as animal studies' founding father; and formulating his "posthumanist" work on animals not only at the expense of ecofeminism but also in explicit opposition to emotionally and politically engaged work on gender, race, and sexuality.

3. "L'Animal que donc je suis (à suivre)" kicked off a series of talks given by Derrida at Cérisy-la-Salle. The English translation by David Wills first appeared in *Critical Inquiry* (2002).

ning to end. He prefers instead to tease us with multiple versions embedded in thickets of puns, repetitions, speculations, and asides. We are warned from the outset that there will be nudity. The basic plot, we learn soon enough, involves a cat who has occasion to look at our philosopher—indeed, to study him coolly as he stands there naked, and not from the side either. Gazed upon so directly by this unabashed creature, Derrida reacts with embarrassment, compounded by shame at feeling so: "And why this shame that blushes for being ashamed? Especially, I should make clear, if the cat observes me frontally naked, face to face, and if I am naked faced with the cat's eyes looking at me as it were from head to toe, just *to see,* not hesitating to concentrate its vision—in order to see, with a view to seeing—in the direction of my sex" (373). The cat in question, he will soon stipulate, "is a real cat, truly, believe me, *a little cat.* It isn't the *figure* of a cat" (374). The "sex" in this scene, we can only assume, is likewise "real" as well as densely symbolic—and it is, moreover, specifically male. It flinches slightly before the animal's riveted gaze; for while the cat looks without touching or biting, Derrida informs us "that threat remains on its lips or on the tip of the tongue" (373). The cat's look and man's blush will recur as a kind of refrain—a personal note recurring in the midst of extended theoretical speculations. A subsequent account elaborates on what is apparently a daily ritual: "The cat follows me when I wake up, into the bathroom, asking for her breakfast, but she demands to be let out of that room as soon as it (or she) sees me naked" (382). This passage leads directly to Derrida's stinging taxonomy, classing together those philosophers unable to acknowledge an animal's gaze. Later he will tie this refusal by post-Cartesians to be seen and addressed by animals to the Holocaust-like violence against them in the modern era (394–95). Citing Descartes, Kant, Heidegger, Lacan, and Lévinas as examples of those belonging to this category, Derrida inserts a striking proviso "(all those males but not all those females, and that difference is not insignificant here)" (382–83).

It is Derrida himself, then, who cues my efforts to articulate the "not insignificant" difference of gender as it functions in discussions of animality.[4] Toward the end of his remarks, attention to gender increases, and its closing paragraphs take the further step of imagining an unashamed "I" capable of presenting himself "in his totally naked truth. And in the naked truth, if

---

4. I use "gender" to indicate a logic organizing "Animal" above and beyond Derrida's characteristic play with the markers of sexual difference. For examples of feminist commentary on "sexual difference" in Derrida, see Leslie Rabine, "The Unhappy Hymen Between Feminism and Deconstruction" (1990); *Derrida and Feminism,* ed. Ellen K. Feder et al. (1997); *Feminist Interpretations of Jacques Derrida,* ed. Nancy Holland (1997); and Anne-Emmanuelle Berger, "Sexing Differances" (2005). As these various works demonstrate, a critique of individual texts does not preclude an appreciation for what Derridean concepts have to offer feminist theorists.

there is such a thing, of his or her sexual difference, of all their sexual differences" (418). Maneuvering beyond binarized to pluralized sexual differences, the conclusion of "Animal" thus echoes the well-known reverie at the end of "Choreographies": "I would like to believe in the multiplicity of sexually marked voices . . . this indeterminable number of blended voices" (108). I would like to believe in this too—and yet, despite several such de-binarizing moves in "Animal," I cannot forget the image of a self-consciously masculinized human, in his bathroom without a stitch, shamed by the gaze of a cat whose femaleness as well as realness is specified early on (375). Like the cat, I cannot help looking—in order to see, with a view to seeing—in the direction of the narrator's "sex." What does it mean to insist on seeing gender doggedly at work in "Animal"? What are the narrative elements that go to shape the gender identities, codes, and politics implicit in this and other works of animal studies? How is this body of scholarship, defined by its interest in animality, nevertheless saturated with notions about masculinity, femininity, and feminism—even (or especially) when not directly engaged with these categories? To pursue these questions, let us juxtapose Derrida's tale with an autobiographical snippet by Barbara Smuts.

Story #2: Barbara & Damien

Like Derrida, Smuts tells of an encounter between human and nonhuman animals in terms that are both highly personal and incipiently paradigmatic. Responding to J. M. Coetzee's *The Lives of Animals*—a fictional academic debate about animal rights—Smuts begins by observing that "none of the characters ever mentions a personal encounter with an animal" ("Reflections" 107). Deliberately eschewing "formal scientific discourse" (108), she prefers to draw on her own experiences as a scientist and pet owner. Ours is the first of two remedial tales, in which Smuts shifts from more general observations into precise mininarratives showing the possibilities of human–animal intimacy. In both cases, their self-contained, suspenseful story-ness is introduced by the phrase "one day," followed by a slowed-down, moment-to-moment chronology along with an increase in spatial particularity and sensory detail.[5] And now for the story that concerns us here. "One day," while living with and studying baboons in Kenya, Smuts finds herself fingertip to fingertip with a juvenile member of the troop. Her hand resting on a rock, she is surprised by

---

5. The second story tells of establishing a connection with a female gorilla, which culminates in an unexpected embrace ("Reflections" 114). Smuts's is one of four responses published alongside Coetzee's work in a 1999 volume edited by Amy Gutmann.

a gentle touch before turning to recognize "a slight fellow named Damien." As Smuts goes on to explain, "He looked intently into my eyes, as if to make sure that I was not disturbed by his touch, and then he proceeded to use his index finger to examine, in great detail, each one of my fingernails in turn. . . . After touching each nail, and without removing his finger, Damien glanced up at me for a few seconds. Each time our gaze met, I wondered if he, like I, was contemplating the implications of the realization that our fingers and fingernails were so alike" ("Reflections" 113).

As I need hardly observe, in Smuts's story, proper names and gendered pronouns serve to denominate the narrating human *female*, the encountered animal *male*. With its first-person, female speaker, it inverts what I have depicted as the relatively stable, normative gendering of Derrida's couple—a gendering that means to bare and implicate the speaker's masculinity along with his humanity, but which also has the further effect of staging a seemingly primal confrontation between masculinized human and feminized animal.[6] The two stories differ, moreover, in depicting and ranking the senses. True that Derrida's cat is accorded the power of the gaze: the singular, discerning "point of view" traditionally tied to cognition and reserved for humans. Yet the bathroom transaction overall—explicitly visual (and visually explicit) but definitely not tactile—leaves intact the old rationalist hierarchy valuing vision/mind/cognition over touch/body/emotion. Illustrating a tendency common to animal rights advocacy, though also routinely criticized, Derrida's cat is granted provisional subject status in implicitly humanist terms— ones that continue to reflect the premium placed by our own upright species on the "higher" faculties. Smuts's account, by contrast, effectively challenges this hierarchy—not only by prioritizing the meeting of fingertips, but also by undoing the opposition between touch and vision, showing instead how these senses overlap and collaborate to bridge the distance between baboon and biologist. As Smuts carefully notes, Damien's gaze adds another level of

---

6. Derrida knows his anecdote has the ring of a primal scene but insists he doesn't intend it as such (380). A further effect of Derrida's masculine first-person is slippage between "man" in the precise sense and "Man" as a false generic meaning "human." Uncertainty as to whether such slippage has occurred is a recurrent feature of "Animal" itself up until its last three pages, due in part to the discursive tradition Derrida engages; for an extended analysis of this equivocation, see Guenther. The problem gets worse in the layers of commentary and metacommentary surrounding Derrida's writing on animals, in which "Man" as representative human is all too easily renaturalized. See Fordham UP's overview of *The Animal That Therefore I Am* (2008), touting Derrida's critique of the distinction "between man as thinking animal and every other living species." Leonard Lawlor's *This Is Not Sufficient* is frequently ambiguous in its usage; at still one more remove, David Wood's blurb for Lawlor is not—Wood praises the author for tracing Derrida's "indictment of man's violence to (other) animals." (By contrast, Cary Wolfe makes a point of avoiding "man" as a false generic.)

contact but doesn't supersede his touch: he raises his eyes to check in visually without breaking the tactile bond. The intimacy thus sustained brings me, finally, to the most striking divergence between these two animal tales: their distinct affective tones and emotional conclusions.

As we have seen, Derrida's encounter is suffused with anxiety and, as he tells us repeatedly, a double dose of shame. This is certainly a reasonable response to our history of defining animals as killable, and Derrida's self-ironizing essay is superb in its wish to hold us accountable. The difference in the emotional and ethical emphasis of Smuts's story is nevertheless telling. The real-time pacing of her narrative, detailing each moment of tactile and visual contact, seems to replicate and reciprocate in formal terms the tentativeness, attentiveness, and tenderness of Damien's gestures toward her. The interaction it models is based on mutual care, in the sense of heightened awareness as well as solicitude. The emotional stance it describes is relaxed, wondering, open to animal overtures and meanings—this in contrast to Derrida's account of his nervous, sheepish impulse to cover himself. Indeed, as Donna Haraway has commented, Derrida's concerns about being exposed are so overwhelming that the cat herself is soon all but forgotten (*When* 20).[7]

This dynamic, whereby interest flips into incuriosity, would not surprise Silvan Tomkins, for whom retreat from another's gaze is the very definition of shameful response. As Tomkins explains, the shame response is marked by a lowering of the eyes that "calls a halt to looking" (Sedgwick and Frank 134). "Such a barrier," Tomkins continues, "might be because one is suddenly looked at by one who is strange, or because one wishes to look at or commune with another person but suddenly cannot because he is strange" (135). Tomkins argues, moreover, that lowering one's eyes and bowing one's head in shame entail a loss of human dignity, since "man above all other animals insists on walking erect" (136). All of this would seem to be applicable in Derrida's case, including Tomkins's observation that shame is frequently experienced as shameful, compounding the original effect (137). As far as human–animal relations are concerned, Derrida's shame thus appears to cut both ways: undermining his sense of human superiority, it puts him on a par with a four-legged creature; at the same time, registering animal

---

7. Haraway comments, further, that Derrida's apt criticism of Western philosophers fails to look for possible counterexamples in areas outside the humanities: "Why did Derrida not ask, even in principle, if a Gregory Bateson or Jane Goodall or Marc Bekoff or Barbara Smuts or many others have met the gaze of living, diverse animals and in response undone and redone themselves and their sciences?" (21). Haraway precedes me in then placing Derrida in dialogue with Smuts. Citing *Sex and Friendship in Baboons* (1999), she contrasts Derrida's limited curiosity about his cat to Smuts's innovative research method of socializing with baboons on their own terms (23–26).

"strangeness," it calls a halt to their communion. What then are we to make of the apparent shamelessness of Smuts's visual and tactile communion with a baboon? Given women's historically embattled relation to full human dignity and entitlement, is it any wonder she finds Damien less "strange" than Derrida finds his little cat? And might she not, for the same reason, be less susceptible to shame at being ashamed, the second-order humiliation brought about by compromised erectness?[8]

Derrida's French title plays on "je suis" in its double sense of "I am" and "I follow": "L'Animal que donc je suis (à suivre)." So saying, he names himself an animal while also questioning the putative precedence of human animals before all others. Smuts, meantime, spent years scrambling to keep up with a very mobile troop of baboons. Before leaving these two figures, I want briefly to differentiate their shared dedication to *following animals*. Derrida's riffs on following animals include tracking animals in the philosophical record; acknowledging our historically predatory relations to animals; and challenging our temporal/ontological priority as humans. Theoretically compelling, all this remains nonetheless at odds with Derrida's image of a cat following him into the bathroom, petitioning for breakfast, only to be left behind as he flies off in pursuit of more abstract game. The result is to keep Derrida, however unwillingly, in the position of alpha animal—putting the philosopher before the feline, the call of the mind before that of the body, and both at the expense of genuine mutuality.

Smuts has, of course, the perhaps too easy advantage of immersion in fieldwork with actual animals. Notably, however, her work with baboons involves far more than literally tracking them across the savannah. As Smuts explains, she learned to keep physical pace with the baboons only by trusting them emotionally and deferring to them cognitively: "Abandoning myself to their far superior knowledge, I moved as a humble disciple, learning from masters about being an African anthropoid" ("Reflections" 109). Following the lead of animals on these multiple levels would come to characterize Smuts's research method overall. Disregarding the protocol of maintaining a "neutral" distance from her subjects, she put herself in baboon hands, yielded to their expertise, and took her cues from them about baboon sociality as well as survival (109–10). Back at the ranch, influenced by her work with primates, Smuts's relationship with her dog, Safi, is similarly guided by principles of negotiation and mutual accommodation rather than ordinary human dominance (115–20). "Because I spent years following baboons around," Smuts says,

---

8. Derrida himself makes some suggestive remarks along these lines later in "Animal," when he contrasts the shame of the mythical Greek hero Bellerophon with the shamelessness of women (413–14).

"I realized that nonhumans tend to have a superior grasp of wild places" (119). It is therefore sometimes Safi who takes them for a walk, sniffing out their route while her person happily brings up the rear (119). In short, the "following" that for Derrida means chasing down the abjection of animals by Western philosophers, for Smuts has meant letting go the lead, drawing closer, apprenticing herself to animal ways of being and knowing.

Clearly some of the variation in these animal stories by Derrida and Smuts may be chalked up to disciplinary training and disposition—no surprise, we might say, that a philosopher would be less in touch with real animals than an ethologist. Disciplinary paradigms also explain Smuts's assumption (in her scholarship) that animal behaviors are naturally tied to reproductive expediency.[9] For a feminist in the humanities like myself, Smuts's evolutionary reasoning, fraught with sociobiological associations, has very little appeal; I get far more leverage from the discursive views of gender (and identities in general) that Derrida's work has helped to formulate. Disciplinary factors aside, however, what interest me here are differences I would parse in terms of gender. Needless to say, I do not mean by this that Derrida's relation to animals is somehow inherently, inflexibly male—or, as my previous point suggests, necessarily less feminist in all of its ramifications than Smuts's. Rather, I offer the examples of Derrida's anxious man and Smuts's interactive woman—his tale of tragic alienation, hers of comic consummation—as tropes for differences between "masculine" and "feminine" approaches to animals and animal studies that are often but not always aligned with male and female morphology. I will also, before we are done, cite examples of divergences within these categories.

If they are not biological, how might we account for the frequent differences, referenced and in some ways illustrated by Derrida, between male and female narratives about humans in relation to other animals? We need not look very far for a sizeable body of scholarship responding to this question in highly theorized, historicized detail. More than twenty years ago, a cohort of ecofeminists—including Josephine Donovan, Brian Luke, Connie Salamone, Marti Kheel, Andrée Collard, Dean Curtin, Alice Walker, Deborah Slicer, Greta Gaard, Lori Gruen, Lynda Birke, Karen Warren, and Carol Adams—undertook to interrogate deeply embedded humanist assumptions

---

9. In *Sex and Friendship in Baboons,* for example, Smuts notes that a psychologist might seek explanations for male–female baboon friendships in individual histories, but for "a biologist interested in the evolution of behavioral tendencies, the question can be rephrased as follows: How might having a friendship with a male increase the reproductive success of a female baboon?" (81). She herself then proceeds to pursue the biologist's question.

about gender and animality.[10] Broadly speaking, these include the beliefs that women and animals are linked together as avatars of nature; that they are similarly debased by their shared association with body over mind, feeling over reason, object rather than subject status; that men are rational subjects, who therefore naturally dominate women and animals alike; that masculinity is produced in contradistinction to the feminine, animal, bodily, emotional, and acted upon; that degree of manliness is correlated to degree of distance from these and other related categories—physicality, literalness, sentimentality, vulnerability, domesticity, and so forth. None of this is news to seasoned feminists, certainly not to poststructuralists bent on deconstructing all such sets of binary oppositions. It is therefore surprising that even someone like Derrida, known for his strategic identification with the feminized, animalized margins, should still in "Animal" flinch at the "threat" connoted by his little cat. Or perhaps it is not surprising, given Derrida's own emphasis on our inability completely to escape this dualistic logic. As a result, men working in the area of contemporary animal studies—men siding with animals—may indeed feel threatened by "castration," may worry lest their manliness suffer from proximity to a feminized realm. They may, in short, be susceptible to a kind of gender/species anxiety I am tempted to call, with a nod to Eve Sedgwick, "pussy panic."

A likely though not inevitable response to such panic is emphatic disavowal of all further, feminizing associations—emotionality in particular—along with the principled affirmation of masculinizing ones. In her incisive 1990 essay, "Animal Rights and Feminist Theory," Donovan identified this gender dynamic at work in two books foundational to the contemporary movement for animal rights as well as to animal studies: Peter Singer's *Animal Liberation* (1975) and Tom Regan's *The Case for Animal Rights* (1983). Donovan begins by citing passages in which each writer explicitly sets off his own carefully reasoned, academically credible defense of animals from the emo-

---

10. I am using "ecofeminism" as a broad umbrella term for analyses linking men's domination of women to the exploitation of planetary resources. It is not, however, a homogeneous category. Adams and Donovan disagree, for example, with those like Karen Warren and Val Plumwood who protest threats to species and ecosystems while ignoring violence against individual animals. They also distinguish themselves as "care" ecofeminists from those like Plumwood and Haraway who countenance meat-eating (*The Feminist Care Tradition* 12–13). For a comprehensive overview of ecofeminism—its roots in 1980s activism, its broad range of scholars and diversity of approaches including materialist ones, its internal debates and development over the last thirty years—see Greta Gaard. Gaard shares my chagrin at the discrediting of ecofeminist scholarship, even as its contributions are appropriated and esteemed under other rubrics. Whereas my focus is the neglect of ecofeminism by Derridean animal studies, Gaard addresses its similar mischaracterization and dismissal as "essentialist" by the feminist academic establishment.

tionally motivated, easily dismissed concerns of "animal lovers." Speaking for himself and his wife, Singer insists they have never been "inordinately fond of dogs, cats, or horses." "We didn't 'love' animals," he repeats, noting that the presumed sentimentality of animal rights views has led to their exclusion from "serious political and moral discussion" (qtd. in Donovan 34). Regan is similarly anxious to counter "the tired charge of being 'irrational,' 'sentimental,' 'emotional,' or worse." He doesn't specify what could possibly be "worse," though I have tried to suggest where his fears are likely to lie. Regan thus advises scholars defending animal rights to make "a concerted effort not to indulge our emotions or parade our sentiments. And that requires making a sustained commitment to rational inquiry" (qtd. in Donovan 35).

As Donovan demonstrates, both men make a point of distancing themselves from "inordinate" feelings clearly coded as feminine, while allying themselves instead with a mode of "serious discussion" and "rational inquiry" no less clearly marked as masculine. It is not that women are inherently kinder to animals, Donovan explains—many are not; nevertheless, those who take up the cause of animals are often more willing to acknowledge the emotional aspect of their advocacy (35–36). Indeed, as designated outsiders to the realm of rationality, women (with less to lose) have often led the way in challenging rationalist frameworks altogether and recuperating their assemblage of subordinated terms—the feminine and affective along with the animal.[11] Regan and Singer, by contrast, are driven by gender norms to make a show of demonizing feeling, thereby basing their defense of animals on the very rationalist schema that spurns animality in the first place. As Donovan concludes, "Unfortunately, contemporary animal rights theorists, in their reliance on theory that derives from the mechanistic premises of Enlightenment epistemology (natural rights in the case of Regan and utilitarian calculation in the case of Singer) and in their suppression/denial of emotional knowledge, continue to employ Cartesian, or objectivist, modes even while they condemn the scientific practices enabled by them" (45).[12] What I take from Donovan's analysis is the following maxim: the more a male-identified scholar is devoted to animal liberation, the more pressure he is under to assert his nonlove for ani-

---

11. For a recent example, see Rosi Braidotti: "Becoming animal, minoritarian . . . speaks to my feminist self, partly because my sex, historically speaking, never made it into full humanity, so my allegiance to that category is at best negotiable" (531). Marianne DeKoven, another longtime feminist theorist, also links her work on animals to her positioning by gender: "Women and animals go together," and her involvement with animal studies derives "in part from that pervasive cultural linkage" (366).

12. Though Singer's reliance on Jeremy Bentham (whose criterion for animal rights is not reason but *suffering*) might seem to exempt him, Donovan argues that utilitarianism remains a pervasively rationalist framework. See also Luke 291–92.

mals. Thinking to find some less panicked narratives regarding our relations and obligations to nonhuman creatures, I turn now to my final two stories.

Story #3: Adams's Pony

Author or editor of more than half a dozen volumes theorizing the relation between hierarchies of gender and species, Carol Adams is best known as the author of *The Sexual Politics of Meat*. *The Sexual Politics of Meat* appeared in book form in 1990, but its origins go back to 1975, when an essay-length version (written for a class taught by feminist theologian Mary Daly) was published in *The Lesbian Reader*. As Adams tells it, the experience leading her to bring feminist and antiracist commitments into dialogue with animal advocacy involved the murder of her beloved pony, Jimmy. Her account of conversion to passionate feminist vegetarianism through Jimmy's death is threaded through her corpus, appearing with slight variations in at least three different contexts.[13] Like Derrida's watchful cat anecdote, it functions as a kind of origin story, emotional touchstone, and paradigm for her work on animals. The time is 1973; the place is Forestville, New York. Adams is already a feminist, alert to the politics of personal life, but still an oblivious consumer of meat. She has just returned to her small hometown from a year at Yale Divinity School when, in the midst of unpacking, she is interrupted by loud knocking—a frantic neighbor has come to report that Adams's pony has been shot. Running to the back pasture, Adams finds Jimmy on the ground, blood trickling from his mouth. "Those barefoot steps through the thorns and manure of an old apple orchard took me face to face with death," she recalls. "That evening, still distraught about my pony's death, I bit into a hamburger and stopped in midbite. I was thinking about one dead animal yet eating another dead animal. What was the difference between this dead cow and the dead pony whom I would be burying the next day?" (*Sexual* 11–12). From that moment on, her view of meat is fundamentally altered.

I have several observations to make about Adams's story as a figure for her overall project. Both confirming and troubling my earlier, gendered generalizations about Derrida versus Smuts, it also sets the stage for some closing thoughts about our fourth animal story and rather different tale of feminist eating. Adams's epiphany comes, first of all, as both disruption and continuation of her theological training. Hers is a feminist theology, but as the blood,

---

13. See *Neither Man nor Beast* (162–63), a brief mention in "Caring About Suffering: A Feminist Exploration" (*Beyond* 171), and the preface to the tenth-anniversary edition of *The Sexual Politics of Meat* (11–12).

thorns, and martyred animal of this story imply, Adams rejects the patriarchal aspects of Christianity while retaining its iconography of suffering along
with its ethic of neighborliness and care for the meek. Caught in spiritual
transit, still unpacking the baggage of her year at Yale, she is brought home
by this act of violence to her calling as an independent activist-scholar—one
for whom the rites of academia will always be less compelling than the justice
issues raised in her own backyard. "Hailed" in what we might be tempted to
think of as an Althusserian manner, Adams is abruptly called into subjectivity
not by a police officer but by a sympathetic neighbor, who effects her interpellation as a dissenting rather than obedient citizen. In contrast to Smuts,
fingertip to fingertip with Damien, Adams's paradigmatic animal encounter
brings her "face to face with death." And this is true across Adams's corpus:
more often than not, the animals we encounter there are neither canny com-
panions nor prurient pets but, as Adams would say, the decaying corpses we
euphemistically call meat. Made suddenly aware, the night her horse is shot,
that she is feasting on dead cow, her first response is similar to Derrida's: a
shrinking back in shame at the "strangeness" of animals, a self-ironizing performance of the nonrecognition enabling animals to be killed for human use.
Like Derrida, her subsequent work proceeds in a critical mode; instead of
celebrating intimacy with animals, she, too, is more interested in tracing the
discursive patterns that help to authorize human violence against them.

Yet unlike Derrida, who blushes for being ashamed, Adams's shame does
not simply double back on itself. In her case, shame as an acknowledgment
of our estrangement from animals yields quickly to a second impulse: "I also
recognized my ability to change myself: realizing what flesh actually is, I also
realized I need not be a corpse eater. Through a relational epistemology I
underwent a metaphysical shift" (*Neither* 163). Exposed in her shame, the
female protagonist is moved not to cover but rather to examine and reimag-
ine herself. The result is a narrative swerving in conclusion from tragedy to
comic redemption. It would be another year before Adams would actually
convert to vegetarianism, some seventeen years before her "feminist-vegetarian critical theory" would be (as it were) fully cooked. But the basis for
these have been laid in the "metaphysical shift" described here—a shift over
to the side of animals, disavowing the identity of meat eater in order to identify, instead, with the eaten. It is, I would note, a shift inextricable from its
occurrence in the early 1970s, underwritten by the civil rights and antiwar
movements and, above all, by the radical wing of the second-wave women's
movement. Thanks to her formation as a 1970s feminist, Adams is primed to
recognize the emotions of shame, grief, and sympathy as sources of knowledge; to imagine herself in relational rather than autonomous terms; and to

bring a sophisticated analysis of patriarchal structures to bear upon human–animal relations.

To summarize the way gender operates in Adams's work: there is no pre-existing, mystical alliance with animals on the basis of her womanhood. Instead, at a moment of crisis in 1973, she makes the conscious choice to be schooled by them and to reposition herself on their side, in keeping with an ecofeminist epistemology. As she will later put it: "I do not value animals because women are somehow 'closer' to them, but because we experience interdependent oppressions" (*Beyond* 173). Smuts, by contrast, does not invoke feminist frameworks, and her emphasis on animal agency and interspecies mutuality might seem to be the inverse of Adams's focus on animal victimization and grief at animal suffering. There are, however, resemblances as well as differences between the two women. Both affirm our "sentimental" ties to nonhuman animals; both claim our liking of and likeness to other animals (in some, though certainly not all, respects). For Smuts, the similarity of Damien's hand and hers reveals our shared ability to navigate our environments and foster friendship through touch. For Adams, the similarity of Jimmy's objectification and her own points to the way animals and women share the position of "other" within a specific discursive and political context.

Story #4: Dining with Donna

Like Adams, Donna Haraway makes good on the ecofeminist and deconstructionist critique of dualistic thinking through work that combines upfront feelings with forceful analysis, political commitments with scholarly ones, care for animals and animal-lovers with theoretical contributions to animal studies. Though gender is not foregrounded in her most recent writing on animals—*The Companion Species Manifesto: Dogs, People, and Significant Otherness* (2003) and *When Species Meet* (2008)—Haraway takes every opportunity to mention her own, long-standing feminism and the pioneering, ongoing importance of feminist scholarship in thinking about species. As she observes in a 2009 interview, "People like Lynda Birke and Carol Adams and others have been for thirty years or more doing feminist theory in the mode of animal studies that gets at the levels of violence and destruction visited on working animals" ("Science" 159). Haraway and Adams are also on the same page regarding animal theorists whose disdain for older women and their domestic animals so obviously stems from masculine anxieties. Citing Gilles Deleuze and Félix Guattari in "Becoming-Animal," Haraway describes their revulsion from "the old, female, small, dog- and cat-loving" as an egregious example of "misogyny, fear of aging, incuriosity about animals, and horror at the ordinariness of flesh" (*When* 30). And despite her reputation as a high-flying postmodernist, Haraway is another theorist who takes a hands-on approach, a thinker very much in touch with the material world. In the opening paragraphs of *When Species Meet,* Haraway introduces herself as a biologist impressed by the lubricating properties of slime, "a creature of the mud, not the sky" (3). Later in the book, we follow her and her canine partner Cayenne into the world of dog agility training, a sport in which most of the humans are women over forty, and "contact zone" refers not only to a technical aspect of the course but also, for Haraway, to agility training as a site of intense bodily and cultural exchange, mutual though not symmetrical, between people and dogs (208–16). Her visceral and intellectual involvement with the female subcultures of dog trainers and breeders suggests another point of comparison with Adams, who works closely with the subcultures of advocates for battered women and fair housing. For both feminist theorists, these women-centered, extra-academic communities with little cultural capital are not written off but valued as sources of inspiration and knowledge.

That said, Haraway and Adams have widely divergent views on two of the most vexed animal issues: meat-eating and animal experimentation. Haraway is highly critical of factory farming, but she looks instead to humane husbandry rather than vegetarianism. More risky and uncomfortable still, as she herself acknowledges, Haraway makes a conditional case for the use and even killing of animals for scientific research (*When* 68–93). Beyond their disagreements on these specific issues, Haraway and Adams are further discrepant in the general emphasis and affect of their animal texts. As I have observed, the emphasis for Adams is typically on animals as victims—disappeared as subjects, feminized and fragmented as objects, so that meat-eating humans are permitted to ignore the violence of their table. In keeping with this view, the emotional tenor of her writing is a mix of sorrow, anger, and compassion. Haraway's emphasis, on the other hand, is on animals as workers and collaborators, creatures with imagination, agency, and influence, even in the context of unequal relations to humans. Like Smuts, her interaction with them is unashamed and fearlessly tactile. Full of wonder, scientific curiosity, and affection, her animal writing tends toward the celebratory, even ecstatic. "Ms Cayenne Pepper continues to colonize all my cells" (15), she declares in the opening pages of *When Species Meet.* For Haraway, moreover, dogs are by no means the only "companion species" to belie the boundaries of our humanness at a cellular as well as conceptual level. As she explains, "I love the fact that human genomes can be found in only about 10 percent of all the cells that occupy the mundane space I call my body; the other 90 percent of the cells are filled with the genomes of bacteria, fungi, protists, and such" (3). Haraway argues, too, that our humanist sense of mastery and autonomy is usefully undermined by technology as well as by animality—by our prosthetic as well as intra-organic ways of being. Challenging the tendency of most ecofeminists, including Adams, to indict science for crimes against nature, Haraway distinguishes creative from destructive uses of science and places us in a companionate relation to the "cyborg" as well as to nonhuman animals. "Ecologies are always at least tripart," she explains: "human, critters other than humans, and technologies" ("Science" 155).[14]

And now for my final animal anecdote, recounted by Haraway as a "parting bite" at the end of *When Species Meet* (293–94). This is no Smutsian tale of intimacy with a dog or baboon in a wild zone remote from other humans, but rather a story of sitting down to dinner with colleagues. The year is 1980, and Haraway has just given a job talk, clinching her appointment as a feminist theorist at UC Santa Cruz. As she tells it, two women arrive at the restaurant fresh from a birth celebration held in the "feminist, anarchist, pagan cyberwitch mountains" (293). Led by a midwife, it had culminated in a feast, prepared by the husband, consisting of onions and . . . placenta. This second group of diners is soon entirely caught up by an intense but inconclusive discussion of "who could, should, must, or must not eat the placenta" (293). Conflicting anthropological, marxist-feminist, historical, nutritional, philosophical, and vegetarian arguments are animatedly canvassed, and after many hours the only thing clear to Haraway is that she has "found [her] nourishing community at last" (294).

What does Haraway's story of feminist eating, ostensibly without reference to species other than our own, have to do with ferreting out gender in animal studies? What are its implications both for theorizing animal–human ties and for specifying the sexual politics of this project? There is, first of all, the placenta as a figure for what Haraway regards as a fundamental aspect of our creaturely lives: our dependence for nurturance, both before and after birth, on bodies other than our own; our need as animals to feed not only with but *on* one another; our interpenetration by organisms that tumble inside us regardless of whether we are pregnant or carnivorous; the phenomenon, in short, of overlapping ingestions, gestations, and embodiments. All of which is

---

14. As author of the influential "Cyborg Manifesto" (1985), Haraway is often identified with "posthumanism." As framed by Wolfe, a posthumanist approach to animals is motivated less by politics or sentiment than by the theoretical goal of deconstructing humanism, and Wolfe includes Haraway along with only a handful of figures representing thorough "posthumanist posthumanism" (*What* 125–26). Haraway herself has insisted, however, "I am not a posthumanist" (*When* 19); likewise, while interested in Derrida on animals, she also describes herself as "not a Derridean" ("Science" 157).

to say that, while for Adams, no one should be considered "meat," one lesson to be drawn from Haraway's account is that we are all somebody's "meat"— even before we are food for worms.

Our two scenes of feminist eating may be contrasted in another way as well. Whereas for Adams eating a burger answers all questions, for Haraway eating a placenta does nothing but multiply uncertainties—chief among them, for my purposes, the conundrum of how "gender" figures in this story. What do we make of the husband, standing (as I picture him) with spatula and grill—so like and unlike your average suburban dad? There is something strange but fascinating about forking up a bite of placenta; we can't help recoiling, and we can't stop talking about it. Digesting placenta, we are made to consider our resemblance to other mammals—only, perhaps, to be reminded of our peculiarity as humans, hemmed in by culinary, familial, academic, and narrative protocols. By deliberately birthing/eating like a nonhuman animal, do we render ourselves more or less animalistic? In short, if the placenta as an organ confuses self and other, inside and outside, *eating* the placenta adds further confusion regarding the "biological" and "cultural," along with our human relation to these categories. Haraway remarks that "kin relations blurred" (293), and for me even the apparently natural, definitively "female" act of giving birth is defamiliarized and denaturalized by this narrative, transmuted into something less reliably gendered. If everyone was once inside a placenta, now male and female guests alike have a bit of placenta inside of them. Finally, while Haraway's "parting bite" helps to blur notions of "gender" as well as "species," it also brings something else into focus: the exciting, passionate, cross-disciplinary, and open-ended character of feminist conversations circa 1980, precisely the moment they began to infiltrate the academy, leaving no discipline unchanged. Despite their many differences, Haraway thus echoes Adams in at least two ways: not only in generating work on animals that remains warmly engaged with activist, athletic, and scholarly communities of women but also in recalling and insisting upon the formative context of 1970s feminism.

Feminist Narrative Theory

Returning to my opening remarks on the feminist character of my work on narrative, we have seen that my comments on Derrida, like those of Donovan on Singer and Regan, take the form of feminist critique. In a longer version of this essay, my address is ultimately less to Derrida himself than to Cary Wolfe, leading figure among recent animal scholars who look to Derrida's

"Animal" as the founding document of their field (see note 1). Trading on the cachet still associated with Derrida, Wolfe offers what I see as a revisionary history, distancing himself from earlier animal scholarship and its frankly political ties to late-century liberation movements, including the second-wave women's movement. Disputing this origin story, I turn to Adams with the goal of recovering her neglected contribution and that of ecofeminism generally. I also contrast Derrida's little story with three others written and narrated by women, stressing their relative lack of shame or anxiety in affiliating emotionally and politically with other animals. At the same time, I have been at pains to differentiate among my female figures—noting their divergent affects, epistemologies, and political positions—while also indicating the uses of Derrida's work for feminist theory. Further emphasizing the instability of gender categories, I attribute Derrida's "pussy panic" not to his biological maleness but rather to the risk he takes of "feminization" within a social and discursive context strongly dichotomized by gender. This risk is heightened by the anecdotal form and content of his story: its status as a short, personal narrative, deviating from a lofty theoretical mode to dwell instead on daily, bodily rituals of bathing/feeding. Derrida pauses to tell us the cat in his story is "real," and at that moment he drops, however briefly, into a mode of realist narrative.

Derrida's shift from a high-status genre associated with mind/abstraction to one associated with body/literalness, brings me to a final, feminist aspect of my readings: their challenge to a host of conventionally gendered oppositions, including those underlying our judgments of narrative forms. Contesting, for example, the dichotomy between mind and body, I begin by agreeing with those who understand the terms of such binaries as intertwined rather than antithetical. As a feminist, I would note not only the hierarchical relation between these two terms but also the way embodiment is marked as "feminine" and subordinated thereby to a notion of masculinized intellect. Beyond this deconstructive project, however, I am also out to vindicate the subordinated "feminine" half of such pairings. Elaborated by 1980s "difference feminists" (Nancy Chodorow, Carol Gilligan, Adrienne Rich, among others), this move has more recently been regarded with suspicion as incipiently essentialist. I want to insist that it need not be so. Accordingly, my recuperative project encompasses not only female figures but also feminized categories—categories which, functioning pejoratively in relation to women, are even more damning when associated with men. These disparaged categories include the bodily, animal, tactile, emotional, vulnerable, small, dependent, nurturing, and intimate, among a great many others. Over against the lauding of autonomy, my readings would therefore redeem relationality as both ethical stance and scholarly method—Smuts's reciprocity with Damien, Adams's choice to identify with animals, Haraway's insistence on overlapping bodies, and Derrida's wished-for communion. In contrast to the premium placed on "objective" intellectual inquiry, I have also sought to illustrate the way feelings of shame, anxiety, sorrow, anger, and love necessarily infuse scholarship by men as well as women.

As a further aspect of redeeming categories disparaged as "feminine," I have also wished to redeem feminized modes of narrative—modes devalued, for example, as slight, personal, confessional, gossipy, sentimental, comic, popular, miniature, middlebrow, domestic, narrow, local, and/or literal. In the preceding pages, I have pointedly preferred the light to the heavy, the comic to the tragic trajectory, and I have argued specifically for the significance of anecdotes feminized by their brevity and intimacy. Though I deploy them in part allegorically, I have also valued them for their attentive, detailed, domestic materialism. Brevity aside, the stories I cite resonate closely with a particular novelistic idiom. Pausing over the minutia of daily life, they invoke the mode of domestic realism that has long attracted me to certain nineteenth-century novels. Indeed, the political/aesthetic sensibilities informing the discussion above are pretty well summed up by the famous passage from George Eliot's *Adam Bede,* in which the narrator stops to celebrate "faithful pictures of a monotonous homely existence" (223). In keeping with Eliot's dictum, a key goal of my own project has been to parse and appreciate humble accounts of everyday life wherever they appear: "old women scraping carrots with their work-worn hands . . . their brown pitchers, their rough curs" (224)—or, as the case may be, old men washing up, their susceptible bodies, their unfed cats.

Works Cited

Adams, Carol J. *Neither Man nor Beast: Feminism and the Defense of Animals.* New York: Continuum, 1994.

———. *The Sexual Politics of Meat: A Feminist-Vegetarian Critical Theory.* 1990. New York: Continuum, 2000.

Adams, Carol J., and Josephine Donovan, eds. *Beyond Animal Rights: A Feminist Caring Ethic for the Treatment of Animals.* New York: Continuum, 1996.

———. *The Feminist Care Tradition in Animal Ethics.* New York: Columbia UP, 2007.

Berger, Anne-Emmanuelle. "Sexing Differances." *differences: A Journal of Feminist Cultural Studies* 16.3 (2005): 52–67.

Braidotti, Rosi. "Animals, Anomalies, and Inorganic Others." *PMLA* 124.2 (Mar. 2009): 526–32.

DeKoven, Marianne. "Guest Column: Why Animals Now?" *PMLA* 124.2 (Mar. 2009): 361–69.

Derrida, Jacques. *The Animal That Therefore I Am*. Ed. Marie Louise Mallet. Trans. David Wills. New York: Fordham UP, 2008.

———. "The Animal That Therefore I Am (More to Follow)." Trans. David Wills. *Critical Inquiry* 28.2 (2002): 369–418.

———. "Choreographies: An Interview with Jacques Derrida." Ed. and trans. Christie V. McDonald. *Diacritics* 12.2 (Summer 1982): 66–76.

Donovan, Josephine. "Animal Rights and Feminist Theory." *Beyond Animal Rights*. Ed. Josephine Donovan and Carol J. Adams. New York: Continuum, 1996. 34–59.

Eliot, George. *Adam Bede*. 1859. New York: Penguin, 1980.

Feder, Ellen K., Mary C. Rawlinson, and Emily Zakin, eds. *Derrida and Feminism: Recasting the Question of Woman*. New York: Routledge, 1997.

Fraiman, Susan. "Pussy Panic versus Liking Animals: Tracking Gender in Animal Studies." *Critical Inquiry* 39.1 (Autumn 2012): 89–115.

Gaard, Greta. "Ecofeminism Revisited: Rejecting Essentialism and Re-Placing Species in a Material Feminist Environmentalism." *Feminist Formations* 23.2 (Summer 2011): 26–53.

Guenther, Lisa. "Who Follows Whom? Derrida, Animals, and Women." *Derrida Today* 2 (Nov. 2009): 151–65.

Haraway, Donna J. "Science Stories: An Interview with Donna J. Haraway." By Jeffrey J. Williams. *the minnesota review* 73–74 (Fall 2009–Spring 2010): 133–63.

———. *When Species Meet*. Minneapolis: U of Minnesota P, 2008.

Holland, Nancy, ed. *Feminist Interpretations of Jacques Derrida*. University Park: Pennsylvania State UP, 1997.

Howard, Jennifer. "Creature Consciousness." *The Chronicle of Higher Education* 18 Oct. 2009. <http://chronicle.com/article/Creature-Consciousness/48804> Accessed 3 Apr. 2011.

Lawlor, Leonard. *This Is Not Sufficient: An Essay on Animality and Human Nature in Derrida*. New York: Columbia UP, 2007.

Luke, Brian. "Taming Ourselves or Going Feral? Toward a Nonpatriarchal Metaethic of Animal Liberation." *Animals and Women: Feminist Theoretical Explorations*. Ed. Carol J. Adams and Josephine Donovan. Durham: Duke UP, 1995. 290–319.

Rabine, Leslie Wahl. "The Unhappy Hymen Between Feminism and Deconstruction." *The Other Perspective in Gender and Culture: Rewriting Women and the Symbolic*. Ed. Juliet Flower MacCannell. New York: Columbia UP, 1990. 20–38.

Sedgwick, Eve Kosofsky, and Adam Frank, eds. *Shame and Its Sisters: A Silvan Tomkins Reader*. Durham: Duke UP, 1995.

Smuts, Barbara B. "Reflections." *The Lives of Animals*. By J. M. Coetzee. Ed. Amy Gutmann. Princeton: Princeton UP, 1999. 107–20.

———. *Sex and Friendship in Baboons*. Cambridge: Harvard UP, 1999.

Wolfe, Cary. "Human, All Too Human: 'Animal Studies' and the Humanities." *PMLA* 124.2 (March 2009): 564–75.

———. *What Is Posthumanism?* Minneapolis: U of Minnesota P, 2010.

KAY YOUNG

Sex–Text–Cortex

Sex and the Single Brain

> Once upon a time there was a female brain cell, which by mistake happened to end up in a man's head. She looked around nervously but it was all empty and quiet.
>
> "Hello?" she cried, but got no answer.
>
> "Is there anyone here?" she cried a little louder—still no answer.
>
> Now the female brain cell started to feel alone and scared and yelled at the top of her voice, "HELLO! IS THERE ANYONE HERE?!"
>
> Then she heard a very faint voice from far, far away . . .
>
> "We're down here."[1]

Sexed and personified, the "female brain cell" in this fairy tale discovers (or confirms) the real location of her male counterparts and so, too, the real basis of sexual difference. One sex, it turns out, thinks from her head. The other sex, it turns out, thinks from his . . . little head.

Is there a pink brain? A blue brain? A gay brain? A straight brain? Such questions are currently being asked and responded to not just as a joke but as

---

1. "The Female Brain Cell."

science. What seemed a commonplace assumption in earlier centuries, particularly in the nineteenth century when mind-brain theories and research were just beginning to emerge as modern sciences—that the brain is sexually determined and determining—has returned to appear somewhat commonplace.[2] Why might this be? How are the claims of the early nineteenth-century phrenologist Franz Joseph Gall, who analyzed the bumps on scalps to determine mental faculties, any more a quack science or potentially any less harmful than the current work by psychologists, psychiatrists, and neuroanatomists who assert that the woman's brain is organically different from the man's, or that there is a "gay brain" or a "straight brain"?[3] If Gall's chief contribution to the history of the mind-brain sciences was to emphasize the possibility that discrete faculties of mind are discretely localized in the brain, his method for its exploration reflects the limitations of the science and technology of his day.[4] The remarkable advances made in neuroscience since Gall's day that have enabled a fuller exploration of the brain from the *inside* stem from evolving techniques in neurosurgery, new forms of neuroimaging, and advances in neurophysiology research which, together, continue to revolutionize our understanding of the brain and its relation to mind and body. But it is an

---

2. See in particular Anne Moir's and David Jessel's *Brain Sex: The Real Difference Between Men and Women* (1991); Deborah Blum's *Sex on the Brain: The Biological Differences Between Men and Women* (1998); Melissa Hines's *Brain Gender* (2004); Louann Brizendine's *The Female Brain* (2006) and *The Male Brain* (2010); and Simon LeVay's *Gay, Straight, and the Reason Why: The Science of Sexual Orientation* (2011). For a more openly questioning, integrating, and complex account of the mix of brain biology with culture in the construction of sex and sexual orientation, see Judith Horstman's *The Scientific American Book of Love, Sex, and the Brain: The Neuroscience of How, When, Why, and Who We Love* (2012).

3. Gall, a neuroanatomist, physiologist, Vienna-trained physician, and originator of phrenology (from the Greek "*phrenos*," meaning "mind" or "brain"), believed the mind had a set of twenty-seven faculties which were located in the brain. This opposed earlier concepts of the four humors of the Renaissance, for instance, or Descartes' notion of the pineal gland as responsible for identity. For Gall, the size of one's mental faculties directly corresponded to their size in the brain and was reflected in the shape of the cranial bone, which presented itself through the scalp. Gall believed that by touching a person's scalp and measuring its bumps, like a Braille of the brain, he could "read" the brain and know the person's quality of mind. Very quickly, phrenology came to be used as a "behavioral science"—as a predictor of the future course of an individual's life—from a child's trajectory to a prospective marriage partner's suitability. For further study of phrenology, see Gall's tome, whose title is a summary of its premise, *The Anatomy and Physiology of the Nervous System in General, and of the Brain in Particular, with Observations upon the possibility of ascertaining the several Intellectual and Moral Dispositions of Man and Animal, by the Configuration of their Heads*, first published in German in 1819. Phrenology found its chief home in the Edinburgh Phrenological Society of 1820 and was at its most influential as a "discipline" from about 1810 to 1840. See "Gall and Phrenology" in Robert M. Young's *Mind, Brain, and Adaptation in the Nineteenth Century*.

4. The Greek Pythagorean Alcmaeon of Croton (6th–5th century BCE) is considered the first to have asserted the organic source of the mind was the brain.

understanding that is still limited and imperfect: brain function remains more mysterious than "solved." Why narrate sex difference and sexual orientation in terms of the brain—as "the brain's story"? As narrative theorists, in particular, as queer, feminist, and cognitive narrative theorists, how do we read this story and why should we be invested in its telling?

In a set of contemporary pioneering articles collected by the editors of *Scientific American* and under the subject heading of "Behavior" in *The Scientific American Book of the Brain* (1994), two papers stand out for their early, defining claims of a hard-wiring of sex difference and sexual orientation, while a third is distinguished for its early critique of the science of those claims and their accounts. In "Sex Differences in the Brain," psychologist Doreen Kimura states:

> Women and men differ not only in physical attributes and reproductive function but also in the way they solve intellectual problems. It has been fashionable to insist that these differences are minimal, the consequence of variations in experience during development. The bulk of the evidence suggest, however, that the effect of sex hormones on brain organization occur so early in life that from the start the environment is acting on *differently wired brains in girls and boys*. Such differences make it almost impossible to evaluate the effects of experience independent of physiological predisposition. (157; emphasis mine)

Kimura's strongly generalizing claim asserts that girl babies and boy babies are wired differently from *in utero* and that their future mental lives will reflect that inherent wiring. Is such a claim supportable or provable—in other words, is this science or a hypothetical narrative of explanation? In "Evidence for a Biological Influence in Male Homosexuality" by neuroanatomist Simon LeVay and biological chemist Dean H. Hamer, they write:

> Probably no one factor alone can elucidate so complex and variable a trait as sexual orientation. But recent laboratory studies, including our own, indicate that *genes and brain development play a significant role*. How, we do not yet know. It may be that genes influence the sexual differentiation of the brain and its interaction with the outside world, thus diversifying its already vast range of responses to sexual stimuli. (172; emphasis mine)

On what is this bold hypothesis based? LeVay and Hamer acknowledge, "We do not yet know." But what they present as evidence is a small group of cells of the hypothalamus that is generally larger in male brains than female brains and smaller in homosexual male brains than in heterosexual male brains.[5] In the same collection of papers, William Byne, the psychiatrist and neuroanatomy researcher, casts doubt on both sets of claims. About the "female brain" and "male brain," Byne writes in "The Biological Evidence Challenged": "Of the many supposed sex differences in the human brain reported over the past century, *only one has proved consistently replicable: brain size varies with body size.* Thus, men tend to have slightly larger brains than women" (185; emphasis mine). And about biological evidence of "the gay brain," Byne writes:

> What evidence exists thus far of innate biological traits underlying homosexuality is flawed. *Genetic studies suffer from the inevitable confounding of nature and nurture that plagues attempts to study heritability of psychological traits.* Investigations of the brain rely on doubtful hypotheses about differences between the brains of men and women. Biological mechanisms have been proposed to explain the existence of gay men often cannot be generalized to explain the existence of lesbians (whom studies have often neglected). And the continuously graded nature of most biological variables is at odds with the paucity of adult bisexuals suggested by most surveys. (184; emphasis mine)

Byne's objections to claims about brain-based determining of sex difference and sexual orientation directly calls into question the science on which these claims are based. If the science is questionable, what seems to me not questionable is the desire by some to narrate the brain's having a role in the making of sexual identity, a desire that has to do with wanting to find an organic answer to explain the origins of sexual difference and orientation. Brain-based evidence becomes invoked as that ultimate answer, irrefutable because it's the brain and tangible because it's an organ, to "solve" these complex mysteries of identity. *Brains, however, are not sex organs and sex organs are not brains.*[6] To suggest that they are is to distort not just our understanding of the human body but of how we imagine and, therefore, narrate sexual identity, orientation, and their formation.

---

5. Writing in the third person, LeVay and Hamer write: "LeVay examined the hypothalamus in autopsy specimens from 19 homosexual men, all of whom had died from complications of AIDS, and 16 heterosexual men, six of whom had died from AIDS. (The sexual orientation of those who had died of non-AIDS causes was not determined. But assuming a distribution similar to that of the general populace, no more than two or three were likely to be gay)" (173). Not only is their hypothesis-conclusion based on an assumption, their unusually small study number negates the possibility of knowing with any reliability that their hypothesis is proven.

6. But they can be in the stories we tell about them.

Reading for the "Unquestioned Theory"

Here's a brief summary of structural and functional differences in male and female brains that seems not to be controversial. About brain structure, male brains tend to weigh somewhat more than female brains, which is in keeping with male overall larger body mass. A small group of cells of the hypothalamus which regulates metabolism, called the third interstitial nucleus of the anterior hypothalamus, or INAH3, may be larger in male brains than in female brains. With this single exception over an enormous set of anatomic features, including cortex folding, fiber connection patterns, and localization of function, male and female brains are remarkably similar.[7] Little else has been found that distinguishes the anatomic structure and fundamental physiology of male and female brains. About brain function, three central findings continue to bear themselves out: (1) women, on average, perform better on tests of verbal fluency than men (60%–40%); (2) men, on average, perform better on tests of spatial relations (60%–40%);[8] and (3) there seems to be a little less extreme lateralization of function in female brains on average and thus there is a little more interhemispheric connectedness, which helps account for how women on average recover better from strokes and childhood brain injury (Miller et al.; Frith and Vargha-Khadem).

I don't think these findings tell us very much, or tell us things that feel like "*news*," unless one takes it to be news that there are *few* notable distinctions between male and female brains. What *is* controversial are the much stronger claims that sex the brain or attribute to the brain the origin of sexual orientation. Rebecca Jordan-Young's important study, *Brainstorm: The Flaws in the Science of Sex Differences*, addresses these controversial claims "head on" when she writes:

> Human brains, unlike genitals, cannot be "sexed," meaning that they cannot be sorted reliably into "male-type" and "female-type" by observers who don't know the sex of the person they came from . . . . This is not to suggest that there is no intrasex variety in genital size and shape, nor to ignore the existence of intersex people whose genitals might not be so easily categorized, but simply to underscore that in a group of only a thousand people, it will be possible to clearly place almost all human genitals into one of two main types. *Human brains are another matter entirely.* In spite of much trumpeting that there exist "female brains" and "male brains," the extent and nature of physical

---

7. For further explanation of brain anatomy and function, see *Principles of Neural Science*.

8. Doreen Kimura summarizes these known findings in her paper and bases on them her hypothesis about male-female brain difference beginning from *in utero*.

differences in the brains of human females and males is highly controversial. (49; emphasis mine)

What makes Jordan-Young's book news, or why it stands out from other works on sex and the brain and suggests why that relation might be of interest to queer and feminist narrative theorists, is what her analysis of the three hundred research projects on sex difference and the brain uncovers. It is their shared, tacit assumption of what Jordan-Young calls *"the unquestioned theory"* that informs their research. Here's a description of that unquestioned theory:

> Prenatal hormone exposures *cause* sexual differential of the brain—that is, early hormones create *permanent* masculine or feminine patterns of desire, personality, temperament, and cognition. Further, hormones later in life could *"activate"* behavioral *predispositions* themselves, but the dispositions themselves result from the initial *"organizing"* effect of hormones very early in development, before birth. (xi; emphasis mine)

To assume the brain gets organized by prenatal and postnatal hormones in ways that cause sexual differentiation, or that "fix" the brain to inalterable patterns of desire and cognition, or that activate predispositions organized from before birth is to tell a *partial* account of the brain's story and to do so in distorting ways. Such an account gives no consideration to personal history and experience—that is, to the contributions of environment over time to the evolution of identity, behavior, and the brain itself. Such a deterministic account takes the brain to be *hardwired at birth* and *unevolving*. While the weight of scientific evidence suggests there are probably modest differences in brain structure on average at the group level of males and females, the *intervariation* between individuals is much larger than the subtle differences that exist between groups. The narrative of crude biological determinism of a strongly differentiated hardwired male-female brain constraining male-female behaviors is *not* consistent with the science. Instead, there are subtle differences that nudge things slightly in a few directions. Human behaviors are more greatly determined by history, development, and education in the larger culture. About that narrative of crude biological determinism, Jordan-Young writes:

> Hormones don't directly *determine* behavior, but create a small push in one direction, which can be *either enhanced* or *eliminated* by subsequent experience, such that development from that point forward would proceed as though the early hormone exposure had never happened . . .

. . . The point is not that hormone effects are not "real." Hormones are important growth mediators, and they do figure in development, in a variety of important ways. Nor is the point that males and females aren't "really" different. There are demonstrable differences, on average, between males and females in a variety of characteristics, including some limited cognitive abilities, personality traits, and interests, including sexual interests. The problem is the way that brain organization theory brings together ideas about hormones with observations of male–female differences. *The story attributes an unrealistic specificity and permanence to early hormone effects, as well as demonstrably false inevitability and uniformity to sex differences,* which are inaccurate even for those animals whose sexual and other behaviors may turn out to be mechanistically less complicated than ours. (288; emphasis mine)

This is a narrative worth knowing, telling, and retelling in revision. "The story," as Jordan-Young describes it, privileges an underlying theory of prenatal hormonal exposure to the brain which determines identity. Not only is such a privileging questionable as explanation, it is as well distorting of the ongoing, complex role that environment plays in the ongoing shaping of brain function and of identity. However much Rebecca Jordan-Young has done in *Brainstorm* to uncover the deficiencies in method and distortions in the conclusions drawn that assert there is a sexed brain or a sexual brain, there is more to do. As critical readers of narrative, in particular of scientific narratives which define us in terms of a crude biological determinism, we have an important role to play in their interrogation and analysis. To bring queer and feminist narrative theory to scientific narratives of sex difference and sexual orientation would help uncover the underlying belief(s) informing their claims and would help to renarrate by complicating any definitions and assertions about what sexual difference and orientation mean with regard to identity. Feminist and queer narrative theorists are particularly well poised to question an overnarrated role of biological determinism and an undernarrated role of cultural exposure, engagement, and embeddedness in the scientific account of the brain's story with regard to identity formation—in fact, who better?

Brain-*Extravagant* Narrative

It is oddly easy to imagine that the brain has a sex or sexuality. While just a part of our whole anatomy, the brain's overseeing role in the maintenance of homeostasis, in the managing of environmental adaptation, in the acquiring of knowledge, and in the generating of the minded self grant it a special status—it *is* the "organ king." All these defining, essential attributes and forms of assistance to our being and to making possible being who we are tempt us to imagine the brain in reified terms, to make *it* be who *we* are. But it is not. It is important to set next to the more deterministic narrative of the sexed brain other recognitions in current research in neuroscience that address how *adaptive* or *plastic* an organ the brain is. Until recent developments in brain imaging techniques, the brain was understood to be "hardwired" and unchanging.[9] The psychiatrist and analyst Norman Doidge summarizes this past understanding of brain anatomy as "fixed": "The common wisdom was that after childhood the brain changed only when it began the long process of decline; that when brain cells failed to develop properly, or where injured, or died, they could not be replaced. Nor could the brain ever alter its structure and find a new way to function if part of it was damaged" (xvii–xviii). His book *The Brain That Changes Itself: Stories of Personal Triumph from the Frontiers of Brain Science* is devoted to revealing the brain's fundamental plasticity through his representations of what I'm calling in this essay "the brain's story." Doidge's version of that narrative is of brain change and recovery that he recounts through tales of rehabilitation, altered brain image, and therapeutic manifestation of change in mental states and behavior. One of the leaders in the field of brain imaging, Alvaro Pasqual-Leone, reports to Doidge: "'Even when we do the same behavior day after day, the neuronal connections responsible are slightly different each time because of what we have done in the intervening time . . . . The system is plastic, not elastic.'" From hardwired machine to elastic band, part of Doidge's project is to find the best *metaphors* that will help him narrate the brain's inherent fungibility and help us imagine it, too. He writes: "An elastic band can be stretched, but it always reverts to its former shape, and the molecules are not rearranged in the process. The plastic brain is perpetually altered by every encounter, every interaction" (208–9). However "directed" the brain is by genetics and hormones, experience goes full shares in shaping brain structure and

---

9. New brain-mapping techniques that depict dynamic alterations in brain function, rather than just fixed brain structure, include (1) Functional Magnetic Resonance Imaging (fMRI), a technique developed in the early 1990s that delineates regional brain activity by detecting changes in blood flow; (2) Positron Emission Topography (PET), an imaging technique developed in the 1980s tracing gamma rays emitted by a positron-emitting tracer atom attached to a biologically active molecule, such as glucose, which is taken up by functionally active nerve cells; and (3) Optical Imaging of Intrinsic Signals (OIS), a technique developed in the 2000s that maps the brain by measuring activity-related changes in tissue reflectance of light.

function—in how we mind being alive—throughout *the whole* course of our lives.[10]

To bring the narratives of determined nature and dynamic nurture together is to retell the brain's story to be one of interactive entrenchment and plasticity. For the brain to function organically and for us to have a sense of self, there must be entrenchment. For the brain to function relationally as the great integrator of information within and without by adapting and growing, and for us to be the adaptive, fluid beings we are, there must be plasticity. We come into the world as *products-in-process,* in flux, where that which "is" is becoming, shifting, changing, responding, adapting, and emerging—not according to plan, but in relation to plan and in response to experience. I assert then that to tell the brain's story as a narrative theorist means to attend to *our determined limits* AND *our dynamic potential*—to tell the narrative of "that brain" and how that brain minds the complexity of human experience.

To narrate the brain in terms of the metaphors of entrenchment and plasticity has everything to do with how the brain functions and how narrative functions. Darwin offers a third extended metaphor of entangled diversity to help us hold the brain and narrative together in mind—both for their functional similarities and for narrative's capacity to tell the brain's story. In *The Origin of Species,* Darwin imagines an *extravaganza of relations* between all organic beings causing an infinite diversity in structure, constitution, and habits and calls this "Nature's way":

> If under the long course of ages and under varying conditions of life, organic beings vary at all in the several parts of their organization, and I think this cannot be disputed; if there be, owing to the high geometrical powers of increase of each species, at some age, season, or year, a severe struggle for life, and this certainly cannot be disputed; then considering the infinite complexity of the relations of all organic beings to each other and to their conditions of existence, causing an infinite diversity in structure, constitution and habits, to be advantageous to them, I think it would be a most extraordinary fact if no variation ever had occurred useful to each being's own welfare, in the same way as so many variations have occurred useful to man. (67)

---

10. Other works of interest on neuroplasticity for the general audience include *Synaptic Self: How Our Brains Become Who We Are* (2003), by Joseph LeDoux; *The Mind and the Brain: Neuroplasticity and the Power of Mental Force* (2003), by Jeffrey Schwartz and Sharon Begley; and also by Begley, *Train Your Mind, Change Your Brain* (2008); *Rewire Your Brain* (2010), by John Arden; and *The Woman Who Changed Her Brain* (2012), by Barbara Arrowsmith-Young.

I understand narrative to be the human aesthetic of the extravaganza of Darwin's evolutionary Nature.[11] Rich in form, variety, style, substance, and meaning, narrative makes possible perhaps the most interactive study of mind-brain/cultural accounts of being male/female/queer/straight/trans—and human. It is in our work as narrative theorists—working as feminist theorists, queer theorists, and cognitive theorists—not only that we *can* talk to one another about how to reveal the profoundly interactive narrative of the mind-brain and culture, but that we *need* to do so. We need to help inform and shape the emerging "story of the brain"—through how *we* read, write, and understand the story the brain tells as narrative art and as life narrative.

Works Cited

Blum, Deborah. *Sex on the Brain: The Biological Differences between Men and Women*. New York: Penguin, 1998.

Brizendine, Louann. *The Female Brain*. New York: Broadway, 2006.

———. *The Male Brain*. New York: Broadway, 2010.

Byne, William. "The Biological Evidence Challenged." *The Scientific American Book of the Brain*. 183–94.

Darwin, Charles. *On Natural Selection*. Excerpts from *The Origin of Species*. New York: Penguin/Great Ideas Series, 2005.

Doidge, Norman. *The Brain That Changes Itself*. New York: Penguin, 2007.

"The Female Brain Cell." <http://1funny.com/the-female-brain-cell/>. 5 May 2009. Accessed 11 Nov. 2012.

Frith, Uta, and Faraneh Vargha-Khadem. "Are There Sex Differences in the Brain Basis of Literacy Related Skills? Evidence from Reading and Spelling Impairments after Early Unilateral Brain Damage." *Neuropsychologia* 39.13 (2001): 1485–88.

Gall, Franz Joseph. *The Anatomy and Physiology of the Nervous System in General, and the Brain, in Particular, with Observations upon the possibility of ascertaining the several Intellectual and Moral Dispositions of Man and Animal, by the Configuration of their Heads*. Trans. R. Willis. London: S. Highley, 1826.

Hines, Melissa. *Brain Gender*. New York: Oxford UP, 2004.

"History of Neuroscience." <http://en.wikipedia.org/wiki/History_of_neuroscience/>. 12 August 2014 at 20:38. Accessed 11 October 2014.

Horstman, Judith. *The Scientific American Book of Love, Sex, and the Brain: The Neuroscience of How, When, Why, and Who We Love*. San Francisco: Jossey-Bass, 2012.

Jordan-Young, Rebecca M. *Brainstorm: The Flaws in the Science of Sex Difference*. Cambridge: Harvard UP, 2010.

Kimura, Doreen. "Sex Differences in the Brain." *The Scientific American Book of the Brain*. 157–70.

---

11. I develop this idea further in "The Aesthetics of Elegance and Extravagance in Science and Art."

LeVay, Simon. *Gay, Straight, and the Reason Why: The Science of Sexual Orientation.* New York: Oxford UP, 2011.

LeVay, Simon, and Dean H. Hamer. "Evidence for a Biological Influence in Male Homosexuality." *The Scientific American Book of the Brain* 171–82.

Miller, John W., Suman Jayadev, Carl B. Dodrill, and George A. Ojemann. "Gender Differences in Handedness and Speech Lateralization Related to Early Neurologic Insults." *Neurology* 65.12 (27 Dec. 2005): 1974–75.

Moir, Anne, and David Jessel. *Brain Sex: The Real Difference between Men and Women.* New York: Delta/Dell, 1991.

Principles of Neural Science. 5th ed. Ed. Eric R. Kandel, James H. Schwartz, Thomas M. Jessell, Steven A. Siegelbaum, and A. J. Hudspeth. New York: McGraw-Hill Professional, 2012.

The Scientific American Book of the Brain. Introd. Antonio R. Damasio. Guilford, CT: Lyons, 1999.

Young, Kay. "The Aesthetics of Elegance and Extravagance in Science and Art." *Narrative* 19.2 (May 2011): 149–70.

Young, Robert M. *Mind, Brain, and Adaptation in the Nineteenth Century.* Oxford: Oxford UP, 1990.

PART V

Challenges
UN/DOING NARRATIVE THEORY

ABBY COYKENDALL

Towards a Queer Feminism; Or, Feminist Theories and/as Queer Narrative Studies

> It is now possible to imagine [queer people to have] a history; . . . to negotiate a future in which [women enter] the wage-time of the professions, and lesbians and gay men . . . the repronormative time of parenting; [to] move among [sexual] identities (or abandon them), or between or beyond genders; [or to] elaborate ways of living aslant to dominant forms of object-choice, coupledom, family, marriage, sociability, and self-presentation and thus out of synch with . . . narratives of belonging and becoming.
>
> —Elizabeth Freeman, *Time Binds: Queer Temporalities, Queer Histories*

> Queerness irreverently challenges a linear mode of conduction and transmission: there is no exact recipe for a queer endeavor, no a priori system that taxonomizes the linkages, disruptions, and contradictions into a tidy vessel.
>
> —Jasbir K. Puar, *Terrorist Assemblages: Homonationalism in Queer Times*

One critical intervention of feminist theory since the 1970s, an intervention quite pronounced in queer theory of the last few decades as well, is its destabilization of the host of hegemonic regimes that constitute what passes as order and sense. Feminist theorists of all stripes, but in particular feminist narrative theorists, have succeeded in demonstrating how the very framing of fields of inquiry can jury-rig and short-circuit underlying systems of thought. For example, scholars no longer deny the crucial importance of seemingly innocuous discursive maneuvers like naming, listing, or archiving, or in other words, the various mechanisms and manifestations of the Lacanian symbolic, especially when disciplines newly authenticate or, for that matter, newly delegitimize emergent academic fields. Feminist theorists have accordingly shown how the mere placement of one term before another can induce an arbitrary ascendance of that term above and against the term to follow, despite the ostensible equivalence of the "and" usually serving to unite them. Reversing the customary syntax of the catchphrase "husband *and* wife," or referencing two of either spouse as a viable conjugal unit without need of a sexed antithesis, illustrates how little egalitarian such familiar couplings can be. Combining feminist and queer studies together can consequently divorce as much as unite those fields in conceptualization and application: constructing feminism *qua* feminism as not itself queer, or queer studies as not itself feminist, and thereby rendering the association between them simply an aggregation of one species of activity onto the presumptive alterity of the other. The slash between queer and feminist in this volume's original working title, *Queer/Feminist Narrative Theory,* encapsulates the suspicion that feminism has rightly wrought on the often blinkered intercourse between language, knowledge, and power: simultaneously coupling and decoupling fields otherwise registering as discrete in substance and therefore, by implication, oppositional if not hierarchical in alignment.

It is in that same metacritical, skeptical, and, I believe, eminently feminist spirit that I would like to underscore the paratextual facets of this book collection. For almost without fail, the elements hovering on the fringes of a forum will condition the range of possible concepts unfolded within its precincts proper. What this approach reveals is that the tacit primacy granted to narrative theory over either feminist or queer theory, whether in the original title of the collection or in the title of the symposium first inspiring it, contravenes one of the signal achievements of feminism during the second half of the twentieth century; namely the comprehensive subversion of epistemological givens, not the least being the unexamined axioms of narratology as a structuralist discipline. Regrettably, in whichever sequence the adjectives "feminist" and "queer" happen to fall, the compound noun which they together modify, "narrative theory," remains the implicit center of gravity and unspoken rationale for each. That arrangement in turn demotes feminist and queer theories to mere adjuncts of narrative theory—secondary, subsidiary, superficial figures to its seminal ground—and, more problematically, positions them as derivatives of the historically phallocentric institution of narratology. All of which belies the fact that by now feminist and queer theories, not just narrative theory, have proved self-sufficient, even seminal, paradigms in and of themselves.

In the wake of poststructuralism, and in light of the increasingly intersectional, multidisciplinary, and yes ever more curiously queer climate of university research and teaching, neither narrative theory nor feminist theory, nor the comparatively recent array of queer theories, can assert explanatory authority over other modes of critical engagement. As with the reversible vase-face engraving through which Edgar Rubin famously elucidates Gestalt psychology, any one of these theoretical approaches is able to serve as the conceptual ground of the others; the partition established between figure and ground, foreground and background, is arbitrary yet uniquely adaptable, hinging less on the positive qualities of the subject at hand than on the particular lenses most suited to accentuating those qualities at specific times for specific audiences and purposes. Nor would situating any one of these approaches as the ground, and any one or more of the others as the figure, necessarily endow greater importance to that approach or render still other, quite possibly as viable, approaches less salient. If, for instance, some aspect of narrative is the main subject under investigation, feminist and/or queer theories, not just narrative theory, may afford the most suitable concepts and methodologies through which to attend to it; if, in contrast, some aspect of sexuality, gender, or embodiment is the main subject under investigation, narrative theory, not just feminist or queer theory, can lend that seemingly discrepant subject a kindred service in turn.

Hilary Schor, alluding to the late resurgence of intersectionality as a paradigm, has cautioned that the central figure of the intersection is a place not simply of contact or collaboration, but of conflict and contention, "a place where there are traffic accidents" and, therefore, she advises, "a place where you need a cop." Schor maintains that narratology "has been and should be" in command of that position, personifying it as a "kind of protector," a "guardian of justice," capable of supervising relations between feminist and queer studies, and adjudicating impartially whenever disputes arise. I would posit, on the contrary, that appointing a traffic cop, or any other authority figure, to oversee the proper ebb and flow of feminist and queer inquiries is neither warranted nor beneficial: feminist and queer studies are alike autonomous fields proficient in debating their own protocols and premises without deference to extrinsic fields. Moreover, each approach is, by nature, deliberately improper and quite properly so. The paternalistic disciplinary gaze that Schor ascribes to narratology, not to mention the infantilized, rivalrous terrain which that gaze projects upon feminist and, most especially, queer studies, would no doubt prove unhelpful regardless. A pluralist, contextually attuned paradigm would trust no single theoretical lens to be any more uniformly objective or holistic than others; in fact, those perspectives granted most perspicuity may well prove least trustworthy precisely because of that exalted status.[1]

A sure sign of the efficacy with which narrative, feminist, and queer studies can be interwoven without any one approach subtending or subordinating the others is the frequency with which pioneering work in narrative studies has also been at the same time pioneering work in feminist and/or queer studies, and vice versa. Indeed, narrative studies can function as a specialized application of the latter fields as much as either can function as a specialized application of it. Notable examples of scholarship drawing upon narrative theory for feminist/queer purposes would be the chief inspiration for the current chapter, Susan S. Lanser's phenomenal "Toward a Feminist Narratology" (1986), which I initially encountered in a gender-studies anthology, *Feminisms: An Anthology of Literary Theory and Criticism*, as well as Robyn R. Warhol's *Gendered Interventions* (1989), Judith Roof's *Come As You Are* (1996), or Lanser's follow-up article in queer studies "Sexing the Narrative" (1995). Of course, this kind of scholarship likewise includes so-called "interdisciplinary" work, provided, that is, we follow two recent anthologies, *A Companion to Narrative Theory* (2005) and *Postclassical Narratology* (2010), in viewing feminist and queer studies as "external stimuli" that can somehow enter into "exogamous unions" with the principal discipline of narrative studies (Alber and Fludernik 11); or, almost worse, see them as autonomous if subaltern entities functioning within that discipline surreptitiously, a tenuous yet indigenous "series of subdisciplines" (Fludernik 37). Perhaps in consequence of the ongoing devaluation of feminist and queer studies, the latest collection in the discipline, *Current Trends in Narratology* (2011), features no contributions with an emphasis on gender or sexuality studies, while the preceding collection, *Postclassical Narratology* (2010), contains a lone chapter, Lanser's own "Sapphic Dialogics," which comprises less than 10 percent of the volume. Judging from the table of contents of these collections, exemplary scholarship in narrative studies only broaches feminist or queer issues on an ad-hoc basis, as outlying regions towards which a specialist need not ordinarily venture or logically stray. Seldom acknowledged are the profound structural ramifications that feminist and queer studies have had on the discipline of narrative studies as a whole, most tellingly, on its persistence

---

1. The position articulated in this paragraph is greatly indebted to Donna J. Haraway's "Situated Knowledges" in *Simians, Cyborgs and Women* (New York: Routledge, 1991), 149–82, and Rey Chow's "Interruption of Referentiality" (*South Atlantic Quarterly* 101.1 [2002]), 171–86.

as a discipline in need of discipline, as a territory rife with boundary disputes, stanch surveillance, and periodic efforts towards decontamination and quarantine.[2]

Arguably more consequential at the present time than the supposedly inter-, intra-, or sub-disciplinary scholarship above is the extensive amount of multidisciplinary scholarship in cultural studies that adapts and hones narrative theory for its own purposes rather than importing it deferentially from an extrinsic or superintendent discipline of narratology. This scholarship encompasses everything from the two books cited in the epigraphs above, Elizabeth Freeman's *Time Binds* (2010) and Jasbir Puar's *Terrorist Assemblages* (2007), to the numerous works in discourse studies proliferating during the 1990s—for example, Judith Butler's *Bodies That Matter* (1993) or Eve Kosofsky Sedgwick's *Epistemology of the Closet* (1990)—to such groundbreaking feminist reassessments of the novel as Nancy Armstrong's *Desire and Domestic Fiction* (1987) or Sandra Gilbert and Susan Gubar's *Madwoman in the Attic* (1979). It remains a mystery why the authors of these works have not been hailed as fellow specialists in and practitioners of narrative studies, as opposed to extradisciplinary, albeit hospitably welcomed, visiting scholars and guests.[3] Are the authors of *The History of Sexuality* (1978–1986) or, for that matter, *Nation and Narration* (1990), namely Michel Foucault and Homi Bhabha, not also authentic, even perhaps superlative, narrative theorists? Recognizing these and similar figures as narrative theorists in their own right would nonetheless require coming to terms with the fact that the vast majority of scholarly works published in narrative studies over the past few decades have emerged far afield of the official auspices of narratology, flourishing without overt sanction or appreciation from a conventional discipline.

It is important to remember that the sole center of gravity around which queer or diasporic subjects can circulate is their collective resistance to normativity, or, in other words, to the dominant cultural *narratives* that regulate

2. The editor of *Current Trends*, Greta Olson (Berlin: De Gruyter, 2011), and the editors of *Postclassical Narratology*, Jan Alber and Monika Fludernik, each discuss the vexed relation between feminism and narratology in their introductions; however, earlier editors, such as Susana Onega and José Ángel García Landa of the 1996 *Narratology* (London: Longman, 1996) and David Herman of the 1999 *Narratologies* (Columbus: The Ohio State UP, 1999), include more chapters with sustained—and hence unmediated—treatments of gender and sexuality.

3. Ostensibly incidental gestures, like addressing scholars as experts in neighboring fields rather than as *de facto* members of the field itself, can make for immeasurable differences in constituting the identity of the scholar as well as the discipline as a whole. As Louis Althusser persuasively argues, institutions come into being through the incremental practices of subjects interpellated by and engendered through them: "ideas are [the subject's] material acts inserted into material practices regulated by material rituals which are themselves defined by the material ideological apparatus" in which that subject is hailed (186).

identity and difference. As a result, queer theorists tend to utilize narrative theory extensively in their reconceptualization of sex, gender, and sexuality, as the high correlation between "queer" and "narrative" in any MLA Bibliography or Google Books search will quickly confirm. In contrast, experts working in Women's Studies or in Lesbian, Gay, and Bisexual Studies retain the option of basing their research on apparently pre-existent, pretextual identity categories clearly delineating who does or does not count as a woman, or as a woman-loving woman or man-loving man, and thence as a potential object of scholarly inquiry. While many if not most of these experts choose to cultivate some degree of proficiency in narrative theory, or advance a social-constructivist, non-identitarian ethos in their scholarship, their colleagues in queer or transgender studies must do so by necessity. Extricating oneself or one's academic field from heteronormative frameworks entails reading and re-reading cultural scripts as scripts, and rescripting those scripts accordingly.[4]

Unfortunately, even as feminist and queer studies have transformed the range and contours of what we regard as narrative and thus narrative studies within academe and beyond, the residually structuralist discipline of narratology continues to treat gender and sexuality as peripheral to its core research interests and practices. For instance, while the 2010 *Postclassical Narratology* collection grants the salience of these forms of study to narrative studies generally, and condescends to "accommodat[e]" them within the official province of narratology, the editors characterize them as "thematic" subcomponents with which the main cohort of the discipline can "cross-fertiliz[e]" and "innovative[ly] blend" (Alber and Fludernik 11, 3, 6, 15)—or, in short, with which it can marry and mate exogenously as Claude Lévi-Strauss might say. Some strands of feminism have regrettably followed suit vis-à-vis the comparatively new fields of queer and transgender studies: shoring up feminism as a discipline by disciplining the dissent perceived as encroaching upon feminism's proprietary domain. The still disproportionate amount of scholarship produced on eighteenth- and nineteenth-century British women's domestic fiction, which, importantly, is likewise research on bourgeois Anglo-American heterosexuality, usually without the class, sexual, or geopolitical parameters of that demographic explicitly acknowledged as such, is here a case in point. As

4. Critical race specialists, from bell hooks in "Postmodern Blackness" (in *Yearning: Race, Gender, and Cultural Politics,* Boston: South End, 1995; 23–31) to José Muñoz in the forthcoming *Feeling Brown* (Durham: Duke UP) likewise treat the process of racialization, not racial identity per se, as the focal point of their research. My own work in progress, "Class Camp and the Queer Imaginary," explores the possibility of a critical *class* studies established along similar lines, that is, without the materialist critique presuming a stable material ground for the object of critique.

Lanser remarks in "Of Closed Doors and Open Hatches," eighteenth-century women's studies remains "quite heavily heteronormative to the impoverishment and perhaps distortion of the field" (275)—a problem extending to feminist and literary studies generally.[5]

The trend towards *postclassical* narratology, a neologism positioning narrative studies against what might be called *poststructural* or *postmodern* narratology, is further symptomatic of the marginalization of the typically poststructuralist approaches of feminist and queer studies. A narratology thus named is at once under- and over-representative in scope. Everything, except the customary classics of Greece and Rome, would be post-"classical" in the classical sense—a tautology compounded by the fact that this narratology's own classical forerunners, the twentieth-century structuralists Gérard Genette and Roland Barthes, would, from a historical perspective, be virtually as postclassical as their professed descendants. Meanwhile, the unspoken foil of postclassicism, poststructuralism, remains vital and dynamic, diversifying and transforming a wide array of fields notwithstanding its lack of an equivalently lofty rubric. The taxonomy of postclassicism may therefore signal less contemporary advances within the discipline than a conservative gesture to temper if not thwart them; that is, to reactivate the structuralist core of the once-dominant narratological orthodoxy, albeit with a minimally original, poststructuralist guise. What better way than the tendentious tidying-up apparatus of periodization to make that discipline's by now irrevocably postmodern milieu disregard the long unadorned truth that narratology, like all other master narratives of modernity, is an emperor without clothes? Postclassicism essentially co-opts the insights yet domesticates the critique that poststructuralism continues to pose to narratology as a discipline.[6]

The characterization of feminist and queer studies, and cultural studies generally, as "extrinsic developments" from which an otherwise apolitical, history-free zone of narratology can be immune suggests that the upshot of this rubric is to obfuscate the world-making, world-replicating power of discourse, which, I believe, can and should be a prime object of narratological concern. In addition, it serves to safeguard the expedient fallacy that ideology taints only *some* minoritarian narratives, allowing investigations of more

---

5. Lanser's essay is reprinted in the collection *Heteronormativity in Eighteenth-Century Literature and Culture,* coedited by myself and Ana de Freitas Boe (Burlington, VT: Ashgate, 2015; 23–39). I am judging the disproportionate amount of scholarship on normative subjects based on the number of submissions which I receive each year as an editor of *JNT: Journal of Narrative Theory.*

6. For an astute analysis of periodization, see Homer Brown's "Why the Story of the Origin of the (English) Novel Is an American Romance (If Not the Great American Novel)" in *Cultural Institutions,* ed. Deidre Lynch and William B. Warner (Durham: Duke UP, 1996), 11–43.

mainstream narratives to proceed apace without assessments of how they too may be situated materially and culturally. Nevertheless, those very texts seeming to elude sociopolitical trappings, those so tightly enmeshed in hegemonic customs and canons as to pass as universal, are also those necessitating the most critical scrutiny. Moreover, whether heeded or unheeded, discourses of gender and sexuality, not to mention race, class, and geographical region, will continue to inflect the entire expanse of narrative studies, not just the diminutive portion set aside for feminists, queer theorists, or other cultural critics to study. Feminist theory, like other forms of critical theory, "expands the terrain of narrative theory not because it enumerates variously sexualised authors and characters, but rather because it provides alternative models of narrative structure and notes the queerness already registered in the classic models of structuralist narratology" (Herman, Jahn, and Ryan 478). The feminisms of the 1970s thus did not stop short in seeking the inclusion of women's works within the then highly homosocial enclave of narratology, but sought as well to expose the self-authorizing, self-replicating force of phallocentrism engendering and rationalizing that homogenization.

The difference between postclassical and other narratologies is ultimately of less magnitude than that between *narratology* and *narrative studies*. Whereas the framework of postclassical narratology implies an unbroken genealogy from classicism to postclassicism without any counter-discourse of poststructuralism intervening—the "ology" symptomizing the outmoded affectation of the new narratology as a positive science—that of narrative studies underscores the *integral* interdisciplinarity distinguishing it and analogous fields like postcolonial or disability studies. Narrative studies, unburdened with the exclusionary legacy of an "ology," is better suited for the intersectional, intellectually porous landscape of today. Whatever rubric adopted, however, feminist and queer studies should not be treated as extraneous, extradisciplinary addendums to narrative studies proper, much less as subaltern or subdisciplinary quasi-constituencies within the larger narratological fold. Despite the apprehensions of some participants at the Queer and Feminist Narrative Theory Symposium, the demise of narratology as a master discourse transcending and translating the lay vernaculars of other fields need not portend the dawn of nonsense or chaos. Multidisciplinarity, like multilingualism, lends narrative theorists more expertise and fluency, not less, while also fostering dialogue among the divergent constituencies invariably interacting within any discipline.

I would like to close by cautioning that after forty years and counting of what Robyn Warhol calls the "feminist-epistemological critique of objectivity" (342), neither narrative studies nor feminist studies—nor, for that matter, queer studies—can feign the authority or claim the prerogatives of a positive science. As Warhol rightly notes, "systems of meaning are never neutral," of necessity "bear[ing] the (gendered) marks of their originators and their receivers" (ibid.). To these inscriptions of gender, I would add those of class, race, nation, sexuality, among a host of other hierarchical classifications that remain operative even after feminist narrative theorists have transitioned from emergent outsiders to relatively mainstream players of the once tacitly, now tenuously, dominant stronghold of narratology. If, having gained that comparative security, feminist narrative theorists were to forsake their oppositional stance and seek the kind of institutional cachet which they earlier obliged structuralist narratologists to abandon, they would jeopardize feminism's systematic and, by this point, successful dismantling of structuralism as a disinterested, metadiscursive science. That would be a pyrrhic victory indeed in deterring other emergent scholarship and feminism's own more resistant formations from joining, transforming, and perhaps altogether abandoning the narratological field.

Works Cited

Alber, Jan, and Monika Fludernik. *Postclassical Narratology: Approaches and Analyses.* Columbus: The Ohio State UP, 2010. 1–31.

Althusser, Louis. *On the Reproduction of Capitalism: Ideology and Ideological State Apparatuses.* Trans. G. M. Goshgarian. Brooklyn, NY: Verso Books, 2014.

Fludernik, Monika. "Histories of Narrative Theory (II): From Structuralism to the Present." *A Companion to Narrative Theory.* Ed. James Phelan and Peter J. Rabinowitz. Malden, MA: Blackwell, 2005. 36–59.

Freeman, Elizabeth. *Time Binds: Queer Temporalities, Queer Histories.* Durham: Duke UP, 2010.

Herman, David, Manfred Jahn, and Marie-Laure Ryan. Introduction. *Routledge Encyclopedia of Narrative Theory.* Boca Raton, FL: Taylor & Francis, 2005. ix–xii.

Lanser, Susan S. "Of Closed Doors and Open Hatches: Heteronormative Plots in Eighteenth-Century (Women's) Studies." *Eighteenth Century: Theory and Interpretation* 53 (2012): 273–90.

Puar, Jasbir K. *Terrorist Assemblages: Homonationalism in Queer Times.* Durham: Duke UP, 2007.

Schor, Hilary. "The Conference So Far." Ohio State's Project Narrative Symposium: Queer and Feminist Narrative Theory. Hyatt Regency Hotel, Columbus, OH. 12–14 May 2011. Address.

Warhol, Robyn R. "Guilty Cravings: What Feminist Narratology Can Do for Cultural Studies." *Narratologies: New Perspectives on Narrative Analysis.* Ed. David Herman. Columbus: The Ohio State UP, 1999. 340–55.

MARTIN JOSEPH PONCE

Queer/Feminist/Narrative

On the Limits of Reciprocal Engagement

*T*hese remarks come from someone who does not work in the field of narrative theory but pursues research in queer and, to a lesser extent, feminist studies. Indeed, my ambivalence extends not only toward narrative theory but to queer theory itself, since my own work explores the lines of inquiry opened up by queer of color and queer diasporic analysis. A number of scholars have addressed the default, constitutive "whiteness" of queer theory as it emerged in the late 1980s and early 1990s out of AIDS street activisms, Foucauldian approaches to histories of sexuality, and poststructuralist critiques of essentialist identity categories (e.g., Cohen, Hames-García, Perez). I will come back to the question of race momentarily. First, I wish to consider whether the framing questions of this collection—What is feminist or queer about one's work on narrative? What is "narrative" about one's work on sexuality and/or gender?—can generate research that is mutually reciprocal across these specific areas of expertise.

That I was invited to contribute to this volume speaks to the possibilities and generosities of cross-field dialogues. But I suspect that those of us represented here have various and differing commitments to its three framing concepts: feminism, queer, and narrative. As I consider our variety of topics—feminist narratology, morphings and perversity, affect and emotion, the brain and sexuality, queer (counter)archives and historical fragments, religion and transnational feminism, interracial intimacy and "post-race" discourse, 1970s women of color novelists and empathy, queer futurity and the "It Gets Better" project, queer temporality and rupture, and queer causality and etiology—my curiosities are aroused less by the internal developments and anxieties of narrative theory *per se* than by the way that those ideas are being broached and are perhaps breaching narrative study from somewhere else, however distant or proximate. Given the wide range of work represented here, I wonder whether these key concepts (intersectionality, systems, cortex, diaspora, affective labor, negativity, retrograde vocabulary, to add a few more) end up telling a story—a story of a shared project—or evoke a productive incoherence.

Several of these essays voice propositions that similarly speak to issues about inter- or cross-disciplinarity. Judith Roof suggests that we need to break down the terms being used lest we cover over the differences and hierarchies that constitute them. Sue Kim calls for narrative theory to widen its scope of texts and consider seriously the scholarship and intellectual traditions that have grown up around them. Is our project to theorize feminist and queer narratologies, subordinating "feminist" and "queer" to kinds or styles of narrative study, or to explore what happens when feminism, queer studies, and narrative theory as distinct fields in their own right converge or collide? Is there a built-in hierarchy of "feminist" over "queer" if only by virtue of the longer and more robust history of feminist narratology? What about the tensions between the potential of narrative theory's imperialist appropriation (its treatment of narratives by women, sexual dissidents, or racial and colonized others as "raw material" for testing out the reach of theoretical frameworks), on one hand, and a genuine commitment to accounting for and historicizing racial, class, religious, and national differences and practices, on the other? Is the goal to explore how tools from narratology can bring renewed attention to issues of narrative form in feminist and queer expressive cultures? Or are we asking that narratology be impacted and reshaped by the urgencies presented by feminist and queer studies and politics?

These questions use the conjunction "or" and recur to a mode of binary thinking that the very project of this volume might seem roundly to criticize. But by phrasing these possibilities as *not* reciprocal, not moving freely and energetically in both directions, I am suggesting that the organizing principle of the volume—narrative—necessarily demotes other terms and fields to secondary status. Is it really possible, to focus on the fields I'm most familiar with, to break down the current conundrums and competing interests operating in queer studies and ethnic studies and their encounters with narrative theory? If we could, I would ask: What and *whom* are queer archives for?

If Monique Truong's novel *The Book of Salt* (2003) is an extended improvisation on an archival fragment, an attempt to produce enduring presence where there was only fleeting ephemerality and interchangeability of colonial laborers, is it also a wishful desire for a permanent legible archive as well (Cvetkovich)? To what extent is Randa Jarrar's novel *A Map of Home* (2008) a critique of Anglo-American queer literary history (Friedman)? Why is there such a noticeable disjunction between women of color fiction and lesbian of color critique during the 1970s and 1980s (Kim)? Does it matter who speaks in the highly mediated, and peculiarly individualized, construction of community of the "It Gets Better" project? What if the world that Chris Colfer, Margaret Cho, and Barack Obama represent is a world I can do without (Matz)? What difference have social differences in addition to class made in the construction of male same-sex desire across the twentieth century (Morrison)? What happens to the category of "queer youth" when the etiology of homosexuality is traced not to biology, god, or bad influences but to a practice of repressing the disorder of *sexuality* as such, resulting in a social disciplining whose effects are the very identity categories that incite violence, depression, and sentimental acts of YouTube charity (Rohy)?

If these questions imply a doubtfulness about the possibility of reciprocal engagements across queer, feminist, and narrative theory, my reservations stem less from imagining the respective practitioners' disciplinary isolationism, defensiveness, or stubbornness, or from positing that an individual scholar cannot be well versed in more than one field, than with the incongruous intellectual histories and political commitments of the different fields. It seems to me that the central issue with which each field grapples—sexuality, gender, narrative—inevitably inflects the emphasis, if not the full content, of the analysis. Such argumentative emphases or "interventions" are made legible and intelligible when framed within a given field's internal developments and trends—in short, within its respective intellectual tradition. This is not to say, again, that disciplines are autonomous, impermeably bounded, and monolithic, but that the specificities of what makes a piece of scholarship "new," "original," or even meaningful is determined by its place within a particular intellectual genealogy. And those genealogies are themselves informed by certain political aims that overlap only partially, at most.

To return to the field in which I work, queer studies has rapidly traversed a great deal of ground in its relatively brief academic existence, quickly moving past the essentialism versus social constructionism debate to investigate such questions as citizenship, colonialism and postcolonialism, race, ethnicity, religion, age, able-bodiedness, affect, popular culture, archives, counter-publics, cultural differences, tourism, international migration, political economy, political asylum, biopolitical governance, indigenous sovereignty, and "terrorism," among others. Given this wide array of issues, it would be rather misleading or reductive to ask what impact queer studies might have on narrative theory since "queer studies" is itself heterogeneous and self-contentious. To be sure, many queer studies scholars examine narratives of all sorts evoked in all sorts of media. And some of the sophisticated analytical insight examining "how narrative works" drawn from narrative theory might very well enhance and enrich the study of those expressive practices. But it is another thing to ask whether the knowledge produced in queer studies scholarship will be (or has been) directly routed back toward narrative theory as a field, or whether narrative theory would welcome and rigorously take that knowledge into account.

One way to put this point is to say that the limits of reciprocal engagement may lie in the orientations of our scholarly modes of address, those fields with which we aim to be in dialogue. It may be perfectly conceivable that an individual scholar is able to converse with equal facility with narrative theory and queer studies. But it seems to me that unless queer studies (to continue with my example) views narrative theory as a significant and necessary analytical framework for coming to terms with its most pressing problems, and incorporates and adapts its insights into its critical repertoire, such an "intervention" would be heard as a mere whisper in the wind. That is, narrative theory would need to become an indispensable part of queer studies' intellectual genealogy. The same would be conversely true, I would surmise, in order for the full range of queer studies to influence the shape and practice of narrative theory.

In this regard, we might compare, in highly abstracted terms, how narrative theory and queer theory narrate their respective histories. As I understand it, the former story begins with classical, structuralism-based narratology dominated by "male theoreticians" and "male writers" and moves to postclassical narratology that has refocused attention on gender, sexuality, social context, and the role of readers in making meaning (Herman and Vervaeck 130), and has interfaced with "ideas from fields that did not extensively cross-pollinate with earlier research on stories" such as feminism, Marxism, and postcolonialism (Herman 16). Although queer theory's origins, according to one version of the story, have not been dominated by male theorists (Eve Kosofsky Sedgwick, Teresa de Lauretis, and Judith Butler, among others, are frequently cited among early influential practitioners), and although queer theory has acknowledged intellectual and political debts to feminism, it has nonetheless tended to elide the work of theorists and activists of color (James Baldwin, Audre Lorde, Cherríe Moraga, Gloria Anzaldúa, and so on) as constitutive of its genealogy in favor of (white) poststructuralist thinkers.

In this connection, I am reminded of Barbara Christian's classic essay "The Race for Theory," in which she challenges the academic ascendancy and presumptions to totalizing authority of what she calls the postmodernist "New Philosophy" for excluding the thought and expressive practices of the Black Arts and feminist movements of the 1960s and 1970s, for example, and for coming to prominence at precisely the moment "when the literature of peoples of color, black women, Latin Americans, and Africans began to move to 'the center'": "Because of the academic world's general ignorance about the literature of black people, and of women, whose work too has been discredited, it is not surprising that so many of our critics think that the position arguing that literature is political begins with these New Philosophers" (71). Christian's argument, however, is not just about struggles over the history of ideas and who is granted the legitimacy to be recognized for them; it's also about the very practice of "theory"—what it is, what it's for, and what forms it takes: "For people of color have always theorized—but in forms quite different from the Western form of abstract logic. *And I am inclined to say that our theorizing (and I intentionally use the verb rather than the noun) is often in narrative forms,* in the stories we create, in riddles and proverbs, in the play with language, because dynamic rather than fixed ideas seem more to our liking. How else have we managed to survive with such spiritedness the assault on our bodies, social institutions, countries, our very humanity?" (68; emphasis mine).

What I am suggesting, in the end, is that the relations of feminist, queer, black, and other ethnic studies to narrative and to narrative theory are highly contingent and variable, engaged with varying degrees of investment. As Christian's essay indicates, even the fundamental terms "narrative" and "theory" can be conceptualized and valued in radically different ways, and what it means to tell stories and theorize about a certain social group's experiences can be a matter of power and survival. If seen as alien and threatening to a specific culture's intellectual, artistic, and social traditions, narrative theory proper may not attain the sort of validity in the corresponding academic field that it has acquired in others. At the same time, there's no reason to believe that its postclassical iterations and widening directions may not eventually be taken up by a critical mass of queer and ethnic studies scholars to the point where those theoretical tools and insights, translated and transformed to address relevant problems in the field, become integral to the field's self-conception, critical lexicon, and modes of analysis.

Works Cited

Christian, Barbara. "The Race for Theory." *Feminist Studies* 14.1 (1988): 67–79.

Cohen, Cathy J. "Punks, Bulldaggers, and Welfare Queens: The Radical Potential of Queer Politics?" *GLQ: A Journal of Lesbian & Gay Studies* 3.4 (1997): 437–65.

Cvetovich, Ann. "The Affective Turn, the Archival Turn, and Queer Historical Fictions." Ohio State's Project Narrative Symposium: Queer and Feminist Narrative Theory. Hyatt Regency Hotel, Columbus, OH. 12–14 May 2011. Conference Presentation.

Hames-García, Michael. "Queer Theory Revisited." *Gay Latino Studies: A Critical Reader.* Ed. Hames-García and Ernesto Javier Martínez. Durham: Duke UP, 2011. 19–45.

Herman, David. Introduction. *The Cambridge Companion to Narrative.* Ed. Herman. Cambridge: Cambridge UP, 2007. 3–21.

Herman, Luc, and Bart Vervaeck. *Handbook of Narrative Analysis.* Lincoln: U of Nebraska P, 2005.

Perez, Hiram. "You Can Have My Brown Body and Eat It, Too!" *Social Text* 23.3–4/84–85 (2005): 171–91.

CLAUDIA BREGER

Critically Affirmative Reconfigurations

Twenty-First-Century Turns, or:
Queer and Feminist Work in an Age of Affirmation

In mapping recent theoretical developments, scholars have proclaimed a range of overlapping turns—including, in alphabetical order, the "aesthetic," "affective," "biological," "cognitive," "ethical," "evolutionary," "(neo-)formalist," "neurological," "phenomenological," and "religious" turns. In all their disparity, these twenty-first century paradigms share, I will suggest, orientations that have also been associated with the end of (capital T) Theory (see Elliot and Attridge). While obviously no less theoretical, in the sense of speculative and analytic, than their predecessors (postmodernist, discourse-oriented, linguistic, ideology-critical, cultural studies paradigms . . .), they disband the reign of critical reflexivity—or, the challenging of commonsense notions— that may have united the diverse branches of late twentieth-century Theory.[1] Without necessarily ignoring the legacy of these critical reflexivities, twenty-first-century approaches have variously argued for reaffirming experience, art, nature, or tradition, to the effect of championing both universal and smaller-

---

1. See Culler, who makes this reflexivity into a crucial part of his definition of (critical) theory (14–15).

scale collective identifications. To the internal "hermeneutist of suspicion,"[2] it must perhaps seem questionable whether these returns to the evolutionary or religious foundations of culture, the shared human capacity for empathy, or the value of classical art forms leave significant conceptual room for a continued exploration of sociosymbolic regimes of difference and inequality. And if new universalisms thus evidently threaten to displace feminist (as well as antiracist) investigations, the fate of queer studies in the twenty-first century seems even more dubious, given the assault on identity inscribed in their very conceptualization, as well as their focus on sexuality.[3] Is the category of sex, in the very moment of its heightened politicization in this country, not pushed into renewed critical marginality by the combined forces of the cognitive turn against psychoanalysis, the evolutionary focus on reproduction, and the shift to the formations of affect in experience?[4]

The fantastic news brought by this volume, however, is that the assembled, heterogeneous community of scholars interested in feminist and queer concerns is still and ever-differently doing it. We see here how deeply involved queer and feminist work is in the emerging twenty-first-century paradigms and, conversely, how deeply provocative (or imaginatively surface-reading)[5] feminist and queer work undertaken through them can be, especially if developed in the spirit of what I will call critically affirmative theoretical bricolage. Taking up the challenges articulated by recent paradigm shifts (for example to the automatized responses of a "hermeneuticist of suspicion") without forgetting the crucial insights of late twentieth-century critical reflexivity enables complex modes of participation in twenty-first-century theory. As Kay Young demonstrates in her work on the gendered imaginaries of new brain research, such a qualified participation allows queer and feminist scholars to explore the diversity and complexity of contemporary approaches, critically engaging with individual premises and conclusions rather than redrawing global frontiers (including those old ones between the humanities and the sciences).

Such detailed engagement may in fact result in the identification of conceptual breaking points, or at least in a cautious close-up on conceptual regions of serious friction, for example regarding the degree to which the centrality of reproductive heterosexuality in most, if not all accounts of evo-

---

2. See Sedgwick's plea for a reparative epistemology overcoming what Paul Ricoeur called the "hermeneutics of suspicion" (Sedgwick and Frank 124).

3. See, e.g., Sedgwick, *Tendencies* 8; on queer theory's contemporary perspectives, see Halley and Parker.

4. See also Edelman's critique of the discussion about an "after sex" moment even in queer theory itself ("Ever After").

5. See Best and Marcus's critique of depth models.

lution threatens to newly marginalize not only nonreproductive sexualities but also nonsexual layers of gender. Simultaneously, however, this detailed engagement allows for exploring productive alliances, for example by returning to Darwin's fascination with the beauty of "endless forms." While the list of promising research foci in the spirit of such bricolage is no less endless, this volume explores a few in particular. Instead of choosing between investigations of affect versus sexuality, there is a lot of productive work to be done in investigating what are perhaps not so much conceptual marriages as "polyamorous relations" between affect and sexuality in the study of culture: that is, in mapping the multifaceted, plural, and contextually changing ways in which feelings are sexualized and desires imbricated in affective orientations (see also Cvetkovich 172). Sue Kim's work underlines the need for analyses that detail the equally multifaceted relations between affective engagements, social structures, and histories. If the twenty-first-century turn to "positive feelings" threatens to displace attention to the histories that block such positive feelings (see Ahmed 50), then a challenge for queer and feminist, or more broadly egalitarian and critically engaged, scholarship in the present condition is to equip our investigative sewing kits (and butch tool belts) for weaving these histories into cautiously reparative theoretical assemblages, that is, a mesh of conceptual devices that chain together disparate critical moments and modes of engaged thought. As I argue below, narrative theory can play a central role in these endeavors. But that very suggestion demands a quick detour.

Queer–Feminist–Narrative: Arrangements (beyond Althusser & Co)

The privileging of "queer" over "feminist" in the title of this volume may seem warranted as a political gesture of "affirmative action," given the research results that Susan Lanser notes, which demonstrate that "feminist narrative theory" has in fact developed into a relatively established paradigm, whereas "queer narrative theory" remains severely marginalized. Such a (situational) political move should, however, not congeal into some neo-fundamentalist theoretical positioning of one category against the other. Rather, the larger theoretical as well as political task at hand is continuously to imbricate the two—as well as to plan follow-up forums that foreground the analysis of racism, class inequality, or the significance of religion in the interplay with both.

As to the privileging of "narrative theory" over its "queer" and "feminist" modifiers, Coykendall's critique made me wonder how my own lack of discomfort with this arrangement indicates my entanglement in the twenty-first-century theoretical trends outlined above. As someone whose academic trajectory took her from an initial focus on "cultural studies" approaches (or, specifically, the interrelations between gender, sexuality, and race) to a sustained interest in contextually informed aesthetic theory, I admittedly love to attend variously modified narrative theory conferences these days, while also importing narrative approaches to queer and feminist conferences. Nonetheless, I suggest that we think about other metaphors than those suggested by Coykendall. Affirming narrative theory not as "traffic cop" but as "elected chairperson with constitutionally circumscribed rights (to be amended as needed), for a set period of time, with the possibility of reelection," might allow us to escape the Althusserian ghosts haunting the police metaphor, perhaps even without immediately falling prey to charges of naïve (Habermasian) ignorance vis-à-vis power. (A chair certainly has power, but as many of us know from our respective departmental contexts, it is a service position.) Seriously: In a spirit of critical affirmation once more, I suggest that we remain aware of the implications inscribed in our framings of the theoretical field (as Coykendall suggests) and that we emphasize their historicity and provisionality along with our agency in changing them, but simultaneously calm the inner hermeneutist of suspicion to the degree that we can comfortably work within a productive framing for, minimally, the duration of a specific occasion.

Reconfiguring Narrative—Narrative Reconfigurations

What, then, is the campaign message of hope offered by narrative, or its qualification for office? The contributions to this volume suggest little consensus in this respect as well. Whereas Susan Lanser powerfully insists that the art of telling a story is queer as such, Judith Roof answers her related question on whether otherness is already part of the story with a much more skeptical "I don't know." Such hesitations are haunted by long-standing controversies in cultural theory at large, echoing some of the post/modernist critiques of narrative which, in the age of Theory, forcefully challenged its authority in the name of categories like performance or space. At the same time, the fact that this critique echoes in question marks rather than programmatic statements these days may indicate that it has become overshadowed by the contrary vectors of narrative's forceful return onto the critical stage in the 2000s.[6] At

---

6. On these (with a closer look, rather complicated) vectors, as well as some of the following, see my *An Aesthetics of Narrative Performance.*

its worst, this return, which has certainly fueled also the transdisciplinary expansion of narrative theory (beyond early proclamations of a "narrative turn" as part of the postmodern regime of reflexivity) can appear as part of the backlash scenario (with respect to a renewed marginalization of queer and feminist investigations) unfolded above. In the wake of Ricoeur's phenomenological definition of narrative as the work of ordering "our confused, unformed [. . .] temporal experience," some cognitive conceptualizations have, in fact, foregrounded narrative's presumed power of establishing coherence and continuity, and told strongly universalizing stories.[7]

However, the overflowing "home/world improvement belt" of narrative theory—including recent cognitive narrative theory—also offers quite different perspectives to queer and feminist scholars. Itself an object of the suggested practice of critically affirmative theoretical bricolage, narrative can simultaneously become its conceptual framework. Narrative scholars affiliated with otherwise diverging approaches have similarly insisted on the performative dimension of narrative in recent years, on the importance of the practice or "action" of telling (Jacobs and Sussman x; Herman 23; Phelan 4). As an *act* and *process* of worldmaking, however, narrative certainly offers space for "otherness," or queer affects and aesthetics. While I share Sedgwick's impatience with the "always"-proclamations of Theory & Co (see *Touching Feeling* 125), and thus would be careful to claim that narrative is inherently queer or feminist as such, I will make a strong plea for its potential as a medium of egalitarian articulations. In theoretical terms, the conceptual bricolage constituting this model revamps notions of performative resignification through twenty-first-century foci on affect and phenomenology. Thus, Judith Butler's act of localizing resignification at the intersection of Derrida and Bourdieu in *Excitable Speech* can serve as a starting point for a model of narrative as a process of performative reconfiguration. Starting from Butler's insistences that speech acts, including counterhegemonic ones, remain embedded in relatively stable social power structures and histories of signification without therefore becoming entirely powerless themselves, I have conceptualized narrative as a process intertwining rupture and repetition; in other words, as the critically affirmative rearranging and reshaping of sociosymbolic building blocks (see Breger). Although I insist that these building blocks of narrative reconfiguration are necessarily shot through with signification (which puts this model of narrative at odds with some of the antisignification emphases in recent affect theory; see Gregg and Seigworth), there is no need to identify

---

7. Ricoeur xi. Coherence assumes a central status, e.g., in Ryan; for the return to universals, see Hogan.

them primarily as linguistic units and thus remain within the orbit of more or less poststructuralist resignification theories. Instead, I conceptualize the process of narrative reconfiguration as a worldmaking assemblage of affects and variously mediated archival scraps, including memories, images, and sounds as well as words.

Rather than remaining bound to specific, usually hegemonic plots, representational techniques, and temporalities, such a model of narrative reconfiguration recognizes that narrative comes in a vast plurality of forms. Here, aesthetics—in the sense of an intermedial poetics—is promising as a methodology of mapping and evaluating possibilities. For example, it can productively mediate interventions into ongoing debates on queer temporalities. Exploring queer forms of temporality in Dan Savage's controversial "It Gets Better" project, Jesse Matz's essay thus takes on Lee Edelman's radically antinarrative insistences on "dis- or de-figuration," on the "ahistoricism" and "incoherence" of sex, and by extension, his programmatic *No Future* proclamation for queer theory.[8] Matz does so by underlining the prominent use of present tense forms and spatialized tropes, which bring the future into affective proximity. As I would contextualize them, such techniques have more generally been developed in much contemporary culture as a powerful ensemble of *presence*-oriented techniques of narrative performance. Some scholars have articulated discomfort with the imaginary collapsing of actual lapses in time through these rhetorical techniques, with their sentimentalism as well as their disregard for the temporality of trauma ("it doesn't get better"). For my part, I do also see the promise of the presence techniques in reaching many of the LGBTQ youth targeted by the project, but would nonetheless advocate for the continued exploration of alternative techniques. To be sure, the alternative solution of 1990s queer theory, which underlined the *theatricalizing* techniques of parody, camp, and, generally, heightened artificiality, may in some respects seem difficult to reappropriate for the age of affirmation. Nonetheless, more broadly conceptualized theatricality or simply distancing techniques of various kinds should perhaps not be altogether discarded from the multifaceted formal archive of queer narrative reconfiguration. (Perhaps all-too-plainly: "even if it doesn't get better, you can get better at dealing with it").

More generally, exploring the rich ensemble of (performative-)narrative techniques probed in the multimedia archives of historical as well as contemporary queer, feminist, and other egalitarian-minded cultural production allows us to counter the grand theoretical gestures of negativity as well as

---

8. Edelman, "Ever After" 470–71; Freeman xxi; both with reference to Edelman's earlier *No Future*.

"antinegativity." While queerness is certainly not exclusively bound to Edelman's Now, it is also not necessarily "about the rejection of a here and now," as José Esteban Muñoz has suggested in his reconceptualization of queerness in and for the age of affirmation (1). While it is, as I will underline with Muñoz, about "enact[ing . . .] new worlds," theorizing these worlds through the concept of narrative reconfiguration outlined above allows attaching "hope" not only to the realm of utopia but also to the messy and variously compromised, but changing, spaces of actual collective and individual lives.[9] As suggested by Elizabeth Freeman, whose *Time Binds* begins to explore such possibilities for queer narrative, delving into the "pleasure and power of figuration"—or, as I would word it, narrative reconfiguration—provides us with a host of ways of "encountering pasts, speculating futures, and interpenetrating the two in ways that counter the common sense of the present tense" (Freeman xxi, xv; see also Matz). In short, I can certainly see myself voting for that narrative chairperson again: There is a lot of work she can still do for us.

Works Cited

Ahmed, Sara. "Happy Objects." Gregg and Seigworth 29–51.

Best, Stephen, and Sharon Marcus. "Surface Reading: An Introduction." *Representations* 108.1 (2009): 1–21.

Breger, Claudia. *An Aesthetics of Narrative Performance: Transnational Theater, Literature, and Film in Contemporary Germany.* Columbus: The Ohio State UP, 2012.

Butler, Judith. *Excitable Speech: A Politics of the Performative.* New York: Routledge, 1997.

Culler, Jonathan D. *Literary Theory: A Very Short Introduction.* 2nd ed. Oxford: Oxford UP, 2011.

Cvetkovich, Ann. "Public Feelings." Halley and Parker 169–79.

Edelman, Lee. "Ever After: History, Negativity, and the Social." *South Atlantic Quarterly* 106.3 (2007): 469–76.

———. *No Future: Queer Theory and the Death Drive.* Durham: Duke UP, 2004.

Elliott, Jane, and Derek Attridge, eds. *Theory After "Theory."* New York: Routledge, 2011.

Freeman, Elizabeth. *Time Binds: Queer Temporalities, Queer Histories.* Durham: Duke UP, 2010.

Gregg, Melissa, and Gregory J. Seigworth. *The Affect Theory Reader.* Durham: Duke UP, 2010.

Halley, Janet, and Andrew Parker. *After Sex? On Writing since Queer Theory.* Durham: Duke UP, 2011.

Herman, David. *Story Logic: Problems and Possibilities of Narrative.* Lincoln: U of Nebraska P, 2002.

---

9. Muñoz 1–4. Anticipating cynical rebuttals, I should perhaps add that the sphere of contemporary U.S./American politics evoked by my rather incautious metaphorical play may not necessarily present a very strong example for possibilities of effective change.

Hogan, Patrick Colm. *The Mind and Its Stories: Narrative Universals and Human Emotion*. Cambridge: Cambridge UP, 2003.

Jacobs, Carol, and Henry Sussman, eds. *Acts of Narrative*. Stanford: Stanford UP, 2003.

Massumi, Brian. *Parables for the Virtual: Movement, Affect, Sensation*. Durham: Duke UP, 2002.

Matz, Jesse. "The Art of Time, Theory to Practice." *Narrative* 19.3 (2011): 273–94.

Muñoz, Jose Esteban. *Cruising Utopia: The Then and There of Queer Futurity*. New York: NYU P, 2009.

Phelan, James. *Narrative as Rhetoric: Technique, Audiences, Ethics, Ideology*. Columbus: The Ohio State UP, 1996.

Ricoeur, Paul. *Time and Narrative*. Trans. Kathleen McLaughlin and David Pellauer. Vol 1. Chicago: U of Chicago P, 1984.

Ryan, Marie-Laure, ed. *Narrative across Media: The Languages of Storytelling*. Lincoln: U of Nebraska P, 2004.

Sedgwick, Eve Kosofsky. *Tendencies*. Durham: Duke UP, 1993.

Sedgwick, Eve Kosofsky, and Adam Frank. *Touching Feeling: Affect, Pedagogy, Performativity*. Durham: Duke UP, 2003.

ELLEN PEEL

Narrative Causes

Inside and Out

A thread that runs through several of the essays in this volume—
with varying degrees of prominence—is that of *causality.* Long
a key category in narrative analysis, causality itself is a miniature narrative:
"*a* caused *b.*" Suppose we hear the sequence of events: "The queen died and
then the other queen died."[1] We wonder if event #1 caused event #2: "The
queen died, and then the other queen died of grief." Even if the causal link
is not explicit, we wonder if *post hoc, ergo propter hoc.* Some might consider
causality a solved problem or (still worse) a passé one. But in the spirit of
trendiness-fatigue, I want to point out the diverse and rewarding ways that
these essays have brought the notion of causality back to life.

Causality has been examined in detail by narrative theorists such as
Emma Kafalenos in *Narrative Causality.* Because of space limitations, however, I will be discussing just two general kinds: (1) what causes what within
a text, and (2) what a text causes in its readers. The first kind of causality—
what causes what within a text—is addressed most explicitly in Valerie Rohy's
"Strange Influence: Queer Etiology in *The Picture of Dorian Gray.*" Questioning whether the etiology of homosexuality should be the fulcrum of argu-

---

1. I am of course alluding to E. M. Forster's distinction: "'The king died and then the
queen died' is a story. 'The king died, and then the queen died of grief' is a plot. The time-
sequence is preserved, but the sense of causality overshadows it" (86).

ments about gay civil rights, she posits causality as a rule made to be broken, as in Oscar Wilde's *Dorian Gray*. Homosexuality pervades the text but cannot be named. "Influences" are often mentioned, but homosexuality is their absent effect. It is also an absent cause, so readers see a perversion of novelistic form. And in one sense causality stretches outside this text: insofar as the book *causes* Wilde's relationship with Lord Douglas, the creator of the book is created by it. Rohy ends by asking more broadly what work is done by homosexuality in desire narratives. Although she does not see homosexuality as the same as queerness, it might still be valuable to extend her inquiry by asking whether lost causes like those of *Dorian Gray* might be present—or absent—in narratives that are more fundamentally queer.

Causality plays a more implicit role in Paul Morrison's "*Maurice*, or Coming Out Straight." He explains that E. M. Forster resembles Freud in that the novelist sees homosexuality as the prime mover (the cause) in *Maurice*, though the two writers otherwise differ. For Freud, it is as if there are no bad heterosexuals: if a problem arises in human development, he attributes it to homosexuality—in my terms, a perversion of causality. (Morrison also exposes a paradox in Freud's notion of causality: the opposition to familialism is like the reproduction of familialism, presumably because the son's opposition to his father is like the father's opposition to his own father.) In *Maurice*, homosexuality is not phase-based, for it is a *rupture* of stasis and seems "out of time." Morrison concludes by observing that it would be hard to show that as a positive model of queer temporality.

The second kind of causality—what a text causes in its readers—predominates in Sue Kim's work on empathy in 1970s novels by women of color. Kim begins by wondering about allegiances shared by women of color across cultures, though she warns that the term "women of color" risks losing its political valence. She then moves to the theme I am stressing and warns that causality is hard to trace. One complex example is the literary marketplace, which both shapes novels and is in turn shaped by them. Kim draws on the work of Suzanne Keen to ask her main question about causality: "To what extent does empathy aroused by novel reading result in prosocial action?" She explains specific narrative strategies that her authors employ to evoke empathy, but she acknowledges limitations on what empathy can actually do. To use my term: even if a text can "cause" empathy, it cannot "cause" social change unless it is linked to understanding of social circumstances and tied to social movements beyond the text.

Kim's essay brings to mind broader issues about the values in narratives. She apparently shares many of the values expressed in the novels she is examining, and therefore would hope the novels could convey those values to readers. Might her theory change in any way if she applied it to narratives whose values she did not share, as Susan Rubin Suleiman does in *Authoritarian Fictions: The Ideological Novel as Literary Genre*?[2] Others might question whether it is a good thing for novels to convey values, desirable or not, in the first place. Still others might assert that, whether or not conveying values is a good thing, it is unavoidable (although hard to control or measure).

Finally, Jesse Matz's essay, while explicitly about temporality, asks implicitly about both kinds of causality: what causes what within a text and what a text causes in its readers (or viewers). It would seem that the queer narrative temporality in Lee Edelman's *No Future: Queer Theory and the Death Drive* has nothing in common with that in the "It Gets Better" videos and book project, but Matz demonstrates that, surprisingly, the project tries to meet Edelman's demands. For example, the project emphasizes that the future awaits the narratee in the present, shows that change can be sudden, dramatizes the performativity of the promise, conflates the narratee with the past self of the narrator, and employs counterfactuality. The narrators play with temporality *within* the text in order to cause the narratees to do something *outside* the text: to refrain from drastic action, especially suicide.

Matz's method involves finding traces of Edelman in "It Gets Better"; what if we also try the reverse? The project privileges survival: might we find traces of that in *No Future* as well? In a sense, Edelman's work is a paean to negativity (including the death drive), to its ability to persist in the face of the narcissistic fantasies and self-delusions entailed by "reproductive futurism" (2). In fact, he argues that, even if society did not position queers as the figure of negativity, that structural position would remain (27). He ultimately says that everyone occupies that niche anyway, even if unwittingly (153). Ironically, by claiming in effect that "it never gets better," Edelman is asserting the survival of negativity.

I will close by offering a few of my own reflections—less a response to Matz himself than to the two approaches he is analyzing. How might we avoid the "hopelessly convincing" negativity of Edelman and the "hokey" "sentimentality" of the "It Gets Better" project?[3] Perhaps, instead of throwing out the child along with the bathwater of reproductive futurism as Edelman does, and instead of embracing the occasional reproductive sentimentality of "It Gets Better," we can move to a queer version of children and reproduction, if not of futurism. Queerness opens up new possibilities, not only in the literal realm of "It Gets Better," but also in the (mostly) nonliteral realm

---

2. Keen addresses related issues through her concept of "empathetic inaccuracy" (136–40).
3. Matz used the terms "hokey" and "sentimental" during the question period.

of *No Future,* where we can consider queer children and reproduction as figures.[4]

We can open up reproduction beyond Edelman's heterosexual emphasis. Queer adults do reproduce themselves in various ways, either nurturant or procreative.[5] He acknowledges the possibility of nurturing through adoption, but—as Susan Fraiman says in her respectful critique of an earlier version of *No Future*—he suppresses "procreative queerness even as he brings up lesbian and gay parenting. [He ties] this firmly and exclusively to *adoption*" (133). She comments: "What remains unthinkable is queer pregnancy . . . [and] queer men with kids genetically their own" (132). Those possibilities have existed for millennia, and nowadays in vitro fertilization and other kinds of assisted reproductive technology make possible procreative reproduction without intercourse. In the future—for better or worse—procreation may be even less heterosexual, indeed almost asexual, to use a term that Edelman associates with queerness (building on Baudrillard [61] and Lacan [82]). Already turkeys can reproduce by parthenogenesis, and cattle and sheep by cloning. The figurative possibilities of such processes are just beginning to be tapped, as in Margaret Atwood's *Oryx and Crake.*

Moving beyond parenthood, whether nurturant or procreative, we come to subtler kinds of nurturing. Fraiman introduces the concept of "the butch maternal" (147), exemplified in some of Jess's feelings and actions in Leslie Feinberg's *Stone Butch Blues* (1993). One instance occurs "when [Jess is] dreaming of what she would do in an ideal world. . . . This is clearly not a dream of conceiving or even adopting offspring, but it is a dream of tending and attending to children as well as plants" (152). In addition, when Jess takes care of another woman's children, her unconventional gender helps in "their struggle to discard old axioms in favor of the new knowledge [about gender that] Jess embodies" (153). Jess's effect on the children reproduces her knowledge, especially about queer gender.

The idea of nurturant reproduction that passes on knowledge brings us to education. Matz calls the "It Gets Better" narrators "pedagogical" and "parental"; this pedagogy is especially parental because what it aims to give the narratees is (continued) life itself. More broadly, this teaching reminds us that in a sense all education, formal and informal, is a kind of reproduction, a passing on of part of oneself. In the classroom, queer math teachers pass on their

---

4. I acknowledge that Edelman is not talking about literal reproduction and children (11), but he's not not talking about them either. To say his figural Child has nothing to do with the child would be like saying Lacan's phallus has nothing to do with the penis.

5. Edelman does remark, "It is true that the ranks of [queer] parents grow larger every day" (17).

conception of calculus, and queer narrative theorists pass on their conception of storytelling. Nowadays some queer teachers even pass on their conception of queerness. Outside the classroom—in the "It Gets Better" project, for example—queer people teach informally as well; in fact, a major complaint of homophobes is that homosexuality reproduces itself, through teachings about queerness (or through teachings *of* queerness—those unnamed "influences" in *Dorian Gray*).

Thus human reproduction involves causality in two ways. The first is procreation, *causing* a person to live (an act of commission—an almost melodramatic, aorist moment in the case when sperm meets egg; a more prolonged event in the case of labor [not a moment but still, thankfully, a limited time]). We need to recognize that in addition reproduction involves nurturing, *causing* a person not to die (an ongoing, low-key, progressive process that encourages an act of omission). This latter process ranges from feeding an infant to preventing an adult from committing suicide. To use William Faulkner's terms in a queer way, causing a person to live or not to die can mean not only to endure, but to prevail.[6] Queer reproduction can cause a person—causality that has figurative as well as literal power.

Works Cited

Atwood, Margaret. *Oryx and Crake*. Toronto: McClelland and Stewart, 2003.

Edelman, Lee. *No Future: Queer Theory and the Death Drive*. Durham: Duke UP, 2004.

Faulkner, William. "William Faulkner—Banquet Speech." *Nobelprize.org*. Nobel Media AB. 2013. <http://www.nobelprize.org/nobel_prizes/literature/laureates/1949/faulkner-speech.html>. Accessed 20 Apr. 2014.

Forster, E. M. *Aspects of the Novel*. 1927. New York: Harvest / Harcourt, Brace & World, 1955.

Fraiman, Susan. *Cool Men and the Second Sex*. New York: Columbia UP, 2003.

Kafalenos, Emma. *Narrative Causalities*. Columbus: The Ohio State UP, 2006.

Keen, Suzanne. *Empathy and the Novel*. New York: Oxford UP, 2007.

Suleiman, Susan Rubin. *Authoritarian Fictions: The Ideological Novel as Literary Genre*. New York: Columbia UP, 1983.

---

6. "I believe that man will not merely endure: he will prevail" ("Banquet Speech").

SHALYN CLAGGETT

The Human Problem

*I*n the past twenty-five years, queer and feminist narrative theory has covered an incredible amount of methodological and theoretical territory and has been usefully applied in fields ranging from literary studies to neuroscience. It thus seems particularly important to identify those areas of inquiry from which we have the most to gain. We have built *out*; now what will we build *up*? In an effort to provide a partial answer to this question, I want to pinpoint and enlarge upon a particularly knotty issue which, for lack of better terminology, I simply call "the human problem": the difficulty presented by the fact that by virtue of its political and ethical dimensions, feminist and queer narrative theory must take stock of extratextual significance while at the same time distinguishing between real-world context and its representation. I will first attempt to identify why this problem has remained overlooked and undertheorized, and then focus on two potential solutions suggested by participants at the Queer and Feminist Narrative Theory Symposium that inspired this volume.

Throughout this volume, oppositions—whether identified as illusory, heuristic, or reductive—are recognized as a continuing obstacle for feminist and queer narrative theory. As Susan Lanser pointed out in 1986, feminist narratology is itself a refusal to recognize seemingly incompatible methodologies; specifically, the "false opposition" between the ostensibly "scientific, descriptive, and non-ideological" investments of narratology and the "impressionistic, evaluative, and political" interests of feminism (674). Resistance to a host of other oppositions organizes many of these essays, each critique accompanied by its own unique solution. For instance, both Judith Roof and Lanser cite the enduring pervasiveness of essentialist binaries that continue to inform narrative approaches to gender, and both suggest a methodological solution that would allow for a more fluid and holistic conception of identity (Lanser through intersectionality and Roof through systems theory). Suzanne Keen and Kay Young identify the assumption of biologically determined binary distinctions as equally pervasive but also illusory: neither the paradigm of the gay/straight, male/female brain nor the nature versus cultural context divide, it seems, is consistent with scientific research.

Such responses, however, prompt a question: if queer and feminist narrative theory consistently identifies multiple sets of oppositions to which it must respond, is the structure of the response necessitated by the phenomena examined, or is it, too, a product of a convenient organizational logic, albeit one based in well-intentioned critique? In other words, is our poststructural inheritance becoming a rhetorical conceit? If not, it seems that the next step is to discover some larger and more comprehensive set of categories that can embrace, or at least connect, the seemingly disparate ways "out" of binarism without endorsing a single approach. Surely it is neither feasible nor desirable for all feminist/queer narrative critics to become practitioners of intersectionality or unilaterally embrace systems theory—but is it possible to identify the key underlying interests that such approaches share?

The particular terms used to describe what narrative approaches to gender should be aiming at—terms such as "node," "nexus," "vector," "intersection," "product-in-flux"—seem to carry similar connotations, but viewed from a strictly narrative perspective, they suggest a clear division of interest over whether the concept of identity addressed in any given approach exists within or outside of the text. It is often very difficult to tell if feminist/queer narrative critics are talking about human psychology or its representation— or, if both, how those two things are connected. Of course, narrative theory attempts to account for both the text and the various modes through which it is interpreted, but its great strength compared with other approaches making the same claim (e.g., new historicism and cultural studies) is its ability to account for the connection between text and reader with rigor and specificity. Many of these essays connect narrative to a real-world context through analogy, with arguments explicitly or implicitly taking the form "these aspects of the story function in this way, which is similar to / models / calls into question these existing social relations . . . ." As effective as analogy may be, the pervasiveness of this kind of parallelism suggests either a shared belief that it is not crucial to *directly* connect the storyworld to the social world, or (what seems more likely) an ideational impasse. One way to get around (or through) this difficulty is to focus on the actual reader, either through cognitive psychology, neuroscience, or reception studies. The great benefit of such approaches is that they focus on the site of transfer from the textual to the phenomenal world. Narrative, however, is both what affects the mind and is its product. Understandably, narrative's wide-ranging relevance in representing human subjectivity is precisely what the move toward analogy seeks to maintain, even if it is not a viable solution.

Two potentially useful but as yet undertheorized areas of scrutiny might offer a way to more directly address this problem: character and nonfictional narrative. Character, as one of the most basic categories of narrative theory, offers a particularly promising site for analyzing the connection between the actual and the represented world. As Lanser notes, character is lamentably ignored in narrative studies in general and in feminist and queer narrative theory in particular. Situated at the liminal space between the literary and the human, character might offer the most promising entry point into a rigorous application of narrative theory in questions of gender at the level of culture. As Mieke Bal has observed, one of the first major contributions of feminist criticism was the attention it brought to how female characters functioned (often marginally) in certain kinds of texts (124). Such longitudinal examinations of character, however, seem to have fallen away in favor of interpretations of particular cultural works that challenge or complicate narrative conceptions of gender. This is not to say that focusing on such texts is not a valuable and important enterprise, but only that it is equally important to theorize how the arsenal of techniques narrative theory has accumulated since its structuralist beginnings can be used to examine character understood as human personality, rather than exclusively focusing on character as literary device.

The problem with character, as narrative theorists have long and insistently observed, is that characters are not people, although they continually tempt readers to see them as such. As John Frow explains, character has remained "the most undertheorized of the basic categories of narrative theory" precisely because "the concept is not specific to the discourse of literary theory but is necessarily dependent upon cultural schemata defining the nature of the self" (227). Reacting against the tendency of earlier critics who treated characters as independent, expressive agents, structuralist theorists including A. J. Greimas, Philippe Hamon, and Tzvetan Todorov took as their point of departure the premise that the mimetic quality of character is not relevant to serious analysis of the text's structure of signification.[1] Such a perspective, which Alex Woloch succinctly summarizes as the "excision of the human from narratology," has since become "the price of entry into a theoretical perspective on characterization" (16, 15).

To treat character as a technical function within the totality of the text's semantic structure, however, risks relegating the work of narrative theory to considerations of the literary and aesthetic due to the constructedness of the text—something that feminist and queer narrative theory strives not to do. The seemingly obvious observation that characters are not people does not mean that the category of "character" does not come into play for human subjects. People cast themselves and others as characters in their own narratives in accordance with, or in defiance of, the social and cultural scripts available to them. Particularly illuminating in this regard is Jonathan Adler's work on narrative identity in relation to mental health. In a recently published study, forty-seven patients were asked to write short narratives throughout their experience of psychotherapy in order to assess the degree to which personal agency correlated with mental health. As expected, mental health increased throughout the course of therapy, as did the degree of agency formally expressed in the narratives related to the experience of therapy. Far more surprising, however, was the study's finding that the narration of agency *preceded* patient-assessed improvement. As Adler put it at the conclusion of his paper, "the results indicate that individuals begin to tell new stories and then live their way into them" ("Living" 385). The significance of such a finding for feminist and queer studies is twofold: first, it underscores that it is possible for individuals belonging to historically marginalized groups to claim agency within oppressive systems. Second, it identifies narrative as the tool through which self-actualization may be achieved.

Of course, what social and cognitive psychologists mean by "narrative identity" does not quite correlate with any existing narratological concept.[2] Nevertheless, "narrative identity" most resembles direct characterization, when a character's traits are "stated by the narrator [or] the character herself" (Prince 13). In a recent interview about this study, Adler observed that "people tend to really like the realization that they are not only the main characters in their stories, but they're also the narrator," with the protagonist position correlating to an idea of self that acts and is acted upon by external

---

1. For examples of criticism that emphasizes the mimetic and expressivist quality of character, see Q. D. Leavis, F. R. Leavis, Rawdon Wilson, and W. J. Harvey.

2. Adler defines narrative identity as "the internalized, evolving story of the self that each person crafts to provide his or her life with a sense of purpose and unity" ("Living" 367).

circumstances, and the narrator position corresponding to the way in which one "makes meaning" of the things that happen to the protagonist. From a narratological point of view, these distinct modes of conceiving of the self correspond not just to character and narrator, but also to the categories of story and discourse and the actantial roles of object and subject. Of further potential interest to narrative theorists, Adler's study did not focus on what patients reported (content), but rather tracked the way in which they told their stories (form). For example, one of the key ways in which the study identified an increase in projected mental control was the narrator's shift in framing the protagonist from passive object to active agent. In what can perhaps be best described as a close reading of a particular case study, Adler discusses the patient's growing awareness of a "distinct story line," comments on how she "framed herself" as a main character, and draws attention to "agentic narrative constructions" that replace the patient's former tendency to use the passive voice ("Living" 380). He further observes that "Significantly more often than not, participants recounted their experiences in treatment as episodes in an unfolding story, sometimes with compelling imagery, characters, and symbolism" (384). In short, the interpretation of psychological data on narrative identity offers just one example of an area in which narratological techniques might be usefully employed to better understand human identity outside of the text. One way to get around an ideational impasse, after all, is to come at it from the other side—not by examining how the real is represented or how the represented is like the real, but how the represented becomes real, in direct and measurable ways.

The second site of interest for addressing the human problem is through the study of nonfiction, including but also outside of lifewriting. Narrative theory's reluctance to address nonfictional nonautobiographical texts is understandable, since textual construction and social construction are clearly not the same thing. The former arises from a discrete set of information filtered through an individual consciousness and motivated by all the social, historical, and personal imperatives called into play by the more or less conscious construction of an implied author; the latter, from a far more amorphous and ambiguous hailing to assume a limited set of possibilities that exist provisionally within a given time and place. Far more than narratology in general, feminist and queer narrative theory has interrogated this dividing line, but has not yet explained how we can get from one side of the equation to the other. As "analogy" readings have ably demonstrated, social construction resembles and influences the construction of fictional narrative, but narratology proper fiercely guards against this conflation.

This defensive position is perhaps most eloquently and elaborately demonstrated in Dorrit Cohn's *The Distinction of Fiction* (1998), in which she convincingly critiques Hayden White's work by arguing that the shared use of emplotment does not render fiction a subcategory of history simply because the latter plays by one of the former's rules. Here, however, narratology has an advantage, because the fact that rendering history fictional fails to account for the distinction of fiction does not necessarily mean that the tools developed by narrative theory cannot be used to account for how nonliterary historical (and not just literary or cultural) artifacts deploy many of the techniques identified by narrative theorists. In other words, rather than making narratology's claim to relevance through an inductive reading of literary texts and claiming, repeatedly, that the dynamics examined resemble structures in the actual world, narrative theory might usefully deploy the tools it has already developed in laying bare the otherwise implicit agendas or implications of political policy, religious doctrine, scientific research, and legal writing.

Admittedly, the application of narrative theory to nonfiction entails an ethical dimension that has, perhaps, dissuaded ever-vigilant feminist and queer theorists from engaging directly with nonautobiographical referentiality. Asking why nonfiction other than autobiography has been overlooked by feminist narratology, Alison Booth observes that nonfictional modes like biography occupy a "messy" ethical space, whereas autobiography implicitly appeals to a feminist/queer interest in self-fashioning. By the very fact of its existence, particularly when in defiance of heteronormative or patriarchal values, autobiography forcefully announces individual agency. Biography, however, by virtue of the fact that it "speaks" for another, potentially threatens to rob the subject of agency. Yet another reason why the stakes are higher, here, is what James Phelan has termed the "ethics of referentiality," the "tacit understanding between author and audience in historical narrative that the historian's narrative is rooted in the events and facts that have an existence independent of that narrative" (219). Misrepresenting the qualities of a fictional character makes one a poor reader; misrepresenting the qualities of an actual person makes one a liar.

Despite these potential pitfalls, however, it seems crucial for feminist and queer narrative theory to address nonfictional texts not *despite* but *because of* the ethical dimension. The well intentioned desire to be scrupulous about not reproducing the repressive dynamics of a cultural discourse that has historically spoken for disempowered groups has ultimately left a great deal unsaid (and potentially unsayable). One of the seminal questions of feminist and queer studies is how one writes about an unrecorded history. In the paper she delivered at the Queer and Feminist Narrative Theory Symposium, Ann Cvetkovich suggested that queer historical fiction imagines a possible past that does not so much dispense with the ethics of referentiality as productively play with the concept. Booth shows that we may not so much lack historical texts as lack the texts we would like to examine. Verifiable reference is a luxury, and nonfictional texts outside of autobiography can and do tell us something, if not about what "actually happened," at least about how it was represented, and narrative analysis can be usefully employed in determining for what purpose, how, and why. As Lanser remarked in 1986, what feminist and narrative studies most notably share is a commitment to that which is "practical." It seems, to me, that it is entirely impractical to remain reluctant about addressing nonfictional texts. Such texts have and will be written about, by historians who are and are not invested in narrative theory. Now is the time to make a bid for relevance, not merely for the sake of our theoretical commitments, but, more importantly, for the emergent archives that are now coming to light and are more increasingly available to readers of all kinds in the digital age.

I have attempted here, however tentatively, to address the "human problem" from two potentially fruitful angles for narrative theory in general, and feminist and queer narrative theory in particular: first, at the level of individuals who conceive of the conception of self in narrative terms, and second, at the level of how people are represented and understood. These sites are psychological and cultural, but neither is, properly speaking, literary. As Mieke Bal has observed, the reason why narratology has "traditionally been confined . . . to the category of story-telling, mostly literary, mostly novelistic" is largely because narrative's omnipresence in the real world makes it particularly difficult to justify interpretations beyond simply establishing narrative status or classifying types of narratives (226). Feminist/queer critics, however, have a ready answer to the question of which narrative cultural artifacts deserve analysis; namely, those that matter to social equality. As Hilary Schor stated in response to the papers delivered at the Queer and Feminist Narrative Theory Symposium, "justice" is precisely what "feminist narrative theory should be about." Outside of aesthetic judgments, "justice" happens (or fails to happen) outside the realm of the literary, and in that respect, the "human problem" is far more than a theoretical difficulty or omission in scholarship—it is political, social, and ethical. In the coming decades, perhaps the most direct way that feminist/queer critics can address these concerns is through a rigorous narrative analysis of texts that express, contour, or delimit the lived experience of actual people.

Works Cited

Adler, Jonathan M. Interview by Jim Fleming. "Stories of You." *To the Best of Our Knowledge.* 17 Feb. 2012. <http://www.ttbook.org/book/story-you>. Accessed 28 April 2012.

——. "Living Into the Story: Agency and Coherence in a Longitudinal Study of Narrative Identity Development and Mental Health Over the Course of Psychotherapy." *Journal of Personality and Social Psychology* 102.2 (2012): 367–89.

Bal, Mieke. *Narratology: Introduction to the Theory of Narrative.* 3rd ed. Toronto: U of Toronto P, 2009.

Cohn, Dorrit. *The Distinction of Fiction.* Baltimore: Johns Hopkins UP, 1998.

Cvetkovich, Ann. "The Affective Turn, the Archival Turn, and Queer Historical Fictions." Ohio State's Project Narrative Symposium: Queer and Feminist Narrative Theory. Hyatt Regency Hotel, Columbus, OH. 12–14 May 2011. Conference Presentation.

Frow, John. "Spectacle Binding: On Character." *Poetics Today* 7.2 (1986): 227–50.

Greimas, A. J. *Sémantique structural: Recherche de methode.* Paris: Librairie Larousse, 1966.

Hamon, Philippe. "Pour un statut sémiologique du personage." In *Poétique du récit,* ed. Gérard Genette and Tzvetan Todorov. Paris: Éditions du Seuil, 1977.

Harvey, W. J. *Character and the Novel.* Ithaca: Cornell UP, 1965.

Lanser, Susan. "Toward a Feminist Narratology." 1986. In *Feminisms: An Anthology of Literary Theory and Criticism.* Ed. Robyn R. Warhol and Diane Price Herndl. 2nd ed. New Brunswick: Rutgers UP, 1997. 674–93.

Leavis, F. R. *The Great Tradition: George Eliot, Henry James, Joseph Conrad.* London: Chatto & Windus, 1948.

Leavis, Q. D. *Fiction and the Reading Public.* London: Chatto & Windus, 1939.

Phelan, James. *Experiencing Fiction: Judgments, Progressions, and the Rhetorical Theory of Narrative.* Columbus: The Ohio State UP, 2007.

Prince, Gerald. "Characterization." *Dictionary of Narratology.* Lincoln: U of Nebraska P, 2003.

Schor, Hilary. "The Conference So Far." Ohio State's Project Narrative Symposium: Queer and Feminist Narrative Theory. Hyatt Regency Hotel, Columbus, OH. 12–14 May 2011. Address.

Todorov, Tzvetan. *Grammaire du Decaméron.* The Hague: Mouton, 1973.

Wilson, Rawdon. "The Bright Chimaera: Character as a Literary Term." *Critical Inquiry* 5.4 (Summer 1979): 725–49.

Woloch, Alex. *The One vs. the Many: Minor Characters and the Space of the Protagonist in the Novel.* Princeton: Princeton UP, 2003.

AFTERWORD

IRENE KACANDES

The genre of the "after word" is a tricky one. The adverb "after" can indicate location or chronology, and implies that the important things come "before." The singular noun "word" restricts length. And yet there it is: an "afterword," its very inclusion implying that there's still something left to be said. Something perhaps that is "in imitation of" or "in homage to," that is "after" this volume's impressive set of essays. Fortunately for me, there's another way to look at my assignment coming from its homophone: afterward. As Toni Cade Bambara put it in her "Foreword" to one of the most paradigm-changing anthologies of second-wave feminism, *This Bridge Called My Back*: "It's the Afterward that will count" (viii). I grew up in the wake of Second Wave feminism and was cheered to see so many Second Wave feminists referred to in this volume, not so much because of my own personal history as much as because I believe it's important to acknowledge our intellectual genealogies. So with "afterward" and generations on my mind, I humbly share a story about Bambara in order to give some shape to my asking: What comes "after" *Narrative Theory Unbound*?

In May 1995 I had the profound honor of driving Toni Cade Bambara to our local airport after a conference on contemporary women writers and activism at Dartmouth College. I felt nervous because of my admiration for

Bambara, her novels and stories, and what she'd just been saying at the conference, and also because I had moved into the area less than a year earlier, was without a map, and really didn't want to get lost on such an important mission.

I must have articulated some of my anxiety or maybe Bambara was reading it from my face. In either case, she put me at ease by talking about her daughter. I'm not sure what I responded that prompted her to say that the reason she got along so well with teenagers was because she listened to them and didn't claim to have the answers. She asked me what I was working on, and when I voiced my worry about writing a first book so that I could get tenure and keep my job, she reassuringly reminded me that books get written like other things I had already managed: one word, one sentence, one paragraph, one page at a time. She spoke slowly and quietly. The buzz at the conference was that her cancer had metastasized, and at one point she'd gone back to her room to rest. Whether it was the illness or her natural manner, Bambara exuded a calm that seemed so different from that bravura many of us learn in graduate school to help mask our insecurities and also different from the affect I'd observed in the few celebrities I'd met before. I didn't want the car ride to end as I hung on her every word.

There are also three points that I remember Bambara making at the conference itself. Her opening gesture was funny, humble, and biting at the same time. She remarked that she was the one organizers invited when they couldn't get Toni Morrison. We in the audience laughed and then felt awkwardly embarrassed by the way she'd gone right to the heart of the star system. We wouldn't have wanted to admit it, especially not in that moment, but of course we did consider Morrison a bigger star than Bambara. The second intervention I remember her making concerned "ethnic envy," a phrase that I haven't figured out if she coined, but one that I attribute to her. It's functioned for me since as a helpful admonition, especially because at the very time those words were coming out of her mouth, I had been staring at her gorgeous dreadlocks and creamy skin, and thinking how beautiful she was. The third point that pierced me concerned working together. She remarked on the struggles during her own life of activism over/with allies in SNCC, the Black Panthers, and other movements. From looking back, she'd concluded that when different groups discover an issue they feel commonly passionate about, they find each other and figure out how to fight for it together. It's useless and probably doomed to pick your allies in advance based on who you think they are, what you think you have in common, or what you think you know about them, their values, and their priorities. Useless, too, to assume once an ally, always an ally.

Being wary of worshipping stars. Noting feelings of envy. Creating alliances as relevant. Listening to the younger generation. Not pretending to have all the answers. Thinking back myself now, I see how much all the things I remember hearing from Bambara are related as various parts of the same nexus. In my mind I connect them to Sedgwick's first axiom: People are different from each other. We have to acknowledge that fact of difference in order to accord respect to others and in order to effect change, including to hierarchy itself. By writing this out, I am reminded to exercise caution around pronouns. Who is the "we" who must acknowledge difference, listen to and respect others, and work for change? On a pragmatic level, I take my "we" here to involve all those who care to read this volume and these lines to think through with me an "afterward" for queer-feminist, feminist-queer narratologies; taking my cue from Bambara, I'd like to pick at three imbricated issues: breaking down hierarchies, managing envies, and working in alliance.

Breaking Down Hierarchies

The star system doesn't just exist among creative writers, of course. It's well entrenched in academia, with gaps in salaries—to take just one metric—of professors in different fields (most notably between fields like law, medicine, business, economics, and the natural sciences at one extreme and nursing, humanities, and arts at the other) and between staff, professors, and administrators at most schools, opening ever wider.[1] Closer to home, that is, within our literature departments, there are some indications that the spread between the best paid and the least well paid tenure-track people is less wide now than it was when Duke, Emory, and other schools set up our particular version of the star system. As Michael Bérubé in his 2013 MLA Presidential Address, the MLA, the AAUP, and many others have recently been pointing out to us, however, the use of various types of nontenured and part-time lecturers has been increasing at a delirious and exploitative rate, creating salary, benefits, workload, and prestige gaps.[2] Our working toward narrowing those gaps could be one "afterward."

---

1. Data on university salaries are notoriously hard to come by and even harder to compare because they tend to include different groups in the averages given. The AAUP and the MLA both keep databases and offer tools to analyze particular data an individual might want to investigate. For one comparison of salaries by field and rank see "Average Faculty Salaries." On income gaps widening at the top of the professoriate and between university presidents and professors, see "Income Gap Widens."

2. The MLA's adjunct project and the New Faculty Majority <http://www.newfacultymajority.info> offer some sobering statistics on numbers and salaries of non-tenure track teachers in American higher education.

To limit what's under examination even further, we can note that narratology itself never seemed to produce the kind of adulation that led to academic megastars like those in, say, deconstruction or postcolonial theory, though, to be sure, we have our preferred guest speakers and invited contributors. Precisely against this backdrop, the conference organizer as well as this volume's editors are to be commended for the wide range of people they included. Especially at the 2011 conference, individuals occupying every position on the academic ladder not only were present but also were given genuine opportunities to contribute. To my sensibility, nothing in the conference setup or actual proceedings smacked of stars; all interventions were received respectfully and evaluated for their ability to further the dialog. Setting up other conferences in this way could be another afterward.

To take a different indicator of hierarchy, I find the essays here much more legible than academic work being published during my graduate school years, that is to say, during the poststructuralist, deconstructivist reign. Still, I find myself wondering what would shift if we questioned more deeply not only from whom we care to hear, but also to whom we are addressing ourselves and from whom we are willing to learn? What would happen if we tried to communicate more directly with queer youth, worker advocates, animal rights activists, popular lifewriters and biographical subjects, reality-television audience members—a direction indicated by moves of authors of essays in this volume? Finding out what would shift in our rhetoric, in our research questions, in our goals as a result could lead to yet other afterwards.

I take great inspiration from someone we might want to salute as an alternative kind of academic star. Susan Stanford Friedman has certainly achieved success by our profession's markers. Yet her total commitment to her work rather than to her status has impressed me over the many years I've had the opportunity to listen to, interact with, and read her. I'm thinking specifically now of her choices of interlocutors in the many senses of the term in the work we do: topics, narratees, readers, and so on. Consider her essay in this volume and its engagement with novels and novelists concerned with gender and Islam. I remark the outcome of that engagement as calling us, her readers, to rethink our reflex to connect religion with oppression, especially women's oppression, and therefore to replot our foundational concept of intersectionalities. The main lesson of Friedman's work for me is that we mustn't just "add" stories from other parts of the world to our corpuses. Rather, we must be open to the way interaction in the form of genuine I–thou dialog with those stories will inevitably change us and the assumptions and theories by which we operate. More possible afterwards.

Managing Envy

Ethnic envy. Sexuality envy. Theory envy. Field envy. Or to connect more directly with Bambara's point about the star system: status envy. I've experienced all those, as ridiculous as that might sound coming from a full professor at an elite university. Maybe one point is that everybody has these kinds of feelings in some realm at some stage in their education and work life. Was career envy behind Bambara's comment about pecking order with Morrison? Not to let myself off the hook: I've already admitted to my own envy of Bambara's beauty at the very moment she was making this point. I could share numerous additional autobiographical examples. I will never forget my feelings of attraction, wonderment, despair, admiration—in quick succession and also simultaneously—when as a student I read Judith Fetterley's groundbreaking work, *The Resisting Reader: A Feminist Approach to American Literature* (1978) and, as a beginning assistant professor, Toni Morrison's *Playing in the Dark: Whiteness and the Literary Imagination* (1992). The gaps between my own previous readings of the American classics and the readings that Fetterley and Morrison conducted were cavernous. I worried whether I could ever learn to read as they were reading, to myself detect how women readers were positioned to read as men and how American literature was untouched by the black experience. Their readings seemed so much more correct, more interesting, more sexy than mine. Looking back now, I notice how being made aware of my ignorance led to jealousy, to my setting up new hierarchies—that is, that reading for emasculation and intersectionalities is superior to my current methods and me—not to genuine inquiry, at least not at first. I was too embarrassed at where I found myself.

What if we framed our "envies" the way we've learned to frame prejudices (and of course envy is a form of positive prejudice)? That is to say, what if we acknowledged more quickly that we had such feelings and then moved with alacrity to decisions about how we planned to act or not act on them? In the case of my readings of Fetterley and Morrison, I needed to realize these older sisters were not showing off, they were showing the way. They'd made that (missing) road map for me, and I could try to follow it and be grateful. I'm wondering, too, what would happen if we used envy as an additional method to understand our dependencies. I'm thinking about bridge-building between Susan Fraiman's argument from Haraway about recognizing dependence on bodies other than our own as a fundamental aspect of our creaturely lives to Suzanne Keen's discussion of "amae" as the comforting feeling of attachment and belonging. In other words, what if we used (individualistic) envious urges (I don't have x and she does) as a way to query ourselves about possible need for and acceptance of new (social) attachments or alliances (maybe I need to tell her I need x, maybe it's okay for me to depend on her for x, and maybe she will share x or show me the way to it)? Letting go of expertise as the (sole) core of our identities and allowing ourselves to be more dependent on each other, in our intellectual pursuits as well as in our creaturely lives, might constitute other afterwards. Which brings me to the third cue I'm trying to take from Bambara.

Working in Alliance

We need alliances, but which ones and how to make them? What are the issues that will lead us to our future allies? Or, rather, if the point about dependencies above is correct, we'll make alliances for sure, so: which issues will lead which of us to which allies? This volume itself is of course an investigation into and an experiment with alliances: queer and feminist, feminist and queer narratologists talking to each other—or not . . . To take it one step further and to paraphrase a question of Susan Lanser's, could narratology matter to scholars who don't practice it as its own end? Could it ever matter to nonscholars?

Having spent a fair amount of my professional life thinking about the differences between oral and literate cultures, I'm always astounded anew by the linearity of print. I mention that in this context because when I think back to the conference that preceded this book, I immediately re-experience a *din,* a joyous if not delirious, multidirectional, multivoiced set of animated conversations. Threads were spun not only by actual talks and the discussions that followed, but also by the murmured or scribbled side comments during the talks, the formal responses, and most especially the facial expressions, glances, and bodily gestures of scores of participants. It seemed so eerily quiet in my study as I was reading through the first draft of this manuscript.

To be sure, even in print, everyone who writes here argues and confers with interlocutors. Yet the "silence" I was registering weighed on me nonetheless. The monovocalism seemed louder due to the echoes and images from the conference in my head. I longed to develop some new charts, more complex than even the most inclusive diagrams about narrative communications' senders, messages, and receivers; narrators, texts, and narratees. I wanted to map all that oral, visual, and written messaging that had been zooming around the conference room and that I could still feel in my bodily memory. I couldn't quite figure out how to do it and, besides, charting the past din felt slightly less urgent as I found myself desiring and even staging conversations between the essays in the volume before me. I wanted to overhear Fraiman and Kay Young debating the usefulness of neuroscience to narratologists, Frederick Aldama and Judith Roof of systems theory; Friedman and Lanser (and half the other contributors) on redefining intersectionalities; Keen, Peggy Phelan, and Robyn Warhol on using autobiographical anecdotes in academic writing; Hillary Chute and Phelan comparing notes on intergenerational autolove (Eve Sedgwick and Phoebe Gloeckner); Alison Booth and Roof on gallant ladies, carnal misdemeanors, and bawdy overtones; Wendy Moffat, Paul Morrison, and Valerie Rohy tussling about gay icons. I wanted Jesse Matz to take up empathy with Sue J. Kim and Keen.

Most of all, I wanted the whole crowd to pause, stare at each other, and start vigorously interrogating themselves—and me and us—about allegiances across cultures besides feminist and queer ones. To paraphrase Kim: "Can North American academia ever stop being so Anglocentric?" I almost screamed aloud at regular intervals. Some parts of the conversations I'd been imagining were realized through the addition of the "Commentaries" section and the airing of even more voices, those of Abby Coykendall, Joe Ponce, Claudia Breger, Ellen Peel, and Shalyn Claggett. Creating even more chatter or wagering answers to my insistent question about Anglocentrism could become other afterwards to this endeavor.

Let's imagine together a few more. As I write this afterword, the "afterward" of the textile factory collapse in Bangladesh has been announced as more than one thousand dead. Rios Montt has been convicted of genocide and crimes against humanity in Guatemala, but Rodriquez Sanchez, his intelligence chief, was acquitted, and Perez Molina as the current president enjoys immunity from prosecution. The Indian government, police, and justice systems flounder in stemming gang rape of the most vulnerable victims. GLBTQ youth continue to commit suicide across the world at higher rates than their heterosexual counterparts. The ocean rises ever higher on Fiji. The only trees remaining in Malawi are those growing on traditional burial lands. By the time you read this, you might need to switch out some place names, but the crimes, tragedies, and impending disasters are likely to be similar.

Which of these issues will mobilize which groups to try which tactics to address them? What will we need to learn to take effective action? With whom will we narratologists tell new stories? Which idioms will facilitate the creation of those stories? Will our theorizing about those stories impede or facilitate new alliances? Will we be able to "take the narrow out of narratology," as Greta Olson has urged us to do recently, and notice how our specialized terminology might be reproducing ideological biases of our wider culture, as Olson herself has done by exposing the gendered, classist, and racist assumptions behind the idea of "unreliability"?[3]

It would be against the spirit of openness of the kinds of afterwards I'm hinting at to try to tie up all these questions posed with one more story. However, in the concomitant spirit of not letting myself off the hook, I offer the following anecdote from my own recent work, that I hope reflects the permeability of life as lived, stories, and theorizing about stories in the context of hierarchies, envies and alliances.

In the wake of the appearance of Art Spiegelman's genre-breaking *Maus*, numerous memoirlike texts have been offered by the offspring of Holocaust survivors.[4] I got interested in these texts partly due to my work on testimony of Holocaust survivors, partly through my association with Marianne Hirsch and her concept of postmemory,[5] and partly because of my own family's complicated connection to the tragedies of mid-twentieth-century Europe. In reading what I have since proposed we call "Holocaust family memoirs" because of their generational structure,[6] I found myself experiencing all kinds of confusing emotions including jealousy, despair, incredulity. How did those kids get their parents to talk about their pasts? How were they able to produce coherent narratives of their traumas? I was suspicious, but I decided I couldn't really critique these memoirs in print until I had made yet another try at investigating my own family history. While that challenge led to a very satisfying intellectual and emotional process that included producing a "paramemoir" with some interesting data to support theories like the critical influence of the gender of the narratee on choice of stories that get told within families,[7] what I want to emphasize here is how my original negative, critical,

---

3. Presentation at ISSN annual conference held at Manchester Metropolitan University, 28 June 2013.

4. Panels of *Maus* started appearing in 1973, and a two-volume version was published in 1991 (New York: Pantheon). Some other examples include Lisa Appignanesi, *Losing the Dead: A Family Memoir* (London: Chatto & Windus / Random House, 1999); Helen Epstein, *Where She Came From: A Daughter's Search for Her Mother's History* (Boston and New York: Little, Brown, 1997); Helen Fremont, *After Long Silence: A Memoir* (New York: Dell / Random House, 1999); Anne Karpf, *The War After: Living with the Holocaust* (London: Minerva / Random House, 1996, 1997); and Michael Skakun, *On Burning Ground: A Son's Memoir* (New York: St. Martin's, 1999).

5. Hirsch first developed the concept "postmemory" as part of her analysis of the photographs in Spiegelman's *Maus* and tied it to the concept of families (see Hirsch 22). In a volume that she and I edited together, she defines the term more broadly as "an intersubjective transgenerational space of remembrance, linked to cultural or collective trauma which is not strictly based on identity or on familial connection" (Hirsch and Kacandes 14).

6. See Kacandes, "'When Facts Are Scarce.'"

7. Kacandes, *Daddy's War*. On gender of narratees, see 183–85.

unproductive affective response eventually led me back to others' memoirs with different questions on my mind. These concerned paratextual and textual strategies of the authors to authenticate the stories of their parents' lives that for many valid historical reasons related to surviving persecution left little documentation of the type biographers would normally use to recreate personal narratives.[8]

As I was doing this work, these types of memoirs and the idea of post-memory were coming under attack from various individuals inside and outside of academia. Charges of "identity theft"[9] and of claiming someone else's memories as one's own (Weissman 16–17) can only be made, I realized, when a reader fails to appreciate that anchoring parents' stories in "real" history is partially accomplished by foregrounding how that history made itself felt in the offspring-authors' own lived experiences. For this reason, in addition to propagating the subgenre of "Holocaust family memoir," I proposed the concept of "autobiography once removed" as a useful framework for reading certain passages in the texts in my corpus.[10] To explain briefly, I located numerous instances where an event in the parent's life that could not be authenticated in a standard way (that is, by documents like arrest warrants, letters, diary entries, etc.) was narrated rather in terms of how the memoirist herself came to know about the event (e.g., my father told me). By virtue of being narrated in the first-person of the offspring-memoirist, such an event comes under Lejeune's autobiographical pact and thus requires on some level no further authentication (4–5).

In the terms of the discussion here, it seems to me that another way to describe this phenomenon is to consider it as a productive act of alliance on the part of the offspring-memoirist with the parent-biographical subject. Readers become part of that alliance when they accept that the "I"-author-narrator-protagonist is telling the truth as best she knows it. Critics, too,

---

8. The record-keeping-obsessed Nazis put enormous effort into erasing their own criminal trail, especially once it was clear that they were not going to win the war. Thus, documenting certain aspects of the Holocaust has been notoriously difficult. A second and related point is that many Holocaust family memoirs try to trace lives that were preserved precisely through targeted individuals' success in hiding or erasing signs of their (Jewish) existence. Not only generally chaotic circumstances or perpetrators' desire to save themselves from postwar retribution, then, but also survival strategies deployed by the subjects of these texts during the persecution may have been responsible for destroying documents that the offspring of the victims will later search for in vain.

9. "Identity Theft: True Memory, False Memory, and the Holocaust," a review by Ruth Franklin of various types of fiction and nonfiction texts by offspring of survivors, originally published in *The New Republic* (May 31, 2004: 31–37) and eventually republished with other commentary on the Holocaust as *A Thousand Darknesses: Lies and Truth in Holocaust Fiction*.

10. Kacandes, "'When Facts Are Scarce'" 190ff.

could become part of the alliance if instead of accusing the offspring of trying to steal their parents' identities, or claim that their own experiences are
"just as valid," those critics would recognize such narrative moves as ways of
engaging precisely our imaginations and our ethical commitments to come to
knowledge of what the persecuted experienced and how they felt about it. It
seems to me—though I have yet to do the research to prove it—that there is a
good chance autobiography once removed or strategies similar to it might be
mobilized in any range of texts where one group is trying to bear witness for
another. Perhaps in relation to historical and geographical contexts other than
the Holocaust, these moves are also being misapprehended as appropriative
rather than being identified as solidarist. Pointing that out could be another
task of our afterward.

An Afterword / Afterward to the Afterword

I'm not really privy to how they felt about each other, but I note in closing
that after Toni Cade Bambara's death from colon cancer at age 56 in December
1995, Toni Morrison oversaw the publication of various short texts by Bambara under the title *Deep Sightings & Rescue Missions: Fictions, Essays and
Conversations* (1996), as well as of Bambara's posthumous novel *Those Bones
Are Not My Child* (1999). Solidarity in deed.

Works Cited

"Average Faculty Salaries by Field and Rank at 4-Year Colleges and Universities, 2010–11." *The
Chronicle of Higher Education.* 7 Mar. 2011. <http://chronicle.com/article/Average-Faculty-
Salaries-by/126586>. Accessed 19 July 2013.

Bambara, Toni Cade. *Deep Sightings and Rescue Missions: Fictions, Essays, and Conversations.* Ed.
and pref. Toni Morrison. New York: Pantheon, 1996.

———. "Foreword." Moraga and Anzaldúa. vi–viii.

———. *Those Bones Are Not My Child.* New York: Vintage, 1999.

Fetterley, Judith. *The Resisting Reader: A Feminist Approach to American Literature.* Bloomington: Indiana UP, 1978.

Franklin, Ruth. "Identity Theft: True Memory, False Memory, and the Holocaust." *The New Republic* 31 May 2004: 31–37. Rpt. as "Identity Theft: The Second Generation," in *A Thousand
Darknesses: Lies and Truth in Holocaust Fiction.* Oxford: Oxford UP, 2011. 215–34.

Fremont, Helen. *After Long Silence: A Memoir.* New York: Dell / Random House, 1999.

Hirsch, Marianne. *Family Frames, Narrative, and Postmemory.* Cambridge: Harvard UP, 1997.

Hirsch, Marianne, and Irene Kacandes, eds. *Teaching the Representation of the Holocaust.* New York: MLA, 2004.

"Income Gap Widens." The Chronicle of Higher Education. 5 Dec. 2011. <http://chronicle.com/article/Income-Gap-Widens/129980>. Accessed 19 July 2013.

Kacandes, Irene. *Daddy's War: Greek American Stories. A Paramemoir.* Lincoln: U of Nebraska P, 2009.

———. "'When Facts are Scarce': Authenticating Strategies in Writing by Children of Survivors," in Lothe, Phelan and Suleiman, eds. *After Testimony.* Columbus: The Ohio State UP, 2011. 179–97.

Lejeune, Philippe. *On Autobiography.* Ed. Paul John Eakin. Trans. Katherine Leary. Minneapolis: U of Minnesota P, 1989.

Moraga, Cherríe, and Gloria Anzaldúa, eds. *This Bridge Called My Back: Writings by Radical Women of Color.* 2nd ed. New York: Kitchen Table, Women of Color Press, 1983.

Morrison, Toni. *Playing in the Dark: Whiteness and the Literary Imagination.* Cambridge, MA: Harvard UP, 1992.

New Faculty Majority. <http://www.newfacultymajority.info>.

Olson, Greta. "Taking the 'Narrow' out of Narratology: Toward the Integration of Critical, Culturalist Narratologies." International Conference on Narrative (Annual Conference of the International Society for the Study of Narrative). Manchester Metropolitan University, York, UK. 27–29 June 2013.

Spiegelman, Art. *Maus I. A Survivor's Tale: My Father Bleeds History. Maus II. A Survivor's Tale: And Here My Troubles Began.* New York: Pantheon, 1991.

Weissman, Gary. *Fantasies of Witness: Postwar Efforts to Experience the Holocaust.* Ithaca: Cornell UP, 2004.

$\mathcal{A}$BOUT THE EDITORS AND CONTRIBUTORS

ALISON BOOTH, Professor of English at University of Virginia, is the author of *Greatness Engendered: George Eliot and Virginia Woolf* (Cornell University Press, 1992) and *How to Make It as a Woman* (University of Chicago Press, 2004), as well as a book on transatlantic literary tourism and house museums, *Homes and Haunts*. She edited *Wuthering Heights* (Longman, 2008) and *Famous Last Words: Changes in Gender and Narrative Closure* (University of Virginia Press, 1993), and directs the Collective Biographies of Women project.

CLAUDIA BREGER is Professor of Germanic Studies, Chair of Gender Studies, and affiliate professor of Communication and Culture at Indiana University, Bloomington. Her research focuses on twentieth- and twenty-first-century culture, emphasizing media and cultural theory as well as the intersections of gender, sexuality, and race. Her most recent book, *An Aesthetics of Narrative Performance: Transnational Film, Literature and Theater in Contemporary Germany*, was published in 2012 by The Ohio State University Press.

HILLARY CHUTE is Associate Professor of English at the University of Chicago. She is the author of *Graphic Women: Life Narrative and Contemporary Comics* (Columbia University Press, 2010) and *Outside the Box: Interviews with Contemporary Cartoonists* (University of Chicago Press, 2014), Associate Editor of Art Spiegelman's *MetaMaus* (Pantheon, 2011), and coeditor of the *Critical Inquiry* special issue on Comics & Media (Spring 2014). Her forthcoming book is *"Disaster Is My Muse": Visual Witnessing, Comics, and Documentary Form* (Harvard University Press).

SHALYN CLAGGETT is an Associate Professor of English at Mississippi State University, where she specializes in Victorian literature and culture. She is currently at work on two book projects: "The Science of Character in Victorian Women's Writing," which examines how women authors appropriated the popular nineteenth-century science of phrenology to challenge social inequality, and "Strange Science: Investigating the Limits of Knowledge in the Victorian Age," a collection (co-edited with Lara Karpenko) that explores contested sciences and unorthodox forms of scientific inquiry.

ABBY COYKENDALL is Professor of English at Eastern Michigan University, specializing in narrative theory, sexuality and gender studies, and eighteenth-century British literature. Along with editing the international peer-reviewed journal *JNT: Journal of Narrative Theory,* she is co-editor of *Heteronormativity in Eighteenth-Century Literature and Culture* (Ashgate, 2015) and is completing a monograph on queer masculinity.

SUSAN FRAIMAN is Professor of English at the University of Virginia. She is the author of *Unbecoming Women: British Women Writers and the Novel of Development* (Columbia University Press, 1993), *Cool Men and the Second Sex* (Columbia University Press, 2003), and articles in such journals as *Critical Inquiry, Feminist Studies, New Literary History,* and *PMLA.* She is editor of the Norton Critical *Northanger Abbey* (2004). Her latest book, *X-treme Domesticity,* is forthcoming from Columbia University Press.

SUSAN STANFORD FRIEDMAN teaches and directs the Institute for Research in the Humanities at the University of Wisconsin-Madison and is the recipient of the Wayne C. Booth Award for Lifetime Achievement in Narrative Studies. Among her publications is *Mappings: Feminism and the Cultural Geographies of Encounter* (Princeton University Press, 1998). *Planetary Modernisms: Provocations on Modernity Across Time* is forthcoming from Columbia University Press, and she is at work on a book on religion, post/secularism, and Muslim women's diasporic writing.

IRENE KACANDES holds the Dartmouth Professorship in German Studies and Comparative Literature. She is the author or editor of six volumes including *Talk Fiction* (University of Nebraska Press, 2001) and *Daddy's War* (University of Nebraska Press, 2009) and has just completed a book on mortality. Past president of the International Society for the Study of Narrative, Kacandes serves on the MLA division of Life Writing and is president of the German Studies Association. She runs an interdisciplinary book series for de Gruyter Verlag.

SUZANNE KEEN's work investigates narrative empathy. Her books include *Thomas Hardy's Brains* (The Ohio State University Press, 2014), *Empathy and the Novel* (Oxford University Press, 2007), *Narrative Form* (Palgrave Macmillan, 2003), *Romances of the Archive in Contemporary British Fiction* (University of Toronto Press, 2001), and *Victorian Renovations of the Novel* (Cambridge University Press, 1998). She guest-edited a double special issue of *Poetics Today* on Narrative and the Emotions (2011). She is Dean of the College and Thomas H. Broadus Professor of English at Washington and Lee University.

SUE J. KIM is Professor of English and Co-Director of the Center for Asian Studies at the University of Massachusetts, Lowell. She is the author of *On Anger: Race, Cognition, Narrative* (University of Texas Press, 2013), *Critiquing Postmodernism in Contemporary Discourses of Race* (Palgrave Macmillan, 2009), and essays in *Modern Fiction Studies, Narrative,* and the *Journal of Asian American Studies.* She co-edited *Rethinking Empathy through Literature* (Routledge, 2014) and guest-edited "Decolonizing Narrative Theory," a special issue of the *Journal of Narrative Theory* (Fall 2012).

SUSAN S. LANSER is Professor of Comparative Literature, English, and Women's, Gender, and Sexuality Studies at Brandeis University. Her publications include *The Narrative Act* (Princeton University Press, 1981), *Fictions of Authority* (Cornell University Press, 1992), edited volumes, and essays in journals ranging from *Eighteenth-Century Studies* to *Feminist Studies* to *Narrative*. Her most recent monograph is *The Sexuality of History: Modernity and the Sapphic, 1565–1830* (University of Chicago Press, 2014).

JESSE MATZ is Professor of English at Kenyon College. He is author of *Literary Impressionism and Modernist Aesthetics* (Cambridge University Press, 2001) and *The Modern Novel: A Short Introduction* (Blackwell, 2004) as well as a number of articles on modernist literature, narrative theory, and queer representation. His essay in this volume is part of a larger project on "time ecology," or efforts to cultivate the temporal environment.

WENDY MOFFAT is Professor of English at Dickinson College. Her biography *A Great Unrecorded History: A New Life of E. M. Forster* (Farrar, Straus & Giroux, 2010) won the Biography Club Prize in the UK, and was selected as an ALA Stonewall Honor Book. She teaches modernism, narrative, and the history of sexuality.

PAUL MORRISON is a professor of English at Brandeis University. He is the author of *The Poetics of Fascism: Ezra Pound, T. S. Eliot, Paul de Man* (Oxford University Press, 1996) and *The Explanation for Everything: Essays on Sexual Subjectivity* (New York University Press, 2001).

ELLEN PEEL studies English, French, and German fiction and specializes in literary theory, literature by women, science fiction, and utopian literature. *Politics, Persuasion, and Pragmatism: A Rhetoric of Feminist Utopian Fiction* was published by The Ohio State University Press (2002), and topics of her recent work have included the constructed body, Doris Lessing, and unnatural narratology. She is Professor of Comparative and World Literature and of English at San Francisco State University.

PEGGY PHELAN is the Ann O'Day Maples Chair in the Arts and Professor of English and Theatre and Performance Studies at Stanford University. She is the author of *Unmarked: The Politics of Performance* (Routledge, 1993) and *Mourning Sex: Performing Public Memories* (Routledge, 1997). More recently, she edited *Live Art in LA: Performance In Southern California, 1970–1983* (Routledge, 2012).

MARTIN JOSEPH PONCE is an associate professor of English at The Ohio State University. His teaching and research interests focus on U.S. ethnic studies, queer studies, and the relations between the two. His book *Beyond the Nation: Diasporic Filipino Literature and Queer Reading* was published by New York University Press in 2012.

VALERIE ROHY is Professor and Chair of English at the University of Vermont. She is the author of *Impossible Women: Lesbian Figures and American Literature* (Cornell University Press, 2000), *Anachronism and Its Others: Sexuality, Race, Temporality* (SUNY Press, 2009), and *Lost Causes: Narrative, Etiology, and Queer Theory* (Oxford University Press, 2015). She has published essays on sexuality, race, and American literature in such journals as *GLQ, differences, Genders, Twentieth-Century Literature,* and *Modern Fiction Studies*.

JUDITH ROOF is the author of *Come As You Are: Narrative and Sexuality* (Columbia University Press, 1996), which won the Perkins Prize, as well as four other monographs on subjects ranging from psychoanalysis to the shift from analog to digital modes of transduction to Hollywood cinema to DNA. Her forthcoming book is *Remaking Genders*. She is William Shakespeare Chair in English at Rice University.

ROBYN WARHOL is Arts and Humanities Distinguished Professor of English at The Ohio State University. She is the author of *Gendered Interventions* (Rutgers University Press, 1989) and *Having a Good Cry* (The Ohio State University Press, 2003), co-author of *Narrative Theory: Core Concepts and Critical Debates* (The Ohio State University Press, 2012), and co-editor of *Feminisms* (1991, 1997) and *Feminisms Redux* (2009) from Rutgers University Press. Her forthcoming book, co-authored with Helena Michie, is *Love Among the Archives: Writing the Lives of George Scharf, Victorian Bachelor* (Edinburgh University Press).

KAY YOUNG is professor of English and Comparative Literature, faculty member of the Literature and Mind Specialization at University of California, Santa Barbara, and an academic fellow of the Institute of Contemporary Psychoanalysis, LA. She is author of *Ordinary Pleasures: Couples, Conversation and Comedy* (The Ohio State University Press, 2001) and *Imagining Minds: The Neuro-Aesthetics of Austen, Eliot, and Hardy* (The Ohio State University Press, 2010), both part of the Theory and Interpretation of Narrative Series.

NDEX

Aaberg, Justin, 228
Abel, Elizabeth, 108n8
Aboulela, Leila, 13, 110–16, 113n11
actants, 38
action, 28, 47, 48, 54n16, 55, 60–61, 66, 134n13, 170–71n2, 180, 184, 239, 257; prosocial, 136, 140n21, 147, 149
activism, 7, 11, 18, 153, 304, 334. *See also* feminism
Adam Bede (Eliot), 30, 310
Adams, Carol, 15, 294, 300, 301n10, 303–5, 303n13, 307, 309
address, structure of. *See* structure of address
addressee, 70, 85, 88, 93, 137, 240–41. *See also* narratee
Adler, Jonathan, 18, 356–57, 356n2
aesthetics, 31, 36, 135, 343–45, 359; fetishized, 161; queer, 344
affect, 15–16, 79, 83, 298, 334–35; and empathy, 126, 129, 134, 135, 137, 148, 150, 150n4, 163; and gender, 293, 298, 302, 309; and new historicism, 216; and narrative theory, 124; and queer theory, 83n13, 336,

341, 344; and sexuality, 17, 342; and the visual, 201
age, 336
agency, 18, 223, 354
agents, 181. *See also* actants
Ahmed, Sara, 342
AIDS, 85, 90, 315n5; activism, 334
Alber, Jan, 37, 64n10, 124
Alber, Jan, and Monika Fludernik, 328, 329n2, 330
Alcmaeon of Croton, 313n4
Aldama, Frederick Luis, 78n1, 195, 195n2, 367
Aldrin, Buzz, 45, 49
All We Know: Three Lives (Cohen), 225
allegorization, 232
allegory, 44, 44n4, 109, 111–12; and DeMan, 232–33, 232–33n1; and queerness, 232–33; and animals, 293, 310
Allen, Woody, 73n23
Allison, Dorothy, 83n16
Allrath, Gaby, and Marion Gymnich, 61, 68
Althusser, Louis, 304, 329n3, 342, 343

emotional contagion, 129

empathy, 147–64, 218, 335, 341, 349; aesthetic, 130; categorical, 149, 154, 163; cognitive, 127–28; defined, 126–36, 148–49; and emotion (*see* emotion and empathy); failed, 149; fantasy, 134, 142; normative, 150; situational, 132, 149, 154, 163.; strategic, 155–56. *See also* Batson, C. Daniel; Keen, Suzanne; Hogan, Patrick

empathy, narrative. *See* narrative empathy

empiricism, 220

emplotment, 9, 11, 15–16, 358

Eng, David L., and Shinhee Han, 83n13

Eng, David L., and David Kazanjian, 83n13

epistemology, 215

Epstein, Helen, 368n4

equity, 275

E. R. (NBC), 65n12

erasure, 148

eroticism, 261; anal, 86

erotics, 36, 46; and plot, 81–82

escapism, 140

Esrock, Ellen, 134

essentialism, 153, 213, 275, 301n10, 209, 334, 354; strategic, 188n21

Esty, Jed, 108n8

ethics, 135, 358; of reading, 164; of relationality, 310

ethics, narrative. *See* narrative ethics

ethnic studies, 152, 164

ethnicity, 3, 13, 336

etiology, 9, 15, 54, 254, 348–49; queer, 275–90, 335, 336

eulogy, 84

Evans, R. Tripp, 225

events, 181. *See also* actions

Ewert, Jeanne, 195n4

exhibitionism, 44

exogamy, 265, 328

Facebook, 177

fan-fiction, 139

Farwell, Marilyn, 8

Faulkner, William, 352

Feder, Ellen K., Marcy C. Rawlinson, and Emily Zakin, 295n4

Feinberg, Leslie, 351

Felman, Shoshana, 35, 281–82

Felski, Rita, 188

feminine narratives, 294

femininity, 296, 300, 302, 309

feminism, 44; Black, 28n5; and comics, 200; and difference among women, 309; and diversity, 3; Eurocentric, 147; in graphic narrative, 194–206; second-wave, 18, 152, 190, 304, 308, 309, 361; third-wave, 190; white, middle-class, 153–54

feminist activism, 153

feminist criticism, 4, 59, 152

feminist narrative theory, 1–4, 36, 188, 308–10, 333, 342, 359; as collaborative field, 14, 366; and intersectionality, 119–20

feminist narratology, 1–2, 9–10, 24–26, 35, 60, 80n6, 138, 139, 334–35, 353; and the Bildungsroman, 108; and comics, 192n3; in a digital age, 172, 187–92; and diversity, 6, 10, 124; and nonfiction, 358; queer, 30, 40; vs. structuralist narratology, 62

feminist solidarity, 147

feminist studies, 187, 190n24, 341

feminist theology, 303–4

feminist theory, 160, 164, 177; and Derrida, 295n4; locational, 101; and queer theory, 211, 325–33

feminist vegetarianism, 303–4, 307

Feng, Pin-chai, 108n8

Ferguson, Frances, 30

Fetterley, Judith, 365

Fink, Bruce, 284

Finlayson, Mark Alan, 172n3

Fiorenza, Elisabeth Schüssler, 102n2

First National Chicana Conference, 153

first-person narration. *See* autodiegetic narrator

Flaubert, Gustave, 5

Fludernik, Monika, 36, 37, 84, 86, 124, 176n9, 328

focalization, 9, 12, 79, 81–84, 97, 183n17; zero, multiple, and internal, 81. *See also*

Mohanty, Chandra Talpade, 153, 153n7

Mohr, Nicholasa, 152, 160, 162, 152n13

Moir, Anne, and David Jessel, 313n2

Moll Flanders (Defoe), 29

Montez, Lola, 173–76, 174n7, 180, 183n17, 185–86, 190

Monty Python's Flying Circus, 45

Moon, Michael, 94

Moraga, Cherríe, 153n8, 338

moral sentimentalism, 135

Moretti, Franco, 10, 29, 35, 108n8, 188, 191

morphing, 40, 334; in "Little Red Riding Hood," 48–49, 50, 51, 55, 56

morphology, 172, 176

Morrison, Jago, 81n8

Morrison, Paul, 8, 9, 14, 15, 16, 18, 254n1, 280, 336, 349, 367

Morrison, Toni, 133, 148, 152, 152n6, 154, 362, 370; *The Bluest Eye*, 152, 152n6, 157–60; *Paradise*, 29; *Playing in the Dark*, 365; *Sula*, 159

Morson, Gary Saul, 242–43

Mother Teresa, 173

motherhood, policies governing, 27. *See also* maternity

Muir, John, 129

Mullaney, Julia, 108n8

multi-camera style, 63n9

multiculturalism, 160–61

Muñoz, José Esteban, 79n3, 233–34, 246, 330n4, 346, 346n9

Muslim diaspora, 13

narratable, the, 190

narratee, 37, 38–39, 137–38, 241, 350; of television, 66, 68

narration, first-person. *See* autodiegetic narration

narration, second-person, 137, 138

narration, third-person. *See* heterodiegetic narration

narrative(s): born digital, 170; coming-of-age, 44, 201 (see also *Bildungsroman*;

coming-out narratives); conventional paradigm of, 45; conventions (*see* conventions, narrative); empathy, 9, 13, 38, 123–42 (*see also* empathy); ethics, 79, 148; environment, 48; feminized modes of, 310; forms, 9; gaps, 180; grammar of, 4; graphic (*see* graphic narrative); as heteronormative, 8; historical, 36; interdisciplinary approaches to, 34; non-fictional forms of, 4, 18 (*see also* nonfiction); relations, 37; as queer, 23. *See also* graphic narrative

Narrative (journal), 189, 195n4

narrative arc, 15–16

Narrative Causality (Kafalenos), 348

narrative identity, 356. *See also* Adler, Jonathan

narrative empathic inaccuracy, 128

narrative medicine, 34

narrative space, 195

narrative theory, 1, 33, 180, 359; anti-mimetic, 3; cognitive, 9, 344; and digital humanities, 170; ethical, 3; mind-centered, 9; and pedagogy, 351–52; and queer studies, 337; rhetorical, 3, 38. *See also* narratology, feminist narrative theory, queer narrative theory

narrative time, 158

narrative turn, 344

narrative voice, 5–6, 36

narrativity, 127, 139, 198, 231, 233–34, 243, 246–47

narrativization, 79

narratology, 1–4, 11, 16–17, 23, 33–34; as articulated method, 2–3; binary categories in, 2; classical, 4, 5, 238–39, 138, 326; contextual, 24, 32, 188; defined, 35; intersectional, 123–42; as isolated from other approaches, 329; contrasted with narrative studies, 332; phallocentric, 326; postclassical, 124, 170, 188–89, 191–92, 197, 331–32; rhetorical, 124; terminology of, 9, 39. *See also* feminist narratology, queer narratology

narrator, 79, 350, 369; engaging vs. distancing, 5; first-person (*see* autodiegetic narrator); gendered, 15, 30, 37, 80, 293;

THEORY AND INTERPRETATION OF NARRATIVE

James Phelan, Peter J. Rabinowitz, and Robyn Warhol, Series Editors

Because the series editors believe that the most significant work in narrative studies today contributes both to our knowledge of specific narratives and to our understanding of narrative in general, studies in the series typically offer interpretations of individual narratives and address significant theoretical issues underlying those interpretations. The series does not privilege one critical perspective but is open to work from any strong theoretical position.